It was not fresh fruit, sun-flooded beaches, or golden weather that tantalized the Pacific whalemen. It was the women and rum. The women were special. Men dreamed of the wild and strange times they would enjoy with the sunburned women of Hawaii. Rum flowed freely, and freedom was another heady draft. For the Polynesian kingdom was both beautiful and lawless.

Rascals in Paradise

by JAMES A. MICHENER
and A. GROVE DAY

FAWCETT CREST • NEW YORK

A Fawcett Crest Book
Published by The Ballantine Publishing Group
Copyright © 1957 by James A. Michener and A. Grove Day

http://www.randomhouse.com

ISBN 0-449-21459-1

This edition published by arrangement with Random House, Inc.

Cover photo: © Chris Thompson/The Image Bank

Manufactured in the United States of America

First Fawcett Crest Edition: July 1974
First Ballantine Books Edition: April 1983

30 29 28 27 26 25 24 23

To Mari and Virginia

Contents

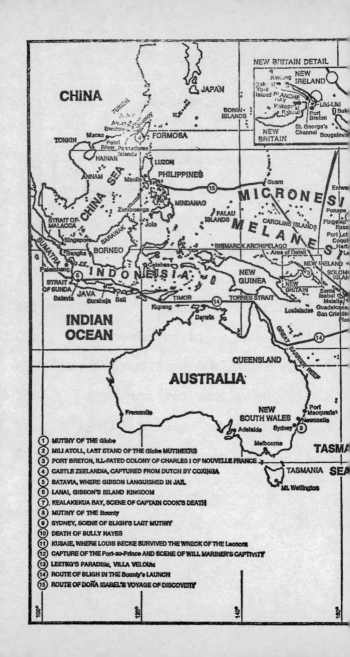

1. MUTINY OF THE Globe
2. MILI ATOLL, LAST STAND OF THE Globe MUTINEERS
3. PORT BRETON, ILL-FATED COLONY OF CHARLES I OF NOUVELLE FRANCE
4. CASTLE ZEELANDIA, CAPTURED FROM DUTCH BY COXINGA
5. BATAVIA, WHERE GIBSON LANGUISHED IN JAIL
6. LANAI, GIBSON'S ISLAND KINGDOM
7. KEALAKEKUA BAY, SCENE OF CAPTAIN COOK'S DEATH
8. MUTINY OF THE Bounty
9. SYDNEY, SCENE OF BLIGH'S LAST MUTINY
10. DEATH OF BULLY HAYES
11. KUSAIE, WHERE LOUIS BECKE SURVIVED THE WRECK OF THE Leonora
12. CAPTURE OF THE Port-au-Prince AND SCENE OF WILL MARINER'S CAPTIVITY
13. LEETEG'S PARADISE, VILLA VELOUrs
14. ROUTE OF BLIGH IN THE Bounty's LAUNCH
15. ROUTE OF DOÑA ISABEL'S VOYAGE OF DISCOVERY

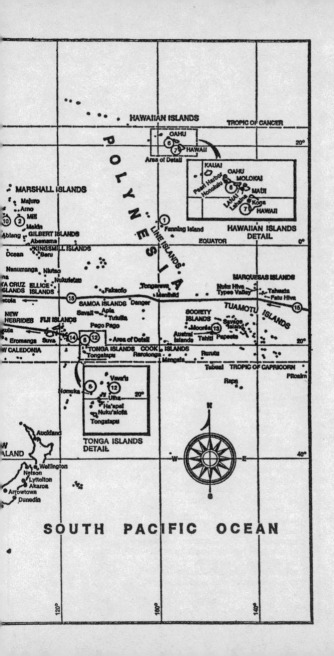

To All Who Seek a Refuge

In an age of anxiety men seek a refuge. Because of some deep urge, constant throughout history, troubled men traditionally dream of islands, possibly because the smallness of an island invites the illusion that here the complexities of continental societies can be avoided, or at least controlled. This is a permanent, world-wide dream.

When the island chosen for refuge happens to lie in the South Pacific, a colorful body of romance often helps to make the idea of escape an absolute obsession. Then, if the chosen island is reputed to contain lovely and uninhibited girls, the obsession is apt to degenerate into a monomania. And if the girls are Polynesians, the dreamer is truly lost.

The authors of this book can testify to the allure of the Pacific. One is a college professor who has served as head of a large department at the University of Hawaii. He has learned that three days after a blizzard in Minnesota, or a week after the explosion of the newest horror bomb, or three weeks after the onslaught of general bad news, his mail will be flooded with applications from professors on the United States mainland who think they could be happy only on a Pacific island. The number of Americans who believe that the islands possess some remedy for our day's malady is staggering.

The other author has reported generally upon the Pacific, and as a result receives a constant stream of mail from citizens of many nations who have grown weary of atomic bombs, dictators, taxes and neurasthenia. His correspondents are united in their conviction that only in the fabled islands of the South Seas can they find the fulfillment that their own society denies them. Were each of the islands a con-

11

tinent, there would still be insufficient room for the defeated people of the world who require refuge.

In fact, this chimerical concept of a haven from the world's dismay is so persistent that the present authors have felt obligated to review the facts. In this book they propose to inspect the histories of certain strong-natured adventurers who actually did flee to the Pacific, and they hope to find from the lives of these worthies some answers to several questions. Was the great ocean ever the refuge it has been popularly supposed to be? Is it such a refuge today? Are those of us who dread the atomic age well advised in seeking haven on some distant atoll?

This book chronicles ten instances in which men—and one woman—sought solace and fulfillment in the broad Pacific. Some fled there to escape complex and overmastering social forces resembling those under which we struggle to survive. Others, driven by the urge to power, hoped to set up private kingdoms where they could rule in accord with their desires. Still others sought refuge in the lonely ocean because they had more or less exhausted the resources of their civilizations, and these men resemble the schizophrenics of our contemporary society, at home nowhere, lured constantly by an alien dream. The remainder were downright juvenile delinquents who prove that this ugly manifestation of a disrupted society is a timeless rather than a contemporary phenomenon.

The characters whose profiles are here sketched differ from each other in most ways. The periods when they play their parts range from 1595 to 1953. The roster includes a Spanish lady explorer, a Chinese-Japanese pirate and filibuster, an Australian writer, a British naval officer, a French nobleman, a young English privateersman and four Americans: a slavedriving buccaneer, a politician of the Pacific, an artist, and a young Nantucket whaleman. The scenes of their operations cover not only the open ocean but also land areas from Peru to the China coast and from Hawaii to New Zealand, with additional episodes played against such backgrounds as the Marquesas, Tahiti, Samoa, the Dutch East Indies, Tonga, the Solomons and Formosa.

Yet, with the exception of Captain Bligh, these ten adventurers had two things in common. They were convinced that, at least for the while, some other part of the world held richer promise than their homeland. And each settled upon the Pacific as his area of escape.

In dealing with these dreamers, we were constantly reminded of a fabled occurrence in recent Pacific history. In the 1930's there was in Australia a learned gentleman who clearly foresaw that a great war was about to break over the world. He had no desire to participate in this foolish war, but he had to conclude from his studies that Europe was going to explode and that the resulting fires would involve Africa and much of Asia. With extraordinary clairvoyance he deduced that Australia, left unprotected because the military men were preoccupied with Europe, would surely become a temptation to Asia and would probably be overrun.

Wishing to avoid such a debacle, he spent considerable time in determining what course a sensible man should follow if he wanted to escape the onrushing cataclysm. He considered flight into the dead heart of Australia, but concluded that although he could probably hide out in that forbidding region, life without adequate water would be intolerable. Next he contemplated removal to America, but dismissed this as impractical in view of the certainty that America would also be involved in the war.

Finally, by a process of the most careful logic, he decided that his only secure refuge from the world's insanity lay on some tropical island. He reasoned, "There I will find adequate water from the rains, food from the breadfruit and coconut trees, and fish from the lagoons. There will be safety from the airplanes which will be bombing important cities. And thanks to the missionaries, the natives will probably not eat me."

Fortified with such conclusions, he studied the Pacific and narrowed his choice of islands to the one that offered every advantage: remoteness, security, a good life, and a storm cellar until the universal hurricane had subsided.

Thereupon, in the late summer of 1939, one week before Germany invaded Poland, this wise Australian fled to his particular South Pacific refuge. He went to the almost unknown island of Guadalcanal.

This book relates the adventures of other people who in their days of hope or torment fled to their obscure Guadalcanals, where, they were convinced, perpetual ease and fulfillment awaited them.

1

Rascals in Paradise:
The "Globe" Mutineers

His name was Samuel B. Comstock, harpooner, of Nantucket, Massachusetts, and he is remembered today because at the age of twenty-two he engineered the most horrible mutiny in the annals of the Pacific. Compared to his gruesome one-man uprising, more notorious ones like that of the *Bounty* seem commonplace and lacking in passion.

Sam Comstock was a Quaker, son of a respectable schoolmaster of Nantucket. The blond-haired, sallow-faced boy had his early training at a fine Quaker school, the Nine Partners, in Dutchess County, New York, where his father was teaching at the time. Here he learned mathematics, reading and other basic subjects which constituted an education for young gentlemen of the day, but the lesson that completely gripped his imagination, and which in time set fire to his brain, was one he heard by the fireside while growing up in Nantucket.

Captain Mayhew Folger, a resident of the town, used to thrill the youngsters with the amazing story of how in 1808, as master of the sealer *Topaz*, he had by chance discovered on lonely Pitcairn Island the survivors of the *Bounty* mutiny against Captain William Bligh. Young Sam Comstock listened with intense concentration as the story of this famous mutiny unfolded.

In Captain Folger's version, the inescapable moral of this yarn was that mutiny never pays, for he described the pitiful aftermath that transpired on Pitcairn, where the successful mutineers quarreled about their native women and brutally stalked one another to death or fell to the muskets and spears of the brown men whose women had been taken.

Young Sam did not listen to this part of old Captain Folger's narration, for dreams of mutiny, high adventure on the seas and sovereignty over some savage island had already inflamed his imagination. He was impatient to be off.

His first sea voyage was a relatively tame one. At thirteen he ran away and joined an inconspicuous ship which carried cargo from New York to Liverpool, but he quickly ditched this job. He had heard that if a boy was to gain great adventure, he must join the whalers.

Sam was fifteen, his education behind him and the blessings of his proper Quaker parents upon him, when he trod the deck of his first whaling ship. His inaugural trip was exciting enough to please even Sam, for in the first months of the voyage the ship was seized by Chilean pirates. Sam, thrown ashore in South America, beat his way back to Nantucket.

Ablaze with dreams, he haunted the water front until, in 1819, he found a berth with the whaler *Foster*, new-built and starting on her maiden voyage. On her he first saw the thundering expanse of the South Seas. From her decks he first spotted a lonely tropical island, rising slowly through morning mists. We are not required to speculate on the deranging effects of such sights on Sam Comstock, for it is recorded that on the voyage he rushed up to Captain Shubael Chase of the *Foster* and pleaded to be set ashore at any one of the islands the whaler was passing. Captain Chase ridiculed the idea and refused.

But Sam never overcame that first almost uncontrollable urge to break loose, invade an island and establish his own kingdom. Pondering the rude manner in which the captain had rejected his friendly request to be put ashore, Sam, who was a brooding boy incapable of forgetting a slight, concluded that there was only one way by which he might succeed in his life's dream. He would have to murder the entire officer corps of some ship, seize it, sail it to some island paradise and then murder the survivors one by one until only he remained, as king.

Sam's plan had three virtues. It was so bizarre that no one would suspect him of it. It was simple and straightforward. And, as we shall see, it was completely practical.

It is possible that Sam contemplated putting his master design into operation against Captain Shubael Chase, in which case Comstock's savage and improbable tale would have lived in history as the mutiny of the *Foster;* but Sam was a wily lad and was the first to realize that as a mere youth of eighteen he lacked one of the prime essentials for success as a mutineer. He could not navigate and would thus be at the mercy of whomever he stationed beside the helmsman of a captured ship.

Accordingly, Sam became a model young mariner. He studied navigation diligently, practiced the difficult art of harpooning until he was one of the best hands in the Pacific, learned to ingratiate himself with ships' crews, and studied patiently for the day when he would commandeer his own ship and send it hurtling through the waves toward some South Pacific paradise, of which he would be king.

When the *Foster* returned to Nantucket, at the end of a successful cruise, it deposited on the docks of that famous port a trim, twenty-year-old harpooner with curly blond hair a little longer than usual, eyes a bit sharper and a burning determination that would never subside as long as he lived.

For several weeks young Sam Comstock loafed along the water front, trying to select a ship for his big adventure. Like a cautious trader picking a horse, he inspected, listened and waited. Then, not long before his twenty-first birthday, he found his ship.

The famous whaler *Globe,* rich in incident and records of sperm oil, was being refitted in Nantucket waters, and Sam Comstock's heart beat wildly. For the *Globe,* only four years before, had opened up new whaling grounds a thousand miles west of Peru, and she was a ship on which any young man would have been proud to sail. Eagerly Sam presented his papers and was signed on as boat steerer, for a cruise of two or more years through the Pacific. His hour had arrived.

Whaling, when Sam Comstock decided to use it for his purposes, was the great American industry. Its ramifications were manifold. For example, the nation was lighted by whale-oil lamps or spermaceti wax candles. Machinery was lubricated by sperm oil, which was also used to make soap and paints. Ladies of fashion were scented with an essence of ambergris, coughed out from the stomach of a sick whale. Their crinolines and bodices were stayed with whalebone.

Big fortunes were made pursuing the largest of all mammals through the most distant oceans. But although there were many families of whale, only two provided real riches: the sperm whale and the right whale. The sperm was found in the more temperate waters of the world. He averaged forty to fifty feet in length, but sometimes ran to eighty-five. A lucky captor might ladle out of the monster's head case as much as thirty barrels of waxy oil. Blubber from his hulking body, when rendered out in kettles on the smoky half-deck, would average 125 barrels of oil, sometimes twice as much. His cousin, the right whale, was found more often among the bergs of the Arctic or Antarctic, and was almost as huge as the sperm. The right whale was sought not only for his oil but also for whalebone. Hundreds of thin blades of this flexible stuff hung in his maw, to be used for umbrella ribs and corset stiffeners. At one time whalebone brought five dollars a pound.

Killing any whale was dangerous work, but killing a sperm whale was especially dangerous. His toothed jaws were quite capable of splintering the hull of a double-ended boat, and tossing out the seamen in the topsy-turvy fashion that Messrs. Currier & Ives loved to depict. The right whale was less dangerous than the sperm, but could defend himself by thrashing his mammoth tail. An old whaling maxim ran: "Beware of a sperm's jaw and a right whale's flukes!" But the rewards were so great that mere men volunteered to row their frail boats close enough to Behemoth to strike his vitals with a needlelike harpoon, and then pursue him with lances until the sea was crimson and the waves violent from his death struggle.

The Pacific, from 1820 to 1870, was to be the main hunting ground of the whalers. Not long after Sam Comstock's day, more than two thirds of the world's whaling fleet prowled this ocean. Most of the ships were American, and most of these were from a few towns on the New England coast. The greatest whaling port, of course, was Nantucket, on an island south of Cape Cod. In the seventeenth century, whaling had been carried on there as an offshore venture by boats which put out from town. But later the seven seas became the Nantucketer's pasture; his herd was Leviathan.

In the 1820's Nantucket sent out about seventy ships a year to pursue the whale.

It was a Nantucket ship, the *Equator*, that along with the *Balaena* of New Bedford was the first American whaler to reach Honolulu, the tropical town that later became headquarters for the Pacific whaling industry. In 1819 these two ships killed a whale off Hawaii. Another Nantucket vessel, the *Maro*, was the first American whaler to cross the middle Pacific; in company with the *Syren* of London it discovered the famous grounds that teemed with whale eastward of Japan. Soon the other main Pacific grounds were discovered. They were scattered within a rough triangle from Cape Horn, at the foot of South America, west to New Zealand and north—including the "on Japan" grounds—to the Arctic, beyond the freezing waters of Bering Strait. Although many whaling operations had to be carried on in cold waters, in winter the favorite cruising belt was along the Equator, where a counter-current stirred up the rich ooze of the ocean floor and attracted the whales. The trade was big business. In the year 1852, for example, the masts of 131 whale ships forested the port of Honolulu, and a man might clamber from one end of the harbor to the other across the decks of the anchored vessels.

That was before the decline—for the Yankee whalers became so energetic that they steadily fished out even the world's oceans. Originally a ship could fill its hold with oil in three months; but soon after Sam Comstock's time a voyage might require three years, or even four, before the return home. Between 1835 and 1872, in the boom years, almost three hundred thousand whales were killed around the world.

The slaughter was a tragedy of waste. The ship *Hope* in 1844 reckoned that only one whale out of every three killed was saved; the rest sank or drifted away. Another vessel lost twenty out of thirty-one killed. Whalers said that not more than half of all they killed could be taken into the ship, and not more than one fifth of those struck were secured.

The lack of skilled seamen to operate the ships and handle the harpoons helped speed the decline of a great industry. The life was so hard that men would not sign on unless they were kidnaped in a drunken coma, and desertions were frequent—particularly in the Pacific, where men were lured ashore by visions of dusky sweethearts and a soft life under shimmering palms. But the death blow to the whaling trade came when the first successful oil well was drilled in Pennsylvania in 1859 and kerosene began to supplant the whale-oil lamp. Today, of course, spurred by the world's need for edible oils, whaling is once more big business, and the famous Pacific grounds now play host to Norwegian, Russian and Japanese whalers.

But in the 1820's the great whalers were from New England, and it was among this group of hardened, able men that Sam Comstock took his place on December 15, 1822, when the whale ship *Globe* set forth on what its crew knew would be a long and possibly dangerous voyage.

The *Globe* did not actually sail from Nantucket, for a sand bar had begun to impair that harbor and large vessels had formed the habit of using alternate ports. The *Globe*, for example, sailed that day from Edgartown, on Captain Thomas Worth's native island of Martha's Vineyard.

As the whaler stood out to sea, Sam Comstock, the chief harpooner and boat steerer, had his first chance to see the four officers whom he would have to murder before he could commandeer the famous ship.

Captain Worth was a competent, salty seafarer with two weaknesses. He was apt to sign men on in a hurry and then to discipline them sharply if they turned out to have been poor choices.

First Mate William Beetle was well versed in whaling life and a good officer, but his men accused him of one fatal weakness: he gossiped about them.

Second Mate John Lumbard was as brave a man as any who ever sailed the Pacific. He was a big man, and to him fell the job of administering such lashes as his captain ordered. For this the men hated him.

Third Mate Nathaniel Fisher was a tremendously strong man well trained in wrestling, a skill that was to call forth Sam Comstock's mad mutiny.

Harpooner Comstock, as he surveyed his future victims, was an inconspicuous, thin-faced, tense young man with the wiry arms needed to plunge the harpoon home and the piercing eyes required for boat steering.

This job of boat steering required exquisite skill. Even before the small whaleboat was launched, Comstock had to coil the harpoon line properly in the tub which stood at his boat's prow—a task which might take several hours, for one kink could be fatal. This line was about two hundred fathoms long. If the chase of a harpooned whale developed into heroic proportions, the lines from six different boats would be joined, and the agonized whale might sound nearly a mile in the distance; but always when he surfaced there would be that gadfly harpoon in his side and that small boat trailing more than a mile astern.

It was also the boat steerer whose steady arm and keen eye probed for the vital spot when the whale was about to be harpooned. It was his savage strength that drove the rapier-like weapon home. And when the whale was safely harpooned, it was the boat steerer's job then to switch places with the mate at the steering oar and guide the boat until the great beast was lanced to death.

The boat steerer was an important person and as such he bunked with the officers and, along with the first mate, headed a watch. In Sam Comstock's case he was particularly important, because the *Globe* also carried Sam's junior brother, George, who at sixteen was making his first whaling voyage. He idolized Sam and enjoyed watching his important older brother swank and swagger among the crew.

The cruise began with bad luck. On the very first day out, the crossjack yard carried away in a high wind, and as if loath to proceed toward its fearful destiny, the *Globe* limped back to port and refitted. Then another omen delayed them—head winds rose and pinned them down inside the breakers for several days.

Finally, when the ship was well at sea, a furious winter gale struck and rolled the *Globe* on its side, so that even the least superstitious seaman could have been forgiven had he turned back from a voyage that had started so unpropitiously.

Bad luck dogged the ship right through the Atlantic, for by the time Captain Worth took his crew around Cape Horn they had bagged only one whale. Far into the Pacific they were still without whales when an excited lookout shouted that a whole fleet of the monsters lay dead ahead. Unfortunately the sea beasts turned out to be only a group of native canoes from Hawaii whose owners wanted to trade yams and coconuts for nails or old hoop iron.

Finally good times arrived. Off Japan the lookout again shouted, "Thar she blows!" and this time he was right. Within a few months Sam Comstock led his boat to numerous kills and the *Globe* began to ride lower in the sea, burdened with 550 barrels of oil.

In celebration of their growing wealth, the officers of the *Globe* hailed a passing Nantucket whaler and the two ships declared holiday and joined in a day's festivities, the highlight of which was a furious wrestling match between wiry Sam Comstock and big Third Mate Nathaniel Fisher. Cocky Sam had issued the challenge, and for a few minutes, on the slippery deck, Sam held his own, but then Fisher's superior size and skill told, and he threw the harpooner firmly to the boards.

Comstock in a blind rage leaped to his feet, swung wildly, recovered, and slugged the officer savagely in the face. Here was occasion for Fisher to reprimand Comstock formally and to punish him according to the accepted rules of the sea, but this was a day of relaxation and fun, so huge Fisher grabbed the wildly swinging harpooner, lifted him high in the air and slammed him onto the deck.

Sam came back trembling with rage to assault the officer. Again Fisher hoisted him into the air and smashed him on the boards.

Stunned, Sam shook the fuzziness from his red brain, then lurched back to strike Fisher once more. This time the patient officer picked Sam up quickly, twisted him for a better grip, and flung him well away.

Sam lay dazed, then stared at Fisher and croaked in an awful voice, "I'll have your heart's blood for this, Fisher!"

The big officer looked down at the harpooner and laughed.

"His blood," Sam muttered. "I'll have his heart's blood."

It was about this time that Captain Worth decided his crew needed fresh food and shore leave. Accordingly he turned away from the "off Japan" grounds and headed back for one of the wildest and loveliest ports that ever flourished in the Pacific; and with every eastward league, the spirits of the crew rose.

For Honolulu, in 1823, was a whaler's paradise. The Hawaiian Islands had the only good ports within a radius of two thousand miles, and in the 1820's about a hundred whale ships called each year at Honolulu. The town lay at the foot of beautiful hills which discharged volumes of good water. Cattle from island ranches were slaughtered for fresh meat. Forests were denuded for galley firewood. Whaling captains spent thousands of dollars a year for fresh vegetables, sugar, molasses, coffee, bananas, coconuts, breadfruit, melons, pineapples, turkeys, hogs and goats.

A shipyard had just been opened, run by two survivors of

the wreck of an English whale ship on a reef in the Hawaiian chain. Spare canvas and spars to replace fittings torn away by tropical storms could be obtained. The ship chandlers of Honolulu also offered for sale the hundreds of items needed to equip a seaworn whaler, including pitch, calking, marlinspikes and supple hemp line for harpooners. Here mail could be picked up in shipping offices where it was held for wandering seamen, and many a sailor rushed ashore at Honolulu to discover that far away in Nantucket he had become a father.

But it was not fresh fruit, or new canvas, or letters from home that tantalized the spirits of Pacific whalemen when word sped through their ships that the next port of call was Honolulu. It was the women and rum.

The women were special, and one of the chief reasons why young fellows like Sam Comstock dreamed of escaping from the rigors of New England was that returning sailors boasted along the Massachusetts coast of the wild and strange times they had enjoyed with the sunburned women of Hawaii.

There were all kinds of women. There were plump Samoan girls who had come thousands of miles north as playmates aboard wandering ships that had touched their islands. There were lovely Tahitian girls who might have crisscrossed the ocean many times. There were some girls from Boston who had broken away from the puritanical groups with which they had come to the islands, and there were the usual roving lights-of-love of German, Scandinavian and British origin.

Rum flowed freely in the low-roofed grogshops and dance halls scattered along the water front. Loafing in these dens or dozing outside under palm trees were at least a hundred beachcombers who had deserted from their ships and were in no hurry to sign on again in the stinking forecastle of a "blubber hunter."

Law and order were not conspicuous in the Polynesian kingdom of Hawaii at the time the *Globe* returned from her western cruise. The young king, Kamehameha II, had just left for a tour of England and America, to talk things over with King George and other fellow monarchs. Far off in London, he and his favorite queen were to die of that horrible foreign disease, the measles. The dowager queen, left behind as regent, could not control the water front. Law enforcement problems are suggested in a surviving schedule of "Fines for Malconduct of Seamen," which included penalties ranging all the way from hanging (for maliciously violating the laws controlling contagious diseases) down through $30 for adultery, $6 for desecrating the Sabbath, $5 for headlong horseback riding, and $1 for hallooing in the streets at night.

In fact, Honolulu was such an alluring port that many strong-minded captains refused to touch there, for desertions of nearly half a ship's complement were not uncommon. In time the problem became so acute that ship owners banded together and paid head money to native gangs for each deserter hauled in from the hills or lush valleys, but some wise Yankee skippers avoided the whole problem by cruising back and forth in sight of land and sending ashore only longboats manned by trusted officers, who accumulated the required provisions and rowed back to their reluctant ships. Occasionally, of course, even such special crews deserted.

Captain Worth of the *Globe* followed neither of these desperate alternatives, but it might have been better if he had. He could not avoid Honolulu altogether, because he needed provisions. And once in sight of land it was difficult to refuse shore leave, because the *Globe* was a favorite ship in this port. On a preceding voyage under another captain, while she was anchored in Honolulu harbor, a dangerous fire had broken out in the town and swept down upon the royal fort, which contained a thousand casks of black gunpowder. Only prompt action by the *Globe*'s crew, acting as a bucket brigade, prevented a holocaust that would have destroyed the mushrooming port.

Therefore on this visit late in 1823 the *Globe*'s crew were treated as heroes and six men promptly deserted. Four were never heard of again and pass from history to some quiet native village or other where they stayed with the languorous beauties who had bewitched them. The other two were tracked down by Captain Worth and were slapped in chains and stowed below decks; but the lure of Honolulu was so great that one of them, by sheer strength, tore himself free of the chains and set his companion loose, whereupon they too disappeared forever.

Captain Worth was thus left short-handed and through either cajolery or crimps lined up seven newcomers. Obviously the quality of sailor available in Honolulu at this time was not very attractive, but the seven monsters that Captain Worth dredged out of the grogshops, the houses of ill repute and the palm-frond shacks were almost unbelievably evil. Three of them played only minor roles in what was to follow—that is, none killed more than one friend and that in no unusual or spectacular manner—but four of them passed from the dives of Honolulu into the history of the Pacific. Lazy and sullen, they caused mischief from the start, and furnished tinder for the fiery soul of Sam Comstock.

We can imagine these four worthies mustering in bright sunlight on their first sober day at sea after the *Globe* cleared Honolulu on December 29, 1823. Tall, unshaven, surly and rugged, Silas Payne of Sag Harbor, Long Island, was clearly a leader. No one knew how he had come to Honolulu or what had beached him. He seemed able and proved himself a first-class seaman, but he hated officers and early in his stay aboard caused minor trouble.

John Oliver was a stocky Englishman, a sailor who had knocked about the merchant fleets of the world and who seemed destined to continue doing so. He was uncommunicative, a very good man in a fight, and one willing to consider anything, even mutiny.

William Humphries was a rangy Negro from Philadelphia. He said he was a steward but showed little aptitude for that work. Probably because he had usually been distrusted by white shipmates, he in turn distrusted them.

The last member of the foursome was something special, a man who, everyone agreed, was destined for hanging. Joseph Thomas, from Connecticut, knew a hundred ways to irritate ship captains. The trick that irked Captain Worth most was Thomas' habit of dawdling at meals and then rising in a surly manner just as the captain's patience seemed about to break. Thomas quickly sensed that this was driving the skipper crazy and perfected his insolence.

Trouble erupted on the morning of Sunday, January 25, 1824, near Fanning Island, far south of Honolulu, when Second Mate Lumbard summoned the men. Thomas snarled, "I'm still eatin' me breakfast!" This was more than Captain Worth could stand. Banging on the scuttle, he ordered Thomas to come above. At this Thomas ambled slowly on deck and started to argue.

Captain Worth well knew what happened at sea when insolence went unrestrained. "I'll have you whipped for that!" he rapped out.

"It'll be a dear blow for you if you do!" Thomas threatened.

That was enough. Captain Worth grabbed Thomas by the

collar. The three mates were ordered to summon the crew aft to witness punishment. Taking the rope in his own hands, Captain Worth personally beat the sailor.

The buntline fell again and again. Soon Thomas was bleeding and limp while the sodden blows of the lash cut into his flesh. Grimly the officers watched the faces of the crew.

Sam Comstock—half officer, half forecastle hand—also studied his mates. Some, like his brother George, were visibly terrified by the thin red spouts of blood that leaped from the back of their fellow seaman. Others, like surly Silas Payne, stared sullenly at the brutal scene and recalled times past when it was they who had been lashed till the blood came.

Apparently it was at this instant, during the flogging of Joseph Thomas, that harpooner Comstock made his decision. From later evidence it seems that this was the time he first proposed to Payne and to Oliver, the willing Englishman, that when the *Globe* reached Fanning Island, those three plus as many others as wished would simply make a break for it. Here Sam would establish his kingdom.

A more unlikely spot for an island paradise than this footprint-shaped atoll could not have been found: knife-sharp coral reef, swampy lagoon, inadequate food and unattractive natives. But Sam was determined.

His next job was to sound out other members of the crew, and when he did, he found that all the seven beachcombers taken aboard at Honolulu were willing to jump ship at Fanning. Toward noonday he edged up to a young boy of seventeen or eighteen who was musing at the maintop masthead. He was an attractive-looking youngster, bright and a willing worker, and during the long voyage he had given some signs of admiring the harpooner.

"What shall we do, Will Lay?" Comstock whispered.

"What do you mean?" the boy asked through suddenly dry lips.

"We've had bad usage, Will! Which shall we do? Run away or take the ship?"

Will Lay, on his first voyage and sickened by what he had seen that day, mumbled something incoherent and turned aside.

From that moment he was a marked man. Later in the day he heard that Sam and Payne had made up their minds. It was to be desertion when they were abreast of Fanning.

Twice Lay attempted to get word of this plot to the officers, but Comstock kept close watch on him. Toward dusk Lay was helping furl the mainsail under Second Mate Lumbard's supervision, but whenever he had a chance to warn the mate, either Sam Comstock or menacing Silas Payne would loom up beside him with a threatening look.

"At midnight!" ran the whisper from one member of the gang to another. At midnight they would jump ship.

In many respects the mutiny of the *Globe* is one of the strangest in seafaring annals, and one of the weirdest aspects is the role played by the whaling ship *Lyra*. On this fateful Sunday the *Lyra*, Captain Joy commanding, was sailing in company with the *Globe*, and in the late afternoon, while the mutiny was being planned in the most casual and careless way, Captain Joy and a contingent from the *Lyra* rowed across the peaceful sea to visit with the officers of the *Globe*. Crew members intermingled freely, and when the *Lyra* men rowed back in the early evening it was agreed by the captains that the two whalers would sail together through the night and that the *Globe* would hoist a lantern toward midnight, whereupon the ships would simultaneously shift to a new tack.

Therefore, during all the events that were to follow that night, a full-rigged consort ship, in complete control of its officers, would be riding with full lights only a few hundred yards away. That no sound of the *Globe* mutiny and no indication of its progress ever reached the *Lyra* is merely another of the sea's many mysteries. But that Sam Comstock would embark upon his great adventure within hailing distance of a fully armed ship is almost incredible.

At ten o'clock that Sunday night Sam Comstock relieved the deck watch and found that his younger brother George was at the helm. "Keep her a good full," Sam ordered. Sometime in the next hour or two the harpooner changed his mind. He would not jump ship at Fanning. Since he was in command of the deck, he would take the ship, murder the officers, desert the *Lyra* and speed away to a better island. He reported these new plans to his fellow conspirators, and they agreed.

At midnight sharp, young George Comstock lifted the rattle by which the steersman traditionally summoned his replacement. He fell back in terror when his brother Sam appeared in the darkness, grabbed the rattle, and rasped: "If you make the least damned bit of noise, I'll send you to hell!"

By the pale light of the binnacle, frightened George saw under his brother's arm a boarding knife—two-edged, four feet long, used for stripping blubber. Then Sam lighted a lamp, shifted the boarding knife to his right hand, and started to go below, where the officers' cabins lay.

More alarmed than ever, George again grabbed for the rattle. But again Sam was at his side, chilling his blood with threats so diabolical that the boy realized he would be killed if he tried to warn the unconscious victims below.

Sam then leaped down the gangway. Behind him loomed up three grimly determined figures, all from the Honolulu beach: Silas Payne, the tall, surly leader; John Oliver, the murderous Englishman; William Humphries, the suspicious Philadelphia Negro. Joseph Thomas, who otherwise would certainly have been with the mutineers, of course still lay in his bunk whimpering with a slashed back into which salt and sea water had been rubbed for therapeutic reasons.

There was a fourth man waiting, armed like a pirate of fiction with a monstrous knife and a hatchet, but when Comstock indicated that the murders were to begin, this would-be pirate gasped, dropped his weapons and galloped back to his berth. He had thought it all a joke and had tagged along only to scare somebody.

To Sam Comstock it was no joke. "This is the captain's cabin," he whispered. Exchanging the boarding knife for an ax that Payne had thoughtfully provided from the forecastle, Sam felt his way through the cabin door.

Things might have gone awry at this critical moment, for the night had turned unexpectedly warm and Captain Worth had forsaken the stuffy berth in his stateroom in favor of a hammock which he had slung from the low cabin ceiling. Thus his head provided only a gently swaying target, and a lesser man than Comstock might have turned away, afraid lest a false stroke merely wound and enrage the victim, whereupon the ship would be alerted. But the harpooner was well versed in striking a shifting target and for a moment his powerful arm swayed to match the motion of the hammock.

At the binnacle George Comstock heard the sickening crunch of the ax as it slashed into the captain's head. The young steersman could not know it then, but that first blow had split Captain Worth's head in two.

Sam Comstock, well launched on his mutiny, kept hacking at the offending head to make sure there was no outcry.

Next Silas Payne burst in the door of First Mate Beetle's cabin and stabbed with his long boarding knife at the man lying asleep in his bunk. But Payne "boned" the knife, and Beetle awoke, wounded and terrified. "What? What? Is this—?" he stammered out. He recognized the grim faces. Was it possible that this nightmare was true? "Oh, Payne! Oh, Comstock! Don't kill me, don't! Haven't I always—"

"Yes," broke in Sam, "you have always been a damned rascal! Tell lies about me out of the ship, will you? It's a damned good time to beg now—but you're too late!"

At this Beetle shook off his despair, sprang up and grabbed Sam by the throat, knocking the stained ax to the floor. The lantern fell and went out. In the darkness Sam choked out an order to Payne to get back his ax, which Payne chanced upon and slipped into the murderer's hand.

Sam broke loose from Beetle's grip and struck the mate a tremendous ax blow that fractured his skull. Beetle fell into the pantry and lay groaning until Sam dispatched him with repeated axings. Oliver, the Englishman, put in a blow with a knife as often as he could, while the black steward from Philadelphia held aloft a lantern which illuminated the grisly scene.

Sam now ordered his henchmen to barricade the cabin where Lumbard and Fisher, the remaining mates, lay listening—fearful of the worst, but hoping to be spared. Comstock then went up to relight his own lantern at the binnacle. There his horrified brother asked if the mutineers were going to kill anyone else.

"Yes," Sam hissed. "We're going to kill them all." At this young George started to cry.

"What are you blubbering about?" demanded Sam.

"I'm afraid they will hurt me!"

"*I'll* hurt you, if you talk that way!" Sam threatened.

By this time the young mutineer had wearied of his ax, so he went to the captain's cabin, took down and loaded two ship's muskets and fixed a bayonet on one of them. Then he went to the room shared by Lumbard and Fisher. Through the door he heard Lumbard cry out: "Comstock, are you going to kill me?"

"Oh, I guess not," Sam joked. He then raised a musket and fired a blast through the door in the direction of the berths. As the smoke cleared, he asked solicitously: "Any of you hurt?"

"Yes, I'm shot in the mouth," mumbled Fisher.

Flinging open the door, Sam burst through and stabbed with his bayonet at Lumbard. But he missed, and staggered clumsily into the stateroom. Lumbard collared him. Sam wrested free. But Fisher had grabbed the musket and, spitting blood, pointed the bayonet full at the murderer's breast.

At this point Comstock's plan should have collapsed. Had Fisher used that bayonet, the mutiny would probably have been over on the spot. Payne and Oliver could truthfully have charged Comstock with the whole affair. But to the third mate, who could see the dead body of Captain Worth in the cabin beyond, it appeared that all was lost and that the whole crew was backing Comstock. At this desperate moment Sam started talking.

"The entire crew is on my side," he said, "but I'm sure I can persuade them to save your life."

After a pause of agonizing indecision, Fisher handed over the musket.

Sam grabbed it with a scream of revenge and immediately began stabbing Lumbard through the body. Again and again he slashed at the stricken second mate. Then, standing in triumph over the writhing Lumbard, Sam broke the news to Fisher.

"You've got to die. Remember how you threw me on the deck during the games? I said then I'd have your blood. Now I'll have it!"

"Is there no hope?" pleaded the third mate.

"None!" Sam cried.

At Sam's order he turned his back, and in a firm voice said, "I'm ready." Sam put the muzzle behind an ear and fired. He almost blew Fisher's head off.

Lumbard, on the floor of the cabin, was still begging for his life, but the fury of killing had driven Sam crazy. "I am a bloody man!" he shouted through the ship. "I have a bloody hand and will be revenged!" Thereupon he pierced the helpless officer several times more. Lumbard begged for water. "I'll give you water!" Sam promised prophetically. He stabbed Lumbard once more and left him dying.

All of this—the gunshots, the screams, the deaths—took place while the *Lyra* drifted peacefully on through the soft Pacific night, only a short distance away. The *Lyra* lookout kept his eye upon the bobbing lights of the *Globe*, but saw nothing more.

The *Globe*'s second boat steerer, a man named Gilbert Smith, also ranked as an officer, so he too was marked as a victim. Sensing this, Smith had been lurking above. Now he heard Sam shout, "I am a bloody man! Where's Smith?"

Smith tried to escape by running forward, but found no place to hide either below or aloft. So he returned bravely to face the ringleader.

To his amazement, Sam embraced him with bloody arms. "You are going to be with us, are you not, Smith?"

"Oh, yes, I'll do anything you require," Smith lied, and by that act saved his life for the tremendous adventure that marked the middle part of the *Globe* mutiny.

Will Lay, the youth who had been approached at the maintop, huddled in his bunk forward until summoned on deck. The mutineers had taken the ship. All hands must turn out. Mustered on the quarterdeck, Will and the rest heard Sam proclaim that he was now master and they must obey his rules. Anybody who would not swear to support him must step to the opposite side of the deck.

Sleepy and scared, not knowing how many of their number were involved in the plot, the poor fellows feared they would be killed at once if they did not swear loyalty to the man with the bloody hand. Each one vowed to follow Sam and obey him.

All hands were now ordered to make sail. Then, almost as if providence were guiding the mutiny, Comstock happened to recall that a light must be hung at the masthead to signal that all was well upon the *Globe* and that the *Lyra* should tack. But when this was done, the *Globe*, under Sam's expert command, hoisted all sail and escaped straight ahead into the enveloping night.

Captain Worth's body was now hauled on deck, where Sam performed a revolting deed. A boarding knife was rammed into the captain's bowels, then driven by an ax until the point protruded at the throat. Then Sam kicked the body overboard. Mate Beetle was found to be not quite dead, but nevertheless Sam shouted, "Throw him in the ocean anyway!"

The sickened crew were now forced to lash ropes around the feet of Fisher and Lumbard and haul them on deck to get the same treatment. But when Lumbard was about to be dropped overside, he miraculously came back to life and clung with both hands to the planksheer, crying, "Comstock, you promised you would save me!"

Sam yelled for the ax. "I'll cut off his hands!" he screamed. When no ax was forthcoming, he kicked with his heavy boots until Lumbard's fingers were completely crushed and the mate splashed into the waves.

But in the growing daylight Lumbard, stabbed repeatedly clean through the body, his hands smashed to pulp, continued, incredibly, to swim after the *Globe*. Sam sang out to lower a boat and he would finish Lumbard off in the water. But on second thought he realized that the boat's crew might try to escape to the *Lyra*, and immediately he countermanded the order. So Second Mate John Lumbard continued to swim after the *Globe*, calling for help until his ship vanished in the pale morning haze and he into the vast bosom of the Pacific.

These savage events left the crew dazed and barely able to function. Furthermore, Sam was the only navigator left alive on the ship, so he was forced to assume control of everything. Yet one night's work had brought him to his goal. Almost single-handed, this youthful desperado had murdered all four of the officers of the whale ship *Globe*, had captured her on the open sea, and had set forth to find his island kingdom.

Early next morning, he ordered the cabins washed down and the bloodstained furnishings brought on deck to air away the smell of mutiny and death. The crew was put to work getting the small arms of the ship ready to repel any attack, and making cartridge boxes.

Brother George was promoted to the job of steward, possibly to protect Sam's food supply. Going into the messroom, George saw the former steward William Humphries, now promoted to purser, secretly loading a pistol. When asked why, the Negro declared: "I have heard something very strange, and I am going to be ready for it."

George at once reported to Sam, who summoned Silas Payne. The two leaders went to the messroom. The black mutineer, who still stood there with pistol in hand, repeated that he had heard something that made him afraid for his life. Pressed, he admitted that a rumor was afloat that the second boat steerer, Gilbert Smith, and Peter Kidder, an ineffective man noted for his timidity, were plotting to retake the ship.

At once these two denied such intentions. The matter, Sam decided, should be settled by a jury trial, with proper legal counsel for both sides—S. Comstock, captain, *v.* W. Humphries, purser, all fair and aboveboard. Sam chose as his advocate the renowned pleader, Silas Payne, while Humphries picked sixteen-year-old Rowland Coffin, the youngest and least influential hand in the crew. The trial was announced for the following morning before an impartial jury.

The next day was one of fair weather for a foul deed. Sam assumed the role not only of plaintiff but of judge. Before evidence could be presented, he stood in front of Humphries, who was guarded by six men with muskets, and declaimed as follows: "It appears that William Humphries has been accused guilty of a treacherous and base act, in loading a pistol for the purpose of shooting Mr. Payne and myself. Now that he's been tried, the jury will give their verdict, whether guilty or not guilty. If guilty, Humphries shall be hanged to a studding-sail boom, slung out eight feet upon the fore-yard. But if he is found not guilty, Smith and Kidder shall be hung upon the aforementioned gallows."

The two-man jury had been primed the night before. In a flash Humphries was judged guilty. His watch was taken from him, and he was dragged forward. A rope was slung around his neck, a cap pulled over his rolling eyes. Sam ordered every man of the crew to help haul at the rope of execution.

In the bright, peaceful sunlight, Sam asked Humphries if he had anything to say. He would be allowed just fourteen seconds to say it in; Sam held a sandglass to measure that brief fraction of time. Humphries barely had begun to gasp out, "Little did I think I was born to come to this—" when Sam impatiently rang a little bell. All hands pulled, and the Negro was slung to the yardarm.

He died quickly, but when he was cut down the gallows rope tangled in the rigging and his body was towed behind the ship for some while, until the rope could be cut. Humphries' sea chest was examined, and in it was found fourteen dollars that he had stolen from Captain Worth. Sanctimoniously, all hands agreed that the hanging had come too late, for the purser was obviously a thief. Thus died the first of the mutineers—executed with pomp and pious justice by his co-plotters.

Now the ship began a zigzagging course along the Equator, headed by navigator Sam in a general westerly direction. Sam invited his henchmen to move, for comfort, into the officers' quarters aft. Here the mutineers sang and feasted and caroused to keep up their spirits. A favorite game involved trying to frighten one another by telling over the details of the murders and relating how their dreams had been troubled by ghosts. Sam in particular gloried in such narrations. He claimed that once the ghost of Captain Worth had appeared to him in a dream and had shown him his wounded, gory head. But, Sam boasted, he had ordered the captain to go away and never return—or he would kill him all over again!

At this point Sam wrote out the new laws of his seaborne kingdom. Everyone who saw a sail and did not report it immediately, and everyone who refused to fight another ship, would be put to death. "They shall be bound hand and foot," Sam decreed, "and boiled in the try-pots of boiling oil." Each man aboard had to sign this document. The ringleaders appended seals of bold black; those still innocent of blood used seals of chaste blue and white.

A fortnight passed and the *Globe* breezed westward, always seeking the perfect island hideaway. On February 7, 1824, she stood off one of the Kingsmill Islands in the Gilberts. Next day she passed the channel between the Gilbert and the Marshall islands, two groups which had been discovered by the captains of the first convict transports returning from Botany Bay in Australia.

Sam dispatched a whaleboat to a nearby island but the crew did not land, for the natives seemed hostile. Those who came out to the boat tried to steal everything in sight and plunge away with their loot. In return, the boat fired a volley of musketry into the canoe fleet. One canoe fled, pursued by the men in the whaleboat, who on overtaking it found one of the two occupants to be mortally wounded by their musket balls. The children of nature held up a jacket, made of a kind of flag, as a bribe to spare their lives, but the whaleboat sheered off and left the wounded man to die in convulsions.

Comstock recalled the whaleboat and ordered the *Globe* to make sail for what turned out to be the kingdom he was seeking. It was a spreading group of beautiful low islands, fringed with coco palms and with heavy white surf breaking on coral reefs. Probably never before visited by a whale ship, it bore the quaint early name of Lord Mulgrave's Range, but later it became better known by its native title of Mili Atoll.*

Because so many men in nations across the world have

---

*Also spelled Milli, Mille, Milly, Milei and, under the Japanese, Miri. Mili lies at the southern tip of the eastern Radak (Sunrise) chain of the Marshall Islands.

dreamed of escaping to some South Sea isle, it might be instructive to pause here and examine the particular paradise Sam Comstock chose. Mili Atoll was a perfect example of the classic atoll. It lay at about 6° north and 172° east, and was thus not far from the Equator but beyond the present date line from Hawaii. It was a small atoll and ran only some twenty-two nautical miles east to west and about twelve across.

Only a small portion, of course, was land, and this consisted of a series of about seventy named islands, all extremely low, and strung together upon a coral reef in the way small green beads might be strung upon a golden necklace cord. The lagoon enclosed by this ring of coral resembed a lake. Below its blue, placid surface lurked dangerous coral heads that could cut a man or a canoe into pieces, but it served two useful purposes: it held many fish upon which the islanders lived, and it formed a pleasant highway from one perimeter island to another. One rarely walked between the reef islets, even when low tide permitted this, for it was simpler to jump into a canoe and cross the lagoon. And, of course, only a fool would try to travel from island to island by means of the outside ocean, for there great waves surged upon the coral as if seeking to engulf the land and the lagoon both, as storms often did.

The islands that clung to Mili Atoll were minute things, only one of which was more than four hundred yards wide. Their highest points did not exceed a man's height above sea level. The white coral sand was blazing and often blinded men unused to it. Land crabs were a nuisance. Drinking water was usually brackish. There was never enough food, and rats fought for what was available. When the weather was good and the trade winds blew, the atoll was magnificent. When storms came they might last for a week and throw great ocean waves completely across the islets, washing away years of work.

The population of Mili was never great, certainly less than a thousand, for there was not enough soil to feed more. What food grew on Mili? Only breadfruit, pandanus and coconuts, plus such meager vegetables as could be painfully nursed along in plots that had to be built up by hand upon a hard coral base. The only animals were the rats, but there were fish, which seemed to desert the lagoon at periodic intervals, when everyone came close to starvation.

Harpooner Comstock first glimpsed his future kingdom on

February 11, 1824, when the *Globe* coasted the edge of Mili Atoll. As dusk approached Sam sent ashore a whaleboat which returned with a cargo of fish, coconuts and—to the joy of the mutineers—women, who were dressed tastefully in tiny woven aprons, each the size of a very small handkerchief. The delightful presence of these women through the soft tropical night quite obliterated the realities that the mutineers would have to face the next morning, when they tried to find a safe anchorage along the forbidding outer edges of the atoll.

Next day the women were put ashore, each with her apron, and the *Globe* began ranging up and down the atoll seeking a haven. Two days later, in some desperation, Sam Comstock was forced to cast anchor in a rocky expanse off the principal islet, which like its atoll was named Mili. Sam was rowed ashore to a spot near the native village, and upon touching land exulted in his triumph. This would be the site of his realm, an island whose total area was less than one square mile.

Sam spent the morning laying out in the sandy soil the master plan for his city, even going so far as to spot the precise sites for his various public buildings. It is recorded that he gave most attention to an eligible situation for the village church.

Then he started to issue orders, and it was probably at this point that men like surly Silas Payne and the hardened Englishman Oliver began to suspect that Sam meant to destroy the *Globe*, align himself with the natives and kill off every one of the remaining mutineers. Sam would then be in a position either to rule Mili Atoll for the rest of his life, choosing such women for consorts as he wished, or to return to civilization as the sole survivor of a harrowing shipwreck, with a tale embroidered by any heroic lies he wished to tell. While Sam tramped across the sands of Mili, Payne and Oliver began to plot steps to protect themselves.

At this point five or six hundred brown-skinned islanders —apprehensive for the last three days because of the big foreign canoe with spreading sails—began to approach. They were people of medium size, with broad dark faces, black hair and eyes and large grinning mouths. One of the *Globe*'s crew later granted that they were well made and handsome but said he found them most indolent and superstitious. "They were morose, treacherous, ferociously passionate, and unfriendly to all other natives," he claimed, but another observer admired their "gentility and fine majestic walk," the latter despite the fact that each footpath on Mili consisted of razor-sharp coral. When the men of Mili were not fishing, they traveled idly back and forth across the lagoon, or swam in the rolling surf.

With these people bloody Sam Comstock displayed a remarkably gentle attitude, and he immediately began to offer the naked men around him fancy officer uniforms, hardtack, rope and nails. When Payne and Oliver, still aboard ship, heard of this, their apprehension regarding Sam's plans doubled and they began talking seriously about specific moves to forestall the harpooner.

Sam had directed that rafts be built of spars, and the *Globe* was steadily being unloaded. Sails, rope, clothing and most of the ship's tools were dumped on the beach, along with a large portion of the ship's hardtack, flour, beef, pork and molasses. For Sam's personal use a large shipment of luxuries was hauled ashore: sugar, dried apples, vinegar, coffee, tea, pickles, cranberries and one box of chocolate. These were extremely useful as gifts to the admiring savages who observed the proceedings. At the end of the first night, harpooner Comstock, his stock of trade goods laid out on the sand, his cathedral well started in his mind, could sleep well.

But aboard the *Globe* there was little sleep, and after long discussions with Oliver, Silas Payne made up his mind. In the morning he sent blunt word ashore that if Sam did not stop trafficking with the natives, particularly if he did not stop making them inordinate presents, he, Payne, would "do something." Comstock ordered Payne to come ashore and explain what he meant by sending such a message.

Payne marched right into Sam's headquarters tent, and seamen some distance away could hear the bitter quarrel that was building up between their leaders.

"You may do what you please with the ship!" roared Sam, "but if any man wants anything of me, I'll take a musket with him!"

Payne jumped at the chance for a duel. "That'll suit me. I'm ready!"

To his surprise Comstock replied, "I'm going aboard ship once more, and then you may do as you please."

Showing considerable courage, Sam boarded the *Globe* for the last time, stood spread-legged on the quarter-deck and bellowed out that he was willing to fight anyone there.

Then he warned them: "I am going to leave you. Look out for yourselves!"

Before the cowed crew he burned the paper on which the laws of the mutineers had been written, then jammed his cutlass into his belt, shouting, "This shall stand by me as long as I live!"

He then grabbed a knife and some fish hooks and lines, scowled at his subdued crew and climbed slowly down into a waiting boat. On the beach he joined a band of fifty natives whom he addressed with furious gestures and then led toward the village huts. Payne, still ashore, watched this performance and that night, fearing a murderous attack by Sam and his new gang, posted guards completely around his own tent.

Sam disappeared till next morning, but Payne's spies spotted him, and Payne decided the time had come for a final settlement. Cautiously he approached the second boat steerer, Gilbert Smith, and proposed that they murder Sam together.

Boat steerer Smith replied, "I'm neutral."

Payne then dispatched a messenger to the ship to pick up the Englishman, Oliver, to whom he made the same proposal.

"I'm your man," Oliver replied.

The two mutineers, supported by two henchmen, crept behind a sand dune, loaded their muskets and waited.

Soon Comstock appeared behind a bush not far from the tent. He turned and saw the muskets leveled at his heart, waved his hand and cried: "Don't shoot me! I won't hurt you!"

It was too late. The four mutineers fired and Comstock fell, with one ball through the breast and another through the head. Silas Payne, a prudent man, feared a pretense. He rushed to the body and severed the young blond head with an ax—possibly the same one with which Sam had done for Captain Worth. The monster was dead.

Sam Comstock was buried, as he had often said he wanted to be, with his cutlass at his side. Wearing his clothes and with all his possessions except his watch, he was sewn in a bit of canvas and stowed away under five feet of sand. He had been murdered without even the legal trial that he had accorded the Negro William Humphries.

When a Nantucket schoolmate, Henry Glover, heard about Sam's death, he wrote a poem about the lad whose "hand was acquainted with daggers," which became famous at the time. It ended:

> *In years that are coming the seamen will tell*
> *Of murders and murdered, and murderer's yells.*
> *The tale, the lone watch of night will beguile*
> *When they sail by the shores of that desolate isle.*
> *And their beacon shall be, as they thitherward steer,*
> *The black rock on the grave of the young mutineer.*

The best epitaph, though, was the despairing exclamation of Sam's Quaker father in a letter which he wrote from New York to break the news to his Nantucket relatives: "O, Samuel! Samuel! Heaven forsaken Samuel!"

It would seem that with such a violent and appropriate climax, the mutiny of the *Globe* might well end. But this particular mutiny is cherished in sea annals because whenever it looks as if the story has ended, some new aspect arises to capture the imagination of the reader, so that there is not one drama of the *Globe* mutiny but many, and we now pass on to two of the most amazing.

Ashore on Mili Atoll, mutineer Silas Payne took command, with the brutal Englishman, Oliver, as his aide. Their first act after stuffing Sam Comstock and his head into a winding sheet was an error in judgment. They summoned the surviving crew, studied them and pointed to the inoffensive boat steerer, Gilbert Smith, saying, "You return to the ship and guard it in case of a native attack." George Comstock, brother of the murdered leader, and four others were told off to go aboard as well.

Payne had selected Smith because twice during the mutiny—once when Sam Comstock needed help for his murders aboard the *Globe* and once when Silas Payne was seeking someone to murder the harpooner—Smith had shown himself to be without courage. He seemed a safe, colorless man who could be trusted with the vital ship.

Nevertheless, Payne took the precaution of telling Smith, "I don't want to run any chances of the *Globe*'s sailing. Send me back both the compasses. I'll hold them here."

But when he reached the *Globe* with his five men, Smith consulted with George Comstock, who sought revenge for the murder of his brother. They secretly substituted for one of the ship's major compasses the "tell-tale" compass that customarily hung in the captain's cabins in those days. Payne, busy with details of organizing the life ashore, failed to notice the deception. That one oversight was his death warrant.

For boat steerer Smith had a most daring plan—to steal the *Globe*. As soon as the day's light began to fade, but with utmost speed, since he must accomplish everything before the moon rose at nine-thirty that night, he organized the five men aboard. One stood with a hatchet by the mizzenmast, ready to cut the stern moorings. One stood by the wheel. Another loafed by the windlass with a well-greased handsaw to sever the anchor cable. Smith anxiously watched the darkness deepen until he was certain that none of Payne's spies ashore could see motion aboard the ship.

Then he gave the signal. He himself grabbed the saw and in two minutes hacked through the bow cable. Others loosed the sails, and the ship paid off. The man astern now severed the hawser and all sails were rapidly hoisted. A stiff offshore breeze held and in the dark the *Globe* stood out from the atoll. Before the shore watchers could detect the theft, boat steerer Smith and his crew of five were headed for South America, 7500 miles distant.

Seafaring men hold this to be one of the most remarkable voyages in Pacific history. The ship had no navigating instruments save the stolen compass, no charts, inadequate food and clothing, no spare rope, no fishing lines, no reserve canvas. No one aboard knew how to navigate, nor where he was going, and it was extremely difficult to handle so sharp a ship as the *Globe* with so few hands. What was most dangerous of all, one of the hands was the very man who had been the cause of the mutiny—the vicious Joseph Thomas of Connecticut, his lashed back now healed, his heart set upon preventing the *Globe* from returning him to the jurisdiction of an American court.

But boat steerer Smith, a quiet, somewhat timorous young man who had shied away from any kind of violence, kept his ship headed roughly southeastward. He traversed seas studded with islands and uncharted reefs. He saw her through the doldrums and drove her through storms. He kept command of his starving men and kept watch upon Thomas, who was often noisy and disobedient. Through manifold troubles Smith continued quietly at his job, determined to send a rescue to the innocent men left behind and to bring the guilty to punishment.

After almost four months, with increasingly poor rations

and only guesswork to go by, he brought his ghost ship
close to the shores of South America. What he intended to
do if required to make port he had not the slightest idea,
but fortunately in early June his lookout sighted a Chilean
merchant ship that put some hands aboard the *Globe* to see
her into Valparaiso harbor.

The American consul there was Michael Hogan, Esq., an
efficient and proper man, and when he heard the harrowing story of the mutiny and the subsequent journey of the
gloomy ship, he officially reported: "This was a voyage most
miraculously completed."

But Consul Hogan's duty was clear. He ordered the six
survivors arrested and put in irons below decks on a French
frigate, there being no American men-of-war in port; but before long he relented and arranged a plan whereby a salty
American sea captain on the beach in Valparaiso was given
command of the *Globe* with orders to run her around Cape
Horn and into Boston. When the time came for this captain
to pick his crew he requested boat steerer Smith as his mate,
and it was Gilbert Smith, a quiet man, who, promoted to
master, finally brought his ship into Edgartown on November 14, 1824.

The mutinous Joseph Thomas was promptly thrown in
jail, and at his trial Smith, George Comstock and the others
who had made the long trip home testified forcefully against
Thomas; but the federal judge acquitted him for lack of positive proof. One thinks of this terrible man dozing in the
Connecticut sun in later years and telling young boys who
pestered him for stories: "I could tell ye lads about such
islands as ye never dreamed of." And for certain, he could
have.

What had happened on the paradise isle of Mili after the
theft of the ship that fateful night? It had been a little past
ten, with a strong moon rising, when a watcher shouted to
Silas Payne: "The ship is gone!"

Payne and Oliver burst from their tent and stared out to
sea. "Maybe she dragged her anchor," Oliver suggested.

"Smith, Smith!" Payne repeated incredulously. But the
Globe was gone, and next morning it was obvious to everyone that she would not return, unless accompanied by some
avenging man-of-war.

Payne fell into a furious rage, and the eight men who
were marooned with him were directed to tell the natives—
in whatever language they could muster—that the *Globe* had

been blown to sea and could be forgotten. But the mutineers knew better, and from that fearful morning realized that they must plan against the day when some American warship would put into Mili with orders to take the mutineers at any cost.

Accordingly, Payne ordered his men to tear one of the boats into planking, which was used to deck over another boat. "It will also be useful," he explained, "if the natives turn difficult."

Payne required his men to sign no articles of piracy, but he made it clear that he was in command and that the Englishman Oliver was his aide. This choice occasioned a good deal of trouble, since Oliver had hidden a whole hogshead of grog, which he appeared determined to finish off in record time. He remained drunken and useless till young Cyrus Hussey, the cooper, secretly stove in the cask and dumped the liquor in the sand.

The natives still appeared to be friendly, even though they mourned the loss of Sam Comstock, who had been extremely generous with them. On February 19 there occurred one of those trivial things which seem to be of no moment at the time, but which in this case was all-important, since the happenstance enabled one of the crew to live to write an account of the amazing things that later transpired.

It was a fine Pacific morning and the lagoon lay like a mirror, with native canoes drifting dreamily from one tiny island to the next. Will Lay, the youngster who had refused to join the mutiny when Sam Comstock approached him at the maintop masthead, casually strolled to a village, where his white skin and odd American jabber caused a good deal of hilarity. One old married couple took particular delight in the young man, and the next day Lay revisited them and was invited to spend the night in their shack. He was kept awake all night by rats, which grew to ferocious size on Mili, but it was clear to him that the old people liked him and were growing to think of him as their son, and he cemented this feeling by bringing them small presents.

Other castaways were less gentle. Silas Payne foolishly tried to overawe the native men by shooting off his swivel gun, but instead of being frightened they were deeply impressed and began plotting as to how they might get such a weapon for themselves.

Then one night Payne and Oliver went exploring and returned with two young native girls, whom they installed as their wives. But next morning Payne's girl fled, so he and Oliver set forth to bring her back. Arming themselves, all the white men marched in formation to the village and began to search the huts. Hidden in a crowd of women, the missing bride was found, and under a shower of musketry fired into the air was hauled roughly back to the tent, where she was publicly flogged and thrust into irons, presumably to show her the superior merits of the white man's way of life.

Payne never learned. Next morning, upon discovering that the camp's tool chest had been smashed and robbed, he demanded the return of every piece, under threat of dire vengeance. That night a native brought back half a chisel, which had been broken. "Where is the other half?" demanded Payne, and kept the messenger as a hostage.

At dawn, Payne sent a company of four men to recover a missing hatchet. They were armed with muskets loaded only with birdshot; Payne, remembering the murder of Comstock, would not trust them with ball. In the village, their threats produced the hatchet, and they started back, followed by a straggling horde.

Then it began. One native threw a big chunk of coral. It hit one of the mutineers. He staggered, fell. These white men, then, were mortal! In a flash, the bombardment started. The fallen man died under a merciless torrent of stones, his face smashed to pulp. The other white men broke, ran for the tent and made ready for war.

The natives brought out their spears and clubs, but, displaying admirable strategy, they attacked not the men but the boats and began smashing them. This threat to Payne's sole means of escape was so great that he bravely ventured out alone and for a whole hour held parley with the chiefs on the beach. He returned with a pact that was a virtual surrender for the white men. In return for their lives, the mutineers would give the natives everything they had, and would furthermore adopt the Marshallese way of life.

The natives at once began to pillage the camp, grabbing knives and bits of iron, smashing the provision casks, tearing clothing into shreds. Oliver objected. He was answered with whoops and howls. Then the massacre started.

Women and even children took part in the killing. An old crone of sixty ran one mutineer through the body with her spear. Other Mili Islanders brought down two of Payne's men, and completely macerated them with great stones. Several natives began to lead Payne away, as if to safety; then one of them seized a stone and struck him on the head.

Payne tried to run, but a second blow felled him, and thus he died, smashed to pieces by chunks of jagged coral. Oliver ran only a short way before he was killed in a clump of brush. In a few moments, seven of the mutineers were slain. If Sam Comstock, the man of vengeance buried five feet below the scene, could have watched the bloody death of Silas Payne, he would have rested content.

Young Will Lay, appalled by the slaughter, found himself dragged from the spot by the old couple he had befriended. They held his hands, threw him on the ground like a log, and squatted on top of him, hiding his white-skinned body from the fury of the mob. One native warrior swiped out at him with a handspike, but was fiercely warned off by his old protectors. Will was then spirited away toward the village, his bare feet lacerated on the razorlike coral.

Now began the strangest part of the *Globe* mutiny. Cowering in a Mili hut, Will Lay understandably considered himself the only survivor of the massacre. But there was one more—the cooper, Cyrus Hussey, a lad of eighteen who had likewise been rescued by an islander with whom he had once made friends. The two youths were soon brought together and exchanged gloomy forebodings. In a sense their fears were justified, for they were doomed to spend almost two years on Mili laboring for their native captors. Ironically, they had come to the island in the entourage of a man who would be king. They alone survived—as slaves.

On the morning after the slaughter, Lay and Hussey were taken under guard to the scene of the massacre. Here they found the pulped bodies of their seven comrades, horribly mutilated and unrecognizable, so furious had been the rain of heavy stones upon their heads. The camp lay in ruins, and all morning the two boys dug graves for the dead mutineers. When the job was done they were permitted to load canoes with flour, hardtack and pork. They also recovered blankets and a few books, including a Bible for each. Most important, they got shoes to protect themselves from the piercing coral edges.

Several days later the boys were hauled to a flat place near the village, where the adults of Mili stood greased with coconut oil and adorned with shells. It was obvious that a feast was about to be held and the boys assumed that they were to be the cannibalized victims, but instead they witnessed a wild ceremony of triumph in which brown women banged on drums in celebration of the victory over the white invaders.

It was then that the boys found they were to be separated and assigned to masters who would keep them as slaves. Yellow-haired Cyrus Hussey was given to a man of thirty—tough, square-built, fiery-natured Lugoma, who carried him off to a distant reef islet. There the boy's shoes were confiscated and his clothing torn up, so that naked he started upon his days of misery.

Promptly his feet were slashed to strips by the relentless coral, while his entire body blistered and caked under the equatorial sun. This his native captor could not understand, since the brown bodies of Mili men warded off both sun and salt water. In time, of course, Hussey's feet and body became toughened, and he served as a fisherman, a farmer, a field hand and a laborer. He seemed clearly destined to a life of perpetual slavery on a desolate and lonely isle.

Will Lay was luckier. His master, Ludjuan, not only lived in a larger village, where there was excitement, but was kinder than Hussey's owner. Ludjuan did, however, insist on two things. Will must destroy his Bible and never read anything again, lest he conjure up evil spirits; and the boy must don native dress, which consisted of a belt of braided pandanus and two horsetails of coarser fiber hanging fore and aft. Will's long black hair was pinned in a bow knot on top of his head, and his skin soon became as dark as that of a Mili man. But Ludjuan supported him when he firmly resisted that final treatment which would have made him a true island beau: he refused to have holes bored in his earlobes and stuffed with rolls of pandanus leaves.

But when Lay acquired some knowledge of Mili speech he got some disturbing news, for while picking breadfruit he heard a small boy shout: *"Uroit aro rayta mony la Wirram."* That meant: "The chiefs are going to kill William."

A previously unknown disease was afflicting the islanders, producing swelled hands, feet and faces. Sometimes cheeks would become so puffed that the victim would go blind for several days. Obviously Lay and Hussey were the cause. Obviously they should be killed.

A council was held at which all chiefs but one voted for death. The negative came from Lugoma, Hussey's owner, who argued that Mili's supreme master, the god Anit, had sent the scourge to punish the islanders for their massacre of the white men. If this were true, would not additional killings infuriate the god further? As a final dramatic gesture, Lugoma swore that if the chiefs insisted upon killing the boy with the golden hair, they would have to kill Lugoma first.

The boys were saved, and the slow abating of the disease was taken as proof that Anit was appeased and that the crime of massacre had been expiated.

Shortly thereafter, at the height of the harvest season, Lay was dragged by a throng of natives to a spit of land, and there, far out to sea, he saw a strange ship standing in for Mili. He was deluged with questions. What was the ship? Where did she come from? How many men would be in such a ship? Lay pretended to be fearful lest the ship take him away from his friends, but all night he tossed and dreamed of rescue. In the morning the ship was gone, and it never returned.

Then, as happened regularly each year, starvation time came, when breadfruit and pandanus bore no food. The day's ration for each person dwindled to one half a coconut. The resulting pangs of hunger were so tormenting that Lay used to sneak out at night, force himself up the steep trunk of a coconut tree, and slide down with a nut in each hand and one held by the stem between his teeth. In the darkness of the night he would wolf the oily meat to stay alive.

But his master found him out, and Lay then resorted to graverobbing, for it was the Mili custom to place a coconut at the head and feet of a newly buried person. Lay stole one of these sacrificial nuts and when the theft was discovered was put on trial for his life. The sacrilege was excused only because of his ignorance.

Suffering constant pangs of hunger, the two boys lived through the starvation time, and like the natives they now resembled, stuffed themselves when the new crops came in. Then, however, an unforeseen problem confronted them, for their island had declared war against a gang of marauders who lived across the lagoon. The boys were summoned and told they must terrify the enemy with white man's guns, but the lads explained that they had no powder.

"I have some," a chief replied, producing a small box of wet gunpowder mixed with mustard seed. Even had the powder been serviceable, it would have sufficed for only five or six shots, but the boys could not refuse. Drying the powder in the sun, they made their cartridges and hoped.

Fortunately, they were not called upon to fire, for when the enemy saw a fleet of fifteen canoes approaching, the front two armed with guns, they capitulated and the boys were returned to Mili Town with full battle honors.

But scarcely had the lads survived the year's expected starvation period than they were faced with an unexpected drought of such severity that even trees perished. Thus they lived in their kingdom—starving, burned by the sun, tormented by rats and persecuted by ignorant natives.

In the twenty-second month of his slavery, Will Lay was awakened by a loud hooting of natives, for a two-masted schooner had anchored at the head of the atoll. Spies, who had been sent out to barter, reported that it carried a hundred men and a row of big guns on each side.

The chiefs immediately guessed that this was a warship sent to capture Lay and Hussey from them, and they concluded that the safest thing would be to kill the boys at once and hide their bodies. But Hussey argued that the ship's crew obviously knew the boys were alive and that if anything happened to them, the ship's guns would begin to fire and blow the atoll right out of the water.

So the chiefs adopted an alternative plan. Two hundred warriors would be sent aboard the schooner to make friends with the strangers. At a signal they would seize the crew and pitch them into the sea. This idea was submitted to the god Anit, who showed his pleasure.

Will Lay, on the other hand, tried to calm the natives' fears, claiming that the ship could not have come from America, because unlike the *Globe* it had only two masts. But as he spoke, a boat was lowered and headed for the beach a hundred yards away. He was promptly whisked out of sight and into the garret of a hut, where forty women crowded around to hide and watch him. The boat's crew actually came to this hut and wandered about beneath the boy, but he was unable to attract their attention—fortunately for him, he learned later, for the women had been ordered to kill him instantly if he moved.

At nightfall Lay was spirited across the lagoon to a distant islet and he assumed that this was the end of his chances with this ship. But on the sixth day, to his surprise, a launch approached his very island.

Lay conceived a bold plan that would either return him to freedom or cost him his life. He said to the chiefs, "Let me lure this boat ashore, and the crew will be so surprised to

see me that they will drop their guard, whereupon you can
fall to and slaughter them all." The chiefs approved. Will
Lay waded a few feet into the water and started calling aloud
in English.

What boat was he hailing? Let us double back to Nantucket, where Gorham Coffin, one of the owners of the
Globe and the uncle of Rowland Coffin, youngest member of
the crew, had been outraged by Thomas' trial and had written to top officials in Washington to demand that the mutineers be apprehended and their innocent victims rescued.
Orders were sent to Commodore Isaac Hull in South America, and as a result, Hull detached one of his ships to pursue
the mutineers and bring them back to justice.

Thus, on August 18, 1825, the U. S. Schooner *Dolphin*,
under the command of an officer whose name is still famous
in Pacific annals—Mad Jack Percival—set out from Peru with
orders to track down the mutineers wherever they might be
and to bring them back in chains. The little topsail schooner
was fast, well armed, well manned and admirably suited for
such a task.

The *Dolphin* stopped at the Galapagos Islands and then
beat westward. In the fabled Marquesas Islands, where another American whaleman, Herman Melville, was to jump
ship seventeen years later and spend a month in captivity
among the cannibals of Typee, the *Dolphin* was greeted hos-
pitably and its men roamed that romantic valley. Marquesan
girls in large numbers swam out to welcome the schooner,
and officers "had to use some violence to get clear of them."

At one island near Mili, savage natives narrowly missed
cutting off several boat crews and the *Dolphin* only just
managed to recover them and escape. But four months after leaving Peru, the schooner hove to off the atoll where
the last survivors still lived as slaves.

Their first searches on Mili, on November 21, 1825, proved
fruitless, but the next day some sailors filling their water casks
ashore discovered on the ground a whaler's lance and several faded pieces of canvas. When the seamen got back to
the schooner, a number of native canoes were clustered
around its side. Some of them were mended with spars of
good New England ash. Most incriminating of all, some of
the canoe seats were obviously made of the lids of sea chests.

The natives refused to talk, but a few days later Mad Jack
ordered a determined search on shore, and during the party's
march an officer found a solitary mitten marked with the

name of Rowland Coffin, youngest member of the *Globe*'s crew. Farther on they came upon a skeleton protruding from shallow sand and a box containing a few Spanish dollars.

That night Mad Jack appointed an unusually brave young officer, Lieutenant Hiram Paulding, to go ashore and find the mutineers. Paulding was warned that they had probably organized the natives and had decided upon war to the finish.

It was a careful Paulding, therefore, who gingerly dropped anchor next morning only a few yards from where Will Lay, playing his own desperate game, waited to be rescued. On the beach beyond sat several hundred impassive Marshallese men. No women or children were in sight—a dangerous sign.

The first suspicious gesture Paulding caught came when a lithe figure, burned brown, with a crown of hair knotted on top of his head, and naked except for a woven mat about his loins, moved out from the assembled warriors and started to shout—in English!

"The Indians are going to kill you. Don't come on shore unless you are prepared to fight!"

This man, Paulding reasoned, must be one of the mutineers. And this was all a trick, else why had the man not disclosed himself before? Even now, why did he not make a break for the boat?

"Who are you?" Paulding shouted back over the open water.

The brown man ignored the question and kept shouting that the natives planned to lure the boat's crew ashore, and when the white men were seated they would be killed by big rocks of jagged coral.

"Who are you?" Paulding repeated.

"William Lay, of the *Globe!*"

Now the natives clustered on the beach behind Lay demanded to know what words he was calling, but he put them off with promises that the trap would soon be sprung and all the white men killed. The natives thereupon edged forward, each spotting a handy rock with which to bash out the brains of the men about to land.

At this point young Lieutenant Paulding made his decision. "Load pistols, and we will march up the beach!" He leaped ashore from the launch and led the way, well in advance. His junior officer, Midshipman Davis, later testified that this was the boldest act he had ever witnessed.

Now Lay was faced with a terrifying decision. If he moved too soon, the natives behind him would transfix him with spears. If he waited too long, the Americans might fire and kill him. Keeping silent, he watched the approaching men, and at the precise moment when his plan had a chance of working, he sped forward and threw himself before the leader.

Coldly Paulding offered Lay his left hand, at the same time thrusting a cocked pistol at the boy's breast. "Now, who are you?" he repeated.

The brown sailor burst into tears. In a babble of English and Mili talk he sobbed, "I am your man. Pardon me, sir, they are going to kill me."

Sternly Paulding turned him around and said, "Notify them that if one rises, or if one throws a stone, all will be shot."

Two or three natives rose and made to advance, but Lay's words drove them back to their places—all except one old man, Will Lay's master Ludjuan, who had many times saved the boy's life. Resolutely the old native came forward; Lay embraced him and told him that they must part. Lieutenant Paulding cut short the farewell and, studying the touchy situation, concluded that he must hurry his men back to their boat.

Among the crew of the launch, Lay, who had talked little English in two years, exploded with words. "Is there anybody here from East Saybrook?" he asked again and again. "That's where I'm from—East Saybrook, Connecticut."

"Where's the rest of your crew?" Paulding interrupted.

"All dead," he replied. Then he remembered Cyrus Hussey and cried, "There's one more alive. Can we go save him right away, before they kill him?"

Will's joy on hearing that his friend might be rescued was as great as his joy at his own salvation. So impatient was he that he begrudged the launch crew the time to eat and rest before undertaking the trip to the island where Hussey lived under the yoke of his master Lugoma.

When the launch grounded on the islet, Lugoma was walking on the beach. Paulding jumped out, pointed a pistol at him. "Where is Hussey?"

The lad happened to be strolling in a grove of coconut trees not far away. Hearing his name shouted, he ran to the landing place. He stood there in amazement, his yellow hair hanging in ringlets to his bronzed shoulders.

"Well, young man," said Paulding, "Do you wish to return to your country?"

Cyrus's eyes filled. "Yes, sir. I know of nothing that I have done for which I should be afraid to go home."

Everybody was happy except Lugoma. He declared to Paulding that he, Lugoma, might as well cut his own throat as to lose this blond boy, his son Cyrus. Nobody else on the atoll was so good at helping catch canoe loads of fish. Now Cyrus was going away with his musket, and Lugoma's enemies would surely come and kill him.

Paulding patiently explained that he would let Cyrus return—provided the boy's mother, back in New England, approved. Then Hussey loaded into the launch his two remaining possessions—his musket and his Bible, which he had saved from destruction by threatening the natives with the vengeance of the Great Spirit. The women of Lugoma's household gave the boy some small mats and shell ornaments, and in return Paulding gave them some cheap rings and glass beads. Paulding presented Lugoma with a treasure such as no other Mili chief owned—a jackknife.

Then Hussey led Captain Percival to the grave of Samuel Comstock, and the chief mutineer's skull and cutlass were exhumed, to be taken back to America.

As the *Dolphin* sailed from this island of terror and vengeance it moved in the direction of an inconspicuous atoll that was then little noted, but which in a later day was to become world-famed for a terror of its own—Bikini.

The celebrated castaways Lay and Hussey were never brought to trial for their part in the drama. First they were taken to South America in the far-wandering *Dolphin*, whose triumphant return proved, in Paulding's words, "that crime cannot go unpunished in the remotest part of the earth, and that no situation is so perilous as to justify despair." Then the lads were turned over to Commodore Isaac Hull and in his frigate, the U.S.S. *United States*, at last returned to their homeland, landing at New York in April, 1827, four years and four months after their departure from Edgartown in the ill-fated *Globe*. They proceeded to publish a little book giving their version of the gory mutiny and a description of their subsequent slavery on Mili Atoll.

Yet in a way it was Sam Comstock, the demon harpooner of Nantucket, who had the last laugh in this grisly affair. New England newspapers always referred to this arch-monster as a man from New York.

2

Charles I, Emperor
of Oceania

Of all the criminals who have pillaged the South Pacific, the most brutal and callous was a gentleman who never reached that region. Cynically, he defrauded thousands of their money, sent hundreds to certain death, and lived in luxury on the proceeds of his villainy.

He was a handsome man, a nobleman of the most ancient French stock. Charles-Marie-Bonaventure du Breil, Marquis de Rays, waited until he was forty-five years old before launching his audacious scheme, and photographs of that year, 1877, show him as he must have appeared to the middle-class people of Europe, whom he bilked so mercilessly.

He was a true Breton, with pale skin, a high and distinguished forehead, a powerful nose set between bleached blue eyes, a wealth of blond hair and a full, strong mouth. He wore a heavy mustache and the trace of a goatee. He had, everyone agrees, a most engaging and forthright manner. He was also a notably pious man.

He loved to wear rich black suits, spotless linen and full bow ties. On public occasions he decorated his chest with a broad silk sash of many colors and wore a gigantic bejeweled star of some noble order, its gold and silver rays making an ornament about the size of an hors d'oeuvre

52

saucer pinned over his heart. He was consul for Bolivia at the Breton port of Brest.

When at the height of his depredations, he solemnly proclaimed himself King Charles I of Nouvelle France and began handing out dukedoms, earldoms and baronetcies, as well as ordinary consular posts around the world, nobody was surprised, for the Marquis de Rays looked and acted much more like a king than any of his European fellow monarchs.

There was, it seemed, nothing spurious about his patent of nobility as a marquis. The de Rays family came of Celtic blood more ancient than that of the French royal family. The ancestors of Charles, forced to flee during the French Revolution, were afterward restored to their lands. His proud coat of arms showed a crowned lion with the Vergilian device: "Spare the conquered, conquer the haughty."

Until the time of the Revolution, the family had lived in one of the most romantic chateaux of northwestern France. Quimerc'h, with its masonry towers, staunch battlements, arched and recessed doorways and stone keep, looked down upon an artificial lake, which reflected the pinnacle glory of the ancient building. It was an aloof retreat for noble dreamers, and its tradition definitely affected young Charles du Breil, born in 1832, only four years after the seigneural chateau had been razed because of the depredations of the Revolutionists.

The future Marquis de Rays actually lived in a much different kind of home, erected on the same site as the old one. It was a solid, ugly, three-storied provincial stone dwelling with dormer windows, six chimneys and a wing aft that looked like a squashed warehouse. Even as a young man, he found this utilitarian substitute for a noble chateau distasteful, and pounded off to remote parts of the world, seeking fulfillment of a prophecy by a Breton fortuneteller, made when he was a child, that he was destined to be a king.

Charles first went to the Far West of the United States and tried to succeed as a rancher. Then he went to Senegal in Africa, and since one must live, he held the lowly post of a peanut broker. Not in Madagascar, nor even Indo-China, did he find the kingdom he sought. It is strange that he did not win for himself a large territory in the jungles of Indo-China, for others did, and without the backing of a noble name. But his failure in Saigon accomplished one thing. It inflamed his mind with visions of an island empire, and thereafter he read widely, tormenting himself with accounts of others who had succeeded where he had failed.

One book that struck his imagination was the account of a French exploring voyage around the world made by Captain Louis Isadore Duperrey in the corvette *Coquile.* A particular section of this book was destined to live in the Marquis' agile brain for years. It told how, on August 12, 1823, the French expedition had stumbled upon a veritable paradise. It bordered a bay at the extreme southern tip of the long and narrow island of New Ireland, northeast of New Guinea, and combined both heavenly beauty and possibilities of wealth beyond description. "We were singularly favored by the weather," wrote Duperrey in his official report. "It rained seldom and we heard thunder only once. The winds came mainly from the east, but only penetrated into the bay as soft breezes. The nights were usually beautiful and calm."

More than half a century had passed since Duperrey wrote that description of New Ireland, but the memory of this gentle paradise continued to haunt the Marquis. He was getting toward middle age, and still the fortuneteller's augury had not been realized. Where should he found his kingdom, and when?

Then, at the end of a sequence of horrible disasters that befell France, the Marquis decided that the time had come for a bold stroke.

In the decade preceding 1877 the French people had been shaken deeply by one crisis after another, and security seemed to have vanished. The tawdry empire of "Napoleon the Little" had suffered fiasco. His troops had been withdrawn from Mexico after the United States ultimatum of 1867. French pride had been humiliated by the disasters of the Franco-Prussian War, the loss of Alsace-Lorraine, and the payment of a crushing indemnity. The radical Communards had taken over during the civil war following the defeat of Napoleon III, and had burned much of Paris. When they were finally overcome, thousands of them were sent to the convict colony of New Caledonia in the Pacific.

The upheavals surrounding the beginning of the Third Republic brought great suffering. Three claimants fought for the nonexistent French throne. After the election of Marshal MacMahon, an old soldier, to the presidency, the Church party began a campaign which resulted in the failure of the *coup d'état* of May 16, 1877. The complicity of the

Church in this affair provoked reprisals by the anti-clericals when they came to power. Many people in France and elsewhere in Europe felt that they would do anything to escape the turmoil and suspicion of the times.

Two months after the crisis of May 16, the following modest advertisement appeared in a Paris newspaper: "Free Colony of Port Breton. Land two francs an acre. Fortune rapid and assured without leaving one's country. For all information apply to M. du Breil de Rays, Château de Quimerc'h, Bannalec, Finistère." Port Breton was the name that the noble promoter had invented for the remote bay in New Ireland that Duperrey had described. The Marquis then began serious propagandizing for a colony of French people who would occupy this region, which he would organize under the name of Nouvelle France, with himself as King Charles I.

As a result of the catastrophes in Europe, many people in France and elsewhere were apparently waiting for some handsome messiah, with an ancient name, who showed an inclination to lead them to a rich and simple life in a more hospitable climate, even though he had never been there himself.

According to one of his propagandists, the Marquis de Rays was just the man for this role. Dr. P. de Groote explained the great man's competence and devotion in these restrained terms: "Possessed of an ample fortune, what would hinder the Marquis from enjoying in peace his vast domain in Brittany? He has preferred to use his position and his administrative talent to promote the founding in Oceania, in the islands of Malaysia, of a free and independent colony. Hardened by numerous travels, the Marquis de Rays is unmoved in the face of danger; calmness and firmness are stamped upon his character. An outward coolness hides a good and compassionate heart which reveals a benevolent simplicity. He is liberally endowed with physical gifts; his manly and serene features, illumined with rays of intelligence, express the frankness, the energy of his character, joined with a fine firmness; these harmonize with a tall stature, sustained by the vigor of an athlete. His outward manner, reflecting a feeling of power, his calm courage, his exquisite kindness, all arouse respect and confidence. The Marquis de Rays was certainly born to command; he has the assurance, the spontaneity, the resolution, the precision of a glance; he has at once in high degree the Christian virtues, the military instinct, the mariner's genius, the forethought of the administrator, and the impartial clarity of the judge. Vigorous in body and mind, arrived at maturity while still young, he has reached by study and reflection that period of life when one enjoys all the fulfillment of physical and moral forces; he has experience behind him and the future before him, in order to achieve, with the aid of God, a great work which has been the preoccupation of his entire life."

Encouraged by such a factual account of his capacities, the Marquis started dreaming on a vast scale and began speaking of his extensive lands, of the Chinese coolies who were going to work like slaves for the enrichment of French proprietors, and especially of the ranks of nobility that he was about to create. All who bought twelve square miles in the new settlement would be issued patents of nobility as dukes or marquises. Those who acquired six square miles, if along the water front, would be honored as earls, viscounts and barons, depending upon the cost of the land. Those who could afford no more than six square miles inland would have to be content with baronetcies.

What made the proposal doubly alluring to people with accumulated money but no sense of adventure was the plan whereby one could purchase land in Nouvelle France, stay safely at home, and have the overseas acres tilled by patient, industrious, and honest Chinese, who would send all the profits back to France by regular steamers. In a few months, the Marquis de Rays picked up for himself well over a million dollars in subscriptions.

But the real glory of the enterprise was to be reserved for Frenchmen with smaller funds who would actually go out to the new kingdom, for theirs was to be a life of sunswept ease under tall coconut palms, with the simple black children of New Ireland hurrying cool drinks to them and fanning them while devout priests and nuns saved savage souls for Jesus and the warm waters of the Pacific hummed a lullaby.

Food? Nouvelle France was composed of land that ached from its burden of succulent riches. A man had merely to call and the natives would rush the produce of the fields to him. The ugly days of buying things from mean shop attendants were ended. Food was everywhere.

Money? The seas abounded in trepang, a crawling slug which could be gathered even by children and which sold in China for $750 a ton. The softly rolling land in from the beach was crowded with mahogany and teak. Copra could be made with almost no effort, since Chinese would do all the work. Vessels of all nations would put into port, hotels would flourish and the citizens of Nouvelle France would reap an enormous profit.

Amenities? When the adventurous colonists reached this paradise they would find schools, churches, stores, factories, a railway, docks, and a lighthouse which would aid large European vessels putting into the colony for trade. There would also be fine roads not less than fifteen feet wide between properties.

Spiritual life? Throughout the fanfare which was built up in Europe for Nouvelle France, the role of God was kept uppermost in everyone's mind. The Marquis humbly announced that he was but a tool in the Lord's hands, destined to create in the savage wilderness a holy settlement which would reflect the glory of Heaven. Each prospectus showed, in moving detail, docile native children gathered together for instruction by priests whose gaze was ever upward. The cross and the church dominated all engraved views of the new kingdom. Rarely has God more certainly supported any adventure; never have the backers of an enterprise been more securely allied with religion.

The grandiose plans of the Marquis de Rays were warmly received, even though they were only on paper. Imagine, therefore, the furor these ideas caused when the nobleman appeared in person at Marseilles on April 4, 1879, his handsome frame decorated with medals, and propounded his project as follows:

"The expansion throughout the world of a nation's ideas has always shown the greatness of a country; it is through colonization that a people becomes great. . . .

"My first concern was to raise the capital necessary for the enterprise. One difficulty arose, insurmountable, it seemed; it lay solely in the need for guarantees. Everywhere arose this cry, unanimous, intense, ironic: 'What sureties can you give us?' And, in fact, what surety could I give for the success of this enterprise except the carrying out of the enterprise? A vicious circle, an insoluble problem.

"The special nature of our enterprise obliged me, in order to ensure its future, to retain within my own hands the supreme direction, in order to keep it from being strangled by industrial and commercial interests whose jealous fetters would soon have destroyed the sacred character of its religious and social baptism.

"I became from then on, by the force of circumstances, the sole representative of my own idea, without sharing control or power. . . . But I am nothing. God alone is powerful—it is by His grace that my voice will be heard. A current of sympathy establishes itself among men united by the same thought; the apostles reveal themselves; one person reflects, the idea takes form, and behold, we become a living unity represented today by the unanimous will of almost three thousand hearts united toward the same goal. . . .

"Gentlemen, I never dared to expect such rapid success in my undertaking; but now that a first step has been made, now that the seed has germinated here in the fertile soil of France, what horizons can we not see for a French idea already supported on its native soil by more than three thousand apostles? God wills it, gentlemen—our enterprise will be great! . . .

"We offer, then, by lot, lands to colonize, to anyone who wishes to associate himself with our enterprise, and we issue bonds for this land, the holders of which pay two francs an acre. The value of these bonds, arbitrarily fixed today, will be created only after colonization. . . .

"No holder of bonds will actually have to go out and settle in the colony. . . . But often the poorest colonist in tropical climes can subsist on one hectare of land cultivated in sugar or in coffee and realize an income of several thousand francs a year. . . . The income will be payable each year on demand at one of the leading banks of Paris, or, for a slight service charge, it will be sent directly to your home. . . .

"The spot is already found; it lies in the southeast part of New Ireland, near New Britain, on the St. George Channel, and on the great maritime route between Australia and China. . . . From Port Breton—at present Port Praslin—our influence can extend over to New Britain, to the Louisiades, discovered by our navigators, to the Solomon Islands, to New Guinea, of which the western part is already occupied by the Dutch, our masters in this new kind of colonizing. Vast spaces will open themselves to us.

"We have, then, a port. The temperature is very moderate, in spite of its proximity to the Equator, and varies only two to three degrees. The country is well wooded, very fertile, admirably watered; it rises rapidly from the sea, which permits everyone to choose the elevation, and consequently the temperature, which agrees best with his own temperament. The abundance of springs and watercourses allows there the economical erection of all industries needing a source of power, and the natural irrigation of the country facilitates, under its exceptionally fertile conditions, all the colonial products which can be sold in Australia much more advantageously than in Europe. Food, provisions abound there, as well as fish. . . .

"We shall blaze the way, be assured, and our country will once again find glory. We shall renew on other shores, by means of our free colonies, the broken chain of our colonial traditions; we shall be great again, and without new burdens on our own country we shall, to the great profit of all, revive our beloved merchant marine, so that the remembrance of a great past will become a source of new glory.

"To work, then, friends, and may God aid us!"

The response to all this propaganda was overwhelming. Within a few months a shipload of volunteers had paid the Marquis all their savings and were ready to embark upon the great adventure. In the meantime, he had picked up, as his aide, an unemployed rogue, one Paul Titeu de la Croix, whom he immediately created Baron de Villeblanche. The name sounded imposing and gave immense support to the fraud that was about to be perpetrated.

In mid-1879 the Marquis had actually spent some subscription money in the purchase of a three-masted ship, the *Chandernagore,* and piled aboard some ninety settlers, including wives and children. There was great excitement as the families assembled for the first time on deck to meet their fellow passengers on this voyage to certain riches. There was more excitement, however, when the sensible French government washed its hands of the whole crackbrained affair and refused permission for the ship to sail from any French port.

The Marquis spirited his vessel up the coast of Europe to Antwerp, where equally sensible government officials termed the adventure suicidal and forced the resignation of the entire crew. Thereupon the Marquis dispatched the ship to Holland, where it recruited a third crew, now under the command of a Captain MacLaughlin of Alabama, who had been a lieutenant in the American Navy. Thus entitled to fly the American flag, the *Chandernagore* none the less sneaked out to sea under cover of darkness. The Marquis, showing the good sense which characterized him throughout the operation, stayed on shore.

At Madeira more trouble developed, for the American consul insisted that his flag be taken off the disreputable ship; whereupon the *Chandernagore* broke out four flags at the same time: American, British, French, Belgian. Under these varied colors the doomed ship started its four-month journey to paradise.

The voyage was not many days old when the passengers began to realize that there were many irregularities about this ship. The food was abominable, so foul and greasy that sometimes diners would get sick merely from looking at it. There was only one officer aboard who could navigate, and he was so permanently drunk that he had to be tied to the mast when taking shots so that he would not pitch overboard. Mutiny developed, and the purser was about to be shot, when the coast of Australia was sighted, and the men of many nationalities aboard forgot their quarrels at a Christmas celebration.

Then, on January 16, 1880, the first settlers of Nouvelle France reached New Ireland, and for the first time saw where they were supposed to build an empire. The contrast between what existed ashore and what the propaganda in France had described was so vast that many never recovered from the shock and lived the next months in a dull stupor.

Here is the way the Marquis de Rays's domain actually looked in 1880.

There was not a single building, no roads, not a footpath, no wharf, not a single sign of habitation. The jungle as it crept down to the foreshore was horribly dense, composed of grubby trees whose prolific branches scraped the earth, from which sprang noisome vines edged with piercing thorns. This mass of vegetation formed a solid wall which no man could penetrate unless he hacked out each foot of his way with a jungle knife. Hemmed in by decayed wood, swamped by interminable rain, this was one of the world's most inhospitable spots.

In the jungle were millions of mosquitoes laden with malaria. Others carried dengue fever, which racked a man to death in sweaty agony. Still others bore the horrible parasite causing elephantiasis, which corroded the blood vessels and quickly loaded the lymph glands of the human body with larval feces. The accumulation strangled circulation and produced arms and legs as big as large tree trunks. In man this foul collection of larval dirt often settled in the scrotum, so that an afflicted man's privates might become as big as the largest watermelon, and as heavy.

Along the ground scurried scorpions and biting insects and snakes. Worst of all the crawling things were the thousand-leggers, ghastly white centipedes whose sticky glands exuded a poison which raised fearful blisters wherever they touched. And there were flies. There were so many flies that a baby left in the sunlight might become black with them in an instant. There were big flies that stung and tiny ones that, unseen, crawled through the hair, and the ears, and the nose. And as if that were not enough, there were the battalions of warrior ants, brutal red-fanged things that rushed for a sleeping man's eyes and tried to eat their way through into his brain.

These things might have been conquered, but there were three fatal weaknesses to the site the Marquis de Rays had chosen for his empire while sitting in his comfortable library sticking pins in a map of Oceania, which he had never visited.

First, the natives surrounding the proposed settlement were all cannibals, and they lurked in shadows until such time as an unwary white man became even slightly separated from his group. Then they clubbed his brains out and ate him.

Second, there was no earth. Literally, at Port Breton there was no earth. A thin strip of land, mostly sand with a little decayed matter in it, clung to the foreshore, but immediately back of it the rocky lower limits of Mount Verron began, so that the settlers were perched on the edge of an inhospitable sea where no fish came. There could be no agriculture, no village, no spacious farms, no network of roads. The sides of the mountain were too steep to conquer. The jungle was too dense to clear away from land which, if cleared, could have produced nothing. The terrifying result of this miscalculation was that there was no food. Nor could there be any. There was not one hectare on which food could be grown.

Third, and most fatal, there was endless rain. The prevailing winds, heavily laden with moisture picked up from the sea, could not escape striking Mount Verron, whereupon their burdens of water were deposited, often in torrential downpours that lasted for seven or eight days at a time, upon the slopes of the bay. During some months the rainfall would total forty inches. Often a foot would fall in a day. Even the stars were denied the colonists, for it rained all night.

Even today, with all modern conveniences, the effect of such constant moisture can be demoralizing. A shoe, left unattended, gains an eighth of an inch of mold within two days. A blade rusts within a week. Clothes, if washed, never dry. Food, if not eaten at once, rots. And a fever, once contracted, rarely subsides. The patient's chest seems to drown in moisture, to collapse with the weight of rain that falls upon it.

No roof can keep out the incessant rain, no coral footpath can be kept negotiable for long. Disease lies everywhere: in the blood stream of mosquitoes, in the dank trees, in the swampy land. And the dreadful rains produce one affliction which even today is particularly terrifying. If anyone scratches or even bruises his shin, the skin is so thin and the moisture so omnipresent that the wound never heals. The tissues cannot dry and heal themselves; for days and months and into years the sore slowly enlarges, until a whole leg becomes a ghastly thing, slowly but inevitably rotting away. The terror of this disease is that everyone knows that even three days of bright, dry sunlight would mend the leg, but the dry sunlight never comes. And, of course, if in scratching the leg one scrapes into the wound any decaying animal matter—a dead scorpion, or a bit of rotting fish—death is quick.

To step ashore at this particular point of New Ireland was, in 1880, almost certain suicide. If there was any spot on this globe entitled to the phrase "Hell on earth," this was it; yet it was here that the unwilling passengers of the *Chandernagore* had to disembark in search of the kingdom of the Marquis de Rays.

When the settlers saw from the ship what awaited them, when they saw that not a single promise made in the prospectus had been fulfilled, they rebelled. But they were forced to land, under the firm orders given the captain by the Marquis. Despite these orders, many remained on the ship, which was now their only home, twelve thousand miles from France.

While the settlers ashore were battling disease and rain, the *Chandernagore* suddenly upped anchor during a storm on January 30, and with no explanation deserted the settlement, finding an anchorage at Liki-Liki on the other coast of the island.

Three days later a native brought the message that the ship was at Liki-Liki. Incredible as it seems, the abandoned settlers hacked their way for twelve miles through the jungle to where the *Chandernagore* was anchored. There, bleeding and nearly dead from starvation and exhaustion, they pleaded to be taken back aboard the ship and evacuated.

They were met at the landing point by one of the Marquis' henchmen, who pointed a revolver at them and reminded them sternly that they had journeyed halfway around the world to live in the Marquis' paradise—and here they would stay. Shortly thereafter the *Chandernagore* forcibly disgorged all passengers and fled the unlucky colony altogether, leaving the colonists marooned on their muddy shore. Captain MacLaughlin had been left behind with the others, but his efforts could do little to save them from their fate.

The settlers bought fifty acres from the natives for a string of beads, and mournfully studied the new site of their colony. If possible, Liki-Liki was even more hopeless than Port Breton. It lay in the middle of a swamp. No land was available for growing food, no hope was at hand. They built a ramshackle blockhouse as headquarters and a few small huts to provide a little protection from weather and other enemies.

Cannibals—some of the fiercest known in the world—started eating off the stragglers, and the most malignant diseases struck nearly all the pathetic band of people. Without food, without adequate guns, and with little shelter from the elements, they began quietly to die. As death approached, so did the warrior ants, whereupon there would be agonizing screams as the vicious insects began to eat their way into the body's openings. Then the screams would diminish, but soon there were no able-bodied men left to dig the graves, and no solid land where they could have been dug.

Forty-two days after the *Chandernagore* had abandoned the settlers at Liki-Liki, an Australian missionary who lived down the channel heard of their plight, and in his own small vessel went to the rescue. His report of what he saw at the settlement is on record.

"There was a rising swell coming from the south," wrote the Reverend Benjamin Danks, "so that the *Ripple* could not anchor, but stood off and on. About twenty men came staggering down to the beach, and stood there awaiting us; some with bandaged legs, all emaciated, sunken-eyed, and mere skeletons, a ghastly sight. Eager questions were asked and answered, and when they knew they were to go aboard the *Ripple* they rushed as fast as their tottering limbs could take them to the places they called houses, and in less than five minutes they were back on the sand with their little all and remained standing in the driving rain. They could not take their eyes off the ship; and do what we would, they madly rushed the boat, each man feebly struggling for a place, nor could any of them be induced to land and await her return. So, loaded down to the gunwales, the boat put out to sea, and I had grave doubts about it reaching the steamer.

"I walked through the settlement with Captain MacLaughlin. It consisted of a road about twenty feet wide and lined with miserable huts. Even to think of sleeping in such a place gave one the creeps. I turned and said, 'Captain MacLaughlin, you ought to thank God any of you are left alive!' . . .

"I went through the storeroom, and examined their stock of provisions, which consisted of biscuits, not of the best kind, and coffee in the berry. The stock of wine had turned sour, the salted fish had become putrid. There were three barrels of salt pork, a few bags of beans, and one or two bags of peas, but no tea or sugar. These were all the stores sixty men had to live upon for an indefinite time. There were a few suits of clothes, some tin basins, and some large flasks.

"Some attempt had been made at cultivation. There was a small banana plantation, also a small patch of sweet potatoes, a few tobacco plants, and some flowers on each side of the path. We returned to the beach, and the poor fellows who had missed the first trip asked again and again: 'Will the boat come back?' They seemed to doubt their own sense of sight, and our word. When we answered them it would, they said: 'We hope so!' and nothing would induce them to seek shelter from the rain which fiercely fell upon us as we stood there, and which, despite my mackintosh, wet me to the skin. It was a pitiful sight."

On the mercy trip away from Nouvelle France, at least

seven men died and two went mad. The rest reached the missionary headquarters on a small island off the coast of New Ireland, but some were so dazed by their struggles against cannibals, mosquitoes, flies, ants and starvation that they would never fully recover. The attempt to found King Charles I's kingdom of Nouvelle France had ended in disaster.

Why did so fair a venture—on paper—come to such a cruel finish? The principal reason was that the Marquis de Rays, when reading Duperrey's account of his stay at New Ireland, had become obsessed with the idea that the southern tip of that island was an ideal spot for a settlement. He never wavered from this judgment, and he so imbued his assistants with this belief that they also became incapable of sound thinking. As we have seen, his aides forced men over the side of the ship when it was obvious that landing at Port Breton meant almost certain death.

But how can we account for the fact that in 1823 Duperrey, an honorable witness, had written such a glowing account of this hellhole set within the encroaching bowl of Mount Verron? The Duperrey expedition had stopped there in what, in that part of the world, was the moment when the rainy season was about to begin. Thus the gloomy bay experienced one of its rare nine-day stretches without heavy rain.

The mountain was beautiful, the sea placid, and the foreshore of the land was warm and inviting. Then one could walk under trees that did not drip a poisonous moisture, and scorpions, startled by the unaccustomed dryness, stayed hidden beneath logs. At night, of course, Duperrey slept aboard ship, and escaped the lethal mosquitoes. After long days at sea, the explorers must have found New Ireland a heavenly place, and so they described it, little dreaming that at some distant date a vainglorious Marquis de Rays would be unbalanced by their favorable description.

Again, the Marquis did not read very carefully the account published by the historian of the Duperrey expedition. The possibility of torrential rains is hinted in this passage from the report: "The channel . . . is protected by two mountains whose elevation appears to be considerable and whose peaks seem to be covered uninterruptedly with black, thick clouds, in such a manner that when it is beautiful weather in Port Praslin"—which the Marquis rechristened Port Breton—"the rain falls in torrents all along the circumference of the bay." Moreover, the same report suggests the horrors of the jungle: "As soon as one steps on the foreshore the vegetation appears so active and vigorous that one sees it as overwhelming the shore and not stopping until the sea disputes the possession of the soil; on this shifting borderline lie enormous trunks of overturned trees rotting into a kind of rich soil, which nourishes another section of gross plants which fight with it for the least little space. This mass of vegetation leaves no clear spot, and it covers this whole place with a single, vast forest."

It is possible to explain the Marquis' self-induced blindness to unpleasant facts, but nothing justifies his callous behavior. In his propaganda he never admitted that neither he nor any one else connected with the venture had seen Nouvelle France. He never told the would-be settlers the truth about the houses and the churches and the stores and the roads fifteen feet wide. Worst of all, he had made no arrangements whatever for title to the land, and thus invited the retaliation of the cannibals who owned it and who promptly ate the most adventurous of the claim-jumping strangers.

It is to the credit of the French government that it suspected some fraud like this and endeavored to dissuade the colonists from leaving Europe. But the lure of quick wealth was so great that the doomed adventurers insisted upon their right to embark upon their Pacific tragedy.

So far, the story of Nouvelle France is the story of something that might have happened anywhere: a smart promoter soft-talks a group of dupes into a catastrophe. That has occurred before and it will happen often again. But what gives this particular swindle an overtone of special horror is the relentless manner in which the great fraud proliferated, the unfeeling manner in which lives were sacrified; and it is in connection with these later developments and refinements that the Marquis de Rays, King Charles I of Nouvelle France, stands forth in particular shame.

To comprehend the proportions of his fraud, we must go back to the moment when the *Chandernagore* deserted the dying colonists, who would certainly have perished en masse had not some been saved by missionaries. The Marquis' henchmen speeded south to Sydney, Australia, where their leader, the recently invested Baron de Villeblanche, had an opportunity to make an honest confession of the tragedy. Instead he cabled the Marquis as follows: "Liki-Liki occupied. Friendly relations entered into with natives. Send money and orders. In hurry. Letter following."

This news was inflated by the Marquis, in a widely distributed prospectus, *La Nouvelle France,* into the following dispatch: "Captain MacLaughlin and his companions are firmly established at Liki-Liki, and are provided with everything necessary to facilitate their establishing themselves in this new country. The officers of the *Chandernagore* have entered into friendly relations with the natives. . . . The Baron has hired the Australian brig *Emily,* and has loaded her with everything necessary for the colonists at Liki-Liki, that they may found a village in a savage country." This brochure became the most popular piece of South Seas fiction of its time, and countless European readers, huddled about their firesides, read it and envisioned owning acres of waving sugar cane in a Pacific Eden.

At this point everyone connected with the Marquis masked the true state of affairs. Instead of evacuating the dying settlers who were recuperating with the missionaries down the channel, the heroic Marquis ordered that they be returned at once to Nouvelle France. And instead of dispatching a rescue ship to save these poor unfortunates from inevitable death, he sent from Europe a second shipload of colonists.

This infamous second vessel, the *Génil,* was in charge of a man whose depths of evil are, even at the present time, impossible to explain. Captain Gustave Rabardy was a young maritime officer of medium build, sturdy character and great devotion to the Marquis de Rays. He wore mutton-chop whiskers, his eyes were close together, and he was a taciturn man. He could not plead ignorance of the South Pacific, for he had made several voyages among the Bismarck group and the Solomons. Looking back upon the disaster in which Rabardy became the central figure, one is tempted to say that out of all the sailors in Europe, the Marquis de Rays had uncannily picked the one officer whose capacities for evil matched his own, but in fairness to the Marquis one must state that prior to Rabardy's return to the Pacific in the *Génil,* there was nothing in his history to indicate that he was on the verge of becoming a hopeless maniac, and one concludes that it was the operation of a malignant fate that brought these two psychopaths together in a mutual enterprise that was to cost the lives of so many innocent and trusting emigrants.

Since most of Europe was now suspicious of the Marquis, he outfitted Captain Rabardy's ship, the *Génil*, in Spain and then seduced the Liberian government into accepting it as a vessel registered by that nation. Consequently, during all the later time when Captain Rabardy was shooting Negroes wholesale, capturing them, selling them as slaves for $100 each, and mutilating black islanders on the ground that they might become his enemies, he was operating under the flag of the Negro republic of Liberia.

Rabardy was given secret orders which, in pursuit of the divine authority which God had vested in his vicar, the Marquis de Rays, empowered Rabardy to execute anyone who questioned his decisions. He apparently read these extraordinary orders before sailing from Spain, for the *Génil* had progressed only a short distance on the long run to Singapore before its pig-eyed captain broke out a complete set of medieval torture instruments, which he used freely in maintaining discipline. He also revived ancient marine punishments and actually strung offending men up by their thumbs so that their toes barely touched the pitching deck. He lashed and swore and terrorized, so that at Singapore he was rewarded by complete desertion; every man except his cook fled, and he had to muster a gutter crew, which finally pushed the worm-eaten little ship to the paradise of Nouvelle France.

Arriving at this bleak, rain-swept beach, Rabardy found nothing but the graves of his predecessors. The *Chandernagore*, after deserting the colony, had retreated to an easier climate in Australia, where the leaders of the expedition were seen dining regularly in the best restaurants; while the settlers who had escaped were still being cared for by the missionaries. At this point it would have been well if Nouvelle France had been abandoned as an evil dream, but Gustave Rabardy was so pigheadedly committed to his Marquis that he stolidly dropped anchor, captured a pleasant little native girl to sleep with, placed two pistols beside his plate, and publicly defied his crew to murder him. When they asked how long the *Génil* would stay anchored at this lonely and forbidding place he replied simply, "Forever." When they tried to plead against such a stupid decision, he threatened to execute them.

Now comes another incredible development in this grisly affair, for the gay Marquis was able to enlist a third boatload of emigrants and to steal from each his entire savings.

This is the more remarkable in that the European public had been made fully aware of the disaster in Nouvelle France. Deserters from Rabardy's hell ship had cabled the true story from Singapore, while from Australia a few refugees who had reached Sydney had sent to Paris circumstantial accounts of the terror they had undergone. Stories from both sources appeared in major European newspapers, but the good Marquis was able to face them down by sanctimoniously charging his enemies with religious persecution, so that he emerged stronger than before. Then, mouthing revolting platitudes and references to God's approval of his venture, he chartered a third ship and with no apparent remorse sent three hundred additional emigrants to hell. They left Barcelona, Spain, on July 7, 1880.

This time he crammed his unseaworthy vessel, the *India,* mainly with people from Italy, where news of his cruel frauds had not yet penetrated outlying villages. He mulcted these Italian peasants of their last lire, jammed them into horrible quarters and with no compunction pocketed the profits. More than a hundred would die even before the *India* reached Nouvelle France. They were the fortunate ones.

When at last they reached that haven they saw only Captain Rabardy's ship. Torrential downpours had made even the narrow strip of sandy soil a morass, and with gasps of despair the Italians pleaded to be taken somewhere else.

But now they were to encounter the iron will of Captain Rabardy. "This is the site," he said coldly. "Disembark."

"But there is no land!"

"Disembark."

"We'll try farther up the coast."

"This is Nouvelle France."

So the Italians were forced ashore, and like their predecessors, many died. One brave man volunteered to scout for better land, and he was eaten by cannibals. Another tried to work at building a house, and he collapsed with malaria. Others, between sobbing laments which their French officers affected not to understand, tried to plant food, and they died of dengue, of chills, of scorpion bites and of starvation.

One of the survivors achieved the distinction of being the first white man to visit the interior of the island of Bougainville in the Solomons. He was an Italian who, after enduring the hardships of Port Breton, decided that any alternative would be preferable. Accordingly, he stole a boat and with several companions made for the Solomons, where on arrival they were all killed and eaten except this one man, whose tears softened the heart of the savage chief. The man was sold to a bush tribe, and became as big a cannibal as any of the savages. After living a year among them, he made his escape to the coast, where he was bought for two tomahawks by the crew of a blackbirding ship. They had thought he was a native, worth £25 in Queensland; but when they found he was an Italian and could not be sold into servitude, they abandoned him at New Britain. The English commissioner there was unable to get much information from the man, however, because he had become a hopeless imbecile and never opened his lips except to ask for food.

The Baron de Villeblanche, safe in Sydney and spending lavish sums intended for the comforts of the settlers, kept cabling to Europe that all was well. In Spain, the Marquis de Rays, who now had three mistresses and untold fortunes gathered from faithful followers throughout Europe, quoted the cables in a new prospectus and collected fresh sums of money from new dreamers whom he was planning to send out to his lethal paradise.

Meanwhile, through a most fortunate stratagem, the doomed Italians finally escaped from Nouvelle France— that is, those who had not died. It had become apparent that since the rains prevented the growing of any food, the entire colony must perish. Captain Rabardy said that was all right with him—let it perish; but the colonists played upon his vanity and he was finally persuaded to sail his ship to Australia for additional food. In his absence, the Italians made such complaint that their own captain agreed to evacuate the entire colony. He would take them to New Caledonia, the French penal settlement. But when the cautious French officials there saw the horrible condition of the *India,* they refused to accept responsibility. Accordingly she limped on toward Australia with her cargo of dying Italians.

On Saturday, April 9, 1881, a Sydney reporter related the condition of the colonists nine months after their gay departure from Spain. "I have just returned from a third visit to the *India,* and the more one sees on board, the more one is struck with the horrors of the whole insane attempt that had been the cause of such misery. An extended inspection between decks revealed more suffering than witnessed on the previous visits. Several poor women—two of them young girls of eighteen and twenty—were stretched helpless, the victims of fever. One was a mother beside a child, lifted up to show me that it was a living, or rather a dying skeleton. . . .

"A few lemons, onions and such trifles distributed by a visitor were eagerly and thankfully received, causing the wish for power to make them rain for a time. Two poor souls less to endure this misery, a woman, weakened by fever and suffering, having passed away last night an hour or two after her confinement—mother and child dead. The deaths in this lot of colonists up to the present, exclusive of the last named, total forty-two. . . .

"Those too ill to work in New Ireland were deprived entirely of their wine. *They were expected to work like slaves,* when the mean range of the thermometer in the shade was 90°. In malarious country, and on an insufficient regimen, the ration of meat per man was reduced to 82 grams (not quite three ounces) per day. Little wonder that in a very short time eighty were on the sick list with fever, thirty of them helpless, the half of the colony in ill health. Yet the doctor is told to 'mind his own business' when pointing out the daily increasing danger and probable mortality."

Now began the final tragedy, and it is difficult, in view of all that had so far transpired, to believe that the governments of Europe would have permitted this additional disaster. But at Barcelona the Marquis de Rays assembled a fourth shipload of colonizers, jammed down the hatches and sent the vessel out to the Pacific with little food, less medicine and no possible hope of survival in Nouvelle France.

It would be needlessly harrowing to recount the familiar and deadly events that overtook this pathetic group. Many died en route, and when the survivors reached Nouvelle France they found a sullen and near-mad Captain Rabardy who, embittered over the escape of the Italians during his absence, was determined that not a single passenger of this fourth ship would ever leave Port Breton.

"Unfortunate beings!" he cried as he stalked aboard their ship. "What brings you here?"

He ordered them ashore, onto the very spot where the other volunteers had died trying to exist with no food, no land, no homes. He then set up a watch to prevent any escape or any communication with the missionaries down the coast, who had saved some of the preceding groups.

After a few days ashore, the utter hopelessness of Port Breton was apparent to all, and a delegation attempted to persuade Captain Rabardy to allow them to try some other

spot, but he answered with loaded revolvers and told them
unmistakably that this was their permanent home and that
here they must either live with what they had or perish. He
then produced his secret orders, signed by the Marquis, which
stated that any critics of the regime in Nouvelle France
should be expelled and left to the tender mercies of the cannibals, concluding: "You may condemn to death anyone who
questions your authority or mine. Not only *may* you sentence
him to death, it is your absolute duty to do so, should there
be the slightest insubordination. By *divine right* I command
you to do so in my name."

Rabardy then roared into his cabin, where he amused himself with his fifteen-year-old black girl, Tani, who was now
his only friend. He insisted that all officers loyal to King
Charles I remain on the ship with him, and in time they too
began merely to wait for the colonists ashore to die.

Students of this amazing chapter of Pacific history—it
occurred when President Rutherford B. Hayes was in the
White House and when cables already connected the main
ports of the world—have suspected that Captain Rabardy
may have had in his possession further orders from the Marquis outlining and approving the course of action he was
pursuing. Others hold that Rabardy was fearful of punishment if any of the victims escaped and brought him to
judgment in a court of law; and that the intolerable situation at Port Breton appalled him as much as it did the
settlers and unbalanced his brain. Although we do not
know what motivated this unhappy man, we do know that he
solemnly announced that he was absolutely committed to
holding the settlers ashore, despite the consequences.

Trading ships arrived and were refused permission to land.
A British warship stood by to see if her crew could help,
but they were ordered to leave the colony alone. The settlers
endeavored to sneak canoes out into the dangerous surrounding waters, but they were stopped and their occupants
threatened with death. Holding his small ship off the mouth
of the bay, Captain Rabardy ate the choice food aboard,
laughed at the settlers and advised them to grow crops or
starve.

He did make one trip. He went across the straits to the
ultrasavage island of Buka, off the northern tip of Bougainville, where he captured a cargo of slaves. These he brought
back, under the Liberian flag, and offered at $100 each to

the desperate colonists, who had not enough food to keep themselves alive.

One bright hope in these dreadful final days sustained the colonists. The captain of the fourth ship was an honorable man, and at great risk to himself had evaded Rabardy's blockade and fled with his ship to Manila, where he cabled the Marquis for funds to save the settlers. None were forthcoming, but promises were made, and on the strength of these, Captain Henry loaded his ship with rescue supplies. Then, as the days passed and no cabled funds arrived, it became apparent to both the captain and his Spanish creditors that the Marquis had finally and completely abandoned the subjects of his kingdom.

In despair, Captain Henry dispatched a most urgent cable, only to get this heartless reply: "We have no funds in hand from the Marquis. Sell or return all you have bought and, if necessary, dispose of the ship itself. Under no circumstances whatever will we be responsible for outlay."

When word of this cable got around Manila, the government made the captain give his word of honor that he would not run away before the merchandise could be unloaded. Captain Henry was now faced with a terrible moral decision. He could surrender his ship and doom the remaining colonists to certain death, or he could break his word of honor, steal the provisions already aboard, and slip out of Manila. He chose the latter—the only time in this sorry affair when anyone in authority, except the missionaries, helped the dying colonists. Captain Henry thus turned pirate to bring back food to Port Breton.

He had scarcely distributed the goods, however, when a Spanish warship hove into the harbor and arrested both him and his ship. But he made such a heartfelt plea to the Spanish commander that, in spite of Rabardy's savage objections, the Spanish warship carried away the most seriously ill, allowing those who survived when the ship reached Manila to find whatever life they could in that capital. After months of questioning, a compassionate judge exonerated Captain Henry of the charges against him.

It is recorded by impeccable authorities that when the Marquis' ship was sold at auction at Manila to cover the bad debts, out of the hold was dragged case after case of the goods that he himself had ordered put there for the sustenance of his Pacific kingdom: a cargo of Punch and

Judy shows; hundreds of pink and white satin slippers to be worn by native beauties who wished to attend the court of King Charles I; twenty-two cases of official-size paper stamped with the royal coat of arms. But even that cargo was less preposterous than part of what the earlier ship, *India,* had carried—three thousand dog collars; while one rescue ship dispatched from Australia by the Baron de Villeblanche contained a few pounds of food and a complete cargo of bricks.

When the Spanish warship sailed from Nouvelle France for Manila, there were forty resolute settlers left on the beach, the last tragic tide of King Charles I's empire. They might have had a chance had they been able to move away from that impossible ledge of land between the sea and the mountain to another part of the island, but offshore stood Captain Rabardy's ship, deserted by its entire crew but still commanded by its mad captain.

Rabardy remained alone with his native girl, Tani, and he now proceeded to make life ashore an added hell. He would issue no food, talk with no one, permit no movement from the beach. Thirty of the forty settlers were prostrated by the fever at one time, and it seemed as if all must perish unless they got away, but Captain Rabardy, alone in his ship, kept his guns trained on the colony and announced that Nouvelle France would be maintained. It was a sacred obligation. To the last, he refused to believe that the Marquis de Rays had abandoned him. To the final day he trusted that a new ship, with new colonists headed for a new death, would arrive. In savage grandeur he remained steadfast to the Marquis who had showered him with honors, position and a promise of great wealth.

At this point, as the last colony is perishing, it is appropriate to speculate on what might have happened to these ventures had the Marquis de Rays, in his Quimerc'h study, selected some spot other than fatal Port Breton.

Suppose he had decided upon nearby Blanche Bay on New Britain Island. Here a ring of volcanoes makes the soil extraordinarily productive. One of the finest beaches in the Pacific invites repose, and palm trees yield abundant coconuts. Large ships can be accommodated in the spacious roads, and the hinterlands provide trading stuff with which to fill those ships. In the years immediately after the Marquis' disastrous colonizing, settlers from England and Germany were to invade lovely Blanche Bay in droves, and all were to prosper. Here, in the city called Rabaul, notable fortunes were made and every promise made by the Marquis came to fruition. The magnificent site of this prosperous settlement is only sixty miles from Port Breton, and had even one ship stumbled upon Blanche Bay, everything the settlers dreamed of and more would have been theirs. Instead, mad Captain Rabardy held the colonists to their doomed strip of inhospitable shore.

Ironically, a monument stands in one of the main streets of Rabaul today to commemorate what might have been. It is a gigantic millstone, shipped out by the Marquis de Rays to enable his colonists to grind their nonexistent grain. In the late 1930's the harbormaster of Rabaul found it on an exploring expedition to Port Breton and hauled it across the channel on a raft. It was erected with an appropriate brass plate, and although the rest of Rabaul was completely leveled by the Allied bombings in World War II, the old stone remained upright as a memento of the folly of King Charles I.

Even closer to Port Breton lay the less spectacular, but equally rewarding, strand of Kokopo, also on New Britain but safe from Rabaul's volcanoes. Here some of Oceania's finest plantations have brought wealth to many, for the climate is good, and down the bay there is an acceptable harbor. Because of the clean winds and moderate rain, tropical diseases were easily mastered. One of the authors has spent many pleasant days in Kokopo. He relished the blazing midday heat and slept refreshed in the breeze-cooled nights. Today Kokopo houses just about the number of families sent out by the Marquis to his hopeless domain a few leagues to the southeast.

As if wishing to demonstrate what might have been accomplished had the Marquis chosen Rabaul, a cabin boy from one of the ships escaped from Port Breton and by chance wandered to Rabaul, got a job with a plantation owner, and later took up land of his own near Kokopo which in the 1930's was sold for a goodly sum. Any of the Marquis' dupes could probably have accomplished as much, had they been permitted to settle at a more promising spot.

Rabaul and Kokopo were on New Britain Island. Were there any promising locations on New Ireland? At the northern end of this island, German colonists later built a splendid capital at Kavieng, with sporting clubs, a harbor for big ships, and stores with goods from Europe. When, during World War I, the British took over, an air base was added.

Particularly along the western coast of New Ireland, a hundred profitable plantations proved that men no more gifted than those who fumbled their way ashore at Port Breton could, with proper planning, cut themselves a home from the rich jungle and prosper. Moreover, New Ireland traders made fortunes collecting turtles, shark fins, bêche-de-mer, bird of paradise feathers and other products of the Bismarck Archipelago.

The tragedy of Nouvelle France can best be comprehended with the aid of a map. Mark in red pencil each of the New Ireland establishments where Germans and Englishmen have lived prosperously along the shores of this wild cannibal island. An interesting pattern develops. The red dots are scattered fairly evenly along the entire coast. This means that a gambler could have pointed to almost any spot along the shore, saying, "That's where we'll settle." And his chances of striking a likely site—move up or down the coast ten miles in either direction—would have been almost one hundred per cent certain.

There was, of course, one unlucky spot to be avoided. There nothing could prosper. Even today, as one studies the map of New Ireland, there remains one spot that has never been settled. Not gasoline, nor penicillin, nor air service, nor government subsidy for copra, nor radio, nor the help of mission schools—not all of these aids together have made this one God-forsaken spot even remotely habitable. During World War II, even the Japanese defenders of New Ireland refused to bother about that unlucky, miasmal, hopeless beach, for they knew that no army could land there and maintain itself.

It was, of course, this spot that the Marquis de Rays chose for his kingdom. But unlucky as this choice was, all would nevertheless have been saved if he had directed his ships to coast even a few miles in any direction. Had they found Blanche Bay, we know that great riches would have come to all. Had they reached Kavieng, all would have been well. A week's exploration—no, two days—and France would have had a powerful colony with a rather fat and ridiculous King Charles I lording it over his black subjects. If the Marquis de Rays and his henchmen had demonstrated one degree of resilience or accommodation to local conditions, no tragedy need have occurred.

But now, in February, 1882, as the last miserable group of colonists huddled on the rain-soaked shore, thirty-five were dying of fever and only five were reasonably well. They stalked the tiny beach and tried to contrive some means of escape. As they plotted, they were watched constantly by Captain Gustave Rabardy, who was more determined than ever that they must remain there and perish.

Finally, in true French fashion, the settlers convened and solemnly declared themselves the Republic of Port Breton. Thus ended the Kingdom of Nouvelle France. Then, with democratic ardor, they defied Rabardy and his little black girl. They established contact with a planter across the bay at Duke of York Island. When he arrived, they were finally evacuated. There was room on the Port Breton beach for not one more grave, and nobody had the strength to hew a tomb from the solid rock of the mountain slope.

Captain Rabardy's resistance had collapsed and, in ungracious surrender, he called his crew back on board and sailed his ship to the plantation on Duke of York Island. Hearing that the three dozen surviving colonists were planning to take the *Génil* to Australia, he fell ill and sulked in his hammock. Then an incident occurred which has never been explained. A daughter of one of the surviving colonists describes it:

"On February 15, 1882, about a quarter past ten in the evening, Mr. Farrell [the planter] came on board, and used all his powers of persuasion to induce the captain to come to his residence and enjoy the comforts of a well-appointed home where he could receive proper nursing. Rabardy resisted every argument, every wile advanced by Farrell. The doctor, rather surprised by the pertinacity shown by the planter, was afraid to allow Rabardy to leave the shelter of the ship, for he knew full well the temper of the colonists who had been so cruelly wronged.

"Next morning the doctor left the *Génil* to visit his patients on board the pontoon. On his return he was surprised to find the captain's hammock empty.

" 'Where is Captain Rabardy?' he asked M. Dessus.

" 'On shore. Mr. Farrell came this morning, and renewed his invitation. He would take no refusal, so finally the captain yielded to his importunity.' . . .

"Although the doctor was uneasy (he could not explain why), he decided to remain on board until after the midday meal. While he was still at luncheon, he heard a voice calling him from afar. He hurried on deck and saw a canoe with Chambaud on board, coming at full speed.

" 'Rabardy is dead!' shouted the surveyor.

" 'Thank God!' exclaimed a colonist standing among a group on deck.

"Without the loss of a second of time the doctor jumped into the canoe, and ten minutes later entered the Farrells drawing-room, where the ex-governor of Port Breton lay dead, extended on a couch, his hands hanging limply by his sides. An empty cup, which had evidently been recently washed and dried, was on a small table beside him.

"The doctor made the necessary examination. Rabardy was indeed dead. Turning to Mr. Farrell, who was watching every movement with the closest attention, the doctor said: 'I must conduct a postmortem.'

"To which Mr. Farrell replied: 'Impossible, in this climate. For reasons that you fully understand, burial cannot be delayed, and must take place before nightfall.'

"Much against the doctor's will, arrangements were made for a speedy interment. By three o'clock all was ready; the pastor, the bier, the candles, and three canoes to convoy the cortege to the neighboring island-cemetery.

"On a brilliant sunny afternoon, with waves dancing in the sun, the final scene in the story of Rabardy takes place. About three o'clock on the sandy stretch between Mr. Farrell's house and the sea, a catafalque is erected. On an open bier, supported by four bamboos, lies Rabardy, dressed in his uniform, hands crossed on the hilt of his sword. The doctor delays the burial until unmistakable signs of dissolution have set in, which happens very speedily under a tropic sun. Officers from the *Génil*, also dressed in uniform, come in their boats, and stand at attention around the open coffin. Little Tani [Rabardy's Melanesian wife], bowed with grief, sobs her heart out at the foot of the bier; Fijian ministers chant their dirges. Rabardy, lying there, is at last at peace, is at last free from the ever present terror of assassination. . . .

"Tani wept for two days, and then played with the light-heartedness of youth among the bevy of young Samoan maidens.

" 'Where is your Capi?' the doctor asked her.

" 'Gone, gone,' she replied; then blithely continued her game."

The Marquis de Rays, meanwhile, was having a delightful time in Spain and France. Altogether he had collected about two million dollars, of which he had probably spent on colonization less than one fourth. Even when his entire colony lay dying, he had refused to cable a single franc to Manila to save it.

What did he do with his money? He maintained several houses in lavish style, paraded three notorious mistresses— one Spanish—around Europe and overwhelmed them with luxuries, and continued to mouth his debt to God for having made possible an empire of religious and forthright men in the Pacific, where noble savages who knew not the ways of the Lord were being saved.

No matter what grim stories filtered back to Europe, his reputation seems not to have suffered. In his three main ships he sent a total of at least 610 European men and women to Port Breton. It is impossible to find out the fate of each of these, although the *Chandernagore* passenger list furnishes a sample: out of 90, no less than 27 died and 21 disappeared. We know that at least 200 survivors, mainly Italians, reached Sydney; 65, mainly Spaniards, reached Manila; and a final 36 got to Australia after Captain Rabardy's death. Of course, many counted as rescued died quickly, as did about half the crew members, who are not included in these figures. That leaves more than three hundred passengers unaccounted for.

If only one of these unfortunates had died as a result of the Marquis' folly, or lack of planning, or downright carelessness, the nobleman would have been guilty of criminal negligence. If, as there is good reason to suppose, he actually gave surreptitious orders to his captains to mistreat the colonists, or worse, he was guilty of murder. That he perpetrated these deeds under the guise of Christianity was nauseating. But that he callously claimed that he and his henchmen, in the year 1881, were above jurisdiction because they acted under the sanctions of divine right, was insane.

Belatedly the French government, which had always opposed the Marquis' schemes, came to the same conclusion. In 1882 he was extradited from Spain on charges of swindling, infraction of emigration laws and homicide through criminal imprudence. At his trial, for certain legal reasons, the last two charges were dropped; nevertheless, under the swindling charge alone the prosecution brought in as evidence no less than twelve thousand documents.

Unbelievably, while the Marquis was awaiting trial and

the newspapers were exposing his heartlessness, many of his adherents refused to believe in his guilt. Here is a translation of an address submitted to him on New Year's Day, 1883:

"Sire:

"The more your raging persecutors torture you in body and soul, the more they attempt to blacken your character in the eyes of your fellow citizens, the more is it our duty to express our admiration for your esteemed person. We humbly pray you to permit us to express the reasons for our love, our fidelity, and our veneration.

"(1) *Veneration.* You are a real martyr; you suffer persecution because you wished to colonize for God.

"(2) *Fidelity.* How disappointed your accusers would be, could they but lift the veil of the future; could their stupefied gaze but see you occupying a throne in Melanesia. But if your enemies could be satisfied only by your death, we would immediately cry: 'The King is dead—long live the King,' and your eldest son would immediately be proclaimed by us Charles II of La Nouvelle France."

On the opening day of the trial in March, 1883, the Marquis made a splendid impression, with his nobility of bearing and his dreamy pale blue eyes—slightly resembling those of Napoleon III, his hearers remarked. They wept when he wept. But the public prosecutor did not spare him, and the frightful tale unfolded.

To his loyal defenders only one item of the shocking evidence seemed to detract from De Rays's reputation, and that only slightly: the prosecutor proved that the supposed marquis was not really a marquis at all. He was really only a viscount.

Nearly a year later, after a sensational trial, he was convicted, fined a sum equivalent to $600, and sent to jail for six years, of which he had already served two. Imprisonment affected the unthroned Charles I very little. Shortly after his release—the unspent portion of his Nouvelle France money stashed away safely somewhere—he offered Europe a medicine guaranteed to heal all known illnesses. It was made of powdered granite rocks from his Quimerc'h estate. The Paris police soon put a stop to its sale.

His jail term did no apparent damage to his reputation, for we last see this engaging nobleman in the evening of his eventful life. Still strutting as King Charles I, he conducted a gala world cruise—probably the first of its kind—on the luxury liner *Tyburnia.* He announced, with studied condescension, that only English and French passengers with titles would be accommodated, since he wished the trip to be free of crudeness or unpleasantness of any kind.

On its triumphant tour the *Tyburnia* did not visit Port Breton.

3

Coxinga, Lord
of the Seas

Sturdy Francis Drake, first Englishman to penetrate the wealth-laden waters of the Pacific, stood on the quarter-deck of his voyage-worn little ship, the *Golden Hind*, which was riding just north of the Equator, in wait for prey off the coast of South America. Drake, already known to the plundered Spanish merchants of the Caribbean as the terror of the Spanish Main, was about to strike anew, here in the Pacific.

It was at dawn on March 1, 1579, that his young cousin John Drake rushed up and cried, "Yonder comes the Spanish galleon!" He had spotted a great prize, for there, a dozen miles astern, loomed the high-pooped Spanish argosy they had been hoping to ambush.

"This gold chain is your reward, coz," cheerily replied Drake, taking the heavy chain from his neck and putting it over the boy's head. The Prince of Buccaneers then gave orders to throw aft some huge jars on ropes, in order to slow down his speedy ship so that the unsuspecting treasure galleon would overtake her around dusk. Drake did not want the captain of the galleon, the *Cacafuego*, to discover that his little ship was English until it was too late to escape or to pitch the treasure overboard.

The galleon creaked and blundered on, its crew never

imagining that ahead lay the ship of Drake, whose name had been translated by the Spaniards as "The Dragon," and that the vessel held a gang of English buccaneers who were already almost sated with plunder after six months of ravaging ships and towns along the exposed western coast of South America. At dusk, the captain of the *Cacafuego* curtly refused to pause at Drake's hail. But when a cannon ball knocked down the Spanish mizzenmast and the navigator was wounded by an arrow from an English longbow, the great galleon abruptly surrendered.

After clapping the Spanish crew below hatches and putting his own men aboard to sail the *Cacafuego* out of the dangerous coastal waters, Drake had to wait two days before he had time to take an inventory of the cargo of the captured galleon. He found aboard fourteen great chests full of coined pieces-of-eight, eighty pounds of gold bullion, caskets of pearls, bars of pure silver weighing twenty-six tons and many rich pieces of massy plate, chains and gleaming jewels. The crew grumbled at the labor of transferring this huge booty to their own ship, for it took several days. Even without the jewels, the cargo of the *Cacafuego* was worth £250,000 sterling—which today would be the equivalent of about twenty million dollars.

Yet even this was not enough for Drake. The dignified old pilot of the Spanish ship privately owned two fine silver bowls. The Englishman eyed them greedily. "Sir pilot, you have two cups here; I must needs have one of them!" Disdainfully the old man gave him one and in stinging rebuke tossed the other to Drake's steward. The great freebooter, already possessed of one of the richest prizes ever taken, could afford to ignore the insult. He ordered the ship to sail to a quiet island where he could divide up the loose money among his men.

There were only forty-five men in his crew and each, the Spaniards later reported, was given sixteen bowls full of coins. But many men heaved their share overboard, because the overladen, hundred-ton *Golden Hind* could not carry it all! No wonder that, when the plundering Drake returned to England after being the first of his countrymen to circumnavigate the globe, he was knighted on his quarter-deck by Queen Bess, who lovingly addressed him in her letters as "My dear pirate."

Western readers are apt to think of piracy as a brutal art which flourished mainly in the Caribbean, where the principal pirates of romance operated. Because names like Jean Lafitte, François L'Ollonais, and "Blackbeard" Teach struck terror in the forecastles of Atlantic trading vessels, we have become accustomed to think of the West Indies pirate as the leading exemplar of his cutthroat trade. But even Sir Henry Morgan, who sacked Panama and switched from being admiral of a pirate fleet to governor of Jamaica, never took booty such as the argosies of the Pacific regularly yielded.

For there the richest prizes sailed—the yearly galleons from Manila to Mexico, laden with spices, silks, Oriental art, gold plate, pearls and other gems. There, too, sailed the silver fleets, overburdened with refined metal from the mines of Peru. The lure of these defenseless treasure ships was too great to resist, and buccaneers from many nations flocked to the Pacific to ply their bloody trade.

The luckiest were those who, like Drake, Cavendish and George Anson, came early. Thomas Cavendish, "The Corsair," who arrived eight years after Drake's voyage and burned nineteen Spanish ships, earned enough to have bought him an earldom when he succeeded in capturing the *Santa Ana*, merely one of the huge Manila galleons. His world-circling little *Desire* returned to London with her topmasts wrapped in cloth of gold and her crew ostentatiously lolling on deck, magnificently clad in priceless silks and brocades. Plunder like this, which the Pacific offered each year, put the pillaging of Henry Morgan into eclipse.

Although Francis Drake never flew the skull-and-bones or made a fat merchant walk the plank, he was nevertheless the most successful buccaneer among a long roster of fellow pirates of the Pacific. Despite the romance of the Caribbean, the pirates of the Pacific levied the greatest toll upon the world's shipping and were also the most fierce and bloodthirsty, fighting and dying for the joy of slaughter.

The Malayan breed of pirate that haunted the Straits of Malacca west of Singapore, for example, was incredibly fiery and persistent. For centuries these devils focused at the northern tip of Sumatra, where their descendants, unconquered even now, wage desultory warfare today against the Indonesian government. It is recorded in American naval history that when one of our warships showed our flag for the first time in the Straits of Malacca, the pirates of Sumatra joyfully leaped into their terrifying craft, sped out to sea, and engaged the American ship in a fierce battle "just to see whether the men in the strange new ship could fight." Toward dusk the pirates were satisfied that the American flag bespoke

a certain bravery, if no great skill, and the marauders retired content.

For terror, for merciless brutality to passengers of captured ships, and for ability to withstand the efforts of European nations to dislodge them, the Malayan pirates were
unsurpassed. One can read of their prowess in the works of
Joseph Conrad, but perhaps the most fascinating account of
their depredations is found in the records of British naval
officers sent to subdue the pirates of Borneo, who were ravaging the newly founded kingdom of the great white Rajah
of Sarawak, the Englishman Sir James Brooke. The Borneo
pirates were an almost indestructible crew, and well into the
twentieth century they defied as much of the British fleet as
could be spared for use against them. Even to this day, at the
slightest diminution of visible police power, the Malayan pirate springs back into action, his courage as strong and as
unabated as it was in the early 1500's, when any ship from
India or from the Spice Islands was likely to be overhauled
and all hands slain.

But the spot where the history of piracy goes back at least
to pre-Christian times, and continues today almost unabated,
is the China Sea, the breeding ground for the adventurer who
became undoubtedly the greatest pirate of the Pacific. This
man, a Chinese-Japanese, could probably be termed the premier pirate in history, for before his untimely death he built
himself a broad empire and made sovereign nations tremble
at his name. His life encompassed not only success in ocean
fighting, not only the winning of incomparable riches, but
also the exhibition of victory and defeat on the epic scale
and a persistence of character—displayed in an unshakable
loyalty to lost causes—which actually won him godhood in
the pantheons of two different nations.

To comprehend the story of this majestic pirate we must
go to the inconspicuous little Chinese village of Anhai at the
opening of the seventeenth century. The mud huts of Anhai
lay not far from the important South China seaport of Amoy,
and were thus only a few miles due north of the strategic island of Quemoy, which in turn lay only about a hundred miles
west of the great and rich island of Formosa. Japan was
about nine hundred miles to the northeast of Anhai, and the
riotous Portuguese enclave of Macao only three hundred
and fifty miles to the southwest.

Anhai, therefore, although itself insignificant, lay along
the principal trade routes that interlocked China, Japan, For-

mosa and Portuguese Macao. Any venturesome boy of Anhai was likely to become involved with this trade. That was
true of one particularly alert child, born about 1603, the
illegitimate son of an obscure Anhai workman.

Little is known of his youth, but he left home to seek
his fortune, and in 1621 he suddenly appeared in the colony
of Macao, where he mastered the Portuguese language and
got a post with a Chinese merchant. Contemplating a permanent residence in that wild, rich city, he had himself
baptized a proper Christian, taking the Catholic names of
Gaspar Nicholas. He was to be known to history as Nicholas
Iquan—the latter name deriving from Chinese words meaning "eldest son."

Of his days in Macao a chronicler wrote: "And as he
wanted not for wit, he every day improved himself, grew
more and more cunning, and capable of higher advance-
ment."

One of the ways in which Nicholas Iquan proved his
ability was by initiating trade, on his own youthful account,
with a tremendously wealthy and powerful Chinese merchant who, escaping the galleys in Manila, had fled to Japan
and made his headquarters in the coastal village of Hirado.
Here he and his brothers traded with Annam and Tonkin,
and were pioneers in the opening up of Formosa. This canny
trader, known throughout Eastern Asia simply as Captain
China, had a vast fleet of ships, monopolies everywhere and
a rugged courage that enabled him to withstand the pressures
of the Japanese, the connivances of the brilliant Dutch
traders who were his rivals and the depredations of pirates
who plagued his convoys. Actually, Captain China was himself a pirate and smuggler on a lavish scale, and he was on
the lookout for promising young men to add to his service. It
soon became apparent to him that in Macao there was growing up another young trader just about as adventurous as
himself.

Captain China was also nominally a Christian, but how he
and Nicholas Iquan first got acquainted we do not know. One
document states: "Icoan [Iquan] or Gaspar seeing himself
at Macao but in a mean condition, and not much considered, returned to his own country; but not being advanced
there, nor contenting himself how to live low and obscure, he
went from thence to Japan, where at that time there was
great freedom to all nations to come and trade, and for this
reason he fixed himself there, and got employment under a

very rich Chinese merchant, whom he served with great fidelity and diligence in all his concerns, and was very well approved of by his master, who found him daily more and more intelligent in all things relating to traffic, and so confided in him that he sent him with some ships, and a great part of his wealth entrusted to his care, to trade in the kingdoms of Cochin China and Cambaye. Gaspar acquitted himself so well of his employment that he returned with great profit to his master and much credit to himself."

From his arrival in Japan, probably in 1622, Nicholas Iquan worked hard. He became Captain China's right-hand man, and thus it was his job to negotiate often with the Dutch, who were among the ablest and most determined traders ever to operate in those waters. Captain China had long been friendly with them and in 1624 advised them to move their base from the Pescadores Islands to Formosa. For several years he acted as a mediator of treaties between the Dutch and the Chinese of the mainland.

It was not surprising, therefore, that Iquan suddenly turned up in 1624 at the Dutch headquarters in the Pescadores, where he served as tailor and interpreter. This latter occupation was extraordinary in that he could speak no Dutch; he was, however, proficient in Chinese and Japanese, and more particularly in Portuguese, the *lingua franca* of commerce in the Far East. He undoubtedly conversed with the Dutch in that language. Under Captain China's encouragement, the Dutch now set up a strong base in Formosa, and promoted migration there of Chinese settlers from the mainland. As an employee of the Dutch, in 1625 Nicholas Iquan was able to squeeze money from the immigrants, but failing to amass any substantial wealth in this way, he dreamed of higher goals. Then his chance came.

His patron, Captain China, died in Japan in the fall of 1625, and by the exercise of prompt and daring initiative Iquan launched his career as a pirate chief. He simply usurped control of the late Captain China's ships and property by pushing aside the claims of his late patron's son and heir. When necessary, he even engaged in the murder of any loyal servants who opposed him, and shortly his swift craft were harrying the Fukien coast. Within four months of murdering off the opposition, the young pirate had consolidated his position as virtual master of the China Sea.

He commanded four hundred heavily armed junks. These he dispersed at strategic points along the sea lanes, while he himself returned to his ancestral village of Anhai to assume command of all operations. Portuguese caravels fell into his hands, and their rich cargoes were sold in the waterfront shops of Amoy. Dutch merchantmen who strayed from the protection of Dutch warships were quickly overpowered and their goods sped into Canton, where traders retained friendly relations with all pirates in hopes of obtaining desirable cargoes. Any vessel setting forth from Japan loaded with the most envied trade goods of Asia—for they were of polished workmanship and difficult to obtain—ran the immediate risk of being quickly overhauled and burned by Nicholas Iquan's disciplined pirates.

By the beginning of 1627 Iquan commanded the entire China coast between the Yangtse and Pearl rivers, and the acting governor of Formosa reported: "Over a year previously a man named Iquan, formerly interpreter to the [Dutch East India] Company, left without notice and became chief of a pirate band. He amassed much shipping and men, and terrorized the whole China coast, laying waste provinces, towns, and villages, and rendered navigation along that part of the coast impracticable."

It had now become painfully apparent to the Dutch that this upstart rival, formerly a mere interpreter and tailor in their employ, would have to be taught a lesson. Accordingly a squadron of nine powerful Dutch warships was dispatched to rout out the pirate and destroy his anchorages off Amoy.

The expedition was a disaster. Iquan, bringing into play all his piratical experience, encouraged his junks to wage such merciless warfare against the more unwieldy Dutch ships that the entire squadron, seeing victory unattainable, turned and fled to Java.

Now Nicholas Iquan was unopposed in his chosen seas, and by the end of 1627 he commanded no less than a thousand sail. He captured outright the island city of Amoy and used it as his commercial headquarters, bringing parts of his extensive fleet to its protecting harbor. Yet his rise to ultimate power did not come without a struggle, for he lost Amoy through treachery and had to call upon his former enemies the Dutch to help him recapture it in February, 1630. Years of hard fighting and of ups and downs elapsed before his position as pirate king was finally secure.

But he never relaxed his ambition and in time gained absolute command of the entire China coast from Shanghai to Canton, and this was not a loosely held control. No ship

hat set out for Japan, Formosa or Macao had much chance
of escaping his pirates. Even small coastal vessels, carrying
on the work of the Ming emperor of China, were likely to
be intercepted, and sometimes the Iquan pirates sailed boldly
into port cities that were supposedly in command of Ming
ground troops and either laid those facilities waste or held
the city for ransom.

This was piracy on the grand scale, and Nicholas Iquan
lived in a style commensurate with his riches. It was estimated by contemporaries that he had more than $5,000,000
in his personal treasury, in addition to a superb palace at
Anhai, which was fitted out with the finest furnishings that
Japan and China could provide.

Understandably, he feared assassination and was constantly guarded by an elite troop of seventy-six Dutchmen who
wore special uniforms and were paid well out of the public
treasury. Later, when he saw that these Dutchmen wanted to
return to their own countrymen in Java, he released them
and conscripted an even more striking personal guard whose
fame was to last in Asia for many years. From Macao
he acquired three hundred Negro slaves who had escaped
from that colony after having been hauled there by Portuguese slavers working off Africa. These giant men, dressed
in startling silks, hovered constantly about the person of the
pirate chief, lending him an air of mystery and power.

The estimate of $5,000,000 for Iquan's personal fortune
at this time is probably conservative, for we know that he
announced himself Lord of the Straits of Formosa and that
he licensed nonpirate ships to trade there under his protection for the staggering fee of $15,000 a year for each
separate ship. He was reported in Japan to be "the richest
man in China." A later historian said of the pirate, "He was
good-looking, a skillful poet, a musician of taste, a dancer
of merit, and withal of pleasing manners."

It was obvious that Iquan's supremacy could not continue
unchallenged, and in fact it was allowed to exist at all only
because Chinese, Japanese, and Dutch could not agree upon
concerted action to cleanse the seas of this gentle, gifted
and well-behaved monster. The problem was solved rather
neatly by the vacillating Ming emperor, who in 1628,
squeezed by both internal and external pressures, sought
some relief by offering Iquan the job of Commander of the
Imperial Fleet with full mandarin rank and a commission
to drive all pirates from the South China Sea.

Rarely has a messy situation been cleaned up so expeditiously. Pirate Iquan moved from his country palace at Anhai and appeared in the bustling city of Amoy as Admiral Iquan. Here he raised a flag proclaiming his new residence to be the naval headquarters of the imperial Chinese government.

It was as admiral of the fleets that in 1633 he engaged in a full-scale war with the Dutch, and a less able admiral never operated, for on July 13 of that year the enemy, by a stratagem which could easily have been nullified by good seamanship, burned his entire military fleet. But if Nicholas Iquan was a miserable failure as a formal admiral, he was still one of the world's great pirates, for by October 22 he had somehow reassembled 150 of his old pirate junks, which slipped in upon the Dutch in a stratagem of their own, and totally humiliated his erstwhile conquerors, destroying their vessels and breaking the blockade of Amoy. His pirates having regained what his legal fleet had lost, Iquan never again abandoned piracy, and from then on the Chinese Navy was a curious blend of imperial warships and pirate junks, all operating to the growing glory of Nicholas Iquan. It is recorded that in 1639, ninety-three Chinese junks put into Nagasaki harbor in southern Japan to pick up the choicest trade goods, and of these about three quarters were trading in the personal name of Iquan. This was the apex of his career.

For the years of tragedy were closing in, requiring this bold pirate to make substantial decisions in the field of moral judgment, and his grievous failure in this respect marred his reputation and cost him his life. These were the trying years when the exhausted Ming dynasty, which had governed China for almost three centuries, was being invaded from the north by the resolute Manchus, who were destined to destroy the Ming rule and to reign successfully as alien invaders down to the revolution of 1911.

Throughout China men in positions of authority were required to take sides. Was the glorious Ming reign entering its final eclipse? If so, would it not be wise to link one's fortunes with the surging, brutal Manchus? On the other hand, had not the Ming often been in difficulties and had they not always triumphed? Would it not be wiser to wait awhile before abandoning their cause as hopeless? Like hundreds of his compatriots, Nicholas Iquan weighed these delicate moral problems.

At first he sided boldly with the Ming and in 1644 accepted from them the resounding title of Count Pacifier of the South. Later he became a full duke, and it seemed that history was about to provide another example in which a land revolution, led this time by the Manchus, would fail to enlist the support of a loyal navy, which in this case would continue to adhere to the dying Ming banners.

But now the Ming cause began to deteriorate rapidly and Duke Nicholas, hearing of the losses ashore, began his fatal vacillation. It was speeded when the Manchus offered him the viceroyship of three major provinces if he would deliver his pirate fleet to their side.

This offer was so appealing to Duke Nicholas that he decided to accept. Accordingly, one morning he left his naval headquarters in Amoy and journeyed to the Manchu city of Foochow surrounded by troops, including his imposing personal guard of three hundred Macao Negroes. Iquan was now about forty-three years old, one of the most powerful figures in war-torn China. His wealth was indeterminable, his fleets vast, his area of control greater than that enjoyed by most European monarchs of his time. Over his dominions he exercised the power of life and death, and over the trade of three nations he was absolute dictator.

We have a portrait of Iquan as he may have looked that day in 1646 while walking through the bright Foochow sunlight on his way to see the Manchu emissaries. He was of middle height and heavy in build. He wore voluminous robes from which his hands did not protrude. He carried a wand of office and a belt of beads hanging over a chunky stomach. He displayed wide-set eyes, bushy eyebrows and a generous nose. He wore a very long, drooping mustache which fell well below his chin, with a broad if not heavy beard and a little square patch of whisker, closely trimmed, right below the edge of his lower lip. He covered his head with a heavily brocaded cap adorned with jewels and ornamented by two scrolls which rose from the rear. His richly made shoes pointed upwards, and if the entire portrait is imaginary, as some claim, it was nevertheless intended to portray a man of substance and authority.

Doubtless he spoke in Portuguese to the giant blacks of his bodyguard, who were arrayed in brilliant costumes which would enhance their impressiveness, so that when Iquan's procession reached the tent of the Manchu general who had been sent south for these important negotiations, the pirate and his bodyguard quite overshadowed the stolid and blunt Manchus.

The Manchu general, having enticed Iquan ashore, proceeded to accord the pirate a series of banquets and entertainments requiring three full days of the most splendid ceremony and concentrated drunkenness. This tickled Iquan's vanity, and while he was preening himself upon the deference paid him by the Manchus, he did not observe that they were inconspicuously separating him from all his troops except his elite Negro guard.

When hidden Manchu soldiers finally fell upon Iquan, a furious battle ensued, in which the Negroes were superb, encouraging each other with the traditional Portuguese battle cry of "Santiago!" This fearfully stirring shout spurred them to extraordinary feats of loyalty and more than one hundred died trying to rescue their master, but in the end the Manchus were victorious, and Nicholas Iquan never again saw the sea.

He was carted, a very special and revered prisoner, to Peking, where he was kept for fourteen long years in loose and luxurious arrest while the alien Manchus systematically subdued and organized the Chinese empire. He was allowed to take a wife, by whom he had a son, and it is recorded that with some of his private wealth he helped Christian missionaries in their work.

Finally, for reasons which will become apparent later, the Manchus tired of their most important prisoner and in 1661 decreed that he should suffer the excruciating "death of the thousand cuts," in which the executioner was charged with slowly hacking away the members of the victim's body, making the required number of cuts before the doomed man died.

At the last moment, possibly inspired by the brave record of this fifty-eight-year-old pirate, the officials relented and allowed him to be beheaded, along with his two lesser sons.

Thus died Nicholas Iquan, one of the most powerful pirates the world has known. His conquests embraced whole seas, thousands of miles of coastline, innumerable ships, vast fleets, an army of many thousands and spoils of such magnitude as to be beyond computation. It is upon the accomplishments of Nicholas Iquan that the authors base their contention that the pirates of the Caribbean were colorful, but the pirates of the Pacific were majestic.

It is with a sense of awe, therefore, that we now state that the man of whom we wish to speak in this chapter outshines Nicholas Iquan in the way the sun outshines the moon. Where Iquan was merely massive in his operations, this man was brilliant. Where Iquan was a pirate merely to indulge himself, this man was a master tactician working on a grand design. And where Iquan vacillated on vital issues, the pirate of whom we write had a constancy of conscience that stupefies the imagination and a devotedness to principle that has immortalized him.

Let us now double back to the year 1622, when the young Chinese merchant Nicholas Iquan grew tired of the confining life of Macao and set out for Japan. He was on his way to that fateful visit to Captain China, whose fleets he would shortly steal in his first great act of piracy.

Iquan probably settled outside of Nagasaki at the village of Hirado, which at this time was the most flourishing center for foreign trade in all Japan. It was not only the main port of call for Chinese merchants, but here the Dutch had chosen to make their headquarters, and in 1623, while Iquan was still there, the English were to open their factory under the flag of the East India Company. Hirado was also the base from which the Dutch and English sent forth a combined fleet to fight their trade rivals, the Spanish and Portuguese. At any rate, wherever he lived the young merchant was faced with one problem that Chinese in Japan face even today: where can a Chinese man get a woman?

After the normal experiments in low dives, and after conversing with the casual girls of the water front, Iquan found a young woman named Tagawa. She was born in 1601 and was thus about the same age as Iquan. Her first name has never been discovered and in Japan and China alike she is known simply as Miss Tagawa. There is bitter controversy in learned circles concerning who she was. Dr. R. A. B. Ponsonby-Fane, an English diplomat, spent many hundreds of words proving to his satisfaction that Miss Tagawa was a lady of excellent background and possibly of the samurai class. Chinese scholars, hoping to claim so notable a girl for their own, contend that she was the daughter of an earlier Chinese merchant and some Japanese girl whom he had picked up along the docks. Enemies of Iquan state bluntly that his wife was a prostitute, and some historians accept the charge: "The 'scion of the proud Tagawa family' was in reality nothing more than the humble inmate of a local brothel in the little fishing town of Hirado." But cooler heads reason that while she was probably a local girl of no distinguished family, the evidence available fails to support the contention that she was a prostitute.

At any rate, this unknown Japanese girl, Miss Tagawa, married the Chinese merchant Nicholas Iquan and became the mother of the greatest pirate Asia, and possibly the world, has ever known. The intense loyalty that characterized her son was doubtless derived from this Tagawa girl: for six years she reared the boy in Japan; for twenty-one years she never saw Iquan. Then, just as Iquan's fortunes were about to collapse with his defection to the Manchu invaders, he summoned this long-forgotten wife to join him at Anhai. Without hesitating, and against all the odds interposed by the reluctant Japanese government, Miss Tagawa emigrated to China, where in the general debacle that overcame her family in 1646, when Iquan surrendered to the Manchus, she preserved its honor by a suicide in the Japanese fashion. Romancers carried word of her gallant action throughout the countryside, embroidering it with lurid details. "She plunged a Japanese sword into herself, then leapt from the wall of the palace at Anhai," whereupon the astounded Manchus are supposed to have cried, "If the women of Japan are of such a sort, what must the men be like?" Exemplifying such constancy, Miss Tagawa passed bodily into Japan's greatest classical drama, where it is said of her, "Even though she was a woman, she did not forget her old home, and paid reverence to the land that gave her birth. Until her last breath she thought of the honor of Japan."

Regardless of her family antecedents, Miss Tagawa was a powerful person and it is recorded that her famous pirate son, although separated from her at the age of six, cherished her as his constant ideal and prayed to her memory during the crises of his life. Says a chronicler: "Every day he would face east and look toward his mother, hiding his tears."

Coxinga,* the name by which this son became known to

---

*Anyone writing of this distinguished adventurer has a plethora of names from which to choose. His name at birth was Cheng Sen, but he acquired the nicknames Cheng Sen-she, Cheng Ta-mu and Cheng Ming-yen. During the Japanese years of his life he was called Tagawa Fukumatsu, but in China he assumed the name by which he is properly known, Cheng Cheng-kung, whose ideographs are read in Japanese as Tei Seiko, by which name he is known in Japan today. In 1645 the Ming emperor bestowed on him his own imperial surname, Chu, which entitled him to the honorific Kuo-hsing-yeh, Lord of the Imperial the world, was thus the offspring of an adventurous Chinese man and a loyal Japanese woman, and much of the symbolic power which was accorded him both during his life and later stems from the fact that he represents the ideal Chinese-Japanese union. There are many today who prophesy that if Japan and China ever unite, it will be for the production of endless Coxingas.

Coxinga was born in Hirado during the Seventh Moon of 1624, the year in which his father Nicholas Iquan left Japan to work for the Dutch in Formosa. At the unlikely age of six the boy was bundled aboard a junk and sent with an older companion to China, where at the village of Anhai he joined his father and became that successful pirate's prize son. He appears to have been a very brainy boy, and at the age of fifteen he was enrolled in the Imperial Collegiate School, where he gained a solid foundation in classical studies and the beginnings of a remarkable education that would have ended in his becoming a learned Confucian scholar and a mandarin. In 1641, at the age of seventeen, the future pirate married a Miss Tung, the first of many wives, and in the next year had a son of his own.

Quickly the moral problems which engulfed and destroyed Coxinga's father crowded in upon the boy. He was forced to choose between the old Ming rulers and the invading Manchu barbarians, and in Coxinga's case the problem of choice was even more difficult, in that his father had already cast his lot with the winning Manchus and enjoyed, for the time being, a position of privilege with them.

For some reason that is not now apparent, young Coxinga chose the dying Ming cause, and defended his choice with passion. One of the most touching features in this confused

---

Surname. These ideographs are read Kokuseiya in Japanese and Kokseng-ya in the Amoy dialect, from which the Dutch derived Coxinga, the name by which he is best known to the West. However, each foreign nation called him according to preference. In Spanish he was often Cotsen; to the French, Quoysim; to the Portuguese, Maroto; to the citizens of Manilla, Pompoan. In Latin he was Quaesingus, and in many works Kuesim. From this welter of names the following alternatives were easily derived, and it is by them that many writers refer to the great pirate: Cheng Kung, Chunggoong, Cocksinja, Cocxima, Cogsen, Cogseng, Cogsin, Conseng, Coseng, Coxiny, Keuseng, Koksengya, Kokusei, Kokusenya, Koshinga, Koxin, Koxsin, Kuesin, Kuesing, Pun Poin, Pumpuan, Punpoan, Quesim, Quesin, Quoseng, Quoesing, Quosing, Tching Tching-cong and Tsung-cheng Shih-lu. After his death, of course, he was accorded an official posthumous name, Chung-chieh.

period of Asiatic history is the resolute loyalty of this pirate
chieftain, for never once, so far as the records show, did he
waver in his steadfastness. Adhering to a lost cause through
agonies of defeat, humiliating retreats, exile from China and
harassment on all sides, he stands forth in his epoch as a
veritable monument to fidelity. It was because of this dedication, persevered in for more than twenty years, that
Coxinga was ultimately created a god in both China and
Japan, and the most remarkable aspect of his deification was
that it was initially promulgated by the very rulers who had
greatest cause to hate him, the Manchus, toward whom his
fiery enmity was constantly directed. When he was dead they
recognized in him the steadfastness they hoped to promote
as a national characteristic.

The steps whereby the youth Coxinga became both the
leading pirate of his age and the head of Asia's largest operating army are fully documented in Chinese sources, but
they parallel so closely the steps taken earlier by his father,
Nicholas Iquan, that to repeat them here would be superflu-
ous. There are, however, certain moments of decision which
are of great interest to students of his character, but unfortunately these have been so inflated by romance and
legend as to be of doubtful historical value. Nevertheless,
the burning of his robes has acquired such symbolic signifi-
cance that most historians accept it. Certainly, something like
this activated Coxinga in his hour of decision.

In 1646, after his father had defected to the Manchus,
and following his immigrant mother's suicide on the walls of
the family castle at Anhai, Coxinga reached his lowest spiritual point, and although the Manchus held out to him rewards of an almost incredible richness and variety, he
spurned them, swore fresh allegiance to his Ming emperor
and disappeared into the hills, attended by only a few close
friends. There he sought out an ancient Confucian temple,
and in a moving ceremony burned his scholar's robes, crying
to heaven, "This one-time Confucian scholar is now an unfortunate subject. My every action must have a purpose,
whether I serve or oppose, stay or go. I now bid farewell to
my Confucian attire. Will the Master in Heaven please
take cognizance of this fact?"

Thereupon, as Coxinga the soldier, he crept down out of
the hills with an insignificant force of ninety comrades and
soon led an army of thousands. No doubt he achieved this

military miracle by simply commandeering his traitorous father's armies; it is certain that he inherited Iquan's imposing pirate fleet, and henceforth he operated as his father had. At the age of twenty-two he constituted the balance of power on the mainland and controlled the China Seas.

So impoverished were the Ming for leaders that young Coxinga was created an earl, with the title Field Marshal of the Punitive Expedition. At the age of twenty-four he was a marquis, at twenty-five a duke and at thirty-one a full prince with suzerainty over an imposing area. He discharged the obligations of these titles gloriously and, while remaining still a pirate whose fleets probed the China Seas for personal loot, he perfected an amazing military machine dedicated to support of the Ming cause. "His force consisted of fifty thousand cavalry and seventy thousand infantry. Of the latter, ten thousand were known as 'iron men,' they being encased in heavy armor decorated with red spots like the leopard, and were always placed in the front rank that they might cut off the feet of the Tartar [Manchu] horses." To support this force, Coxinga personally maintained seventy-two military stations along the coast.

There is a portrait of the pirate leader at this period of his life, and it shows a hefty beardless young man who wears his hair Dutch style and whose armor, joined at the neck in a wide collar, seems also to have been borrowed from the Hollanders. He carries two swords, which he holds before his rugged chest in a strange manner, as if ready to repel an assault. From a heavy leather belt hangs some unidentifiable instrument of war, but it is the man's face that is unforgettable. We see a full-faced warrior who could easily have slipped into the armies of Oliver Cromwell without occasioning much comment, for although his countenance has some Chinese elements, it is not what the Westerner considers an Oriental face. These are the features of an international man who would have been at home anywhere in his contemporary world. It is the face of Coxinga, the Chinese pirate, who by the chances of history had become Coxinga, the timeless adventurer, the lord of the seas.

The Manchu enemy, realizing that they could not subdue China while young Coxinga maintained his power against them, endeavored to seduce him by the same lures that had succeeded with his father. Accordingly, without waiting to see whether he would accept or not, they created him in turn earl, duke and prince. They offered enormous riches and power. They assured him of amnesty and promised him a military command far exceeding what he already had.

His answer was forthright and amazing. He spurned the Manchu offers of nobility, trebled his forces and launched an assault intended to drive the invaders right out of China. It soon became apparent that the crucial battle would be fought at Nanking, for if this redoubt some miles up the Yangtse fell, Peking and the other Manchu positions to the north would be clearly imperiled if not untenable. Coxinga's bold decision was that his fleet should capture Nanking.

It was an unprecedented armada that in 1659 made its way up the coast from Amoy and into the Yangtse under the command of the pirate prince. An observer wrote, "Never before or since was a more powerful and mighty fleet seen in the waters of this empire than that of Coxinga numbering more than 3,000 junks, which he had ordered to rendezvous in the bays and rivers around Amoy. The sight of them inspired one with awe. This squadron did not include the various fleets he had scattered along the neighboring coasts." In addition, Coxinga had a huge land army consisting of 170,000 armored men, 50,000 marines, 5,000 cavalry and 1,000 iron men. His entourage included ten personal concubines, at least one legal wife and three sons. It was a two-pronged thrust by land and river that he made at Nanking, whose outlying centers of resistance soon fell under this pressure. The occupation of the city itself seemed inevitable, and leaders of the Coxinga expedition anticipated the quick humiliation of the Manchu invaders and the restoration of the ancient Ming line.

Then Coxinga, with great victory in his grasp, behaved like a true pirate. On the eve of the final assault he celebrated his thirty-fifth birthday with a wild carouse that soon spread to his entire encampment. The long night of revelry and congratulation was drawing to a close when the Manchus, kept aware of the drunkenness by spies, unleashed a furious attack.

The result was a debacle. Coxinga's mighty force, the most powerful then operating in Asia, was completely demoralized. Manchu cavalry stormed the perimeter of Coxinga's headquarters. Boats in the river were set ablaze. The iron men were stampeded and as dawn broke over the confused and milling Coxinga forces, a disreputable retreat set in.

The high tide of Ming hopes had passed, and as Coxinga led his battered remnants away from the scene of his lamentable birthday party, the Manchu invaders consolidated their control step by step. It was a terrible defeat and unnecessary. It destroyed the Ming and might have been expected to end Coxinga's career.

Certainly the Manchus thought that it had, for they quickly launched a major naval expedition of more than eight hundred ships in a mopping-up operation against Coxinga, whose shabby undestroyed remnants consisted of only about four hundred junks, which were quickly bottled up at Quemoy. The Manchu admirals moved in for the kill.

But now Coxinga's piratical skill manifested itself, and in a fearful day-long battle that recalled Nicholas Iquan's fight against the Dutch in these same waters twenty-seven years earlier, Coxinga toward evening maneuvered his crippled and outnumbered ships masterfully, brought the entire Manchu fleet under two files of cannon and annihilated it. "For many weeks after this terrible catastrophe the beaches of Amoy were covered with rotting bodies and naval debris that the flux and surge of the sea would daily cast on the shores. . . . Not one man lived to tell the tale."

In surly peace, unable to dislodge Coxinga from his harbors or to win him to their side through his father's influence, the Manchus were forced to accept a temporary division of China. They had ninety percent of the sprawling land area. The pirate Coxinga controlled the seas and a thin strip of coast.

Accordingly Coxinga re-established headquarters in Amoy, with his main fleet based on Quemoy, and from here he dominated his realm. But his continued depredations called forth a spectacular retaliation, one that still confounds the imagination.

The Manchus, irritated beyond endurance by this pirate with whom they could not come to grips, foresaw that it might be decades before they could consolidate the coastal areas and cleanse them of his marauders. Moreover, they had cause to suspect that most of the coastal people were both Ming patriots and Coxinga partisans. Accordingly they promulgated one of the most Draconian edicts on record.

All residents of the coast were required on three days' notice to move inland at least seventeen miles. No provision was made for them behind the barrier, and upon arrival they found no food, no water, no housing, no commerce, no government. The law was simple and simply enforced: "Move inland or have your head chopped off."

The misery involved in this countermeasure against Coxinga was appalling. A contemporary writes: "At first the people thought they would return and tried to stay together, but when they saw there was no hope they began to separate. Sons were sold for a bushel of rice, daughters for a hundred cash. Speculators were able to buy people into slavery for practically nothing. Those who were strong and able were made to join the army. The authorities looked on the people as so many ants."

Like ants they crawled inland, away from the life-giving coast. Those who had lived on fish perished, for they could find no substitute. Those who had lived in little shops died of starvation, for there was nothing to trade, and no money to exchange if produce had been available. Death ruled the coast of China for a thousand miles. The entire area was made waste, and it has been estimated that in the first evacuation half the residents who were forced inland died. Any who in despair attempted to return to their homes were tortured and killed, for the Manchus, in order to prevent the rebuilding of destroyed towns, erected watchtowers at three-mile intervals along the entire coast. Each was manned by a hundred soldiers, who were ordered to decapitate instantly and without trial any trespasser caught inside the immense demarcation zone.

The shocking thing about this gigantic dispersal is that it was conceived, ordered and executed on the spur of the moment without any plan or consideration of consequences. For nine determined years and desultorily for ten more, the policy was maintained, and the total loss of life and wealth was incalculable.

Ironically, by the time the law was enforced Coxinga had already left Quemoy and had embarked upon the vast enterprise for which he is best remembered today. In April, 1661, with a fleet of nine hundred ships bearing twenty-five thousand marines, he set sail eastward to resume a battle started many years before by his father, Nicholas Iquan.

He was sailing to Formosa, to declare war against the Dutch and to drive them from that rich and favored island. A stylized portrait of that time shows him as a thirty-six-year-old mandarin seated on a tiger skin and wearing heavily brocaded robes with pointed sleeves. He has a wispy, drooping mustache, tiny beard and separate lower-lip patch. His face is thinner than when he was younger and on his head he wears the ceremonial mandarin's cap. His entire appearance is Chinese and the determination that was to mark his behavior during the events about to occur is easily noticed.

Why did he decide to invade Formosa? Manchu pressure on Amoy was actually not very great and was withstood by Coxinga and his son for many years, so that was not the effective cause. Nor could the removal policy have launched the invasion, for that did not take effect until after he had left. Three dissimilar factors probably motivated him and in them we see a picture of the forces which played upon this powerful man. First, he had an inborn hatred for the Dutch, against whom his father had often warred, and for many years he had apparently entertained ideas of ultimately evicting them from Formosa. Now was a good time. Second, Formosa was a wonderfully endowed island whose location placed it athwart the main trading routes of the Chinese, Japanese, Dutch, Portuguese and Spanish argosies. Coxinga foresaw growing strife in this area and considered the island to be the best available center for his sea-roving occupation. Third, and possibly most persuasive, with China in turmoil and with the Ming loyalists in flight everywhere, Coxinga, as the only important rallying point for the Ming, wished to establish a refuge. In an age of bitter anxiety he sought an island where he could be king, on which he could offer sanctuary for all who were disposed to support the Ming cause, and from which he could harry the Manchus.

The island which Coxinga had chosen for these purposes was a historical curiosity, for although it lay midway between the ancient civilizations of China and Japan, it remained an unclaimed, totally savage island populated by a backward race, each of whose little enclaves along the coast and in the deep mountain valleys spoke a completely different language. The Formosans were merciless head-hunters, and only the bravest visitor to the island would dare move inland without full military protection, which had to be maintained both constantly and with care.

Yet the island was probably the richest in the Pacific, and still is. It contained gold and silver, pineapples and sugar, rice and tea. Its immensely rich forests yielded camphor of the best quality, strong rattan, rare orchids for trade, and more than six dozen kinds of choice lumber. Obviously any power that controlled Formosa's trade had a likely chance of acquiring great wealth.

In appearance the island was as lovely as its appropriate name, derived from the Portuguese word for beautiful. A hospitable western plain rose toward mountains that reached over 13,000 feet into the air. There were ample rivers for water supply, good harbors, and a profusion of wild flowers that could be matched nowhere else in that part of the Pacific. The climate was delightful, and the island was singularly free from tropical diseases.

Why had no Asiatic nation claimed Formosa? Why had neither Spain, active in the nearby Philippines, nor Portugal, ensconced in Macao, occupied this rich island? Apparently the ferocity of the natives had scared away potential settlers, and it was not until 1624 that the Dutch, as we have seen, were persuaded by Captain China to abandon their entrepôt on the Pescadores and to move a few miles eastward onto the main island of Formosa. There, to protect their growing settlement, they had erected a famous fort, which was now to occupy Coxinga's attention.

On April 30, 1661, his powerful armada loomed out of the mists of the Straits of Formosa and anchored off the Dutch fortress, Castle Zeelandia, off modern Anping (Anpin, Ampin) on the southwest coast. This stronghold was located on a curiously shaped island which looked like a club with a large knob on the end. The shaft consisted of a narrow sand spit that almost touched the shore, while the knob, on which the castle rested, faced inshore at another point. The castle was a solid affair of baked bricks, well studded with cannon and defended by determined Dutchmen whose empire in the east had been won only by the resolute defense of such fortresses in Java and elsewhere. These Pacific Ocean Dutch were a heroic breed and, once dug in, were never easy to dislodge.

Coxinga, aware that he faced a stubborn foe, proceeded cautiously. Throwing a sea blockade across the approaches to the island, he landed assault troops who methodically captured one after another of the shore outposts. "He was abundantly provided with cannon and ammunition. . . . He also had two companies of Black Boys, many of whom had been Dutch slaves, and had learned the use of the rifle and musket-arms. These caused much harm during the war in Formosa."

We have a report of the stratagems adopted by Coxinga at this stage of operations, for a Dutch mission sent to him reported that they were led to a tent, where they were told to wait for Coxinga. "Meanwhile, several fine regiments marched past the tent. Then the captain who was with the deputies said they would be received as soon as Coxinga's hair was combed; but that they might now come close to his tent, some distance off. Here also many armed men who had passed the other tent were again paraded before the deputies, from which they saw that the intention was to practice deceit as to the number of soldiers in the field. Ultimately the deputies were brought before Coxinga, who was sitting in an armchair, under an open blue tent, beside a small square table, and surrounded by all his magnates clothed in long garments like popes, without any weapons."

When all the outer defenses had been subdued, Coxinga offered Castle Zeelandia an honorable surrender, adding, "But if you still persist in refusing to listen to reason and decline to do my bidding, and if you wish deliberately to rush to your ruin, then I will shortly, in your presence, order your Castle to be stormed. My smart boys will attack it, conquer it, and demolish it in such a way that not one stone will remain standing."

The Dutch commandant of the fortress replied to this threat, "We understand its contents perfectly well; but cannot give you any answer than the one we sent you on 10th instant, namely, that we are bound for the honor of our omnipotent and true God—on Whose aid and assistance we entirely rely—as well as for the sake of our country and the Directors of the Dutch India Company, to continue to defend the Castle, even at the point of our lives."

Consequently, a siege in the classic manner developed: a powerful invading force applied pressure to a well-entrenched and resolute defensive body, and if that were all the story, the assault on Castle Zeelandia would excite no great attention today. But the commander of the Dutch forces was a man of extraordinary character—in his own way quite the equal of Coxinga—and he was, in addition, one of the truly tragic men in the history of the Pacific, Frederik Coyett, an undaunted fighter whose fortitude in the midst of callous betrayal won him the verdict: "an honorable, brave, but ill-used man."

Coyett was governor of Formosa, but he was subject to orders from his Dutch superiors in Java, where he had a vengeful host of detractors who systematically undercut him on every point, and one of the bitterest aspects of the siege he underwent was that the worst blows were struck against him not by his Chinese enemies but by his Dutch compatriots. From 1646 till the invasion of 1661, Coyett had been aware that ultimately Coxinga's pirates would invade Formosa. This apprehension was reported, by Coyett and others, in 1646, 1652, 1655, 1656 and 1660. In Java the reports were not only ridiculed; each sensible defensive step taken by Coyett was condemned as cowardice. "It seems rather absurd," wrote the experts in Java regarding one fortification which was later to be the means whereby Coyett was enabled to hold Coxinga off for more than half a year, "that, on your own account and without previously acquainting us—far less asking our permission—Your Honor should have built such a strong fortification. . . . We wish reasonably to show our discontent herewith so that Your Highness may be a little more careful in the future and avoid the carrying out of such important undertakings, without previously obtaining our approval and formal consent."

Badgered at headquarters, Coyett was also beset by local superstitions: "The extraordinary and terrible earthquakes of the previous year, lasting fourteen days at a stretch, seemed to portend Heaven's wrath and threatening punishment upon the people; also, a story was circulated that a mermaid had shown itself in the Canal; and the soldiers told each other that, on a certain night in the Company's Armory, there was heard a tumult and sound of all kinds of weapons, as if some thousands of men had been engaged in battle. True: one or two of those alleged circumstances may have arisen from common rumor, and may have had no sure foundation. But to what can we ascribe the statements that, on a certain night, one of the projections connected with the castle was seen in a blaze; that, on the execution ground between the castle and the city, a woeful groaning was heard, as of dying people—the voices of the Hollanders being distinguishable from those of the Chinese; and that the water of the Canal was once seen changing into fire and flames. There were said to be many more such fearful premonitions, and each reader is free to believe whatever he thinks best."

When the attack came, Coyett had only one Dutchman for every thirty attacking Chinese, and of his personnel of 1140 only three dozen were soldiers, but some years earlier a handful of determined Dutchmen had defeated enormous numbers of unarmed Chinese and an insidious myth had taken root: "The Chinese in Formosa were regarded by the Hollanders as insignificant and in warfare as cowardly and effeminate. It was reckoned that twenty-five of them together would barely equal one Dutch soldier, and the whole Chinese race was regarded in the same way, no distinction being made between Chinese peasants and soldiers; if he was but a native of China, then he was cowardly and had no stamina."

Coyett had only one experienced officer inside the fortress, and this captain personified the arrogant attitude against which Coyett had to struggle. Captain Pedel saw nothing foolish in marching two hundred and forty of the castle's best men in parade formation right down the sand spit and into the face of four thousand Coxinga regulars. The result was appalling, and only those few Dutchmen who could swim out to sea and back to the castle escaped. Stubborn Captain Pedel, who had insisted that one Dutchman was worth a score of Chinese, was among the dead and Coyett was reduced to one officer, an impressed baker's assistant of no skill or experience whatever.

But as before, the greater enemy was in Java, and at the very moment when Coyett's best troops were being chopped to pieces by the Chinese, the directors in Batavia were sending their governor in Formosa this amazing dispatch: "Surely if Koxinga cherished any intention at all to come, he would have done so long ago. . . . The statement that Koxinga, hearing of Your Honor's great preparations to resist him, had postponed his intended attack to a better opportunity, is entirely unacceptable, as was shown afterwards. He never appeared on our shore with evil intentions, although he had ample opportunity of so doing, and we would never be able to hold our possessions there in peace if we allowed ourselves to be kept in continual alarm by such idle threats. Your Honor's predecessors never troubled themselves and others in this way, but always kept on their guard as became faithful, courageous men. This example Your Honor ought to have followed, without becoming so shamefully alarmed. . . . Accordingly, Governor Frederik Coyett is instructed hereby to retire from the government, and no longer to interfere in any way with the affairs of state." Rarely has bureaucracy demonstrated such colossal ignorance and bad timing as that displayed in this letter, which, at the height of a siege, fired a brave man—for cowardice.

To replace the dauntless Coyett, his Dutch masters in Java had selected a dandy little hero, one Herman Clenk, who arrived off the besieged castle just as operations reached a furious pitch. His letters of commission stated that he was to assume governorship "of a land basking in peace and plenty," but since Formosa, overrun by Coxinga's troops, clearly failed to fit that description, the redoubtable Clenk scuttled off to the safety of Japan, then doubled back to Java, where as a reward for his courage he was given command of the yearly argosy to Amsterdam.

Still governor by default, the deposed Coyett dug in and defended the fort gallantly. His journal is an epic of human resolution: "This morning at daybreak a soldier named Hendrick Robbertsz came swimming to the Pineapples, and afterwards to the redoubt. Having been carried into this place, he gave us the following account: Last month, the interpreter Druyvendal and a young schoolmaster had each been fastened to a cross [by the occupying Chinese forces], nails having been driven through their hands, the calves of their legs, and into their backs. In this sad condition they were exhibited to public view before the house of the Governor, our own people guarding these victims with naked swords. At the end of three or four days they expired after meat and drink had been forbidden them all that time. The reason for their execution was said to be that they had incited the inhabitants against the Chinese. They, however, denied to their last breath that they had ever done so."

Back in Java the Dutch governors at last reluctantly faced up to the seriousness of the situation in Formosa and belatedly assembled a formidable fleet intended for raising the siege, only to discover that no one would accept the dangerous command. "At last, after many inducements, with great promises of recompense and reward, they found an adventurer who dared to accept the commission, namely, Jacob Caeuw, a person so defective in the power of speech that one almost required an interpreter to understand his words—which were all spoken through the nose. According to his own confession, he had no other experience in warfare than that of having, when in the Academy at Leyden, often run his sword through the stones in the streets or through the windows of decent people's houses."

Caeuw's deportment is an epic of cowardice. On August 12, 1661, he hove to his warships off Castle Zeelandia, saw that the situation was desperate and immediately fled to safer waters. After thirty days' cruising, during which the beleaguered garrison suffered constant assault, Admiral Caeuw returned with the stirring proposal that he evacuate the women and children to Java.

At this Coyett exploded and the dashing admiral countered with the suggestion that he be appointed to visit China to see if the Manchus would help the Dutch fight the common enemy. Without waiting for a commission, he fled to the safety of the China coast, refused to land lest he get into trouble, and scurried away to peaceful Siam, where he announced his arrival with a salute of more than fifty guns, startling the Siamese to such an extent that he was asked to leave. "The powder he wasted," wrote a compatriot, "might have been saved for doing better service at Formosa."

Evicted from Siam, Admiral Caeuw contemplated going back to the relief of Castle Zeelandia, but thought better of it and fled to Java, where the directors, who were charging Coyett with cowardice, levied against Caeuw a trifling fine and suspension from his admiral's job for six months.

Betrayed by fools, abandoned by cowards and badgered by poltroons, Frederik Coyett continued to rally his starving men and settled down to the last stages of a doomed nine months' siege. His behavior was in the great tradition of heroes: in the last days a vote was taken; only one man stood out for continued resistance, and that was Coyett.

In his extremity, Coyett did find one fellow countryman whose courage equaled his own, and in this man the Dutch gained a notable hero whose name is still familiar in storybooks. One of the first prisoners taken by Coxinga upon investing the hinterland facing Castle Zeelandia was a venerable Lutheran minister, Anthonius Hambroeck, part of whose family had fled to safety inside the fort. When Coxinga sought a messenger to deliver his demand that the fort be immediately surrendered he selected Hambroeck, from whom he exacted a solemn promise that regardless of the outcome of the mission he, Hambroeck, would return to Coxinga in person with the message.

Upon arrival at the fort, Reverend Hambroeck, instead of advising surrender, steadfastly urged the Dutchmen inside never to give in. Then, having failed in his ostensible mission, he made preparations to return to Coxinga, although he knew that to do so meant certain death, for his advice to resist had been delivered in the presence of the other Coxinga messengers.

Hambroeck's daughters inside the fort pleaded with their father not to return to Coxinga's camp, but the old man said that he had given the word of a Dutchman and a minister, and that he was thus doubly bound. To the lamenting of his daughters he went forth and, as he had foreseen, he was promptly beheaded. But it was the spirit of men like him that kept

Castle Zeelandia resolute during the worst part of the siege.

When surrender was forced upon him, through the advice of his councilors, Coyett was ignominiously hauled off a prisoner to Java, where his enemies demanded that he be put to death. The bill of indictment against him is a revolting document filled with inconsequential matters, smeared with a lust for personal revenge, and crawling with unction: "The plaintiff should have manifested a feeling of gratitude and loyalty in furthering the interests of those by whom he was treated, not as a servant, but with the affection of a father for his child; and this altogether apart from the terms of his oath. This sense of honor and duty should have impelled him thereto. But as the best-loved children frequently cause their parents the greatest sorrow—as the little lambs fed under their master's table will attack first of all the children of him who supplies their wants—in like manner, the plaintiff and his councilors have so retaliated upon their kind and forebearing rulers that the entire building is shaken to its foundations."

So determined were the enemies of Coyett that the hero of Formosa was actually dragged onto the execution block, but as the headsman lifted his axe, some sanity manifested itself and the sentence was changed to two years of brutal imprisonment followed by exile for life to the fetid islet of Ay, near Banda. Thirteen years after his heroic defense of Castle Zeelandia, Coyett was finally released through the pressure of friends in Holland who knew the true story, but they had to post a bond of 25,000 guilders that he would live only in the Netherlands, would never visit Java and would take no part whatever in Eastern affairs.

Old books show Coxinga as he accepted the surrender of this gallant Dutchman. Under palm trees the brave defenders of the fortress march forth in heavy armor. Across a narrow channel stands Castle Zeelandia, its walls still unbreached, while on a little knoll Coxinga sits in a beribboned tent at a table with a heavily brocaded cloth. He wears a Jesuit cap, becaped robes like those favored by Cardinal Richelieu, and no weapons. Dutch suppliants approach their austere conqueror with no show of cringing or humility, while Chinese soldiers parade and scurry in the background.

That night Coxinga became the first king of Formosa. His rule, which was one of the bright spots of the period, started auspiciously with just and compassionate surrender terms for the Dutch, who were allowed to retire unmolested to their ships, taking with them considerable possessions and all honor.

There was no revenge. Coxinga's rule continued with a series of wise measures for the government of Formosa: "In order to establish our rule over this island we must have food for our subjects. With insufficient food in the house even a family, in spite of ties to bind them, finds it difficult to live happily. So in this island, notwithstanding the patriotic spirit of our subjects, we cannot hope for tranquillity unless we provide them with the necessaries of life. . . . Hence our soldiers, whose occupation is to guard us against our foes, should prepare for battle by engaging, in times of peace, in agriculture." Coxinga's conquest of Formosa was to be used by the Japanese several centuries later as a basis for their occupation of the island, since he was half Japanese.

It is noteworthy that of all the characters in this book who sought dominion over some Pacific isle, the only one who accomplished his dream in full measure was this son of Nicholas Iquan, the illegitimately born Chinese tailor, and he became king of what is probably the most desirable island in this ocean.

Had he continued to make the government of Formosa his main job, he might have constructed there an enduring kingdom as an example to surrounding empires. Even so, because of what he did accomplish, many writers have begun to argue against calling him a pirate. They claim that his official commissions from the Ming government made him a bona fide general rather than an improvising marauder. They believe that his operations in the China Seas had official approval, and were therefore the accomplishments of an admiral, not a buccaneer. And they cap their arguments by pointing out that Coxinga's constructive work on Formosa partook more of statesmanship than of piracy.

But to Coxinga's contemporaries he was a pirate, and they so described him. Naturally, the secondary accounts which were built upon those sources carried over that colorful word. The present authors have concluded that while Coxinga was admittedly a general, an admiral and a statesman, he was also a pirate, and their contention is based not upon the piracy of his youth—when he operated with the fleet he more or less haphazardly inherited from his piratical father—but rather upon his curious relationship with Manila in the closing years of his life. In this bombastic affair with the Spaniards he was certainly neither a statesman nor a general. He was a pirate.

For many years the city of Manila had exercised a strange fascination on the mind of Coxinga, for not only were the Philippine Islands accessible and inviting—they lay less than three hundred miles south of Formosa—but they were also exceedingly rich, and the galleons which lugged away the prolific wealth of Manila were a constant temptation to anyone as piratical as Coxinga.

But in the case of Coxinga there was an added fascination, for as a Chinese he had special reason to want to humiliate proud Manila. The Spaniards in that city had acquired a nasty habit of goading their Chinese settlers into provocative acts and then assassinating the lot of them. Accustomed as Chinese immigrants were to rough treatment overseas, in Manila they underwent barbarities that were matched nowhere else. In fact, slaughtering Chinese had become a kind of national sport.

It is difficult to isolate the causes for this curious Spanish behavior, for the Spaniards readily admitted that their Chinese were skilled merchants, industrious tradesmen and essential artisans. In addition they provided the barbers, the weavers, the fishermen, the farmers and, in some exalted cases, even the bankers. Serious Spanish writers were always careful to report that the Chinese formed the economic mainstay of the Philippines.

But they were Oriental, and at home Spain had only recently expelled her powerful invaders from the Near Orient—the Muslim Moors of North Africa—and a natural suspicion was undoubtedly transferred to the Chinese. But what made any substantial rapprochement impossible was the fact that the Chinese, even when they were converted, simply did not make good Christians, and those who submitted to conversion were doubly suspect. For this reason, the entire breed was feared and abhorred by the Spaniards.

Any trifling scare was more than likely to precipitate a panic and slaughter of the Sangleys, as they were nicknamed.* For instance, in May, 1603, three mandarins arrived in Manila and told the authorities that they had been sent by their emperor to investigate the tale that near Manila was a mountain of pure gold, belonging to no one and rich enough to pay all the taxes of China. Naturally, such an unlikely excuse for travel forced the Spaniards to suspect that these men were spies. In turn, the visiting Chinese feared an attack and this caused the local Sangleys to make preparations for defense.

---

*The Manila Chinese were always called Sangleys, a slang word of perplexing origin. Possibly it derives from two Chinese ideographs meaning "constantly coming," a reference to trading habits.

In the autumn the conflict degenerated into open warfare; a company of more than a hundred Spaniards was ambushed and killed, and Chinese gangs assaulted the walls of Manila. When Filipino troops marched to the rescue, the Chinese were driven into the hills. Spanish historians state that no less than twenty-three thousand Sangleys—most of those in the Philippines at the time—perished in the revolt; and because of their loss to the community, an economic depression followed.

In 1639 Manila was ready for another massacre. Oppression of Chinese laborers in the provinces started an insurrection and the Sangleys plundered twenty-two towns and churches and killed many Spaniards, Filipinos and Christian Japanese. This time they made no attempt to attack Manila, for the memory of their defeat there in 1603 was still fresh. After a year of battles and sieges, the Chinese laid down their arms in February, 1640. The number of Sangleys killed was between twenty-two and twenty-four thousand.

These massacres were much talked about in Asia and seem to have rankled in Coxinga's bosom, so that when he saw a chance to gain an economic advantage as well as exact revenge, he quixotically determined to teach the Spaniards a lesson. He would expel them from the Philippines and take over Manila, possibly making it his capital.

Accordingly he laid plans for a massive assault on the islands, but before actually launching it he made one of the most bizarre gestures of his life. From the European refugees in Formosa he selected a gifted gentleman of wide learning and dispatched him to the Spaniards in Manila with the following bombastic epistle:

> It is a well established custom, in both ancient and modern times, that foreign nations recognize illustrious princes chosen by Heaven and offer them tribute and gifts. The foolish Dutchmen, not recognizing . . . the decrees of Heaven, operated shamelessly, oppressing . . . my subjects and even robbing . . . my sampans filled with goods. I kept sending warnings and exhortations, as from a friend, hoping they might repent of their misdeeds and reform themselves of their sins. But they . . . were corrupt and perverse and did not behave as if they understood. I then became extremely angry and . . . collected a fleet to punish their crimes. When I arrived I captured them, and killed and destroyed without end, and . . . the Dutch humbly asked to become our subjects. . . .

I am, therefore, sending ahead my ambassador with a friendly notification . . . in order that your tiny kingdom, if it wishes to recognize the desires of Heaven and to acknowledge its own errors, may come with penitence to my rule and each year offer tribute. If you accept this . . . I shall be reconciled and will forgive your old misdeeds, and will respect your royal dignity. At the same time I shall command my merchants to fulfill their contracts with you.

But if you mistakenly do not accept, straightway there will arrive at your city a fleet which will burn up your forces, reservoirs, cities, warehouses—everything of value, even to the very stones. I shall destroy you. And if you then beg to pay tribute and tender your submission, you will not be permitted to do so. Let what happened to the Dutchmen be an example. . . . Let your tiny kingdom ponder this speedily. Let it not postpone repentance. I am only giving notice in a friendly way, admonishing and instructing. . . .

Kuesing

The rage of the Spaniards at receiving such a message from an infidel and a pirate was no less great than their astonishment at the man who delivered it. Vittorio Ricci, a resident of the city of Florence, was a Dominican friar who was to serve in Asia for thirty-seven incredible years, during which he encountered so many improbable adventures that merely to recount them seems stultifying. Rather late in his pyrotechnic career he became involved with Coxinga, through the accident of having been on the island of Amoy just as the great pirate was preparing his fateful assault on Nanking, and as a result of one improvisation after another he wound up on Formosa as Coxinga's priest-ambassador, in which capacity he watched the infidel Chinese finally expel the Lutheran religion and establish Confucianism in its place. Old accounts give us good reason to believe that Friar Ricci, seeing the Lutherans at a disadvantage, derived satisfaction from the humbling of this religion that had caused his own such grievous damage in Europe.

But now he was being sent south to help the infidel Coxinga extirpate not Lutherans but Catholics, who had established a strong enclave in Manila, and his appearance in that city created a scandal. He strode ashore, a handsome man in full mandarin robes, bearing documents which could mean the end of his religion in one of the principal cities of Asia, probably the only time in history when a friar served such a contradictory purpose. He delivered his inflammatory ultimatum to the governor, and then—in great confusion of mind, no doubt—sat back to watch the riots.

At first the outraged Spaniards decided to employ their traditional gambit: behead every one of the more than fifteen thousand Chinese. As a contemporary pointed out, this would at the same time insure the peace, gratify religious zeal and advance the personal fortunes of the Spaniards: "One seldom finds a person who is not interested in the ruin of the Sangleys—some on account of the loot that they may obtain; the rest because there are few persons who do not hold property of the Sangleys in trust, or else owe much for merchandise which they have bought on credit. Many have become depositaries for their acquaintances, who, fearing the removal of their property to other hands, give it to their intimate friends to keep; and by slaying the Sangleys all render account with payment. Accordingly, in the insurrection of 1639 it was found by experience that those in whom the Sangleys placed most confidence were the first and most importunate voters for their ruin."

In view of the earlier massacres, it was astonishing that Manila in 1662 held any Chinese, but as in the parallel case of Java, where there were similar repeated extirpations, these seem never to have deterred fresh immigration and thus Manila's sprawling Parián, one of the world's principal Chinatowns, became a scene of intense excitement as Spanish troops, inflamed by Coxinga's maladroit threats, moved to circle the area. The Parián was a remarkable city in itself, of which a contemporary wrote, "Usually fifteen thousand Chinese live there; they are Sangleys, natives of Great China, and all merchants or artisans. They possess, allotted among themselves by streets and squares, shops containing all the kinds of merchandise and all the trades that are necessary in a community. The place is very orderly and well arranged, and a great convenience to the citizens. It is an indication of their greatness that although they are so few, they have so many workmen and servants assigned to their service. The Sangleys live in wooden houses; they have a governor of their own nation, and a Spanish alcalde-mayor and the other officers of justice, with a notary; also a jail. They have a parish church, where the sacraments, the divine word, and burial are administered to the four thousand

Christians among these Sangleys; the rest of them are heathen." Now the Sangleys of the Parián huddled together and awaited assassination.

But, although cannon on the walls briefly bombarded the Chinese quarter, this time no mass execution swept the Parián, for the governor of Manila was a resolute man and he refused to give permission for a general massacre. "From the time when the disturbance began until it was entirely quieted, his lordship had much to do in defending his prudent decision against many Spaniards who desired to break entirely with the Sangleys and make an end of them—not considering that such proceedings would ruin the colony, all the more as, since we had to prepare for the war we regarded as certain, we needed more of the Sangleys' industry for the many labors required for defending and fortifying the walls, erecting temporary defenses, and harnessing so many horses; for it is they who bear the burdens of the community in all its crafts, notably those that are most necessary."

There was complete panic within the Parián, however, for the Chinese there could remember the massacre of 1639 and understandably expected a repetition, particularly when "their desperation was completed by the interpretation which the common people gave to everything—irresponsible soldiers with mestizos, mulattoes, and blacks, telling the Sangleys that they were to have their heads cut off, as if they were men already sentenced to death; and inflicting on them many injuries and uttering a thousand insults."

In despair, the frantic Chinese killed two Spaniards, and when Friar Ricci and a fellow priest who spoke Chinese were sent into the Parián to quiet the storm, the mob of eight thousand Chinese also killed this second priest. Only the most courageous action by the governor postponed the holocaust, but when many of the Chinese fled the Parián altogether, he was prevailed upon to declare war against them, and bands of troops and excited Filipinos tracked the cowering Chinese down and slaughtered them mercilessly. Thus Coxinga's precipitate diplomacy had become the cause of precisely what he had intended to forestall.

Next it was decided to deport all the remaining Sangleys to China, but in the sober light of economic existence this was found to be impractical, since "all recognized our need of that Chinese nation, in the lack and scarcity of all things to which we see ourselves now reduced—all because the number of Sangleys has been diminished, since the natives have neither energy nor strength to support the burdens that the Chinese carry; and much more on account of our dependence upon their trade, for everything. For not only does everything necessary for life come to us from China—such as wheat, cloth, and earthenware—but it is the Sangleys who carry on all the crafts, and who with their traffic maintain the fortunes of the citizens."

Nevertheless, the feeling against Coxinga and the Chinese was so pronounced that three junks were loaded almost to the sinking point with Sangleys and hustled off to China. The remaining Sangleys were holed up in the Parián to await the next outburst against them, and most of them accepted the amnesty offered by the governor. Ambassador Ricci, the bearer of the challenge, was sent back to Formosa with an insulting letter to Coxinga, who was advised to steer clear of the Philippines, lest he be visited with the same punishments already handed his countrymen.

Friar Ricci, who would probably have been beheaded had he delivered such a message, escaped punishment, for by the time he reached Formosa, his great pirate master had mysteriously died. Coxinga, at his death, was not yet thirty-eight years old, a greatly gifted man who could have been presumed to be just at the portal of accomplishment, so that his untimely death has always been variously explained and interpreted.

Spanish Catholics in Manila, of course, contended that God had struck him down in retaliation for his blasphemy against the Church; while Dutch Protestants were sure that it was for his sins against their church that the infidel had perished. Portuguese, Manchus, Japanese and English all added their versions and their moralizings—the French suggested that he died in anger at his generals because they refused to kill Coxinga's eldest son when he had adulterous relations with his younger brother's nurse—so that the facts of his extraordinary death will probably never be known.

One completely muddled account impartially combines his father's death with his and was widely circulated: "Koxinga did not live for more than a year after his conquest of Formosa. It is said that the Tartars imprisoned him; and that he, fearing they would compel him to disclose matters of which he was unwilling to speak, first bit off his tongue and then his forefinger, so as to deprive himself of the ability to speak or write. He afterwards came to a miserable end."

Most of the obituaries agree that Coxinga suffered great remorse at having unwittingly been the instrument for unleashing the Spaniards yet again upon the defenseless Chinese of Manila. He certainly blamed himself for the mishap. Then, too, he probably foresaw the gloomy end of all Ming hopes, and although for the time being he felt militarily secure on Formosa, he must have known that ultimately his island refuge was doomed, and this knowledge added to his depression.

The version of his death which seems completely appropriate, even if one cannot prove it to be true, is found in an unsigned Spanish manuscript of 1663, the year after his death: "With these anxieties Cotsen was walking one afternoon through the fort on Formosa Island which he had gained from the Dutch. His mind began to be disturbed by visions, which he said appeared to him, of thousands of men who placed themselves before him, all headless and clamoring for vengeance on the cruelty and injustice which had been wreaked on them; accordingly, terrified at this vision (or else a lifelike presentation by his imagination) he took refuge in his house and flung himself on his bed, consumed by a fierce and burning fever. This caused him to die on the fifth day, fiercely scratching his face and biting his hands, without any further last will than to charge his intimate friends with the death of his son, or more repentance for his cruelty than to continue it by the orders that he gave for them to kill various persons; thus God interrupted by his death many cruel punishments."

The most provocative account of Coxinga's death, however, comes from a Spanish historian who hated the pirate. He starts with the last days of the massacres in the Philippines: "The Chinese of the provinces who had taken no part in the disturbances at the Parián came out still less luckily. The governor, seeing the internal and external dangers which threatened the entire archipelago, and fearing that the rebellion and the disturbances would spread to other parts of these islands, ordered that all the Chinese found in the distant provinces should be immediately decapitated. This was a cruel and inhuman order, it appears, and far from the benevolent nature of that governor; but he considered it then as a necessity, inescapable if the islands were to be saved from the danger which menaced them in this crisis. Under this power were decapitated various Chinese seamen serving on the ships found in this port. . . .

"On the same ominous day of the bombardment of the Parián there had disappeared from these waters thirteen Chinese ships, under the command of a captain known by the name of Na-chin, a wise man, proud and vengeful. When the flight of the Chinese became known, the governor ordered several ships to go out in pursuit; but, with the start they had, they were not able to capture them, and the ships arrived without incident at Formosa. The malign Na-chin immediately appeared before the great pirate, and revealing in his manner and appearance an extraordinary feeling, he spoke thus: 'Our nation, powerful lord, all your faithful vassals are ruined and dead in Luzon. I alone, with the aid of our gods, have been able to escape from the hands and sword of the cruel Spaniards. In this manner has been paid the tribute which is due you and which you await. What should be done? Your forces are immense, your soldiers valiant, your arms victorious, and our fortune has descended from the heavens, which make you terrible in the face of the nations, and eternal victor over the enemy on land and sea. There is no lack of ships, supplies, munitions or provisions, and your troops are comparable only to the stars in the sky, the blades of grass in the fields, and the seething sands of the abyss [hell]. Let your power wipe out the name of Christian in all parts; let perish at a blow of your sword all the Spaniards in Luzon, our greatest enemies, for heaven does not wish and your justice should not permit that their malignity should go unpunished.' The proud pirate [Coxinga] was furious at hearing such astounding news; the pupils of his eyes were transformed at once into two flashes of lightning, and clutching convulsively the hilt of his cutlass, he ordered that all his forces and his immense military resources should get ready to advance against those islands, swearing by Hell that he would scatter such trifling dust on the surface of the seas.

"However, God, Who watches over and always watched over these Spanish provinces with special concern for their preservation and independence, confounded his ideas and jested with this vow in his counsels. His sudden attack of terrible anger altered the robust constitution of the corsair in such a way that within a few hours he was smitten by a sort of terrifying and astonishing hydrophobia. In his horrifying frenzy he scratched his face, bit his lips and tongue, attacked furiously anyone who came near his bed, and issued death decrees against the Spanish monarchs. Five days passed, filled continually with these horrible scenes, until throttled with rage, he delivered up his perverse soul to the demons, as a manuscript says. Thus died the Attila of the Orient on July 2, 1662, at the age of thirty-nine years."*

The Spaniards understandably feared and hated Coxinga, who was indeed the Attila of the East, but nowhere is their peculiar reaction to this great pirate more clearly expressed than in the following peroration, which neatly combines the anxiety they felt as they saw him encroaching on Manila, and their firm assurance that God held that city in His special care: "Eternal nightmare of the empire, terrifier of Tartary and China, fateful and sinister vestige of the continents and the seas, he made with his shadow to tremble the tyrants of his homeland, and his domination would have been a problem if God had not smashed with His hand the head of this monster in the robust vigor of his existence. He who knew how to face with calm visage the fury and the might of the angry elements; he who in his horrible blasphemy feared neither God nor man, nor the dominions of Hell, succumbed merely at the idea of seeing himself conquered and humiliated by the high dignity of the Spanish nation, even before resorting to the barbarous argument of combat."

If it is difficult to decide how Coxinga died, it is even more difficult to assess his meteoric career. As a general he showed appalling judgment at Nanking, and through his carelessness lost the most powerful land mass in Asia. As a diplomat his boastful handling of the Manila affair was ridiculous and cost him the lives of the very people he was trying to defend. He was a ruthless, cruel man who in 1650 assassinated his cousin, in 1651 his uncle, in 1661 the defenseless patriot Reverend Hambroeck, and who on his deathbed certainly ordered the beheading of his own son, which atrocity was prevented by the fact that the executioners balked at the job. To the Dutch and Spanish, understandably, he was an archfiend.

But that cannot be the whole story of Coxinga's amazing life. If he was cruel, he faced cruel adversaries. When the Dutch caught a Chinese insurgent "he was roasted alive before a fire [in Castle Zeelandia], dragged behind a horse through the town, and his head stuck on a pole. Two of

---

*At his death Coxinga was thirty-seven, but he lacked only a few weeks of being thirty-eight, which by Chinese reckoning would count as thirty-nine.

his chieftains, who had ripped up a pregnant native woman and torn the child from her body, were broken upon the wheel and quartered." It was a violent world in which he operated, and if he did slice off the ears and noses of his Manchu prisoners after Nanking, he nevertheless treated his Dutch prisoners with generosity and honor after the fall of Castle Zeelandia.

The one act for which Coxinga has never been forgiven by European writers occurred after the fall of Castle Zeelandia. Then Coxinga inspected the prisoners before him and his eye fell upon a young Dutch girl, whom all narrators describe as lovely and intelligent. Coxinga kept her as a choice concubine—he had dozens—and in so doing outraged all the decencies. For this girl was the daughter of Anthonius Hambroeck, that Lutheran minister who had ignored his own safety in order to acknowledge his pledge that he would return to certain death.

Asian judges, less punctilious about such matters, quickly saw in Coxinga's vain battle to support the collapsing Ming cause an almost perfect example of fidelity to a principle, and the nations of Asia embraced his memory. In 1700 the Manchu emperor decreed that henceforth Coxinga must be referred to not as a rebel against the Manchus, but as a devoted loyalist to the Ming. In 1875 a later Manchu emperor announced that Coxinga would in the future be called Cheng-chieh (loyal and faithful) and would be the subject of public worship as an exemplar of these attributes. In 1898 one of the first things Admiral Count Kobayama did when taking over Formosa on behalf of the Japanese emperor was to proceed formally to Coxinga's Formosan temple, where he ceremoniously invited the Chinese-Japanese pirate into the Shinto pantheon.

A more substantial immortality came when Chikamatsu, Japan's greatest playwright, presented in the year 1715 a dazzling new drama, *The Battles of Coxinga*. Its instantaneous reception was repeated year after year until Coxinga entered not only the austere pantheons of Shintoism and Confucianism, but also the livelier deification of the alleys, the restaurants and the theaters of Japan. There he exists today, the pirate god.

By now the perceptive reader can probably guess why there has been a reawakened interest in Coxinga. His violent life foreshadowed that of Chiang Kai-shek's. Like Chiang, he tried to resist an invasion of revolutionary ideas and the incursions of the revolutionists themselves. Like Chiang, he suffered debacles in the north and fled to Amoy. Like Chiang, he escaped to Formosa, where he instituted a good government which avoided the excesses that had cost his side the mainland. Like Chiang, he held on to Quemoy and never ceased being a thorn in the side of the mainland victors. Most persuasive of all, like Chiang he was loyal to an idea, from which he never wavered, regardless of the considerable temptations put in his way.

It is therefore little wonder that today on Formosa more scholars study Coxinga than any other figure of Chinese history, for his example is a steady reassurance to the people of that island, whose first king he was. In fact, the scholars have delved so deeply into Coxinga's life that a schism splits them into two groups: some swear that Coxinga wore a beard; others insist that he was clean-shaven. The 1950 exhibition on Formosa of Coxinga's relics prudently showed him in both guises.

Worshiped as a god by two nations, the accidental patron saint of another fugitive regime on Formosa, and the subject of a rapidly growing shelf of learned studies, Coxinga is at last coming into his proper position on the world stage. He was courageous and loyal, and one searches far in history before finding another who combined these two characteristics so steadfastly.

Therefore, it is with no intention of developing inferences applicable to the present—but merely to round out the facts of history—that we conclude our story of this fascinating pirate with one additional observation. Sometime after Coxinga's death his grandson surrendered Formosa to the interlopers in Peking, whither he went as a prisoner. But to his and the world's surprise, he was not beheaded. He was created a duke.

4

Gibson, the King's Evil Angel

One of the most engaging rascals who ever plied the Pacific was an amazing gentleman from South Carolina. Tall, handsome, dressed in black, with sharp, deep-set eyes and a patriarchal beard, he commanded an orotund speaking style, a fine gift for quoting the Bible and a vision of himself as the savior of all the native peoples in the Pacific.

"My heart is with the Oceanican races," he once cried in the oratory that marks even his simplest statements. "I was born on the ocean and I have felt a sort of brotherhood with islanders." He constantly dreamed of uniting the entire Pacific, and incredible as it seems, came reasonably close to doing so.

Think of what he accomplished solely through the exercise of a glib tongue. He plotted a Sumatran war of liberation from the Dutch. He rescued himself from a Java jail after more than a year of doleful imprisonment. Almost single-handedly he brought Holland and the United States to the brink of war. Then, shifting ground, he became one of the most potent missionaries in the Pacific, from which job he was ousted because of public scandal. He thereupon became an extremely wealthy man, and then he entered upon his greatest adventure.

With little more than his charm and cunning to support

him, he became prime minister of a sovereign Polynesian kingdom, held at one time or another all the cabinet positions, and from this point of vantage launched his grandiose scheme for uniting the Pacific. As the power behind the throne for more than a decade, he was indeed the evil angel of the Hawaiian king who reveled in the title of "the merry monarch." And then Gibson boldly challenged the armed might of Germany, Great Britain and the United States, and initiated one of the most hilarious episodes of naval history.

Even in his declining years he was spectacular, involving himself in a notorious breach of promise suit. In addition to all this, he was a vehement writer, a philosopher, a dreamer, a self-appointed expert on tropical medicine, an energetic sea captain, a skillful editor, a fine farmer, a good businessman, a superb orator and a distinguished linguist.

In fact, Walter Murray Gibson was one of the most highblown, dignified and utterly delightful adventurers in history; and if he had not simultaneously accepted two separate bribes totaling $151,000 for an opium monopoly, he might have ruled a fair portion of the Pacific until he died.

As he boasted, Gibson was truly a child of the ocean. Appropriately, he began his adventurous life by being born at sea, during a raging storm in the Bay of Biscay on January 16, 1822. He was the third son of English emigrants bound from Northumberland to the United States.

Growing up in New York and New Jersey, young Walter was fired by the tales of an uncle who had mysteriously returned from long voyages to Malaysia and who was then in the service of an Arab merchant of Muscat. This romantic relative announced that he was making the boy his heir. "And then he spoke," Gibson later recalled, "of a great city in the center of the island [of Sumatra], a city once of mighty extent and population, whose sultans had given laws to all the rest of the Malay nations. But this great city had decayed; and its empire had been divided into many small and feeble portions. Now the Malays looked for the restoration of the sacred city; and their traditions had pointed to fair-skinned men from the West, who should come with wisdom and great power, and who should destroy the robbers of Islam, the evil genii of the woods, and a great plunderer called Jan Company." It is clear that from then on, Walter Murray Gibson was determined to be the fair-skinned man who would restore this romantic city and save Sumatra.

As if such an uncle were not enough to inflame a boy's

mind, young Gibson also went to school to a teacher who had been a missionary among the Indians of the American northwest, and this man's lurid tales committed the lad to a life of high adventure.

When his parents moved to the backwoods of South Carolina, the wild outdoor life gave Walter "independence of spirit and an impatience of restraint." He ran away from home at fourteen and for a while dwelt among the Indians. He went to New York and then back to South Carolina, where he met a Miss Lewis, daughter of a planter. For a sample of Gibsonian prose at its best, no better excerpt could be found than his account of his wooing:

"When I was yet a boy, I met in my wanderings in the backwoods of South Carolina with a fair gentle girl of my own age, who had never been more than half a day's ride from the plantation of her father. We often sauntered together in the still woods of Milwee on summer days; we would wade, barefooted, the shallow pebbly streams; cross the deep and rapid creeks, with mutual help of hands to our tottering steps, as we walked the unsteady swinging trunk that bridged them over. We rambled hand in hand to gather wild grapes and the muscadine, then we would rest beneath the dense shade, and at the foot of some great tree, and talk of our boyish and girlish fancies; and then without any thought as to mutual tastes, character, or fitness, or any thing that had to do with the future—but listening only to the music of our young voices, to the alluring notes of surrounding nature, and having only our young faces to admire—we loved; and long ere I was a man, we were married."

The early death of his wife left him a widower at the age of twenty-one, with three children—a girl, Talula, and two boys, John and Henry. The father of this brood then went to sea, according to one account, as master of the first iron steamship ever built in the United States, which ran from Savannah to Florida. After a year or so he turned up in New York as a commission merchant, and then joined the gold rush to California.

Afterwards he traveled in Mexico, and he seems to have won many influential people there by the charm of his personality. Still feeling his way, he dropped down to Central America, where his pulse quickened, for he became involved in the intrigue of the banana countries. On a secret mission, of the kind he loved, he returned to the United

States and in 1851 bought the cutter *Flirt*, a 96-foot
schooner of less than a hundred tons' burden. But before he
could smuggle it out of the harbor, the *Flirt* was seized by
the revenue service and found to be loaded with arms and
ammunition for General Carrera of Guatemala.

Deprived of his chance to become an admiral in the
Guatemalan Navy, Gibson nevertheless spirited the *Flirt* out
to sea with a crew of eight and a ballast cargo of eighty tons
of ice. After a few weeks of Atlantic weather, a mutiny aboard
caused Gibson to put into Porto Praia in the Cape Verde
island of São Tiago, owned by Portugal. There he avoided
confiscation of his ship as the property of a filibuster by entertaining some officials with "gracious gentility and rare old
wine."

Out of Porto Praia, with his cargo of ice rapidly melting in
the warmer seas, Captain Gibson found that somebody had
vengefully smashed his chronometer and other nautical instruments, and sailing blind, he headed for Brazil to get some
new ones. There, to raise funds, he sold one or two tons of
ice, all that was left of his melting cargo. For the rest of this
unbelievable voyage, the *Flirt* sailed completely unladen. At
the port of Maceió the death of a crew member in a drunken
brawl almost brought confiscation once more, but Gibson's
appeal to the British vice-consul enabled him to escape arrest.

Gibson then sailed the empty *Flirt* eastward around the
Cape of Good Hope. He said that the magic islands he now
passed in the Indian Ocean—Madagascar, Mauritius, Cocos-
Keeling—held no allure for him, as he was drawn almost
magnetically on toward the great island of Sumatra, about
which he had dreamed since youth. His rhapsody upon his
first sight of it is still moving: "On Christmas eve, we were
sailing with a gentle wind over a smooth sea. We were nearing
thick masses of land-clouds, when there came a faint aroma of
sweet woody scents, wafted on the breeze; as we sped through
the yielding vapory banks, the fragrant air came strong and
pleasurable, like distant strains of song; then the retreating
clouds presented to our gaze a dark blue peak, piercing the
skyey blue above; the wood, and blossoms, and gum-scented
breeze came stronger and more thrilling, rivaling in pleasure
sweet melody on the waters; and the peak, and the odor-laden
winds, were the first sight and first welcome breath of the land
of long dreams, the island of Sumatra."

But he was tempted to leave Sumatra by prospects of a
trip to nearby Singapore, where his storytelling uncle, now

dead, had supposedly left him a fortune. Unable to go because the Dutch would not clear his ship, he turned with a profound uplifting of spirit to his main job of setting Sumatra free from Dutch rule. Accordingly he steered the *Flirt* into one of the most sensitive and spy-ridden ports of the Dutch colonial empire, the tin depot of Muntok on the metal-rich island of Bangka.

There followed a hilarious interlude. One practical Dutch official after another tried to figure out what an empty ship, seeking no cargo, was doing in the East Indies. Did mynheer come halfway around the world for a shipment of tin? No? Then perhaps coffee? No, then surely he seeks pepper? Cloves? Cinnamon? Good, then the captain wishes a cargo of lumber? No, then maybe arrack? Perhaps tobacco for the China trade? Ah, yes! Mynheer has come for a boatload of our wild animals for the zoos of America. The great elephant? The fierce tiger? The rhinoceros? The curious tapir? Perhaps the musk deer?

The questioning went on day after day, and one can imagine the frustrating reports filed by the Dutch secret police. At one point it was suspected that Gibson was after a restricted and highly lucrative cargo of birds' nests for the Chinese soup trade, and after half a dozen similarly exotic suggestions had proven vain, the patient Dutch started to repeat the litany. Did mynheer come for tin, for coffee, for pepper?

Gently Captain Gibson gave reply: "I reached out my hand over the rail of the veranda where we sat, and drew towards me the limb of a jessamine bush, which becomes a tree of twenty and thirty feet high in these islands. I inhaled the sweet fragrance of its blossoms. I then pointed to some banana and coconut trees, loaded with their fruit; to a tame musk deer, running about in the yard; to a bird of bright plumage. . . ." These were the things, he said grandiloquently, that he had come around the world in an empty boat to see.

The Dutch gave up and concluded that Gibson must be a wealthy yachtsman traveling solely for pleasure.

A local guide, a native of Bali, now offered to lead Gibson to Palembang, the largest town of Sumatra, a floating city known as the Venice of the East. This was a ticklish proposal, because Englishmen were stirring up native revolts against Dutch rule; and when Gibson indicated that he might go inland, the Dutch concluded that he was a super-smart secret agent. They began to suspect him of being an American spy or deserter, and kept an increasingly attentive eye on his activities.

Gibson, meanwhile, was reflecting upon the success of James Brooke, about whom he had read back in the United States. On the island of Borneo, to the east of Sumatra, Brooke had succeeded in setting up a personal kingdom as Rajah of Sarawak. Gibson felt that he was as good a man as Brooke and began looking around for a similar opportunity in Sumatra.

Trying to get in touch with the Sultan of Djambi, a native prince of the region, Gibson made the mistake of writing a message to that potentate in Malayan, offering to supply weapons and ships to free the natives from Dutch domination. Unluckily, the translator he chose happened to be a Malay spy who had been planted on him by the Dutch government police. Gibson's sailing master, Graham, was sent to deliver this incriminating letter, which was found on his person when he was quickly captured by the vigilant Dutch.

Gibson was clapped into the Dutch prison of Weltevreden at Batavia, Java, on a charge of fomenting rebellion. He always claimed that the innocent letter of greeting he had dictated had been replaced with an incriminating document. He refused several chances to escape and hoped for rescue by the American government, even though there was at the time no American consul near at hand. His trial was postponed indefinitely, because if he were convicted the penalty had to be death, and his execution might lead to trouble with the United States.

Gibson endured sixteen months of imprisonment with fortitude. He learned the Dutch and Javanese languages, invented a brick-making machine, and studied for hours with Sahyeepah, "the winged one," a native princess who visited him often in the free-and-easy Dutch jail.

He was finally brought to trial on February 14, 1852, and judged not guilty of high treason, but was ordered to be put in the pillory for two hours and then to be jailed for twelve years, paying his own board bill during his imprisonment. Other Dutch authorities, trusting that America had decided to abandon her erring son, ignored the sentence, and in April, 1853, a secret tribunal condemned him to death.

Yet the practical Dutch hoped that he would escape and thus solve the problem for them, and so a complicated scheme to get Gibson away from prison with the aid of the princess —who had fallen in love with him—was finally worked out.

An American schooner, the *N. B. Palmer,* was fortunately
being repaired in the vicinity and it was arranged, probably by
the Dutch themselves, for Captain C. P. Low to take the
fugitive aboard on April 24, 1853. According to Gibson's
later account of his escape, the *Palmer* while leaving the
roadstead was fired on by the Dutch cruiser *Boreas* and
after retaliating crowded on sail and evaded pursuit. This
seems highly unlikely, for the ship passed easily through the
Straits of Sunda next morning, leaving behind the confiscated
Flirt, as well as Gibson's hopes of becoming a second Rajah
Brooke.

Two years later Gibson published an excellently written
account of his attempt to free Sumatra, *The Prison of Weltevreden,* in which he adopts the device of recounting to the passengers on his rescue ship, the *Palmer,* the incidents of his
complicated adventure. Like a male Scheherazade, for fifty-
four days of the flight from Java he thus entertains the people
of the *Palmer,* and if any modern reader longs for the old
days of high-flown style, lofty sentiment and rich description,
this narrative is recommended. His cell in the state prison he
portrayed thus: "A narrow den, a foul sweltering oven; ten
feet in length and eight in width, half filled by a coarse platform, its only furniture. No light or air, but from one double-
barred grating in front. The cell stank, the air was dead and
still; I sat down with sickened feeling, on the platform; the
foulness and heat of that place was fearful. . . . The door was
closed, the dead air felt deadlier and stiller, one quaff alone of
the breezy air of the morning was prayed for; and then
water, not thought of when the keeper was in the cell, water,
water, I called for between those bars, but the brutal sentinel
paid no heed; a little water, and a little air, were the craving
wants of a dreadful night passed in the Stad prison of Batavia."

When the *Palmer* arrived in England, Gibson sought out
the American consul at Liverpool and asked for a loan to
enable him to return to the United States. He proclaimed
grandly that he was going to demand high indemnities from
the Dutch government for his mistreatment at Batavia.

The consul, whose name adds luster to the Gibson legend,
listened to tales that threatened to put the consul's own volumes of romance in the shade. After the interview he reported that he found Gibson to be "a gentleman of refined
manner, handsome figure, and remarkably intellectual aspect.
. . . Literally, from his first hour, he had been tossed upon

the surges of a most varied and tumultuous existence, having been born at sea, of American parentage, but on board of a Spanish vessel, and spending many of the subsequent years in voyages, travels, and outlandish incidents and vicissitudes which, methought, had hardly been paralleled since the days of Gulliver or Defoe. When his dignified reserve was overcome, he had the faculty of narrating these adventures with wonderful eloquence, working up his descriptive sketches with such intuitive perception of the picturesque points that the whole affair was thrown forward with a positively illusive effect, like matters of your own visual experience. In fact, they were so admirably done that I could not more than half believe them, because the genuine affairs of life are not apt to transact themselves so artistically. Many of his scenes were laid in the East, and among those seldom-visited archipelagoes of the Indian Ocean, so that there was an Oriental fragrance breathing through his talk, and an odor of the Spice Islands still lingering in his garments. He had much to say of the delightful qualities of the Malay pirates, who, indeed, carry on a predatory warfare against the ships of all civilized nations, and cut every Christian throat among their prisoners; but (except for deeds of that character, which are the rule and habit of their life, and a matter of religion and conscience with them) they are a gentle-natured people, of primitive innocence and integrity." Those are the opinions of Nathaniel Hawthorne as recorded in his book of English observations, *Our Old Home*.

Then Hawthorne describes briefly one of the most completely typical of the Gibson antics. "Meanwhile," he writes, "since arriving in England on his way to the United States, he had been providentially led to inquire into the circumstances of his birth on shipboard, and had discovered that not himself alone, but another baby, had come into the world during the same voyage of the prolific vessel, and that there were almost irrefragable reasons for believing that these two children had been assigned to the wrong mothers. Many reminiscences of his early days confirmed him in the idea that his nominal parents were aware of the exchange. The family to which he felt authorized to attribute his lineage was that of a nobleman, in the picture-gallery of whose country seat (whence, if I mistake not, our adventurous friend had just returned) he had discovered a portrait bearing a striking resemblance to himself. As soon as he should have reported to President Pierce and the Secretary of State, and recovered the confiscated property, he proposed to return to England and establish his claim to the nobleman's title and estate. . . . The English romance was among the latest communications that he entrusted to my private ear; and as soon as I heard the first chapter,—so wonderfully akin to what I might have wrote out of my own head, not unpractised in such figments, —I began to repent having made myself responsible for the future nobleman's passage homeward in the next Collins steamer." Nevertheless, Hawthorne advanced $150 with which Gibson was able to travel to Washington, D. C.

There he persuaded the United States to present a formal claim against the Dutch for $100,000 in damages. When the Dutch refused to pay, the United States virtually threatened war, and conflict seemed imminent. Gibson meanwhile had obtained a post as attaché of the American Legation in Paris, and during rambles around Europe he "read the record of glorious adventure" and dreamed of further feats of daring. His favorite hero was Prince Henry the Navigator. The Emperor Napoleon III, hearing of his exploits, offered Gibson a place in the New Caledonian expedition then forming, but the adventurer declined. He still wanted to fight the Dutch.

Returning to the United States, Gibson aroused public sympathy for his claim by lectures and by the publication of his book, *The Prison of Weltevreden*. But when his case was to be put before Congress, an important letter was found to be missing from the State Department files on his case. Since Gibson himself, who had been given access to the file, was the only person who could have abstracted it, suspicion fell on him.

It just so happened that the Dutch diplomats had a duplicate of this purloined letter and they made it public. Written by Gibson, dated at Batavia on February 25, 1852, and addressed to the governor of the Netherlands Indies, the letter begged for its writer's release and admitted making "vainglorious remarks" to the natives of Sumatra while under the influence of liquor. Gibson also confessed, "I have too often been led away in life by some high-colored romantic idea," and he admitted having indulged in "bravadoes that I would become a potentate in the East." Writing this letter and then pilfering it from the files destroyed Gibson's claim in the eyes of Congress. War with the Dutch was thus fortunately averted.

Throughout the rest of his life Gibson mourned Sumatra as his lost empire, and we can believe that, like Queen Mary

Tudor's Calais, its name was engraved upon his heart. But his rajahdom being irretrievably lost, he spruced up and looked around for other conquests.

It was in Washington that he became interested in the Mormons, or Latter-Day Saints, and observing their difficulties with the United States government, he advocated settling all of them on some Pacific isle of Eden. But his plan was rejected by officials because the cost, five million dollars, was prohibitive. As he often pointed out later, the futile Mormon War subsequently cost the United States three times that amount.

Still, an idea had struck fire in his febrile brain, and he betook himself out to Salt Lake City, where on October 29, 1859, he suggested to Brigham Young that he sell Utah to the United States and move the Mormon state—lock, stock and barrel—to Papua or New Guinea. He told Brother Brigham that his high object was to do good to the natives of those lands, as he had reason to believe they were the Lost Tribes of Israel. Instead of accepting this bizarre plan, Young countered with the suggestion that Gibson become a Mormon and perhaps go to the Pacific islands to convert the natives to that sect.

After some heart searching, Walter Murray Gibson on January 15, 1860, became a member of the Saints. He lectured for a while in Utah and then went to some of the eastern states to recruit converts, but he soon wearied and raised money to bring himself back to Utah, along with his three children. On arrival he heard the joyous news. His great desire had been realized—he had been cleared as a preacher and was appointed to carry the Mormon gospel to all the Pacific islands.

Accompanied by his daughter Talula (the two sons remained for the while in Salt Lake), Gibson headed west, and lectured in California, where because of high tensions he found it expedient to deny being a Mormon. Nor did he admit his affiliation when he landed on July 4, 1861, in the Hawaiian capital of Honolulu after a voyage on the ship *Yankee*. There he gave lectures on Malaysia and passed himself off as a world traveler on his way to the East Indies.

The Civil War had now broken out in the States, and the king of independent Hawaii, Kamehameha IV, had proclaimed his country's neutrality. Union sympathizers in Hawaii quickly became suspicious of this mysterious, energetic, glib-talking Captain Gibson of South Carolina. They guessed that he was planning a privateering venture. On September 2, while calling at the U.S. Legation, Gibson was prodded into a fiery defense of Jeff Davis, and Union spies were convinced they had their man. But two hours later he confounded everyone by leaving with his daughter on the steamer *Kilauea* for the island of Maui.

The United States consul on Maui was alerted regarding the suspicious Southerner and had him followed. He uncovered some highly perplexing data, for Gibson was accompanied by two worthies—one an ex-bartender—whom he had picked up on the ship from California. These two were now found to be wandering around Maui trying to peddle a compendium called *Dr. Warren's Household Physician*. The Union spies were utterly confused and no one knew what to do about Gibson; then suddenly he stepped forth as a full-blown Mormon missionary. His first act was, characteristically, to devise a Mormon flag with individual stars for the eight Hawaiian islands. The Union forces, withdrawing from the field, sneered at it as a "secession flag."

Gibson began his missionary labors among the native Mormon Church members, who had lacked a white leader for three years. Within a few weeks he was presiding over a conference of Mormons on Maui. But now the Hawaiian government became suspicious of him, and the Cabinet Council minute book shows that fifty dollars was authorized for obtaining any information regarding what Brother Walter was really up to. The missionary forestalled them, however, by giving a solemn promise that he would never take any Hawaiian subjects away to New Guinea. Somehow this made everything all right.

Meanwhile Gibson, in a whaleboat owned by a native, had visited the little island of Lanai. Here the heads of the Mormon Church had decided in 1853 to establish a stronghold. A tract of five thousand acres was obtained, a town site was laid out, houses were built and farms started, and slowly the City of Joseph rose. Gibson, viewing the scene, the site of his future grandiose operations, said sententiously: "I will plant my stakes here and make a home for the rest of my days."

He began to work to build up the Mormon settlements on Lanai, and by November 5 he and Talula were living at Palawai on that island. He was now head of a colony of about 180 Hawaiians, ruling under the title of "Priest of Melchisedec and Chief President of the Isles of the Sea," and this robust title seems to have awakened once more the dreams of his youth, for he wrote in his diary on January 31, 1862: "O smiling Palawai, thou infant hope of my glorious kingdom! Blessed is Lanai among the isles of the sea." From that moment, he was on his way to empire.

To further his plans, the Priest of Melchisedec began making a study of Hawaiian history, customs and language, and soon became so proficient that he was venerated by the natives. His style became even more florid: "This is the time when the gentiles of America shall be swept from the face of the earth, as has been foretold in the prophecies of the Prophet, Joseph Smith. As for Zion, her time has come to be set free, and the Prophet, Brigham Young, is to become as the King of Kings. . . . You, the red-skinned children of Abraham, have attained the joy of preparing to found the New Jerusalem."

To build Zion on Lanai and advance the farming projects there, the faithful children of Abraham donated goats, fowls, donkeys, furniture and cash. Gibson supplemented these funds by selling offices in his church; a post as one of the twelve apostles under him went for a price of $150, but other positions could be purchased for as low as fifty cents. At this point Gibson seems to have become more interested in wealth and political power than in erecting a religious Utopia, for in a revealing communication he assured the government that he could influence 2500 votes in the kingdom.

Gibson had his troubles. The two cronies he had picked up on the ship ungratefully denounced him, called him a "black-hearted schemer" and accused him of sympathy with the Confederate cause. What was worse, a drought and a worm pest threatened the harvest in March, 1862, but Gibson resolutely ordered that teams of natives be harnessed to the plough to break new land, and under similar conditions of slavery, most of the crop was saved. Although the Gibson diary now referred to "windy, desolate Lanai," success in raising cattle and sheep helped the colony prosper.

But now a few doubting natives began to wonder if what they were suffering was really the Lord's way, and a committee complained to Salt Lake City about their pastor's methods. In April a grim-faced delegation of Mormon elders arrived at Lahaina, Maui, where their investigations showed conclusively that the church had been betrayed. Gibson had diverted its funds to the purchase of about half the island of Lanai, and all the church property was in his name.

The elders were apoplectic, and Robert Louis Stevenson claimed some years later that "there is evidence to the effect that he was followed to the islands by Mormon assassins." But no Avenging Angel laid Gibson low for his theft and sacrilege. It does seem certain, however, that Elder Joseph F. Smith told the backslider: "Gibson, you will die in a gutter!"

Gibson was excommunicated by the Mormon Church within a month, and he ceased calling himself a Mormon. Most of the settlers left Lanai and went to build the New Jerusalem somewhere else. A much more promising site was chosen at Laie, Oahu, where after some years of hard work the community established a thriving sugar plantation which brought funds that enabled the erection of the imposing Mormon Temple that today glistens among the fields of waving cane. Gibson, however, stayed on Lanai with his fraudulent acres. In 1864 he was joined by his two sons, and thereafter he increased his island estates and flourished.

To the consternation of his enemies, the fruits of his wickedness seemed to multiply, and in a moving passage he recorded his reactions to his new home and its people: "They are material for a very little kingdom. They would not affect the course of trade nor change much the earth's balances of power. They are not material for a Caesar, nor a cotton lord, nor a railroad contractor. They would not be very potent secessionists and surely will seem but small material for me, after all the hope and grasp of my heart. But they are thorough, what they are. There is no cant among the kanakas. They bring a chicken or some yams to make up for their deficiencies in courtesy in approaching me. . . . I hope to influence the government to let us have all of this valley and most of the island to develop, and then we will dig and tunnel and build and plant and make a waste place a home for rejoicing thousands. I could make a glorious little kingdom out of this or any such chance, with such people, so loving and obedient. I would make a port and a commerce, a state and a civilization. I would make millions of fruits where one was never thought of. I would fill this lovely crater with corn and wine and oil and babies and love and health and brotherly rejoicing and sisterly kisses and the memories of me for evermore."

Gibson, realizing that at last he had a good thing, became a naturalized citizen of Hawaii on March 26, 1866. He made a trip back to New York in the fall of 1868, where he turned up as the "commercial agent to the colony of Singapore," trying to encourage the idea of Malaysian immigration into Hawaii, where labor was badly needed on the spreading sugar plantations. He also journeyed to Washington on his own account, where he lobbied for a reciprocity treaty between the United States and Hawaii that would break down the tariff wall on sugar and other articles exchanged by the two countries. Ignoring his Hawaiian citizenship, he tried to get himself a job on an American commission concerned with Oriental immigrants in the United States. And in his spare time he looked for good mainland farmers to bring back with him to the islands, but the few families he brought home to Lanai did not want to work very hard and the idea was a failure.

Gibson moved to Honolulu in September, 1872, and, supported by his hefty income from Lanai, entered politics. His first move was the promotion of a scheme for repopulating Hawaii. He advised importing people from the Orient or Malaysia—he strongly recommended Sumatra—to replace the declining Hawaiians and to supply labor in the fields. He founded a Hawaiian Immigration Society which advised the government on such matters, and the fact that Hawaii is today so strongly Oriental stems partly from his activity.

But sending memorials to the government was not his idea of politics. He had a much grander field of operation in mind, but for such achievement he required that the Hawaiian throne be occupied by the kind of king who would fit in with his grandiose plans. The present king, Kamehameha V, had not the commanding mind of the great ruler whose name he bore, but even so, Gibson could not make any headway with him. Fortunately for Gibson, Kamehameha V died without having named his successor, so Hawaii was free to elect a king.

Gibson looked over the two candidates, Prince William C. Lunalilo, a high-born chief with liberal opinions, and Colonel David Kalakaua, a politician and newspaper editor. Apparently he thought highly of neither, for there is some evidence that before the election he tried to organize a revolution which would have established a republic with Gibson as president; but this scheme failed, so he came out strongly for Lunalilo, and his candidate won overwhelmingly.

Yet Gibson had made a poor choice, for Lunalilo proved himself to be a fairly good king and one quite unprepared to follow Gibson's leadership in anything. Gibson, now fifty-two years old, a wealthy, influential man with a handsome black beard and commanding presence, decided to attain power without the king's assistance. His skill in oratory, and especially his mastery of the Hawaiian language, gave him command over the popular imagination, aided by his editorship of a paper called *Nuhou*, or "gossip." He appealed to the natives' fear of foreigners and missionaries, and for his own ends stirred up racial hatred. Ironically, the cry of this Caucasian messiah was "Hawaii for the Hawaiians!" and his demagogic articles and lectures poured scorn on the "grasping and unscrupulous whites." Clearly aiming at the private goal of "Hawaii for Gibson!" he stirred up hatred of all non-Hawaiians, but particularly those who had long resided in the islands and were prominent in business and social life.

Then Lunalilo died after less than thirteen months of sovereignty, and Gibson had another chance to pick himself a king. This time he made no mistakes. Backing David Kalakaua vigorously, he opposed the more logical candidate, Queen Emma, a brilliant woman and widow of Kamehameha IV. Of her Gibson shouted piously that she should refrain from running, for "the Hawaiian people will love her as a benefactress and hate her as a politician." When the legislators met, thirty-nine voted for Kalakaua and only six for Emma. The queen's supporters attacked the Courthouse and a riot broke out that was quelled only by the landing of forces from British and American warships in the harbor.

At last Gibson had the king he wanted. Kalakaua, destined to be the last male monarch of the Hawaiian kingdom, was truly a "merry monarch," but also a visionary, one who believed in Hawaii's high destiny. Fourteen years younger than Gibson, he had been born on November 16, 1836, in Honolulu; but he came of a prominent family of the Big Island—Hawaii—and could trace his ancestry back to legendary times when chiefs had reached there from Tahiti. He was a practiced public speaker and writer in both English and Hawaiian, and had once edited a newspaper, *Star of the Pacific*. In 1888 his name was to appear as author of *Legends and Myths of Hawaii*, edited by R. M. Daggett, the first important book in English dealing with these old tales. He also loved music, and composed the words of the national anthem, "Hawaii Ponoi."

Kalakaua started his reign auspiciously, and won wide popularity by attaining a reciprocity treaty with the United States. To aid the cause he made a visit to that country, and thus became the first king of any nation to do so. Americans, of course, have always gone mad over royalty, and King Kalakaua was widely hailed as a democratic king. But he dreamed of restoring the strong personal rule of the early Hawaiian monarchs, and his reign was marked by an increasing march toward autocracy.

Burly in figure, with luxuriant side whiskers, Kalakaua Rex was imposing in the glittering uniforms in which he loved to dress. He was a living paradox, both kingly and democratic. Stevenson, who spent six months in the islands in 1889, called Kalakaua "the finest gentleman I ever met" and "a very fine intelligent fellow," but added, after the king had lunched on the writer's yacht *Casco,* "what a crop for the drink! He carries it, too, like a mountain with a sparrow on its shoulders." Henry Adams, whose education was advanced by a visit to Hawaii in 1890, noted that Kalakaua "talked of Hawaiian archaeology and arts as well as though he had been a professor." Charles Warren Stoddard, another author, remarked: "Oh, what a king was he! Such a king as one reads of in nursery tales. He was all things to all men, a most companionable person. Possessed of rare refinement, he was as much at ease with a crew of 'rollicking rams' as in the throne room." John Cameron, who as master of a steamer running to Kauai often found His Majesty seated among his retainers on mats on the afterdeck, termed him "easy to approach and difficult to leave; unfailingly genial; kind to high and low alike; beloved by his subjects. . . . It was not strange, I think, that many adventurers took advantage of Kalakaua's liberality and joviality to intrigue for their own miserable ends." The chief intriguer was Walter Murray Gibson.

Under Kalakaua, as under Lunalilo, Gibson continued his intrigues to obtain favorable leases on more Lanai lands. He was elected to the Legislative Assembly in 1878 from Lahaina, and took an active part as a supporter of the king and a champion of the natives. He worked for sanitation and better care of lepers.

Further, Gibson supported an appropriation to build a more commodious palace, observing in his rich prose that it was "essential to the dignity and security of a throne that it should be upheld by appropriate surroundings of domain and mansion." He also took the lead in proposing a fitting celebration of the centenary of the discovery of the islands by Captain James Cook, and an appropriation of

$10,000 was made for a statue of Kamehameha I to be erected in Honolulu. Some people commended Gibson's efforts in this session, but the *Hawaiian Gazette* sourly wrote: "He got up more special committees, made more reports, and by his officiousness and vanity kept the legislature in a continual ferment of excitement, merely to enable him to air his inordinate ambition to shine as a leader of the Assembly; and par excellence, the special friend and protector-general of the remnants of the Hawaiian race."

The statue turned out to be a typical Gibson project. As committee head, he felt he had to go to the United States, and in Boston commissioned the sculptor Thomas R. Gould to design an idealized statue of Kamehameha the Great, which would be erected across from the new palace in downtown Honolulu. Somehow, the expense of this statue ran into big money; the pedestal alone cost the kingdom $4,500, and the statue itself sank when the ship that carried it caught fire off South America.

Now occurred one of those accidents which try the politician's soul. And Gibson must often have contemplated wryly the irony of a situation in which he introduced into Hawaii his own worst enemy. Some years before, while knocking around Washington, he had met an ingratiating Italian adventurer, Celso Caesar Moreno, whom he had casually invited to Hawaii. Long after the invitation had been forgotten, Moreno turned up brightly on the Honolulu docks. He immediately charmed King Kalakaua, and with Gibson's support wangled $24,000 for a steamship line to be run by Moreno, showed how an opium concession in Hawaii would make millions, tried to borrow $1,000,000 to lay a transpacific cable to China, and set up a plan for educating likely Hawaiian boys at overseas universities at government expense.

This was the kind of big thinking that appealed to King Kalakaua, and startling as it seems, exactly 274 days after the enterprising Celso Caesar Moreno landed in Hawaii, the king prorogued the Assembly, forced his entire cabinet to resign, and appointed Moreno premier of Hawaii!

A tornado of protest at once arose against the interloper. Various people advocated the crowning of Emma, the abdication of Kalakaua, the lynching of Moreno, or immediate annexation of the kingdom by the United States. Under this storm of indignation, the king reluctantly dismissed Moreno, but to save face gave him the position of escorting some young Hawaiians abroad to study in Italy. Moreno departed, suspected of some sinister mission.

Gibson must have breathed a sigh of enormous relief when the gallant Italian disappeared, for Moreno had done exactly what Gibson wanted to do, and only the popular revolution against the appointment made it possible for Gibson himself to attain the post of premier. His election, however, was to come more slowly than Moreno's dazzling rise.

Posing as the savior of the declining Hawaiian race, Gibson had been busy giving medical advice toward that end. He rightly asserted that the race "which cared not for the chastity of its females must not hope for independence or perpetuity." Completely without the aid of the medical profession, he wrote a book of sanitary instructions for the native Hawaiians, which would help them avoid malaria, smallpox and leprosy. The main source of his rules was, as he wrote to one editor, "the first and most eminent writer on sanitary conditions known to us—and that is Moses." Gibson made a good deal of money on this volume and obtained a post on the Board of Health.

Gibson's real power began to accumulate when he acquired the influential newspaper, *Pacific Commercial Advertiser,* in whose columns he continued to play the champion of the Hawaiian people, the enemy of grasping Caucasians, and the only logical savior of the islands. He had plenty of space in which to advance these views, for all the respectable business leaders had pulled their ads out of his paper.

Kalakaua Rex departed in January, 1881, on a trip around the world, the first king to make such a tour. He was accompanied by his chamberlain, Colonel C. H. Judd, and his attorney general, W. N. Armstrong. His valet Robert, a decayed German baron who was an accomplished linguist, went along as interpreter. The king went abroad presumably to study the immigration problem, but one of his ministers said his only object was to gratify his curiosity and that it was "pure poppycock and Gibsonese" to say otherwise. Kalakaua went first to San Francisco and then visited Japan, China, Siam, India, Egypt and the capitals of Europe. In all of these places he was given royal honors and hearty entertainment, and in Tokyo nearly succeeded in arranging a marriage between his lovely niece, the Princess Kaiulani, and one of the imperial princes of Japan.

During the king's absence, Gibson built up his political power and came to be considered a public leader. He was appointed a member of the privy council, and when Kalakaua returned, Gibson continued to instill in him a love of pomp and aggrandizement, for the king was easily dazzled by show.

While in England the king had ordered two golden crowns, set with precious jewels. On February 12, the ninth anniversary of Kalakaua's election to the throne, the coronation was held in a pavilion on the grounds of the new Iolani Palace. While eight thousand people watched, the elected king, Napoleon-style, put on his own head and that of his queen the royal crowns. Years later, runs the legend, on the night the Hawaiian monarchy was overthrown, an officer of the Provisional Government forces found his men in the palace basement throwing dice for jewels gouged out of these royal diadems. The biggest diamond was sent by an Irish sergeant to his Indiana sweetheart, who always considered it just a lump of glass.

During the election of 1882, Gibson's opponents tried to overwhelm him by publishing a satirical exposé entitled *The Shepherd Saint of Lanai*. It revealed in lurid detail the shadiness of his early career and predicted a revolution if Gibson continued to stir up hatred. This pamphlet failed to ruin him, however, because it was printed in English, and few of his native supporters could read it! Again his political cunning and his oratory enabled him to be elected by a large majority.

The 1882 session of the legislature was one of the most corrupt that had ever met in Honolulu. One of its first acts was to convey to Claus Spreckels, a California sugar magnate, a large tract of crown lands at Wailuku, Maui, to settle a claim he had bought from a local princess for $10,000. Gibson supported an opium-licensing bill, another big loan bill, a bill to permit sale of spirituous liquors to natives and another for nonsegregation of lepers. Another bill led to the minting of the silver coins which in 1884 were put in circulation bearing the bust of Kalakaua; on this coinage deal, Spreckels made a profit of $150,000, and the dumping of silver currency for a time threatened the entire Hawaiian economy.

Such flagrant misgovernment could not be tolerated by sensible men, and Kalakaua's entire cabinet resigned. This was Gibson's supreme chance, and he prevailed upon the king to appoint him premier and minister of foreign affairs. Thereafter, until his sudden downfall five years later, Gibson had everything his own way. He proved himself an adroit politician and held each of the cabinet posts in turn, occasionally several at once. Whenever the conservative elements in the kingdom tried to unseat him, he threatened them with his staunch Hawaiian supporters, and made his position secure by continuing to flatter the hula-loving, poker-playing king.

The Gibson rule was one of utter confusion, but slowly a Reform party, solidly organized, began to coagulate and it managed to defeat some of the wildest Gibson measures, even though the premier used patronage and government funds shamelessly to support his program. He favored his son-in-law with sinecures and showered the young man's father with building contracts. Among the more trivial scandals of the Gibson regime were the sale of public offices, the ruination of the civil service by purges, misuse of royal privilege to defraud the customs revenue, illegal leasing of lands to the king, neglect of the roads of the kingdom and the sale of exemptions to lepers, who could thereby escape confinement on Molokai.

Now Gibson was in a position where he could revive the dreams of his youth, and he launched a systematic program of corrupting Kalakaua's judgment and subtly introducing his own grand design. Hawaii must head a vast coalition of island states including Tahiti, Samoa, Tonga, the New Hebrides, the Solomons, the Gilberts and all the islands in between—and the king of Hawaii would become the emperor of the Pacific.

Gibson's studies had shown him that in the past, the Hawaiian Islands had not only striven for their independence but had at times tried to play a bigger role in Pacific politics and to annex other regions. He recalled that Kamehameha the Great, the "Napoleon of the Pacific," had dreamed of going far beyond his unique achievement of uniting the baronial, war-torn Hawaiian Islands under himself as ruler. During the last years of his reign that powerful monarch, who died in 1819, was reported to have opened negotiations with King Pomare II of Tahiti on the project of having a son and daughter of Kamehameha marry Pomare's offspring. An alliance of that kind might have been the first step in organizing a spreading Polynesian League in the Pacific before too many islands had been grabbed by European powers.

Gibson also remembered the disastrous expedition of Governor Boki and his two Hawaiian brigs in search of a sandalwood island in the New Hebrides in 1830. Trying to recoup his lost fortunes, Boki and nearly five hundred of his followers had mysteriously disappeared in the South Seas. Gibson deduced that Boki had probably carried secret orders to annex some of those islands to the Hawaiian kingdom. Could Boki's tragic trip be used as an excuse for annexation?

But most of all, Gibson was familiar with the exploits of one of the strangest men in Hawaiian history. Charles St. Julian never saw the Islands, probably never saw a Hawaiian. He was an underpaid law-court reporter in Sydney, Australia, with little schooling and only an inordinate personal vanity to build upon. As a result of writing innumerable letters to different governments, he was—almost accidentally —allowed to serve as *de facto* consular agent for Hawaii in Sydney.

That was all the purchase he needed, for he thereupon launched a veritable blizzard of reports, fantastic plans, involved negotiations and scatterbrained attempts at consolidating most of the island groups in the Pacific under Hawaiian rule. With his own money he purchased a lovely atoll just east of the Solomons called Sikaiana, and tried to give it to Hawaii. It is doubtful if any kingdom ever had a more loyal servant than Charles St. Julian. For twenty years he tried to get the Hawaiian kings to accept the "Primacy of the Pacific" and take the lead in establishing protectorates over islands that had not yet been seized by the great powers.

But Hawaii, without a Walter Murray Gibson on hand at the time to appreciate the Australian's energy, treated St. Julian badly. He got little or no pay, no support. Not even his atoll was accepted, but he did enjoy moments of grandeur. He was allowed to design his own uniforms, and by all accounts was one of the handsomest and most glittering consuls ever to operate in the Southern Hemisphere. He also initiated, on his own account, a florid, bejeweled decoration, the Order of Arossi, which he gave to himself for extraordinary services to the people of Polynesia.

Usually such dreamers reach a bad end, but Charles St. Julian gladdens the heart by his accomplishments. Despairing of getting anywhere with the unimaginative Hawaiian kingdom, he transferred his cyclonic talents to Fiji, where he appeared grandly as "Charles, Muara of Arossi and Sovereign Chief of Sikaiana." He completely bedazzled that island group and talked himself into the job of lord high chief justice. Then, as he was about to leave Sydney for his new post, he received notice that Hawaii, whom he had pestered for years seeking some kind of honors, had finally awarded him "a Cross and Diploma as Knight Commander of the Order of Kamehameha I." With tears of gratitude overflowing upon the paper, he reported that he would accept the offer, because he would now be able to appear in Fiji as Sir Charles, which would "look better" and be "more fitting."

We see St. Julian for the last time as he enters the judicial chambers of Fiji. It is said that this flamboyant man, who was totally unschooled in law, appeared in a tremendous scarlet gown, a full-bottomed wig, and all the glittering accoutrements of a proper English judge.

Walter Murray Gibson, who became premier eight years after St. Julian died in Fiji, was apparently haunted by the Australian's concept of what might be accomplished in the Pacific by a determined Hawaiian leader. He would be that leader. Accordingly he began to indoctrinate King Kalakaua with the idea of empire, and in 1880 the astonished United States minister at Honolulu reported to his superiors that Kalakaua's imagination was actually "inflamed with the idea of gathering all the cognate races of the Islands of the Pacific into a great Polynesian Confederacy, over which he will reign." On June 28, Gibson had inserted into the preamble of a resolution adopted by the Legislative Assembly a statement that "the Hawaiian kingdom by its geographic position and political status is entitled to claim a Primacy in the family of Polynesian States." But this statement passed unnoticed by the press, and nothing further was done until Gibson came to power as head of the cabinet in 1882.

In this year Gibson received an inquiry from the chief of Makin, one of the Gilbert Islands, concerning a possible protectorate. He answered favorably and the upshot was that this chief and one from Abiang were invited to come to Kalakaua's coronation, but they were unable to do so.

As might be expected, Gibson's first overt act of empire was a disaster. Hearing that Captain A. N. Tripp, of the blackbirding ship *Julia*, was about to leave Honolulu for a native-stealing expedition to the New Hebrides, Gibson officially appointed him as "Special Commissioner for Central and Western Polynesia," with the job of inquiring whether any Gilbert Islands kings wanted to affiliate with Hawaii.

The *Julia* was wrecked on a Gilbert Islands reef while the captain was spying out the prospects, and the ship was a total loss; but when Special Commissioner Tripp beat his way back to Hawaii in another ship, he was quite excited about the prospects for a United Gilbert Islands nation under Hawaiian protection. The only lasting result of his mission, however, was the introduction into Hawaii of grass skirts from the Gilberts to adorn the palace hula dancers.

Soon after sending Tripp on his mission, Gibson took the first big step toward empire on August 23, 1883, when the Hawaiian government issued, in the form of a protest to the representatives of twenty-six nations, what was really a sort of Monroe Doctrine of Oceania. It proclaimed that Hawaii as a free Polynesian state should take the lead in guiding less fortunate neighbors. Only eight nations even bothered to reply. The document had no immediate effect, except to give Gibson's enemies a chance to ridicule the idea of his "calabash empire," referring to the Hawaiian expression of "calabash cousin" to indicate a non-blood relationship.

Tired of fooling around with paper measures, in 1886 Gibson decided that a likely region to begin in was the wartorn Samoan Islands, south of Hawaii, and he proposed that these islands should be taken under King Kalakaua's protection. Accordingly, he requested a $30,000 appropriation to send a government mission to Samoa and the South Pacific to demonstrate Hawaii's right to take the lead among Polynesian states. Opponents said it was "a policy of sentiment, show, and nonsense," and that "it was a ridiculous farce for this one-horse kingdom to maintain consular offices in all parts of the world." Gibson responded: "What was Rome but a one-horse state at its beginning? . . . The Great Powers never think of us as a one-horse state." Using steamroller tactics, Gibson put through a final appropriation of $35,000 for the purpose, and in a gesture which he no doubt later regretted added on $100,000 for the purchase of a steamboat to overawe the other Polynesians and $50,000 for its running expenses.

The mission, which was about to stumble blindly into the fury of Prince Otto von Bismarck, chancellor of Germany, was appointed on December 22, 1886. Its totally inadequate head, John Edward Bush, a Caucasian-Hawaiian, was created

"Envoy Extraordinary and Minister Plenipotentiary to the King of Tonga and High Commissioner to the Sovereign Chiefs and Peoples of Polynesia." He was accompanied by his wife; his daughter; some servants, at least one of whom could play a guitar; Henry Poor as secretary; and the artist Joseph D. Strong, husband of Robert Louis Stevenson's stepdaughter. Strong was commissioned to paint Polynesian portraits and scenes. The group left on Christmas Day on the S. S. *Zeelandia*. A fancy carriage, a gift to Malietoa, the leading chief of Samoa, was unfortunately left behind on the wharf at Honolulu.

Rarely has a mission headed so hopefully for an arena where only disaster could result. Not only was Samoa torn by internecine strife between two claimants to power, Malietoa and Tamasese, but Great Britian, the United States and Germany were also involved in the bickering, and the last, a late-comer on the imperial scene, was determined on a showdown. Samoa would be German, or there would be war. It is pitiful to contemplate John Bush's fumbling group as it prepared to back into the German lawn mower.

Of all the places in the Pacific to which such a mission could have been sent, Samoa was in many respects the most appropriate, for there a heady brew of intrigue, romance, assassination and adultery was provided in a rich tropical setting, of which Stevenson's wife was to write, "Socially, Samoa was certainly not dull. Diplomats and officials, many of them accompanied by their families, rented houses in the vicinity of Apia and entertained as they would at home. I have known Apia to be convulsed by a question of precedence between two officials from the same country, who each claimed the place of honour at public functions; burning despatches on the subject were written, and their respective governments appealed to. Well has Apia been called 'the kindergarten of diplomacy.'" With the arrival of the Bush party, the children in the kindergarten were going to play rough.

On arrival in Apia, Bush began building a spacious house that would serve as a permanent Hawaiian legation. In a show of glittering splendor he decorated Malietoa, the warring chieftain whom he had decided to support, with the "Grand Cross of the Royal Order of the Star of Oceania," a knightly order that Gibson had whipped up in imitation of St. Julian's abortive Order of Arossi. Bush then confided to Malietoa his breath-taking design: Samoa and

Hawaii would form a federation under King Kalakaua. Then Tonga and the Cook Islands would join up, followed no doubt by Tahiti, whereupon the Gilberts would be annexed outright. In celebration, Malietoa and his supporting chiefs were given their first taste of Ambassador Bush's secret weapon: large bottles of square-face gin. The party lasted till five in the morning.

The Treaty of Confederation between Hawaii and Samoa was actually signed by Malietoa on February 17, 1887, and Bush celebrated the occasion with another all-night party. Stevenson, who arrived in Samoa two years later, wrote in *A Footnote to History* that Malietoa withdrew at an early hour, but "by those that remained, all decency appears to have been forgotten; high chiefs were seen to dance; and day found the house carpeted with slumbering grandees, who must be roused, doctored with coffee, and sent home. As a first chapter in the history of Polynesian Confederation, it was hardly cheering, and Laupepe [Malietoa] remarked to one of the embassy, 'If you have come here to teach my people to drink, I wish you had stayed away.'"

Bush went ahead to establish a virtual protectorate over the naïve Samoans. He obtained the defection of one of Malietoa's chief enemies, the father-in-law of rival Tamasese. Of this man Poor wrote that he had become "a generous admirer of our cheap gin and has even offered me his virgin daughter." Moreover, Tamasese's position was greatly weakened when his wife left him, and having "become charmed with the guitar music and songs" of one of Bush's Hawaiian servants, went to live with the latter as her paramour. In early March, Malietoa himself even proposed marriage to Bush's daughter Molly, offering to make her Queen Molly of Samoa, but unfortunately for her own future, the young lady declined that honor.

This extraordinary sequence of events infuriated the Germans, who had already secretly decided to back Tamasese and under his chieftainship to incorporate Samoa directly into the German Empire. But for the present Captain Brandeis, in charge of the German manipulations, had no clearcut commission from Bismarck, and so had to fight off the Bush mission as slyly as he could. He had reason to believe, however, that when a squadron of the German Imperial Navy reached Apia, things would be different.

But Ambassador Bush also had a rather terrifying trump card up his sleeve. The Hawaiian fleet was about to appear in Samoan waters, and Bush felt certain that this redoubtable force would sway the balance of power definitely away from Germany and toward Hawaii.

The fleet consisted of one wormy ship, the 171-ton British steamer *Explorer,* which Gibson had bought for $20,000. It had been launched in Scotland in 1871 and had since seen good service in the guano trade. The government got possession of this vessel on January 21, 1887, and for $14,000 more fitted her out ostensibly as a naval training ship. Gibson's detractors hailed it as an expensive folly to "saddle the country with a toy ship for which she had as much need as a cow has for a diamond necklace."

The ship, whose name had been translated into Hawaiian as *Kaimiloa,* was armed with four muzzle-loading six-pounder saluting guns from Iolani Barracks, and two Gatling guns. Among the sixty-three-man crew it was decided to include twenty-four boys from the Oahu Reformatory School, twenty-one of whom would comprise a ship's band to "awe the natives with martial strains." Not much was known about the captain of the gunboat, George E. Gresley Jackson, except that he claimed to have been a British naval officer, was lately master of the reform school, and was indubitably one of the worst habitual drunkards in all Hawaii.

After many delays, H.M.S. *Kaimiloa* departed from Honolulu on May 18. She had been commissioned March 28 by Gibson "for the Naval Service of the Kingdom." Criticism arose against the use of the reform school boys and this vessel of the Hawaiian navy, which critics ironically predicted would "shortly strike terror into the hearts of the natives, and teach the pigmy national ships of France, Germany, and Great Britain, in those waters, a necessary lesson."

Even before sailing, a disturbance on board upset discipline, and led to the dismissal of three officers. A marine officer was drinking with some sailors; he refused to return to his cabin, and called his marines into action to aid him. This was the first of the *Kaimiloa* mutinies.

That the *Kaimiloa* ever reached Apia to challenge Germany's imperial might was a miracle, for during the first eleven days at sea Captain Jackson hid out in his cabin, blind drunk. None of the other officers knew anything about navigation, but they kept the ship in what they thought to be a southerly direction, so that when their captain finally staggered out to shoot the sun he found that his loyal crew had wasted not more than a week. A journal entry runs: "The captain took sights occasionally but never attempted to work out his longitude."

By some miracle, he and his crew sighted Apia on June 15, 1887, after a sickly twenty-nine-day passage. The German gunboat *Adler* was found at the anchorage and signaled inquiry as to the Hawaiian ship's identity, but the *Kaimiloa*, unaware of naval courtesies, drove gaily onward until checked by a shot across her bows.

The *Kaimiloa*'s first function was the presentation to Malietoa of a gorgeous uniform, which he wore when inspecting the ship, where a twenty-one-gun salute was offered. To everyone's astonishment, the guns fired.

Then came intrigue of the highest order. The German corvette *Adler*, which had been met in the harbor, was ordered to maintain constant vigil upon the intruding Hawaiian gunboat until the German squadron, which was on its way, had time to arrive and take command of the situation. A game of hide-and-seek developed when Ambassador Bush dispatched his warship to the neighboring island of Tutuila, where it was trailed by the suspicious *Adler*. But halfway to Pago Pago the *Kaimiloa* suddenly hove to and sent up a distress signal. Here was a chance for the Germans to board and inspect the Hawaiian menace!

But what the *Kaimiloa* wanted was a doctor. Captain Jackson, after having lived exclusively on gin for weeks, had finally eaten some food and it had given him galloping dysentery. Accordingly, a German medical officer, commissioned on the spot to spy out Hawaii's intentions, was rowed over to the wallowing *Kaimiloa*, where Captain Jackson was found doubled up in his bunk. For the remainder of the cruise the German officer more or less took charge.

Early in July, the second mutiny took place on board the *Kaimiloa*. A gunner, returning drunk, decided to rush the magazine and blow up the ship, just for the hell of it. Since trouble seemed inevitable, three officers promptly went ashore and presented their resignations to Captain Jackson, who was drinking gin, as usual. Ambassador Bush convinced them it was their duty to stay in service and quell the mutiny. But to safeguard his navy, he took the precaution of sending Poor and Jackson on board to see what they could do to save the *Kaimiloa*. Apparently the peacemakers got rough handling; according to Stevenson, "for a great part of the night she was in the hands of mutineers, and the secretary lay bound upon the deck."

After Poor had been chained for three hours and it seemed that the ship might actually be blown up, the Germans intervened. The *Adler* hove alongside and restored order. Her captain warned that if the uprising did not end, he would have to take over the rebellious ship and sail it back to Honolulu with the mutineers in irons. Where Poor and Jackson had failed, the Germans succeeded, and finally quelled the disturbance on the vessel sent to overawe European gunboats in Samoan waters.

Later Bush took the *Kaimiloa* on a cruise to the large island of Savaii to impress the outlying chiefs. He used up seven cases of gin, and the only result, according to one observer, was "to gratify the several chiefs visited by a sight of the ship, and by having the band sent ashore to entertain the people."

Now the Bush mission began to experience those heartaches which at times overtake even the best-planned operations. It was discovered that the ambassador had built his imposing legation on the wrong piece of ground and that it no longer belonged to him. Consequently a protracted lawsuit was initiated which annoyed him greatly. Then an enemy secretly reported to Gibson in Hawaii that Bush was "the most dissipated man who has held a high position at this place for many years. His associates here are mostly of the lowest kind of half-castes and whites." Later Bush found that the instigator of this canard was his own secretary, Poor, but in a dispatch that must be unique in diplomatic history, he explained everything away by pointing out that Poor was living with Bush's daughter Molly and had got her pregnant and was thus somewhat irritated with her father, the ambassador.

As if the troubles ashore were not enough, the *Kaimiloa* now produced its third mutiny, for on July 22 the marines refused to load coal without being paid a bonus. Secretary Poor later called the vessel "a disgrace to her flag. . . . There was a state of continuous insubordination on the ship and utter disregard of all order and discipline. With a few exceptions the marines and white officers behaved badly, the marines continually breaking liberty by swimming ashore and disturbing the town with their drunken conduct." In fact, impartial observers reported that, if one took into consideration the behavior of the captain, the officers and the marines, the only people aboard the *Kaimiloa* who behaved even reasonably decently were the reform school boys; but this was probably due to the fact that early in the visit to Samoa all the troublesome boys deserted the ship and were never heard of again.

Ambassador Bush's cup of trouble was brimming, for he found that his underlings had spent far more money than he could supply, and Apia merchants refused to do business on credit. The Germans were becoming stronger and more arrogant, and it seemed only a matter of time until Hawaii's friend, Malietoa, would be thrown out of power. Consequently it was a gloomy delegation that Bush led to say farewell to Chief Malietoa on the last night ashore; but the evening was made lively by Captain Jackson, who fell into a violent attack of delirium tremens.

That was enough. In disgust Ambassador Bush ordered the captain to take his warship back to Honolulu, and that, presumably, was the last of the *Kaimiloa.* Henry Poor wrote in his diary on August 8, "It was with a feeling of intense relief that I watched her disappear from sight."

But a few days later when Bush and his party, who had borrowed and scraped up enough money to pay their steamer fares back to Honolulu, reached Pago Pago on the way home, they found the *Kaimiloa* snugly berthed in that majestic anchorage. The enlisted men, fearing that they might have inadequate food for the trip north if their captain got drunk again and lost the way, were bartering all the ship's muskets for pigs, while Captain Jackson, also dubious about his own comforts on what might turn out to be a long voyage, was hocking the ship's silverware for bananas and other food.

In later years, when the *Kaimiloa*—which had once defied simultaneously the three greatest nations of the earth—was an inglorious hulk rotting on the Honolulu water front, Captain George E. Gresley Jackson turned up in various American ports. He dressed like an admiral and accorded himself that title. He was utterly contemptuous of the Hawaiians as sailors. "They were," he snorted bitterly, "far too fond of gin."

Thus ended Walter Murray Gibson's boyhood dream of a South Seas empire. The recall of the Bush mission and the abandonment of "gin diplomacy" occurred just in time, for Otto von Bismarck had endured enough. Around the end of July the Iron Chancellor confided to an associate: "We should not have put up with insolence of the Hawaiians any longer; if a German squadron were at anchor before Samoa, it could sail to Hawaii, and King Kalakaua could be told that, unless he desisted from his insolent intrigues in Samoa, we should shoot his legs in two, despite his American protection."

On August 19, only eleven days after the *Kaimiloa* had departed, a squadron of four German warships did arrive at Apia. The American consul there believed that, had the Hawaiian ship lingered until that time, it might well have been blown out of the water. Even Hawaii itself, as Bismarck had threatened, might have been attacked. On August 25, the squadron proclaimed Tamasese as King of Samoa, and unlucky Malietoa was deported. The Germans proclaimed martial law, and they threatened war with Hawaii if it aided the Malietoa faction in any way. Gibson's vision of Hawaiian empire had led only to a very real danger to Hawaii's home islands from German cannons.

But Gibson was not around for the final debacle. Weeks before the collapse of empire, the man's follies had come home to roost, and his own neck was in danger. Had Germany known the true state of affairs, she might well have thought of armed intervention in Hawaii, for a revolution was simmering there. Gibson's attempts to use Kalakaua for his own selfish ends, plus his cabinet machinations and his stirring up of racial prejudice for political purposes, made *pilikia*—trouble—inevitable.

The election campaign of 1886 had been a riot of vilification by both parties. Gibson's royalists had the edge, however, because they could use the king's privilege of importing liquor duty free. Their henchmen served waiting lines of thirsty voters from a galvanized washtub full of straight gin, poured into tumblers from a coconut-shell ladle. The going price for votes was five dollars. Gibson won.

During the legislature of 1886, Gibson found the government heavily in debt to Spreckels and faced by the need to mortgage its revenue to the man who was being called "the second king of Hawaii." Public money continued going down the drain. The appropriations bill passed in 1886 exceeded four and a half millions. As the *Gazette* wrote: "The money borrowed has been used for every folly that the brains of a vain and foolish man could invent."

Now a worse scandal was about to break. For many years Gibson had abetted Kalakaua in reviving native customs and traditions, which opened the leaders to charges that they were "licensing sorcery and the hula and sacrificing black pigs." They had also founded a society which, it was charged, was set up "for the propagation of idolatry and sorcery." This was the Hale Naua or House of Ancient Science, a secret society combining aspects of Masonry with the rites of pagan chiefs. According to its charter from the privy council, it was organized forty quadrillions of years after the foundation of the world and 24,750 years after Lailai, the Hawaiian Eve. One historian believed that it was intended "partly as an agency for the revival of heathenism, partly to pander to vice, and indirectly to serve as a political machine."

The king dabbled in "scientific" theories such as the notion that Hawaii was the remains of a large Atlantis-like continent which his race had once dominated—a theory that would appeal to the Mu enthusiasts of today but which evoked contemporary laughter. Kalakaua also founded a "Hawaiian Board of Health" which his critics termed an organized body of *kahunas,* medicine men. Gossips whispered of palace orgies at which the heathen pastimes were revived, including the *hale ume,* in which the companion of a night's pleasure was chosen by rolling a ball of twine in the direction of the selected charmer.

Other gossip concerned the private life of Gibson, who was still the Lothario. The sixty-four-year-old premier was courting a twenty-eight-year-old widow, Flora Howard St. Clair, who had come with her sister from their home state of California in February, 1886. She was a book agent and while canvassing for sales soon met Gibson. They immediately found a common interest in British painters. He told her that his life was lonely and remarked, "There is nothing like a true, loving heart." A day or two after Christmas, according to her testimony in court, he proposed marriage to her on the veranda of his home; but later he denied the engagement, and in May, 1887, when Gibson had his hands full with politics rather than with affairs of the heart, her lawyers brought a suit for breach of promise and asked $25,000 in damages. The suit did not come to trial until after Gibson's downfall, and in October, 1887, a jury awarded Mrs. St. Clair the sum of $10,000 heart balm.

As if no collapse were imminent, on November 16, 1886, Gibson had helped to celebrate King Kalakaua's fiftieth birthday with a grand *hookupu,* or gift-giving. Each guest brought a present suitable to his station. Premier Gibson led off with a pair of elephant tusks on a koa-wood stand with the inscription: "The horns of the righteous shall be exalted." The police department, more practical, tendered a bank check for $570. The ensuing jubilee pageantry and hula performances lasted more than a week.

Such scandals and the drain on public funds had hopelessly alienated most of the white residents as well as many of the natives. Early in 1887 a secret society called the Hawaiian League had been formed to fight for a less autocratic constitution. Hundreds of islanders joined, and as a last resort were ready to overthrow the monarchy, set up a republic and apply for annexation by the United States. The League members obtained arms and drilled regularly, and were ready to fight if necessary to obtain their rights.

The immediate occasion for the Revolution of 1887 was an act of blatant corruption. A disgruntled rice merchant named Tong Kee, alias Aki, disclosed that he had paid a bribe of $71,000 to cabinet officials for an opium monopoly in the kingdom, but that the license had been given to the Chun Lung syndicate, who had paid a bribe of $80,000. Both Gibson and the king were unquestionably involved. When the news broke, one firebrand advocated a march on the palace by the Honolulu Rifles, the armed militia of the League. Instead, the aroused citizenry held a mass meeting on June 30. Unanimous resolutions were passed demanding that the king dismiss his cabinet and other officials concerned, and that he pledge himself never again to interfere in politics.

There was no bloodshed. Most of Kalakaua's troops had deserted him, and the battery of field guns he had bought in Austria on his world tour for $21,000 was of little value in defending him from his irate subjects. Hurriedly he fired Gibson and appointed a new cabinet, which drew up a less imperious constitution that he signed on July 6. The unfortunate Aki never got his money back, for the supreme court decreed that the king could not be sued.

What happened to the deposed premier? Taking advantage of the fear and confusion of the revolution, his opponents came within an ace of lynching him. The leader of the Honolulu Rifles dragged Gibson down to the docks and announced that he must hang from the yardarm of one of the vessels at the wharf, as a horrible example to those who would seek to overthrow the new government. But at the last minute the British consul intervened and the aging ex-premier was rescued from hanging.

He was hurried off to jail, where he remained until brought to trial on July 12 on charges of embezzlement, but the government decided not to prosecute. To save embarrassment, Gibson was allowed to leave Hawaii on a ship headed for the United States. His dreams of empire had vanished.

If Gibson's sense of drama had inspired him to seek out a proper death, he would have died in a California gutter, in accordance with the Mormon malediction directed against him. Instead, he died comfortably in bed, in St. Mary's Hospital, San Francisco, on January 21, 1888.

His body was embalmed and returned to Honolulu, where it was put on view at his late residence on King Street. Hordes of mourners came to pay their respects to the dreamer of the Pacific. "Native Hawaiians," reported a newspaper, "exceeded all other nationalities in numbers, and their manifestations of sorrow and grief were touching." A solemn funeral was then held at the Catholic Cathedral. Among the dignitaries who attended in formal attire were diplomatic representatives of the United States, Great Britain and Portugal. The bishop who conducted the services, aware of the tensions accompanying this funeral, ended his peroration with an admonition: "Let him who is without fault among you cast the first stone." Gibson's estate, according to local rumor, totaled more than a million dollars.

In writing of Gibson, one is constantly tempted to dismiss him as another of the confused visionaries who have tormented the Pacific, but to do so is to blind one's self to the authentic magnificence of this foolish man. True, he was the gaunt dreamer; but he was also an inspired prophet.

It is amazing how often Gibson was right, and if we tick off the areas in which he clearly foresaw the future, we find ourselves in the presence of a remarkable man.

The people of Sumatra won their independence from the Dutch in much the way that Gibson had envisaged. The Malaysian islands he loved have confederated into a powerful nation, as he predicted. No doubt the Malays of neighboring Malaya will one day do the same.

Hawaii has developed pretty much along the lines he predicted. The role of the native Hawaiian has diminished under the very pressures he foresaw and warned against. Concurrently, the Oriental population has achieved a status which in some respects he anticipated, for it was he who paved the way for their entrance. If he did not foresee the dominant role to be attained by these Chinese and Japanese immigrants, he was aware that energy like theirs was needed if Hawaii was to prosper.

He was right in his theories about the need for treatment of leprosy, in his general ideas on the health of native peoples, and in many of his advanced views on agriculture. He also foreshadowed the essential role to be played by Caucasians in politics—at least during the early years—and was one of the ablest practitioners of this difficult art of convincing full-blooded Hawaiians that they should elect a Caucasian immigrant to represent them. That he held power so long proves his gift of persuasion.

In one nebulous but increasingly important field he was spectacularly correct. With unexpected insight he explained the precautions that ought to be taken by a white, highly organized, mechanized, capitalistic society to preserve the existence of a primitive, non-mechanized, communal group. Gibson was one of the first to see that the native cultures of the Pacific were threatened with extinction, and although he himself did many things contrary to his own preachments, he clearly perceived that the native Hawaiians would have to be supported and protected in many psychological ways if they were to maintain themselves. He advocated the preservation of ancient Hawaiian artifacts, the cultivation of Hawaiian culture and the study of indigenous songs and chants. The museums of the Pacific and the work of various cultural commissions exemplify his dreams.

Gibson's vision of a united Pacific under the leadership of Hawaii has not come to pass, but if he were alive today he would applaud the logic of America's governing hundreds of the islands west of Hawaii, some of them from naval headquarters in Honolulu. This is close to what he advocated.

The important South Pacific Commission operating out of New Caledonia in the interests of the entire South Pacific is a fulfillment of his plans, and within the next hundred years we can expect some kind of South Pacific federation similar to the one he envisaged, although it will probably not depend upon Hawaiian leadership.

Curiously, even the Mormon Church, which he abused so badly, has developed its Pacific missions largely as he predicted it would; and the church, in spite of the hurt Gibson did it, has accomplished about what he had originally hoped for it.

In view of Gibson's excellent foresight, and his accomplishments as a practical politician and his marked success in business, one might expect him to have enjoyed the reputation such attainments merit. Instead, by most people except his beloved Hawaiians, he was hated during his lifetime and ridiculed in death. Two grave defects in character nullified his accomplishments. First, he was cursed with an intemperate enthusiasm and imagination. The modern reader shares Nathaniel Hawthorne's amusement as he watches Gibson in England, his mind inflamed by the obsession that in infancy he had been swapped for a baby of noble lineage. We can also imagine the self-delusion in which Gibson dispatched the pathetic *Kaimiloa* to ensnare Samoa. His ridiculous enthusiasm constantly invited ridicule. Second, he was driven by an insatiable personal vanity. Most of his political excesses stemmed from this, as did most of his bitter enmities.

Time and again in his stormy career, Gibson allowed these two defects to seduce him into real folly. His mistakes then became so blatant as to invite condemnation, and his real accomplishments were overlooked.

Gibson's day in court will come when his voluminous and elegantly written diaries are published. They will disclose a poetic dreamer, an Old Testament prophet and a contentious man whose ambition destroyed him. No more moving passage will be found than a prophecy he uttered at the age of forty on the island of Lanai. A powerful conspiracy of his enemies had humbled him momentarily and in his despair he caught a glimpse of his destiny: "There will be treasons as now, I shall die in the isles by the deed of an island foe, but I shall love them to the end, and it shall be said of me he was a worker of good among his fellow men and above all a lover of the weak island races that had no friend."

5

Bligh, Man
of Mutinies

During World War II, several million Americans experienced the crushing boredom of troopship life. While their rolling transports plodded back and forth across the vast wastes of the wartime Pacific, they yearned for recreation, and almost without exception their tedium was lightened by some enthusiastic amateur who could make barking noises like Charles Laughton.

This Thespian in khaki would grab a microphone, plant himself athwart an after hatch and dig up some straight man who could mimic Clark Gable. Then, in burlesque that was frequently excellent, these seafarers would shout selected scenes from "Mutiny on the *Bounty*," a film which had recently enjoyed great popularity.

"Mis . . . ter Christ . . . ian!" the improvised Captain Bligh would bellow. "Who stole my co . . . co . . . nuts?"

"Are you suggesting, sir—" the long-suffering mate would plead.

"Suggesting? Suggesting, Mis . . . ter Christ . . . ian? Damn your filthy eyes, I'm charging you with rob . . . ber . . . y!"

Our men never tired of this act, and there must be many in civilian life today who recall with nostalgia the terrifying shout that so often swept their doleful ships: "Mis . . .

ter Christ . . . ian!" It was an appropriate cry for the Pacific.

Those who heard the bellow at sea were apparently only slightly more impressed than the general public, to whom Captain William Bligh had become the arch tyrant of the oceans. Moviegoers around the world have enshrined him as the demented bully, the terrible-tempered ogre.

But was he a tyrant and a monster? Or was he a highly competent naval officer cursed by an evil fate which moved him into positions of command whenever a violent mutiny was about to erupt? To answer these questions, let us look at the evidence. Perhaps the real Captain Bligh is a more dramatic figure than the stereotype of the silver screen.

Bligh first strode onto the pages of history in an episode that reflected much credit upon both his bravery and his common sense. That was in the year 1776, when he was selected, at the age of twenty-one, to serve as sailing master for Captain James Cook. That great and gentle explorer was about to set forth on his third expedition to penetrate the farthest reaches of the Pacific.

Cook always felt that he had chosen wisely in selecting young Bligh for so important a position, and had the great explorer, in his hour of mortal peril, been fortunate enough to have had Bligh in his launch, Cook would surely have lived for even more profound explorations. Unfortunately, a lesser officer commanded the guard boat, and the world lost its noblest explorer.

At that fateful time, Cook's flagship, the *Resolution,* dismasted by a sudden tropical storm, rested in Hawaii's spacious Kealakekua Bay, where the natives were beginning to steal much precious equipment from the white visitors. "I am afraid," the reluctant captain told his aides, "that these natives will oblige me to use some violent measures."

The night of Saturday, February 13, 1779, was filled with alarms. A marine on guard at the shore camp where the *Resolution*'s foremast was being repaired saw creeping figures and fired. At dawn Cook found that the sailing cutter anchored a dozen yards away from the bow of his other ship, the *Discovery,* had been stolen. The time for "violent measures" had come.

This sparkling blue bay where Cook had anchored near the jagged lava cliffs of the Kona coast was a long way from the Yorkshire farm cottage where he had been born fifty-

one years before. Cook had learned seamanship as a boy
in a North Sea collier. His skill in navigation and in mapping
the coasts of Newfoundland had qualified him to head the
famous 1768 expedition to Tahiti, where astronomers
wished to observe the transit of Venus across the face of the
sun. During the next ten years he became the foremost discoverer in the Pacific region. The tracks of his ships crisscrossed the world's largest ocean. He was the first man to
set foot on all of the six major continents, and only bad
luck—stormy weather when he was seventy miles from its
ice barrier—kept him from discovering Antarctica.

In January, 1778, he had discovered the Hawaiian Islands,
and now, returning from an exploration of Alaskan and Si-
berian waters in search of the Northwest Passage, he had
come back to these hospitable shores. And just as he had
been worshiped as a god when he had discovered the northern Hawaiian islands of Oahu and Kauai ten months before,
so when the *Resolution* reached Kealakekua he was greeted
with divine honors.

The Hawaiians had decided that he was the reincarnation
of one of their most beloved demigods, Lono. A former
king of Hawaii, Lono had killed his wife in a moment of
anger, and had gone mad with remorse. He wandered
throughout all the islands of the Hawaiian chain, working
off his irritation by boxing and wrestling with the local
champions. Then he set out, in an odd-shaped canoe, for
distant lands. His people had made him a god, and in his
honor set up an annual sports festival, a kind of Hawaiian
Olympics, at the time of the *makahiki*, or harvest season.

As Cook's ships first coasted the main island, Hawaii, at
makahiki time in November, 1778, the sails hanging on the
yards looked like the traditional processional banners of the
priests of Lono. The cry arose, "Lono is come again!" When
the white-sailed floating islands came to rest at Kealakekua,
ten thousand Hawaiians shouted and sang greetings as they
swam out in shoals like fish, or rode canoes and surf-
boards. Cook had not seen such a large crowd in all his
Pacific wanderings. It is not strange that he wrote in his
journal—the last words he was fated to write—that his expedition had made a discovery "in many respects the most
important that has hitherto been made by Europeans
throughout the extent of the Pacific Ocean."

At Kealakekua, Cook made a fatal mistake. It did no

harm, he thought, to let these joyful heathens think he was
a god.

The deification took place casually, as he stepped ashore
at Kealakekua. A skinny old priest named Kuaha, red-eyed
from drinking too much awa—made from the roots of a
pepper plant—took charge. He led the captain to the rickety top of a temple platform hung with the skulls of men
sacrificed at the dedication of this most famous shrine of
Lono in all the islands. Here the embarrassed Britisher was
wrapped in a robe of red tapa and, encouraged by signs
from Kuaha, was led to kiss one of the hideous wooden
images that decorated the scaffold. By that act Cook unwittingly assumed godship, and the Hawaiians officially recognized him as the god Lono. Thereafter he must act as
one more than human.

The king of Hawaii accordingly exchanged presents with
Cook and bountifully supplied the sailors with needed provisions. In exchange, the Englishmen furnished the warriors
with two-foot iron daggers made by the ships' armorers on
the pattern of the native *pahoa*, sharpened at both ends.

After a fortnight of feasting, Cook's two ships, the *Resolution* and the *Discovery*, departed to the north on February
4. But four days later the storm struck, and there was
nothing for it but to limp back to Kealakekua to refit. This
time the natives were not so friendly as before, and the
petty thievery began. And now, on the morning of February
14, with the sailing cutter missing, Cook decided to teach
a violent lesson.

Cook planned to use a scheme he had tried successfully
in other parts of the Pacific. He would lure the king on
board the flagship and hold him as a hostage until the cutter
was returned.

Cook himself took charge of arrangements. He loaded both
barrels of his gun, one with light birdshot, the other with
deadly ball. Then, placing a cordon of boats to guard the
bay, he left in a six-oared pinnace, accompanied by Lieutenant Molesworth Phillips and nine marines. A second boat,
a launch under the command of Lieutenant John Williamson, was to stand by in case of trouble.

Cook and the marines landed on the cruel lava rocks
edging the water and marched to the king's house. The
ruler had just wakened, and his friendly manner made it
clear that he was innocent of any plot. He and his two

sons agreed to visit the big canoe of the foreigners. But before the party could reach the shore, the queen and several chiefs pleaded with the king not to go. They argued that Lono was acting strangely.

A great crowd of natives gathered, brandishing clubs, spears and the newly made iron *pahoas*. The king sat down and pondered. During this hitch in the proceedings, bad news came. A native rushed up crying that a chief, while attempting to run the blockade on the bay, had been killed by a shot from one of the boats.

The warriors began tying on their armor of matting. Women and children slid out of sight. Cook was forced to abandon his plan, and looked about for a way to withdraw, but his retreat was almost cut off by the shouting throng. He placed his marines near the rocks by the water and ordered them to remain ready for firing, but since these natives had never seen the power of a bullet, he could not be certain that a fusillade would halt their attack.

Cook faced the brown-skinned horde. A burly chief made a pass at him with an iron *pahoa*. Cook first fired his charge of birdshot, which fell harmlessly off the woven armor. The peppery shot merely enraged the warriors, who became bolder. Lieutenant Phillips struck down one of them with his gun butt. Another aimed a dagger at Cook, who pulled the trigger of his second barrel. The man fell dead.

Now the sailors in Lieutenant Williamson's launch offshore fired at the crowd, but the sound was lost in the shouts of the Hawaiian attackers. The marines on the beach were able to fire one volley only; then they were overwhelmed. Four were killed by the mob; the rest were pushed into the sea, and swam to the pinnace. Phillips, stabbed in the shoulder, was the last to make it. Williamson refused to move in to provide support.

In this manner Captain Cook was abandoned on the island he had discovered. He turned his back on his attackers and shouted an order to the boats to cease firing and come in closer. Lieutenant Williamson's armed launch was not twenty yards away. Prompt action would have saved the captain, but Williamson, craven with fear, yelled to his oarsmen to pull back to the safety of the ship.

As the rescue launch drew away, a club struck down Captain Cook. He tried to rise. An iron dagger tore into his back. Blood spurted. He groaned. But gods must not show pain.

"This is not truly Lono!" the natives cried.

Cook, still trying to reach his boats, staggered into the water. Even then a daring move might have saved him. But none was made, and the great captain fell forward into the water. A howling mass of Hawaiians stormed over him, each eager to have a hand in his destruction.

Finally the boats took action and the native warriors retreated under a heavy fire. But they dragged Cook's body with them, and proceeded to treat it like that of a god. It was cut into pieces, and each chief received a part. Not until after a week of desultory fighting were Cook's men able to negotiate for the few remaining parts of his body, enough to enable a sea burial to be performed in the waters of the archipelago that Cook had discovered.

What part had William Bligh taken in the tragedy? When Cook fell, Lieutenant James King of the *Resolution* was in charge of the camp a mile down the bay, where the broken foremast was being repaired. He heard the distant firing, and tried to reassure the Hawaiians who crowded around him. But King's fellow officers aboard the *Discovery* learned of Cook's death and fired several cannon balls at the natives and set them scampering. King dispatched a boat asking that the firing stop, since all was well with him.

The boat returned with a strong party of marines led by William Bligh. He carried to King the sad word of the commander's death, along with orders to strike the tents at the shore camp and send the sails on board. The remaining party was placed in a strong position on top of the temple platform, and Bligh was left there with positive orders to act entirely on the defensive. King departed for the *Discovery* to make a report. He had barely reached the ship when he heard the marines under Bligh open fire.

The natives had begun throwing stones at the Englishmen. A few daring Hawaiians then crept around to the side of the enclosure next to the beach and tried to storm the flank. Bligh was not the sort of person to brook such an attack. He promptly ordered the marines to shoot. Eight natives fell. The rest retreated to muster reinforcements. Lieutenant King hurried back on shore, and soon Bligh's alarming position was relieved by the arrival of his own reinforcements. His musket fire had made a deep impression, and the Hawaiian priests sought a truce, under which Bligh recovered the mast and sails and took them back to the ship undamaged.

On the long return voyage to England, Bligh did most of the navigation work and arrived in London with a reputation for both bravery and competence. It was obvious to all that when the next important command arose, he would have to be considered.

By this time Bligh had spent more than half his life at sea. He had joined the Navy at the incredible age of seven, when he appeared upon the articles of His Britannic Majesty's warship *Monmouth* as captain's servant. This was a prudent move, common at the time, on the part of Bligh's father, a customs collector. It enabled the boy to fulfill the time requirements for a lieutenancy and thus more quickly gain command of his own ship.

At sixteen young Bligh was actually at sea, but not as a common foremast hand, and six months later he was a midshipman well on his way to becoming an outstanding officer. At twenty-two he was a full lieutenant, thanks to his father's foresight, and an officer under Captain Cook, in whose company he first tasted the tropical fruit that was to make him famous.

Breadfruit—an excellent starch food about the size of a cantaloupe—has a hard green rind and grows on spreading trees. Boiled it is tastier than a potato; fried it is delicious; and roasted it is best of all. Easily digested and rich in carbohydrates, it is still one of the finest South Pacific products. Bligh promptly agreed with previous experts that such a likely food should be transported from Tahiti, where the best variety flourished, to the British West Indies, where there was insufficient food to feed the slave population imported there from Africa.

In 1787 the British government decided that the breadfruit should be transplanted and appointed the ship *Bounty* for the task. Many of Cook's former officers longed for this command, but to Bligh's surprise and pleasure, it fell to him, and he proceeded to enlist a strong crew.

A man of below average height, Bligh was at this time robust and active, but inclined to corpulence. His forehead was high, and his black hair was usually concealed under a wig. His lips were taut. The most prominent of his features were his jutting nose and a pair of brilliant blue eyes. His complexion was "of an ivory or marble whiteness." His face, though, exposed for years to all climates, was not weatherbeaten or coarse, probably as a result of his temperate habits. Living in a time when drunkenness was a gentlemanly vice,

Bligh was never accused of excesses. His family loved and respected him, and he was to bring into the world six beautiful daughters who were devoted to him. He was to have all through his life many admiring and loyal friends, some in the highest positions, including even the royal family.

He was, unquestionably, a man with a terrible temper, prone to sudden storms of anger. A contemporary described him as being "so uncertain in his manners, so violent in his conduct, and at the same time so eloquent in diction, that he overpowers or affrights every person that has any dealings with him; and particularly as he desires and expects all the deference and submission to be paid him that the proudest despot would covet." Bligh himself knew he was of a choleric nature, but attributed his righteous anger to zeal for efficiency in service. He obeyed orders given him, and expected others to obey orders he gave them. Once, while defending himself against court-martial charges, he growled, "I candidly and without reserve confess that I am not a tame and indifferent observer of the manner in which officers placed under my orders conduct themselves in the performance of their several duties." And he could swear—like a sailor, as Nelson swore. He was a martinet, but by no means harsh or unamiable. He wanted his orders obeyed on the double, but surprising as it may seem, he was always anxious for the comfort and happiness of the men under his command.

Combined with his choleric temper he had one unlucky trait: he seemed always to be on hand when mutinies were afoot or when lesser disciplinary problems were about to erupt into court-martial cases.

When Bligh heard that he had gained the breadfruit job, he energetically set to work to put his ship into the best possible shape for the long voyage to Tahiti. He was not completely happy about her. "Government, I think, have gone too frugally to work," he wrote; "both the ship and the complement of men are too small, in my opinion."

The *Bounty* was a 215-ton merchant vessel which had originally been the *Bethia,* owned by Duncan Campbell, an uncle of Elizabeth Betham, whom Bligh had married in February, 1781. Bligh had commanded vessels for Campbell in the West Indies trade for four years, and it was probably Campbell who recommended Bligh for command of the *Bounty.* The ship was ornamented with "a pretty figurehead of a woman in a riding habit," and her chronometer was the most famous in England, for it had been twice around the world in the *Resolution* with Captain Cook. Unfortunately when the *Bounty* was refitted, the comfort of the crew was subordinated to the safe transportation of the plants to be taken on at Tahiti, and throughout the voyage breadfruit was to be more important than the forty-six souls who made up the ship's complement.

The *Bounty* was delayed in the Channel, much to the irritation of Bligh, who foresaw that he thus ran the risk of arriving at Cape Horn during the period of foul weather. She did not leave Spithead until December 23, 1787. Bligh wrote to Campbell from Tenerife in the Canary Islands early in January that "I have her now the completest ship I believe that ever swam." But he still feared Cape Horn.

Whatever Bligh's faults of personal manner, no sensible critic can complain of his efficiency as seaman, navigator and officer. The safety of his vessel and the comfort of her crew were his chief concerns. The ship's passages were continually aired, and fires were kept burning to dry out the crew's quarters. Cook had discovered the cure for scurvy, and his apt pupil Bligh achieved a record on his voyages for the health of his crews at a time when other vessels arrived in port with most of the crew too sick for duty.

Upon leaving Tenerife for the run to Cape Horn, Bligh divided his crew into three watches instead of two. As he wrote: "I have ever considered this among seamen as conducive to health, and not being jaded by keeping on deck every other four hours, it adds much to their content and cheerfulness." Control of the third watch was given to one of the mates, a Mr. Fletcher Christian, who had sailed with Bligh on two previous voyages and whom the captain trusted. Christian had a bright and pleasing face and a tall, athletic figure. Bligh described him as "strong made and rather bow-legged," but "subject to violent perspirations and particularly in his hands, so that he soils anything he handles."

Bligh also demanded that the men relax and obtain mirthful exercise. "After four o'clock," he wrote, "the evening is laid aside for their amusement and dancing," to the tune of a forecastle fiddle. In fact, his advocacy of the dance as a therapeutic measure for sailors was so great that he was later charged with cruelty in that he stopped the grog of John Mills and William Brown for having refused to dance one night.

But more serious matters soon attracted his attention, for as he feared, he arrived at desolate Cape Horn at a season when breasting that fearful point was impossible. From March 24 until April 22, 1788, the *Bounty* log records nothing but furious gales of rain, hail and snow.

The ship had to be pumped every hour and many men were injured or fell sick. At this point Captain Bligh surrendered his own cabin "to the use of those poor fellows who had wet berths." Under their captain's ministrations the crew remained in good spirits and were willing to tackle Cape Horn for another month, but there was real relief when Bligh passed the word that they would abandon the attempt. Instead, to save the men, he gave the order to weather the helm and run clean around the world via the easier Cape of Good Hope. In this way he entered the South Pacific.

After stops at Capetown, Tasmania and New Zealand, the *Bounty* sighted Tahiti on October 25. This lovely "new Cytherea," as the French explorer De Bougainville called it, was destined to be the home of the mariners for the next six months.

De Bougainville, who missed by a few months the fame of discovering Tahiti, had found it a paradise filled with noble savages, who came out to his ships in the costume of Eden and offered close friendship with no uncertain gestures. "It was very difficult, amidst such a sight," he wrote, "to keep at their work four hundred young French sailors, who had seen no women for six months. In spite of all our precautions, a young girl came on deck and placed herself upon the quarterdeck, near one of the hatchways, which was open in order to give air to those who were heaving at the capstan below it. The girl carelessly dropped a cloth which covered her and appeared, to the eyes of all beholders, such as Venus showed herself to the Phrygian shepherd, having, indeed, the celestial form of that goddess. Both sailors and soldiers endeavored to come to the hatchway; and the capstan was never hove with more alacrity than on this occasion."

The sea-worn mariners of the *Bounty* were greeted with similar affection by the Tahitians, whom Rupert Brooke later described as "the brown lovely people who sing strange slumbrous South Sea songs and bathe in the soft lagoons by moonlight." Captain Bligh himself gave a good deal of space to descriptions of the sports and amusements of the people, such as the *heiva* dance performed by two girls and four men, "which consisted of wanton gestures and motions." The moral Bligh found it shocking but not uncommon for brothers to dally with each other's wives, particularly elder brothers with the wives of their younger brothers, without causing offense. "Inclination," he remarked, "seems to be the only binding law of marriage at Otaheite."

Cunningly the captain persuaded the head chief, Tinah, to think that it was the chief's own idea that he should send a great many breadfruit trees to King George. "I had now," Bligh wrote, "instead of appearing to receive a favor, brought the chiefs to believe that I was doing them a kindness in carrying the plants, as a present from them to the Earee Rahie no Britannee."

The midsummer season was not favorable to the transplanting of the breadfruit plants, and against his inclinations, Bligh was forced to wait around until the proper time. Six months of exposure to the Society Islands was too much for the morale of his crew. For example, upon arrival at Tahiti, no members of the crew were suffering from any venereal disease; yet, after a short stay, a considerable number, including many of the future mutineers, had become infected. What was worse, attachments had been formed that were to lead to tragedy. While the *Bounty* was still anchored off Tahiti, three crewmen stole a cutter and some arms and deserted.

To what extent did Bligh himself cause the mutiny of the *Bounty?* He has been pictured as a sadistic monster whose unnatural brutality forced a fine, innocent crew to revolt. When the motion picture was made of the mutiny, the captain was described in the publicity in these restrained terms: "Bligh! His very name struck terror to the hearts of all his crew. A seagoing disaster, begotten in a galley, and born under a gun! His hair was rope, his teeth were marlinspikes, and the seamen who dared disobey his mad, ruthless orders seldom lived to do it twice."

But looking at the mutiny from the viewpoint of facts uncovered by recent documentary research, we see that William Bligh, as befitted one of Captain Cook's star pupils, handled the entire affair with much credit to his training and to the traditions of the navy he served. Today it seems likely that the mutiny was a hot, spur-of-the-moment affair, arising much more from the loveliness and allure of Tahitian maidens than from Bligh's quarter-deck tyranny.

True, Bligh had cursed at his crew, and he had perhaps stinted them on provisions issued during the voyage. Certainly he seemed to prize his breadfruit more than he did his men. He had punished some of his crew for serious breaches of discipline. But although flogging was common in the British Navy in those days, when crews were recruited mainly from the gin shops and prisons, Bligh flogged nobody until eleven weeks after he sailed. Before the mutiny, only seven men were flogged—three of them for the high crime of desertion, and one for striking a native. Bligh's conduct certainly did not justify the taking over of one of His Majesty's ships and abandoning nineteen men to almost certain death in a crowded open boat on the Pacific.

Usually the *Bounty* story has for its romantic hero the Byronic mate, twenty-four-year-old Fletcher Christian. He was certainly the ringleader, but not of a group of men suffering nobly under a tyrant's whims. Christian led the young bloods who wanted to get back to their native sweethearts. And certainly Bligh had no suspicion that what he later called "one of the most atrocious acts of piracy ever committed" was brewing.

True, several brushes had recently occurred between the captain and Christian. Three weeks after leaving Tahiti, the *Bounty* called at the island of Nomuka in the Tonga Islands to take on wood and water. That night Mr. Christian, who was in charge of the party, was blamed by Bligh when a native stole an adz which could not be recovered. On the afternoon of April 27, according to the journal kept by James Morrison, boatswain's mate, Bligh missed some coconuts and scolded the officers for carelessness. When Christian asked if Bligh thought him so mean as to steal the captain's coconuts, Bligh was supposed to have responded: "Yes, you damned hound, I do! . . . God damn you, you scoundrels, you are all thieves alike, and combine with the men to rob me. . . . I'll make half of you jump overboard before you get through Endeavour Straits!" But a short time later, when the captain cooled off, he genially invited Christian to have dinner with him in his cabin. Christian pleaded illness and refused.

That night the brooding officer, recalling the charms of his lovely Tahitian "wife" Isabella—who was later on lonely Pitcairn Island to bear his son, Thursday October Christian—apparently made up his mind to desert in a boat. But a series of extraordinary chances caused him to elect mutiny instead.

First, there were no marines or other guards on board. The two mates of the watch were criminally asleep. The arms chest was in the center of the main cabin, to make room for the breadfruit plants; and Christian, on the plea of a shark scare, could easily get the key from the armorer. Most providential of all, the more violent characters in the ship happened to be members of Christian's watch, which took over at midnight. In that watch were all seven of the men who had been flogged for derelictions of duty since the voyage had begun.

On the spur of the moment, Christian broached his bold project to the hardened Matthew Quintal, who agreed and swung others to the idea. The delights of Tahiti, where the men had lived like sultans, were recalled. Both men and officers were young and lusty, and had made many Polynesian friends, who would welcome them back. Their yearning memories of Tahiti were contrasted with the dangerous year-long voyage ahead. The ringleaders spread disaffection, and the remainder of the crew were weak-willed or bewildered. Not one officer was able then or later to rise in the defense of discipline. As for Christian, he is reported to have said, when setting his captain and eighteen shipmates adrift in a leaky boat: "It is too late; I have been in hell for this fortnight past and am determined to bear it no longer."

Captain Bligh was asleep in his cabin before sunrise on April 28, 1789, when he was seized by the gang of mutineers. Holding naked bayonets at his heart, they tied his hands behind his back, threatening instant death if he made the least noise. He none the less cried out, but the officers were also prisoners and could not come to help him. He was then forced on deck in his shirt and nightcap, hemmed in by men with cocked muskets. He demanded of Christian the cause of this violent act, but the only answer was: "Not a word, sir, or you are dead this instant!" At the same time the mate often threatened to stab the bound man in the breast with a bayonet.

The small cutter was hoisted out, but since it was a worm-eaten carcass of a boat, the launch was put out instead and loaded with sails, twine, rope, a grapnel and a small cask of water. Bligh tried several times to rally the men to a sense of duty, but was saluted by shouts of "Damn his eyes! Blow his brains out!" Eighteen other officers and men not concerned with the mutiny were hurried overside. The carpenter was allowed his tool chest, and the captain's clerk managed to load in 150 pounds of bread, some wine, a quadrant and a compass, but no maps or chronometer or any of Bligh's precious drawings and surveys. He did, however, salvage Bligh's journals, his commission and some ship's papers, as well as the captain's uniform. Four cutlasses were thrown into the boat when it was veered astern.

Holding the captain by the cord that gripped his hands behind his back, the diabolical-looking Christian and his bayonet-wielding gang forced Bligh over the side. The crowded launch was then cast adrift in the open ocean, thirty miles from the nearest land. Symbolically, the mutineers threw overboard the offending breadfruit plants and shouted, "Huzzah for Tahiti!"

The *Bounty* was fated to return to that luscious island. Then, when Christian feared retribution, it was to sail onward with eight of the mutineers in search of a secret hideout, leaving sixteen of the crew behind. Its final destiny —to be burned and sunk in the deep waters off Pitcairn Island—and the story of the crimes and murders of the pirates on that lonely rock were not to be revealed until twenty years later, when the tale was told by old John Adams, the one mutineer who survived.

Undoubtedly Fletcher Christian had originally intended to toss his captain and the loyal men to the bottom of the Pacific, but others among the mutineers had qualms and Bligh's party were given a fighting chance to make land in the launch—which was only twenty-three feet long and was loaded to within seven inches of the gunwale. Even then death seemed certain, and only the bravery and seamanship of Bligh avoided it.

Bligh's bitterest critics marvel at his feat of bringing that perilous launch to safety. For length, privations and heroism, the story of that voyage—told in Bligh's salt-stained log, which has miraculously survived—is unsurpassed in sea history. In forty-one days the open craft traveled 3618 miles, across waters almost uncharted, through tempestuous weather—on half the days of the trip there was either gale with heavy seas or else pouring rain—with provisions not exceeding a gill of water a day and an ounce and a half of bread, weighed out with a musket ball. They passed through some of the most dangerous waters of the world, including the cannibal Fiji Islands, the Great Barrier Reef of Australia and the deadly Torres Strait. Undefended by a single firearm, they faced daily threats from savage islanders; yet only one life was lost on the voyage, that of the fat quartermaster, who was stoned to death in a battle with the fierce natives of Tofua, one of the central Tonga Islands.

The crew of the launch, who were half dead during the last days of the voyage, survived only because their captain had superhuman courage. He got no help from his officers—in fact, the behavior of his sailing master Fryer and his carpenter Purcell was so exasperating as to amount to revolt, and finally Bligh had to take a cutlass and face them down, "determined to strike a final blow at it and either to preserve my command or die in the attempt."

Yet even when at last the launch arrived at Kupang on Timor on June 14, Bligh's troubles did not end. He bought from the friendly Dutch, with bills on the British government, a small schooner. With the *Bounty's* launch in tow, this vessel left Kupang on August 20, and reached Surabaja on September 12. And here the continued mutinous behavior of the master and the carpenter forced Bligh to call for a court of inquiry, at which the two were judged to be held as prisoners to stand trial when they arrived in England. The complicated affair at Surabaja, during which Bligh seized a bayonet and personally put Fryer and Purcell under arrest, can be counted as at least a minor mutiny to add to Bligh's growing list.

Bligh was back home on March 14, 1790, his name on every tongue for his open-boat exploit, the narrative of which he published before the end of the year. The formal court-martial on the loss of the *Bounty* was held at Spithead on October 22, and the verdict was that "the *Bounty* was violently and forcibly seized by the said Fletcher Christian and certain other mutineers." The court honorably acquitted William Bligh and those tried with him of responsibility for her loss. On the same day, Purcell the carpenter was reprimanded for his behavior during the open-boat voyage.

At about the time of the trial, Fletcher Christian, on far Pitcairn, was learning that mutiny never pays. He had won the detestation of his fellows because of his cruelty and disregard of human rights—the very crimes of which he had accused Captain Bligh. His native wife had died on the island, and to replace her he forced the wife of one of the Tahitian men to live with him. This native retaliated by shooting Christian, and thus died the exiled mutineer, whose distinguished connections among the gentry of Westmoreland had begun a campaign to defame Bligh as a way of defending the reputation of their kinsman.

Bligh, in England, was riding high. He was introduced to the king at court. The Admiralty recognized his services by promoting him to the rank of commander and appointing him captain of the fourteen-gun sloop *Falcon*. Exactly a month later he was given an unusually rapid promotion to the rank of post-captain—the customary three years' service as commander required by naval regulations having been dispensed with in his case as a special recognition of his valor.

On April 15, 1791, he was appointed captain of H. M. S. *Providence*, and charged with making a second attempt to transplant the breadfruit tree to the West Indies. This time Bligh saw to it that nineteen marines were aboard; he was taking no chances of having his ship pirated from him again. The *Providence* sailed on August 3, carrying among the officers young Matthew Flinders, who under Bligh's instruction was to learn his trade in a way that enabled him to become Australia's foremost maritime explorer. Flinders later recalled that on this second breadfruit voyage the ship's complement often suffered from thirst, so that in quest of water "he and others would lie on the steps and lick the drops of the precious liquid from the buckets as they were conveyed by the gardener to the plants."

During Bligh's absence on this trip a number of the *Bounty* crew, survivors of the sixteen who had remained in Tahiti, were hauled back to England for trial. These were not the ringleaders, who by this time had settled on Pitcairn, but lesser figures who had been abandoned by Christian. At Tahiti one man had been murdered by a companion, who was then killed by the natives. The remaining fourteen were rounded up in March, 1791, by the twenty-four-gun frigate H. M. S. *Pandora*, under Captain Edward Edwards. The retributory arm of the British Admiralty had reached across the world to bring back for court-martial as many men as could be found of those who had stayed behind on the *Bounty* on that fateful April morning. But of course not even the determined *Pandora* could find the eight ringleaders.

The fourteen prisoners that were taken experienced a living hell, penned up like animals in what they came to call "Pandora's Box," an iron-barred roundhouse built on the frigate's deck. In this cage they were shackled in irons and

treated by Edwards with greater severity than Bligh had eve
exercised. Morrison wrote of it: "The heat of the plac
when it was calm was so intense that the sweat frequentl
ran in streams to the scuppers, and produced maggots in
short time. The hammocks being dirty when we got them
we found stored with vermin of another kind, which we ha
no method of eradicating but by lying on the plank. An
though our friends would have supplied us with plenty o
cloth, they were not permitted to do it, and our only remedy
was to lay naked. These troublesome neighbors and the tw
necessary tubs which were constantly kept in the place helpe
to render our situation truly disagreeable."

Seeking a passage through the Great Barrier Reef, th
Pandora was wrecked on the night of August 28. For man
hours after she struck, Edwards, disregarding the Admiralty'
orders to pay "proper regard to the preservation of thei
lives," kept the *Bounty* prisoners in the cage, still in chain
and guarded by sentinels with orders to fire among them i
they made any motion. When the ship broke up, four o
the *Bounty* men perished, still in manacles. The surviving
ten, with the eighty-nine crewmen of the wrecked *Pandora*
were finally brought back to England.

Three months after their arrival, the prisoners were put o
trial on a charge of mutiny. By this time a good deal o
public sympathy had been aroused in their favor, particularly
through the activities of the friends and relatives of young
Peter Heywood and the brother of Christian, a professor o
law. The Admiralty committed an error in not waiting unti
Bligh's return to prosecute the prisoners, and hence public
opinion became definitely anti-Bligh. He has sometimes been
accused of avoiding this trial through cowardice, but his
absence cannot be charged against him. He had reported
the mutiny; he had faced his own court-martial and been
honorably acquitted; and he had published his account of
the affair. He did not appear in court against the accused for
a very good reason: the mutineers were not brought back
until June, 1792, by which time Bligh was again at Tahiti,
seeking another load of breadfruit.

The court-martial met at Portsmouth on September 12,
1792, and ran until the eighteenth, attracting a crowd of
spectators. At the end, four of the men were acquitted. Six
were found guilty and condemned to death, but Heywood
and Morrison were recommended for mercy. They were later
pardoned, along with William Musprat. Three others were

executed in Portsmouth Harbor on October 29—three and a half years after the mutiny had taken place.

Bligh returned with the *Providence* in September, 1793, after a highly successful voyage. He had collected twice the number of breadfruit plants in half the previous time, and had transported them to the West Indies. His voyage had also contributed to Pacific discovery. He had introduced the apple into Van Diemen's Land (Tasmania), where it still prospers. He had discovered Mount Wellington and D'Entrecasteaux Channel, between Tasmania and Bruny Island. He had reported on the customs of the Society Islands, and was also the author of the first description of the natives of Fiji, first called Bligh's Islands, which he further explored and mapped. In the waters between Australia and New Guinea he discovered a passage into Torres Strait which is now called Bligh's Channel. In nineteen days his two ships safely traversed the island-dotted Strait, a region of which Flinders wrote: "Perhaps no space of three and a half degrees in length presents more danger." Subsequently they passed around the Cape of Good Hope and on January 23, 1793, anchored at St. Vincent in the West Indies, where the first consignment of breadfruit was delivered. Though the fruit was soon sold in the markets of those islands, the people did not take too kindly to its flavor, and stubbornly preferred their own plantain.

During Bligh's third mutiny, he had the company of other distinguished captains. At the end of the century, the treatment of seamen in the British Navy caused a growing series of outbreaks. The first big one was at Spithead, and lasted from April 18 to May 15, 1797, but it was put down. The mutiny of the Nore, which began as that at Spithead ended, was not so easily suppressed. Bligh's ship, the sixty-four-gun *Director*, was, as might be expected, to play a leading part.

The sailors had many serious grievances. Their wages had not been raised since the time of Charles II, when prices had been thirty percent cheaper. Provisions were often of poorest quality and frequently deficient in weight. No vegetables were issued to ships in port. The sick were not well cared for, and luxuries from the ships' stores intended for them were embezzled by the surgeons. Pursers cheated the men and usually amassed a fortune, while the crew lived in a chronic state of irritation.

Worse were the charges against cruel officers; the inhuman Lieutenant Irwin once gave a seaman thirty-six lashes

for expressing "silent contempt." Other impetuous officer
had men keelhauled, a punishment which consisted of tyin
a long rope to the man's hands, passing it beneath the kee
of the vessel at midships, and then dragging the unfortunat
victim slowly across the barnacled bottom of the ship. I
the sailor did not drown, as was often the case, he lived th
next weeks in agony as rotten material from the needle
sharp barnacle shells festered and suppurated in his body
Adroit twisting of the rope while keelhauling insured tha
his face and back alike would be well torn by the poisonou
shells.

Further complaints were that enough liberty in harbor wa
not commonly granted; that men wounded in action were de
prived of their wages while incapacitated; and that th
amount of prize money paid them was out of proportio
to that paid the officers.

The mutiny of the Nore, which broke out off the mouth c
the Thames on May 12, during the Dutch war, had th
aspect of a modern strike. The men chose two delegates fror
each ship to a general strategy board, with Richard Parke
as president, and on each ship elected a committee of twelv
to manage its special affairs. The delegates and committe
men tried to gain popular support by going ashore daily a
Sheerness, holding meetings, and marching to a brass ban

The first outburst of organized mutiny came when Bligh'
ship, the *Director*, was refitting at the Nore, "the ship
company ordering that Lieutenants Ireland and Church an
Mr. Birch, the master, be dismissed from duty for ill usag
to them as they alleged." No charges were made at thi
time against Captain Bligh, however, and exactly a wee
passed before he also was compelled to surrender his con
mand and go ashore. He was far from inactive, though, an
was appointed to the Admiralty's board of strategy for sup
pressing the mutiny.

As the mutinous month passed, the position of the rebe
became more desperate, and they were goaded into foo
hardy actions. First they blockaded the Thames, and the
helped themselves to provisions from passing merchant ship
Parliament acted summarily to deal with the mutiny at a
costs. New batteries of guns were erected at the mouth c
the river, the navigation marks were removed and a nun
ber of loyal vessels were ordered to the attack. The mutinee
at last recognized their position as hopeless. Their overture
were rejected. Some of the crews tried to take the ships t

sea, and during the next few days some bloody struggles took place. But by June 13, most of the mutineers had hauled down their red flag and asked for a general pardon. Thus the mutiny fizzled out. As might have been expected, Bligh's ship, the *Director*, was the last to capitulate.

Parker and many other leaders were executed, several were flogged from ship to ship, a few were even transported to Australia. Captain Bligh was not removed from his command by the Admiralty, as he would have been if he had been guilty of undue harshness leading to mutiny. He was again put in charge, and soon after led the *Director* into a battle which enormously enhanced his reputation as a good officer.

This was the Battle of Camperdown on October 11, when Bligh's ship had a single-handed encounter with the Dutch flagship *Vryheid*, a seventy-four-gun ship which, it is true, had been somewhat battered by others before being tackled by the smaller *Director*. Not one of Bligh's men was killed, and only seven were wounded. It was in this engagement that John Williamson, who when in charge of the launch of Kealakekua had refused to rescue Captain Cook, was in command of the *Agincourt*. He was accused of cowardly behavior, and put out of the service; Lord Nelson thought he should have been hanged.

Four years later Bligh accomplished his greatest naval success, in command of H. M. S. *Glatton* at the Battle of Copenhagen on April 2, 1801. This vessel had been chosen to lead the third line, and she slugged away at the Danish commodore in a long, hot action. Damage to the ship was serious, and seventeen men were killed and thirty-four wounded, but Bligh held on tenaciously and achieved a victory. After the battle he proudly recorded in his log: "Lord Nelson in the *Elephant*, our second ahead, did me the honor to hail me to come on board, and thank me for the conduct of the *Glatton*." In the following month Bligh was put in command of a fine seventy-four-gun ship, and on May 21 the Royal Society bestowed upon him the honor of electing him a fellow "in consideration of his distinguished services in navigation, botany, etc."

On May 2, 1804, Bligh was on active service in command of H. M. S. *Warrior*, on guard to defend England against the invasion being prepared by Napoleon. Here again he was involved in a court-martial, this time defending himself from the accusations of a disgruntled lieutenant, John Frazier.

As a result of a squabble during which Bligh accused Frazier of neglect of duty, the lieutenant was brought to a court-martial on November 23 for "contumacy and disobedience." Frazier may have been a malingerer; at least he was the sort of man who was fond of hugging a grievance and willing to ruin his own career if he could make his commanding officer suffer in retaliation. He therefore launched a countersuit, charging Bligh with "calling me rascal, scoundrel, and shaking his fist in my face," and claiming that at various times Bligh had "behaved himself towards me and other commissioned, warrant, and petty officers in the said ship in a tyrannical and oppressive and unofficerlike behavior."

Bligh was brought to trial in February, 1805. The evidence showed that he was certainly subject to outbursts of wrath and profanity accompanied by violent gestures. On cross-examination, Lieutenant Alexander Boyack agreed that Bligh was accustomed "to use a great deal of action with his hands, without having any particular meaning in it." Boyack also deposed: "I have heard Captain Bligh call Mr. Keltie, the master, a vile man, a shameful man—'Oh, you are a disgrace to the service, damn you, you lubber!' . . . I have frequently heard him damn Lieutenant Johnston and call out, 'Oh, you, Mr. Johnston, God damn you, sir, what are you about?' . . . I heard him often call the boatswain an infamous scoundrel, an audacious rascal, a vagrant and a dastardly villain." Lieutenant William Pascoe affirmed that he had heard Bligh "call the master a Jesuit and an old rogue, and say, 'Let me have none of your rigadoon steps here.' "

On the other hand, Mr. William Simmons, a gunner, stoutly vowed that "to his knowledge Captain Bligh had never called him a 'long pelt of a bitch.' " Lieutenant George Johnston, who had served under Bligh for three years in other ships, firmly defended the captain's conduct. The court dismissed Frazier from the Navy, and adjudged Bligh "to be reprimanded and to be admonished to be in future more correct in his language." With this rap over the knuckles for intemperate diction—a not uncommon failing in the British Navy, from Lord Nelson on down—Bligh was restored to command of his ship. This court-martial had little effect on his career, for less than two months later he was signally honored by an appointment to one of the best and toughest positions available to any naval officer, even though some of his contemporaries suspected that he was being kicked up-stairs.

The advisers who drew up specifications for this job said they needed "one who has integrity unimpeached, a mind capable of providing its own resources in difficulties without leaning on others for advice, firm in discipline, civil in de-portment, and not subject to whimper and whine when se-verity of discipline is wanted to meet emergencies." An additional drawback to the job was that it would require the holder to relinquish active connection with the Navy, which in Bligh's case would mean sacrificing his chances of becoming an admiral.

Nevertheless, when the job was offered, Bligh quickly ac-cepted and thus launched himself into an extremely violent position that would be the occasion for his fourth and most serious mutiny.

The task which presented so many challenges was that of serving as civilian governor of England's mushrooming new penal colony in New South Wales on the recently settled continent of Australia. The government in London foresaw that a rigorous man like Bligh could, in these formative years, establish significant patterns upon which the entire future of Australia might be built, and many historians have felt that Bligh might have accomplished that feat had he not run into an adversary who, for ability, determination and malice, made Fletcher Christian look like a weak-kneed, vacillating village vicar.

In fact, William Bligh in his new job had two mortal enemies. The first was John Macarthur; the second was an extraordinary regiment of English soldiers. Bligh never took on a tougher adversary than the New South Wales Corps.

It had been raised in England for special service in Aus-tralia and had been assembled under a private contract with one Major Francis Grose, who made a lot of money peddling the officerships to the highest bidders. These men, in turn, gained extraordinary privileges, most noteworthy be-ing that of a monopoly on the right to import rum. Thus the officers of the Corps came to Australia not primarily as military men but as business adventurers determined to make their fortunes quickly. A contemporary described them as a body of men "banded together on every suitable occasion to maintain by violence and injustice what they had ob-tained by the sacrifice of honor."

In fact, the ship that brought the Corpsmen to Australia

in 1790 was loaded to the gunwales not with ammunition or stores, but with cheap goods brought out as the officers' private luggage for huckstering among the few free settlers and the many convicts. Quickly the Corpsmen obtained an all-powerful grip on the economy, becoming intimate with the convicts they were supposed to be guarding and enticing the women into concubinage through the judicious scattering of small presents among the young girl convicts. By the time Bligh arrived, New South Wales boasted of 395 legally married women and 1035 convict concubines.

More important, perhaps, was the strangle hold the Corpsmen attained on the economy of the young colony, for they were officers only by accident; in truth they were sheep breeders, farmers, merchants, shipbuilders, speculators and grogshop owners.

Around 1795 the officers of the Corps obtained a virtual monopoly on all alcoholic spirits arriving in the colony, which they bartered, at a profit of four or five hundred percent, to the settlers and thus kept them in a state of peonage. Bligh's predecessor, Governor P. G. King, had found that despite his efforts, the colony was inundated with imported liquor.

The anomaly of a line regiment in the liquor business worked this way. The government, controlled by senior officers of the military, claimed the right to purchase all spirits arriving in the port. The officers could buy all they wanted on favorable terms. They obtained convict women as barmaids and opened grogshops. It was a matter of common knowledge that the chief constable of the territory held a license and sold rum right opposite the jail door.

The demand for spirits was brisk, for there were few other forms of entertainment for the ticket-of-leave man or the hard-laboring settler. "Individual powers of consumption were incredibly great," wrote a visiting surgeon. "The expiree farmer, and his not more intemperate prisoner servant, broached the vessel, poured out its contents into buckets, and drank until they were insensible, or until, roused almost frantic, they were swift to shed blood." For rum, the settlers would sell or mortgage their farms and their bodies. And the officers of the Rum Corps got all the profits. They would send peddlers throughout the country districts to offer liquor against the future crop, at a good rate of interest. Consequently the farms sooner or later fell into the hands of the traders in uniform. All grain and general produce was

put into the royal storehouse and the officers would draw
inflated bills against the treasury, thus robbing not only the
settlers but the government at home.

The officers of the Rum Regiment even exploited the men
under them. The privates were paid not in cash but in goods
from the stores, often worth only half what they were entitled to; if a soldier objected, he might be sent to the
guardhouse, tried and sentenced to imprisonment. Thus the
smart soldier would take anything that was issued to him,
and use it to barter for whatever he needed. Usually he
needed rum, which served in place of money in this isolated
colony across the world from London.

What made the situation intolerable was that these same
Corpsmen, who in Bligh's time contained in their ranks no
less than seventy ex-convicts, formed the only law enforcement agency in New South Wales, and the governor had to
rely upon them in his supervision of the convict colony.
Bligh was acquainted with the above facts when he accepted
orders to rehabilitate the settlement, but it is unlikely that
he even dimly foresaw the amount of trouble into which
he was heading when he sailed from England in February,
1806, leaving behind his wife and all his daughters except
one, Mrs. John Putland, who accompanied her Navy husband.

Bligh's dignity promptly involved him in a new quarrel on
the voyage. His civilian transport, the *Lady Sinclair,* was in a
convoy under the charge of H. M. S. *Porpoise,* commanded
by Captain Joseph Short. This officer interpreted his instructions as meaning that he would command the convoy, subject
to Bligh's orders concerning course and ports. Bligh as senior
officer considered himself in supreme command of all the
ships, even though he was no longer an active naval officer.
A series of violent quarrels arose. At one time Bligh, without consulting Short, went so far as to alter the course of
the *Lady Sinclair,* and Short finally had to fire two shots,
one across Bligh's bows, and another astern. Although Short
attempted some reconciliation at the Cape, he had unfortunately also quarreled with some of his own officers. As soon
as the vessels reached Sydney, Bligh appointed a court of
inquiry, and Short was found guilty of some breaches of
naval discipline. Bligh thereupon had Short arrested and sent
back to England. After a court-martial a year later, Short
was honorably acquitted, but his brush with Bligh had ruined
his career.

Bligh's new command was the tiny settlement of Sydney, which did not even foreshadow the great metropolis of today. In 1806 it was a jumble of dwellings and barracks, dotted here and there with a windmill. On its rutted roads jostled gangs of convicts at work, sailors off the trading ships in the Cove, lounging soldiers of the Corps, a few free settlers and various officials of the penal colony. Around the gun battery on the east side of the Cove was a region where Bligh's writ did not run. This slum, called The Rocks, was termed by a contemporary "that fortress of iniquity more like the abode of a horde of savages than the residence of a civilized community." Every other hut was a tavern haunted by grog-swilling seamen, thieves and runaway convicts, and this human jungle also housed gambling hells and brothels, humorously called "cock and hen clubs."

In contrast, in the center of the village, facing the Cove, was the dignified edifice of Government House, a two-storied, whitewashed building, with a hill behind it whose trickling springs caused an unpleasant dampness in the rooms. Here reigned as chatelaine Bligh's beloved and respectable daughter Mary, nursing her invalid husband and acting as her father's hostess.

She was not only the first lady of the colony but the leader of fashion, for by every ship her mother sent her dresses from London. One of these was the cause of the first unpleasantness that was to arouse tension between Bligh and the officers of the New South Wales Corps. It was a clinging, diaphanous French gown which revealed so much of her figure that, to forestall colonial criticism, she wore in place of petticoats a pair of long pantaloons. As she entered the church one Sunday morning on the arm of her father, the soldiers of the Corps nudged each other, sniggered and then laughed aloud. Blushing and feeling faint, Mary rushed from the church. The rage of Bligh on realizing that these upstart soldiers had ridiculed his favorite daughter soon subsided, but this insult added fuel to the flame of enmity that was shortly to arise between the Corps and the governor.

Bligh assumed his post in Sydney on August 14, 1806. His Excellency settled in Government House and at once started to institute the two difficult reforms which he had been firmly ordered to make. The first of these was to suppress the notorious rum traffic in the colony. The second was to replace the pernicious system of barter with the use of currency. Both these orders put Bligh squarely against the entrenched selfish interests of the profiteering New South Wales Corps; and this headlong collision was to produce Bligh's greatest mutiny, the famed "Rum Rebellion."

Even though the forces ranged against Bligh were formidable, he would probably have won except that his enemies were led by one of the most unprincipled and able men in the history of Australia. In John Macarthur, Bligh was to find an adversary as egotistic, irascible and bullheaded as himself. Here were the irresistible force and the immovable object. Macarthur today is acclaimed in Australian schoolbooks as the great pioneer sheep raiser of the country, the one who developed the merino breed that later became the main source of Australia's great wool industry, and he was undoubtedly an able and far-seeing man. But his personality was not of an endearing kind, and during the three years that Bligh knew and fought against him, Macarthur played a less than heroic role.

In England, Macarthur had been apprenticed to a staymaker, whence came his Sydney nickname, "Jack Bodice." He had previously served in the army before he bought an ensigncy in the New South Wales Corps and arrived in the colony with it in 1790. He was just twenty-three years old and married to the daughter of a country gentleman. He was swarthy, with determined square jaw, compressed lips and a pug nose. His nature was cold and harsh, that of a man on the make. He was described as being "as keen as a razor and as rapacious as a shark," and anyone who stood in his path was likely to fall a victim to "his overweening vanity, lust for wealth, aggrandizement and possession of landed property."

Although quickly promoted to captain, "Jack Bodice" had retired from the regiment after a violent quarrel with an earlier governor, who had put him under arrest for wounding his commanding officer in a duel and had sent him to England for trial. On his return, although keeping in touch with the regiment, Macarthur devoted himself to making a fortune by raising wool on his five-thousand-acre estate called Camden. The governor bitterly pointed out that, for a full-time officer, Macarthur had earned a goodly income. "He came here in 1790 more than £500 in debt, and is now worth at least £20,000. . . . His employment during the eleven years he has been here has been that of making a large fortune, helping his brother officers to make small ones (mostly at the public expense), and sowing discord and strife. . . . Experi-

ence has convinced every man in this colony that there are
no resources which art, cunning, impudence, and a pair of
basilisk eyes can afford that he does not put in practice to
obtain any point he undertakes. . . . One half the colony
already belongs to him, and it will not be long before he
gets the other half."

One foundation of that fortune was indicated in the testimony of Joseph Holt: "Every soldier got twenty-five acres of
land. Many of them when intoxicated sold their tickets for a
gallon of rum. Mr. Macarthur used to supply them with
goods, and so obtained from these improvident and foolish
men their tickets, by which he acquired an enormous landed
property." On his own behalf he carried on trade with China
and the South Sea Islands, and was the biggest rum retailer
of them all. His defiant temper, his paranoiac conviction that
anyone who opposed him was seeking his ruin, his gift for
magnifying a personal slight into the status of a national
wrong—all these qualities had aroused such animosity in every corner of the colony that it is remarkable that he had
any supporters left; but people followed him through gulli-
bility or fear of reprisal. Macarthur's life had been a series
of quarrels, duels, grudges and almost fatal feuds. He boasted
that he had caused the government to dismiss Governors
Hunter and King. He had flouted all local ordinances and
challenged all comers. But now he was to meet Bligh.

"John Macarthur was very like Bligh in character," C.
Hartley Grattan once wrote. "He too was of a violent temper, though it was a 'cold' temper that found release not
in curses that died away as uttered, but in calculated vitupera-
tion that lived on. He too was a stern disciplinarian, contemptuous of the whims and weaknesses of ordinary men.
He too was self-confident and self-righteous. He too never
committed any sincere self-doubts to paper. He too formu-
lated his ends and set about realizing them by bending men
to his will. But he differed from William Bligh, one may de-
duce from the records, in confusing personal advantage with
justice, and in knowing how to manipulate the 'fools' among
whom he found himself, for his own purposes. His position
was strengthened when his ends coincided in part with those
of a powerful minority in the community."

During Bligh's first year of rule, when this energetic sailor
was clearing the decks and making everything shipshape, he
got along fairly well with everybody, even with the provok-
ing John Macarthur. But gradually the opposing interests

showered sparks. Captain Charles Walker testified that once, when Bligh had found it necessary to refuse Macarthur's request for something from the government stores, Macarthur had told Walker that "Governor Bligh was giving the government property to the settlers, a set of rascals who would deceive him; it would be better if he gave it to me and some of the other respectable gentlemen of the colony; if he does not, he will perhaps get another voyage in his launch again."

A whispering campaign was begun against Bligh. An omen of the coming storm was a "pipe," or lampoon, circulated by Macarthur's friends against "Bounty" Bligh: *"O tempora! O mores!* Is there no CHRISTIAN in New South Wales to put a stop to the tyranny of the Governor?" This sounds as if a mutiny was brewing, with Macarthur cast to play the role of the aggrieved Fletcher Christian.

Macarthur's monomania was to create a sheep industry in the new land, but Bligh's attitude was unmistakable: "What have I to do with your sheep, sir?" Bligh roared at him. "What have I to do with your cattle? Are you to have such flocks of sheep and herds of cattle as no man ever heard of before? No, sir, I have heard of your concerns, sir. You have got five thousand acres of land, sir, in the finest situation in the country, but by God you shan't keep it!"

Another series of episodes involving Macarthur caused the community to break into uproar. There was a disagreement over a certain promissory note and over an illegal copper liquor still which Macarthur wanted to keep, minus its head and coils. The immediate *casus belli*, however, was the seizure of Macarthur's trading schooner *Parramatta*.

This vessel had broken port regulations by allowing a stowaway, a life convict named John Hoare, to escape on her from Sydney and then to get ashore at Tahiti. When the case was tried, Macarthur and his partner were condemned and a £900 bond was declared forfeited. Macarthur determined to abandon the vessel rather than lose the money, and on December 7, 1807, he notified the crew that he would no longer pay or support them. When they came ashore in defiance of orders, Macarthur tried to evade responsibility by saying that the government was now owner of the ship he had abandoned.

Acting on instructions from Bligh, the judge advocate, Richard Atkins, summoned Macarthur to appear in Sydney to answer charges. Since Atkins was not a lawyer, the indictment, which specified a long list of complaints and termed Macarthur "a malicious and seditious man, of depraved mind and wicked and diabolical disposition," was drawn up with the aid of the only lawyer in the colony, an emancipated forger named George Crossley.

There had been bad blood between Judge Atkins and Macarthur, and the latter refused to obey the summons, on the grounds that Atkins would not give him a fair trial—even though the remaining six judges of the panel were all officers of the New South Wales Corps and open supporters of the Macarthur faction. Macarthur's contemptuous and scornful response to the summons foreboded bloodshed, and was an open defiance of the authority of the governor. Bligh, who never evaded clear duty, supported his arrest, and Macarthur, burning with hatred at such an insult, decided on the spot that Bligh would have to be overthrown.

Out on bail, Macarthur began fomenting trouble and laying the groundwork for revolt. He revived and demanded payment of a fifteen-year-old debt owed him by Judge Atkins, amounting to £26 plus £56 interest. The judge agreed to pay even though the debt had long since been legally outlawed, but Macarthur was not satisfied and complained that it was unfair that he could not sue Atkins, who presided over the only court that could handle such a case. Macarthur then uncovered another grievance against Bligh, who had canceled an illegal lease that Macarthur had obtained on a plot of land in the Government Domain next to the church. Macarthur refused to accept another piece which Bligh offered in its place, and hired some soldiers to put a fence around the original plot, which included a public well. This was another act of calculated defiance.

When Macarthur was brought to trial on January 25, 1808, before a panel of six Corps officers and Atkins, he refused to be tried by a court presided over by his personal enemy. The officers accordingly objected to sitting with Atkins, who retired and then maintained that there was no legal court without him—an attitude that Bligh upheld. In this way, Governor Bligh was maneuvered into the paradoxical situation of opposing the military power of the colony which alone could carry out his orders. The six officers insisted that they had the right to judge Macarthur without the presence of Atkins; Bligh said they had not. Their defiance was probably a symptom of a deep plot to challenge Bligh's position and try to restore the good old days of rum and rackets. Their secret leader was certainly Macarthur, the prisoner before them, whom they had vowed to judge impartially.

The next day Judge Atkins presented Governor Bligh with a memorial which indicated that the six officers had committed an act which amounted to a usurpation of the government and which tended to incite or create rebellion or other outrageous treason. On the basis of this report, Bligh summoned the six officers to appear before him at Government House to explain their behavior. At the same time he wrote again to ask the aid of Major George Johnston, in acting command of the Corps, requesting him to come into town and take charge of his rebellious soldiers. Johnston, who had retired to his estate four miles from the barracks, had pleaded the previous day that he was dangerously ill and could not even write a reply. Yet now he miraculously recovered and was able to ride to town in a carriage. But Bligh was to get no help from him.

The major later claimed that on his arrival at the barracks, soldiers and civilians were in a state of terror, and they convinced him that there would be a bloody insurrection unless he immediately put the unpopular Governor Bligh under arrest. Johnston did not go and talk to Bligh about the situation, or even report to him as he was obligated to do, since Bligh was his superior officer. Instead, Johnston usurped the title of lieutenant governor of the colony. Then, under this title, he ordered that John Macarthur be liberated from custody at once.

When that firebrand joined the group in the barrack square, Johnston is reported to have said: "God's curse! What am I to do, Macarthur? Here are these fellows advising me to arrest the governor." Macarthur answered: "Advising you? Then, sir, the only thing left for you to do is to arrest him. To advise on such matters is legally as criminal as to do them," implying that the whole group were now committed to the rebellion.

Then Macarthur, using a cannon barrel for a desk, wrote out a petition asking Johnston to arrest Bligh. This requisition, on the basis of which Johnston led a mutiny against constituted authority in New South Wales, was probably signed by only two or three people at the time it was

drafted; other signatures were gained after the rebellion wa
over, some of them at the point of a bayonet. But documen
or no document, Bligh had to be overthrown immediatel
after Johnston had unlawfully released Macarthur from pris
on.

Johnston placed himself at the head of his regiment o
three to four hundred men, with bayonets set and musket
loaded with ball. The redcoats marched to the tune of "The
British Grenadiers," with the proud colors of the Rum Corp
floating in the air. Macarthur ran alongside, urging the me
on. Less than half a mile from the barracks they came to
Government House. Here they were drawn up in line oppo
site the gates, with pieces of artillery aimed at the building
Four officers and a number of troops were sent inside to
arrest one man, Governor Bligh. Their capture of Govern
ment House was the first and last victory in the field in the
history of the New South Wales Corps.

The entrance of the soldiers was delayed for a while.
Mary Putland, the recently widowed daughter of Bligh, beat
them off with her parasol, exclaiming: "You traitors, you
rebels, you have just walked over my husband's grave, and
now come to murder my father!" She clung with her little
hands to the gatepost and, even when forcibly dragged
away, returned to the defense. Hers was the only hand to
strike a blow in Bligh's defense that afternoon. The soldiers
soon overran the house, including Mrs. Putland's room, and
arrested the small group of magistrates conferring in Bligh's
study. But where was the governor himself?

Bligh, in spite of previous experiences, still refused to believe that anyone would mutiny against him. But here they
were, on the march. From an upper room he had watched
the enemy approach, and was determined not to give them
the satisfaction of arresting him without a struggle. In fact,
Bligh kept a whole regiment busy hunting for him for almost
two hours. Again and again, in a grim game of hide-and-
seek, they plunged their bayonets into likely lurking places
in the house and grounds. Finally they found him in a
little lumber room, in full uniform with his medal on his
breast and his sword by his side. He was behind or under a
bed—accounts differ.

The mutinous populace, of course, made propaganda by
publishing broadsides showing their governor being dragged
forth from under a bed. But it is unlikely, in the light of

his whole career, that Bligh concealed himself as an act of
planned cowardice. Piecing together various testimonies, it
is probable that the following events took place. His first
impulse at the alarm was to face his attackers. He went
upstairs and donned his naval uniform and his Camperdown
medal. Then he began collecting valuable papers to destroy
or hide for future use. Hearing the search begin when a
party of soldiers rushed upstairs, he retired to the back room
with the idea of escaping to the Hawkesbury River settlements and striving to maintain his authority.

That proved impossible. At this point he lost his head,
and took refuge ingloriously under a bed which was high
enough to enable him to brace himself out of sight; indeed,
the soldiers searched the room twice before finding him,
and he might have escaped, but the Corpsmen found him
on the third try. His friends have argued that this conceal-
ment was not the act of a poltroon; a coward would have
surrendered without an effort to escape. But his enemies
never let anyone forget the bed story.

That night, with Governor Bligh under arrest, Johnston
proclaimed martial law and seized the government papers.
The downfall of Bligh was celebrated with an issue of free
liquor. Bonfires blazed, Bligh was burned in effigy, the military band played a piece called "The Silly Old Man" and
John Macarthur was carried around the streets in a chair
to receive the cheers of his faction.

Johnston took over the governor's functions, but the power
behind the throne remained Macarthur, who got himself appointed to the newly invented position of secretary to the
colony. The treasonous regime at once set about restoring
the old days of plunder and rum, and so distant were they
from the authority in London that for two years they were
able to maintain an interregnum filled with corruption.

Macarthur's trial was resumed, and turned into a smear
attack on Governor Bligh, still under arrest at Government
House; the judges were the same officers who had led the
overthrow of the government. The new regime elevated
Bligh's enemies to office and persecuted his followers. For
example, the provost marshal and the emancipated forger
who had compiled the list of complaints against Macarthur
were dragged off to start seven-year sentences in the coal
mines north of Sydney.

Friends of the ruling gang were rewarded by wholesale

grants of public lands and cattle from the government stores. Even the naval officers were corrupted by land grants. Liquor once more flowed freely; it was reported by the Reverend Samuel Marsden that "since the governor was in arrest, ninety houses have been opened in the town of Sydney, eight and twenty in Parramatta, and fourteen at the Hawkesbury, to sell spirits." Thefts and robberies became common. A ship was captured by forty convicts and used to escape from the colony.

The rank-and-file rebels had hoped that there would be a restoration of the old spoils system, but the new dictators they had set up were grabbing everything on their own behalf. Their greed was insatiable, and even Macarthur said that "the whole of the public property would not have satisfied them." The administration alienated even its friends; feuds broke out; and the colony slowly fell apart.

The government in London was slow to act even when the news of the mutiny reached them; and not until December, 1809, did Bligh's successor arrive in Sydney. Bligh did not leave for England until April, 1810, on a ship loaded with household goods and bundles of papers—his evidence in the forthcoming trial—and accompanied by no less than sixteen witnesses who were to testify in his behalf.

Major Johnston was taken to England to answer courtmartial charges brought against him for deposing Bligh. He was convicted of mutiny and sentenced to be cashiered from the service.

Macarthur had also gone to England, to organize Johnston's defense. Although it was clear that he had been the main undercover promoter of the whole affair, Macarthur was not tried, since he was not then a military officer. He attempted but failed to hold the spotlight as a champion of civil liberties, and merely played the role of a minor witness. He was forced to remain in exile from his Australian estate for eight years, under threat of arrest there for treason, and possible hanging. He did not return until 1817. During his last few years he degenerated into a hopeless lunatic.

What of William Bligh, who thus weathered his fourth mutiny and fifth major court-martial? As usual, he was not only exonerated but was also restored to his naval rank and promptly promoted. As a mark of signal honor, on July 31, 1811, which was conspicuously one day earlier than the year's general promotions, he was gazetted a rear admiral of the

Blue Squadron. Three years later he was upped to vice-admiral and became a prominent figure in the British Navy.

At the comfortable age of sixty-four, laden with glory and befriended by most of the great figures of England, Admiral William Bligh died peacefully in bed.

6

Dona Isabel, the
Lady Explorer

The Pacific has never been noted for its women adventurers, primarily because the native Polynesian woman was such an utterly delightful creature that no mere stranger from Europe could hope to match her. When the first white men sailed their exploring craft into the warm waters of Polynesia one of the most striking aspects of that wonderful new world was the brown-skinned native women—and you could see all the skin—who swam out to the anchorages, their long black hair festooned with flowers and streaming out behind them, and who made the most provocative gestures, understood in any language, inviting the water-weary sailors ashore for a frolic under the palm trees.

And when these beautiful children of nature were allowed to climb aboard the ships—some captains made their men fight them off with boat hooks—the girls promptly sought out the bunking quarters, to which they took the sailors, one at a time.

It was pretty difficult for a white woman to compete against such experts, and that explains why the literature of the Pacific is so replete with wild and improbable stories about the men of the West and so barren of good tales about the women of Europe and America.

Actually, there is a considerable body of story material

about white women in the tropics, but unfortunately most of these lively girls are of such recent vintage that delicacy and respect for immediate families forestall the writer of this generation. Regretfully he puts aside his notes on the *soi-disant* queens, the wild women of the gold fields and the would-be litterateurs who ploughed a deep furrow through the broad wastes of the Pacific. Their delightful stories will have to be shared with the public a generation from now.

But there is one adventuresome lady who set forth to win a Pacific empire sufficiently long ago that a brief narrative of her behavior will embarrass no one, and fortunately for the modern reader, she was one of the supreme bitches of all time.

She participated in a particularly turbulent exploring expedition that set out from Callao, Peru, in 1595. It was headed by her fumbling, well-intentioned husband, Don Alvaro de Mendaña, and was piloted by a superb gentleman who was to leave a distinguished though tragic mark upon the Pacific, Pedro Fernandez de Quirós.

But the most important member of the expedition turned out to be Mendaña's wife, Doña Isabel Barreto, who, in pursuit of designs which no husband has ever understood since the world began, insisted that many of her relatives accompany the expedition in positions to which their abilities did not entitle them. Rarely has an expedition set forth so clearly marked for disaster: a vacillating leader, a fiery wife, a horde of incompetent relatives, maps that had been doctored to hide true longitudes and sails that tended to rot quickly in the tropics. In addition, the convoy carried with it a special complication, for Don Alvaro's intention was not only to explore but to colonize as well, so that he took with him a number of unmarried Peruvian women. This created problems.

Fundamentally, Don Alvaro's theory was a sound one. Ever since the Pacific had been discovered by a Spaniard, Balboa, more than eighty years before, Spain had held a virtual monopoly on this mighty ocean. Only a few intruders like the Englishman Francis Drake, whom the Spaniards considered a pirate, had entered its waters. Most of its great expanse was unknown even to the Spaniards. And its islands remained uncolonized, its natives ignorant of Christ.

As for discovery, anything might still be found in its watery leagues. Gold, pearls, spices, hundreds of black slaves— wealth that might make old King Solomon seem a beggar by comparison. And Doña Isabel Barreto's secret purpose in

joining this expedition was to win treasure that would make
her and her family rich beyond the dreams of anyone, even
those who had seen the inexhaustible treasures of Mexico
and Peru.

The islands of King Solomon! That was the glittering
name that had been passed from mouth to mouth ever since
Doña Isabel's husband had returned, twenty-six years before,
from his discovery of those islands in the South Pacific.
Doña Isabel knew that Mendaña had not actually brought
back any gold, but the miners he had taken with him insisted that plenty of it was there. Furthermore, the islands
were stuffed with valuable woods and creamy tropical fruits
and pearl shells, and the black natives could easily be captured and put to labor for Christian rulers, even though it
was known that they were cannibals like those of neighboring New Guinea. For all these reasons, Doña Isabel
yearned to go with her husband to rediscover the Solomon
Islands, to colonize them and to reap that waiting wealth.

Many times since her marriage she had listened to her
tedious husband repeat the story of that troubled voyage.
In those far-off days, Don Alvaro's uncle, the new viceroy
of Peru, had appointed him, though he was only twenty-six,
to be the commander of the expedition. It was in the autumn
of 1567 that the two ships had sailed and for eighty long
days had pushed westward, without sighting any land.

At last, on February 7, 1568, they had discovered the
volcanic islands that later were to be called the Solomons.
The first of them, nearly a hundred miles long, they
christened Santa Isabel. To explore the shallow waters of
the group, the men built a five-ton brigantine and in it
discovered other islands, including Guadalcanal and Malaita,
all of which were claimed by Mendaña in the name of the
king of Spain.

What about the gold? Mendaña had on board experienced
miners, who had seen plenty of gold back in Peru, and
when the ships joined the brigantine, he sent them ashore
to prospect in various streams. The miners declared that
the country showed signs of gold, but they could not be
sure, because the river currents were turbulent and when they
tried to wash out the gravel in pans, the stream almost
carried away the pans. The prospectors assured Mendaña that
there was plenty of gold in the Solomons, but what they
could not have foreseen was that more than three hundred
years would elapse before that gold was found.

The first exciting days of prospecting were cut short, however, by the attempts of the natives to massacre the invading white man. Mendaña discovered to his horror that the Solomon Islanders really did feed on baked human flesh. One story Doña Isabel had been told a hundred times: "There was one Indian who actually came to feel the legs of a soldier who stood there, by way of testing whether he were tender for eating, as he would be his share in the distribution which they had made."

To punish the cannibals, Mendaña had ordered their villages to be set on fire, and a canoe load of them had been killed. But when this first expedition stopped at the next big island, San Cristóbal, where the ships were drawn up ashore to be caulked and scraped, the natives were still hostile. Therefore, since the vessels were leaky and the rigging was badly worn, Mendaña decided to return home to Peru for the time being and to colonize these islands on some later trip.

Thereupon the ships headed north for hundreds of miles in search of a wind to blow them to California. They found a hurricane. The two vessels did not sink, but they became separated, and each alone pushed through the North Pacific for two months, with their crews suffering from frightful hunger and thirst.

A few drops of mingled water and powdered cockroaches, a few crumbs of rotten hardtack, one or two black beans —on this daily ration the men existed. They were tortured by scurvy. Their gums swelled until the putrid flesh hid their teeth. They could not move for weakness of their bones. They fell blind. The blood left their veins and rotted just under the skin. "We threw a man overboard every day," Mendaña used to recall sadly, "and their chief consolation was to call me to watch them die."

The ships were hopelessly lost, but luckily each stumbled upon the coast of California, and at last made its way back to Peru. Mendaña's superb patience and dedication had enabled many of his men to survive and to return after two years in the unmapped Pacific, at a time when most people in Peru had long given them up for dead.

Immediately the story spread that Mendaña had brought back a treasure of forty thousand pesos' worth of gold. That was, of course, untrue. But everyone was sure that the isles of Solomon must be filled with gold. Mendaña set about trying to form another expedition to settle there.

It took him a quarter of a century to complete the

arrangements. Times were becoming harder. Spain was no longer the sole proprietor of the world's oceans. English sea dogs were fighting and looting even in the sheltered seas of the oldest Spanish colonies. The defeat and scattering of the Great Armada had intervened in 1588 and had made the king of Spain much more cautious about risking the loss of his ships, especially in further explorations of the distant South Seas. But at last Mendaña won his long game of petitioning at court, and was given the right to sail to the Solomon Islands, and as governor set up a colony there for God and for Spain. If he achieved his purpose, he would be given wide grants of land and the noble title of marquis.

Governor Mendaña was not a youth this time. He was a man of fifty-four, weighed down with responsibilities. He had acquired a wife and a heartbreaking host of in-laws. To finance the expedition, he volunteered all the money he had in the world. His wife's family, the Barretos, had helped a little and the group had raised the great sum of forty thousand pesos and had spent it on ships and supplies for the new expedition. The settlers who were invited along had to outfit themselves and bring their household goods, expecting, when the Solomons were reached, to be given large estates and many slaves to cultivate them.

The Barreto family, led by Doña Isabel, were the dominating power in the preparations, and their two strongest traits, pride and clannishness, were to shape the destiny of the venture from the start. The pride of a Spaniard is proverbial, but the Barretos overdid it. Although the Barreto line was not actually of much social prominence back in their home province of Galicia, they felt that any slight upon their pretensions should be resented to the death. In this spirit, the Barreto clan stuck together. Doña Isabel was the wife of the Governor, of course, and therefore in position to see that her family got high value for every peso they had invested in the enterprise. Her brother Lorenzo was appointed captain of the flagship, the *San Jerónimo,* and two other brothers were shipping in the same vessel. To add to the complications, Isabel's unmarried sister, Mariana, was also a member of this family party. And anybody who threatened the pride, the family unity or the possessions of the Barretos was instantly an enemy.

Among the warring factions that arose, the capable Chief Pilot, Quirós, tried to remain neutral, but from the start he had his hands full keeping peace among the leaders of the expedition. Quirós suffered under one grave handicap; he had been born not in Spain but in Portugal, before that country had come under the rule of His Majesty Philip II of Spain, and gossips muttered that Quirós had grown up in the waterfront alleys of Lisbon. Nevertheless, he had served in many ships as clerk and supercargo, and there was no doubt that he was one of the most skilled navigators of his time. Now only thirty, he left behind in Peru his wife, the daughter of a Madrid lawyer, and two children.

Our main source of information regarding this ghastly expedition is the Chief Pilot's narrative, from which it is clear that his patience was sorely tried by the conflicting demands of the ill-assorted mass of humanity that was packed into the four ships setting out on a difficult mission of discovery and settlement in the far Pacific.* He was clearly the most sensible person in the party, and everyone was dependent upon his sailorly advice. But Doña Isabel in particular did not appreciate that advice, and was bored by his efforts as a peacemaker.

By far the most troublesome member of the expedition— the one who made the voyage hell instead of mere purgatory —was the Campmaster, who was in charge of the force of soldiers that had been provided by Governor Mendaña's friend the Marquis of Cañete, Viceroy of Peru at this time. This Campmaster was a crusty, white-haired veteran of about sixty, named Pedro Merino Manrique. Even before the ships departed, this terrible martinet began to interfere with the sailors in their work. He scolded the boatswain, and when the man objected, the Campmaster started to punish him. Doña Isabel, looking on, remarked to the Pilot: "The Campmaster is certainly severe. If that's the way he tries to handle things, he may possibly come to a good end, but I'm far from thinking so."

The Campmaster marched up to them and said to the Pilot: "Do you know who I am? Understand that I am the Campmaster, and if we sailed together, and I ordered the ship to be run on some rock, what would you do?"

The Pilot replied: "I don't recognize any other leader than the Governor. If you want to be lord of all that is

*Actually the Quirós report was apparently set down by a young poet, Luis de Belmonte Bermudez, who acted as the Chief Pilot's amanuensis aboard ship.

about to be discovered, rather than be under the orders of a person who shows such little judgment I would give up this voyage!"

Later, both the Chief Pilot and the Campmaster separately threatened to resign, but Governor Mendaña smoothed them down and promised that he would take steps to settle their grievances.

After a lofty speech by the Viceroy of Peru, the four ships left the port of Callao on April 9, 1595. But more provisions were needed, and more people had to be collected along the coast, people who wished to take their goods and settle in the islands of Solomon. At one port, where Captain Lope de Vega had enlisted a group of married people, this captain himself was married to Doña Isabel's sister Mariana. Now a member of the family, he was given command of the consort ship, the *Santa Isabel,* but for some reason his wife still lived on the flagship, the *San Jerónimo.* The remainder of the fleet consisted of two smaller vessels—the galiot *San Felipe* under Felipe Corzo, and the frigate *Santa Catalina* under Alonso de Leyva.

At the same port the Campmaster got into another quarrel with Mendaña, who had put ashore several couples that he thought were not respectable enough to make good colonists; the Campmaster took their part and said they were as respectable as some others on the ships. The old soldier then managed to get into a rage against the Vicar, one of the two priests in charge of the religious side of the expedition. Next he disputed with Captain Lorenzo Barreto because he thought there wasn't enough room in the ship for the soldiers to stow their luggage in. The Campmaster's favorite method of addressing a subordinate was first to crack him heavily over the head with his cane and then to speak, and all except the soldiers, who idolized him, were soon heartily tired of the old bully.

At last the four vessels, with many flags flying and trumpets playing, left Paita on the northern coast of Peru and sailed toward the southwest. Aboard were 378 persons, of whom 280 were listed as capable of bearing arms. Soldiers and sailors, men, women and children—all enjoyed a feast in anticipation of great success and wealth to be found in the South Seas.

The people got acquainted with their shipmates, and at first scarcely a day went by without a wedding ceremony. Doña Isabel must have felt grievously the lack of a hundred comforts that she had been used to during nine years as the wife of Mendaña; but she demanded as her proper due a continuous obeisance from the people of the ship, who were constantly reminded that her family had put much money into the expedition.

No land was sighted for three whole months. Then on Friday, July 21, 1595, the cry "Land ho!" rang out, and Mendaña was so delighted that he asked the Vicar and his assistant priest, the Chaplain, to chant the *Te Deum*, while all the people knelt on the deck.

In the gathering dusk the expedition had a chance to see their first Pacific island, a glorious remnant of two ancient volcanoes whose entire western rims had fallen into the sea, leaving inspired peaks, deep valleys and wonderfully wooded bays. Here was an island whose physical beauty far exceeded anything the expedition had hoped for, and a thrill of discovery ran through the four crowded ships, for accidentally they had come upon an island which through the long history of the Pacific would be treasured as one of the most hauntingly beautiful retreats in the ocean. It was the island of Fatu Hiva, a lonely, savage, terrible and doomed place, yet one which has lured all travelers who have seen it. As night fell on this moment of discovery, Mendaña and his crew tried, from their little craft, to pierce the mystery that has forever shrouded Fatu Hiva.

In the bright sunlight of the next day, the boats sailed in close, and Mendaña christened the island Magdalena. It was found to be inhabited, and although nobody in the ships was aware of the fact, they were seeing for the first time the members of a race previously unknown to the world. These were the Polynesians, who still inhabit the Pacific within a great triangle whose apexes are Hawaii, Easter Island and New Zealand.

Doña Isabel watched at the rail as seventy outrigger canoes came out, bringing about four hundred natives, paddling or else swimming and hanging to the canoes. Surprisingly, they were almost white in skin color, and their graceful naked bodies were tattooed with fish designs and other patterns. Among them was a boy of about ten, who paddled one of the canoes. He had long locks, and his face seemed like that of an angel. "Never in my life," the Pilot was heard to remark, "have I felt such pain as I do now, to think that such a fair creature might be left to go to perdition!" There were souls to be saved in these lovely isles.

The natives surrounded the ship and shouted, and made gestures inviting the strange visitors to go ashore. They handed up gifts of coconuts and fine bananas, and bamboo canes full of fresh water. Then one of the natives was coaxed to climb aboard the flagship, and the Governor got him to put on a shirt and a hat. As he capered about in this garb, many others laughed and came aboard, staring in wonder.

Some forty of the natives strolled around the deck. Their bodies were well proportioned but so large that the Spaniards seemed dwarfed by comparison. The natives were confused by the fact that the Christians wore clothing, but the soldiers bared their breasts and let down their stockings to show the skin underneath, and finally the Polynesians were convinced that these were human beings like themselves.

They began to dance and sing and grab at things they saw, and the Governor ordered them to leave the ship. But they stayed until he ordered a cannon to be fired; at the sound, in great terror they jumped overboard and swam to their canoes. Yet one persistent man clung to the main chains and would not let go until his hand was struck with a sword. At this the natives got angry, and under the urging of an old man with a long beard, the warriors in the canoes approached the ship with raised spears and began throwing stones. A bullet from the arquebus of one of the soldiers hit the old man's forehead. He fell dead, and the canoes retreated to the shore.

Mendaña at first thought that he had prematurely arrived at the Solomon Islands, but he soon had to admit that he did not recognize these shores. Soon other beautiful islands were sighted, and the group was christened Las Marquesas in honor of the Marquis of Cañete, Viceroy of Peru, who had aided the expedition. Mendaña's fame as discoverer of the romantic Marquesas will always be respected in Pacific history. Unfortunately, the impact of the brutal and senseless behavior of these first Spanish adventurers upon the quick-witted Polynesian inhabitants was never forgotten, and made later contacts with Europeans an unhappy ordeal.

The island of Tahuata, which the Governor called Santa Cristina, was discovered on July 21. Here the Campmaster was sent ashore with twenty soldiers to find a watering place. Becoming fearful when many natives paddled out in canoes to greet them, the soldiers began to fire unwarrantedly at

he Marquesans. One native jumped into the sea with a child
n his arms, and clasped together they were sent to the bot-
om with one shot. Later the Pilot asked the soldier who had
lone this needless murder why he had not fired into the air.
The man answered that he did not want to lose his reputa-
ion as a good marksman. "What good will it do you to enter
Iell with the fame of being a good shot?" asked the Pilot.
Iut that first indiscriminate shooting of helpless natives was
out a sample of what was to come.

The following day the Campmaster's party actually landed
on the island, and surrounded one of the villages. Three
lundred natives approached, but were warned not to cross
a line drawn in the sand. When asked for water, they
orought coconuts for the men to drink from, and the women
prought other kinds of fruit. The women were very pretty,
and with true Polynesian hospitality they came close to the
nen and flirted with them. But the natives did not welcome
he idea of being put to work lugging the water jars that the
Ipaniards had brought with them to be filled. When they
saw that the Campmaster was about to order this task, they
an off with four jars. To punish them, the soldiers fired a
volley into a helpless and unoffending crowd, and a number
of the villagers were killed.

A better landing place was found up the coast, and Doña
Isabel and her husband and most of the people of the fleet
went ashore on Santa Cristina, to hear the first mass said.
The natives flocked around and quietly imitated everything
he Christians did, kneeling and folding their hands at the
oroper times. Near Doña Isabel sat a very beautiful Marquesan girl, whose long hair was such a startling red that the
ady took her scissors and tried to snip off a few locks as a
keepsake. The girl did not like this and Doña Isabel had to
stop for fear of making the natives angry.

The soldiers who attended the church service immediately
noticed that the women of the Marquesas had beautiful legs
and hands, fine eyes, fair countenances, small waists and
graceful figures. They wore nothing but a single garment
hat covered them from the breasts downward. The Spaniards
pointed out some girls that they thought were prettier
han the ladies of Lima, who were famed for their beauty.

After mass, Mendaña, in the name of His Majesty, took
formal possession of all four of the islands of the southeast-
ern Marquesas. He walked about in the fields, planting seeds

as a ritual act. Then he and Doña Isabel went back to sta
aboard ship. But the Campmaster and all the soldiers re
mained on shore.

Soon the men began to quarrel among themselves an
with the natives. When the aroused Marquesans threw stone
and lances in self-defense, the soldiers chased them into th
hills with their women and children. The Spaniards the
took over the village and fortified it. A few bold native
skirmished with the troops, but when they saw how littl
harm their missiles did, and how easily they were killed b
the bullets of the Christians, they tried to make peace

They brought fruits and other offerings to the soldier
and by signs asked when the Spaniards would go away, s
that they could move back into their homes. Each nativ
picked out one Christian as his special comrade—a chumm
custom that Melville later noted among the Marquesans—
and would sit with him and try to talk, asking the Spanis
names of the sun and the stars and the palm trees an
everything else in sight.

The Spaniards learned that these natives lived together i
big houses formed of wooden posts interwoven with can
and roofed with leaves. They had canoes seating thirty c
forty men, and in them went to other islands far away. On
of the natives, seeing a Negro on the ship, pointed towar
the south and made signs to say that in that direction ther
were many people like the Negro, who used arrows, an
the Marquesans went south in canoes to fight these blac
people.

The climate in these islands was healthful, and the nativ
fed well on pigs and chickens and fish. The mainstay c
their diet was an amazing food, part fruit, part vegetabl
and in the Quirós narrative we find the first description c
the breadfruit, so vital to the economy of the South Pacific
"The trees . . . yield a fruit which becomes the size of a boy
head. Its color, when it is ripe, is a bright green, and whe
unripe it is very green. The rind has crossed grooves like
pineapple; its shape is not quite round, being rather mo
narrow at the end than at the base. From the stem grows
stalk reaching to the middle of the fruit, with a sheath c
tissue. It has no core or pips, or anything inedible except th
skin, and that is thin. All the rest is a mass of sapless pul
when ripe, not so much when green. They eat much of it i
all sorts of ways, and it is so palatable that they call it 'whit
food.' It is a wholesome fruit and of much importance. Th

leaves of the tree are large, and deeply cleft, like those of the papaya."

One day eleven natives came out to the ships in canoes and offered coconuts for trade. When they got within range the soldiers wantonly fired into them and chased them back to the beach. The bodies of three who had been abandoned were taken on shore and mutilated. Then the Campmaster hung them on trees as a warning, so that the natives might be terrified by seeing the wide gashes of swords and the ugly wounds of the bullets. At night the natives took the hanged bodies away.

As one instance of the bloodthirsty treatment of the natives by the soldiers, Quirós mentions that a soldier had an arquebus in his hut, and a friend of his came in, loaded it and pointed it at some visiting natives. The man took the weapon away from his friend and asked him what he was going to do with so much diligence. The friend said that his diligence was to kill people, because he liked to kill. "What harm have these natives done you," asked the man, "that you should be so cruel? It is not valorous to show yourself a lion among lambs. If you do not know what a foul and sinful thing it is to murder a body which contains a soul, it is high time you learned." But other soldiers were not so kindhearted, and shot the natives down for fun, since they found pleasure in testing their skill on moving targets. The most that can be said of such behavior is that it set the pattern for all subsequent European visitors to these tragic islands, which explains why, today, one native survives where in 1595 there were fifty. During the two weeks the fleet stayed in the Marquesas, at least two hundred natives were murdered for sport.

Mendaña was impressed by the Marquesas and wanted to leave thirty men and their wives to colonize these lovely islands, but the soldiers complained and he gave up the idea. Thereafter, until Captain James Cook rediscovered the Marquesas in 1774, no white men visited this group for a hundred and eighty years; but when they returned, the natives still retained memories of the horrors perpetrated by their first white visitors.

On August 5, 1595, Mendaña's small fleet headed once more for the Solomons. But for a whole month no land was to be found except some dangerous reefs that almost took the bottoms off the ships. The Campmaster continued to wrangle with everyone and to wield his cane, trying to run the flagship as if it were a besieged garrison in Flanders.

Among the company the grumbling increased. Many said they despaired of ever finding land in this deadly ocean, which might well be empty all the way to Great Tartary. Others said that Mendaña had obviously forgotten where the isles of Solomon might be found, or else the sea had risen and covered them. Still others said that Mendaña, in order to earn the right to be made a marquis, would let them all starve on these waters, or make them go to the bottom and fish for those pearls he gabbled about. Pilot Quirós knew that the ships had already passed far to the west of the longitude given him by the Governor as that of the Solomons, but he assured the complainers that he would navigate as well as he could, for he did not intend to lose his own life.

The consort ship *Santa Isabel* had by this time grown so short of firewood for the galley that the crew was burning the upper spars of the vessel, and was short of water as well. Captain Lope de Vega came to the flagship and pleaded for twenty jars of water, but Mendaña could not believe he was so short, and refused to give him any from the remaining supply of four hundred jars. Captain de Vega was worried also because without ballast the consort could not sail well. As it turned out, he had good cause to worry.

On September 7 the lookout on Mendaña's flagship sighted a mass of dark smoke dead ahead. The two smaller ships were dispatched to explore cautiously, and at nine that night those on the flagship briefly glimpsed Captain de Vega's *Santa Isabel* standing out from a thick curtain of smoke reaching to the horizon. The night was passed in praying God to send the daylight, but at dawn there was no sign of the *Santa Isabel*.

For many days—and at intervals later—the expedition sought this lost ship, but she had disappeared and nobody was ever to see her again. With a hundred and eighty souls aboard, the vessel vanished into the bosom of the Pacific. Doña Isabel's sister Mariana, who still lived on the flagship and was thus a widow before she was a wife, mourned for her lost Captain Lope de Vega, and blamed herself for not having shared his fate.

Now, 1085 leagues from Peru, the expedition at last sighted land, a perfect cone-shaped mountain rising from the ocean. It was the active volcano of Tinakula, rising three thousand feet and spouting out great flames and sparks, more than enough for ten ordinary volcanoes. The mountain thundered in its bowels, and from it came an immense cloud of smoke that blanketed the world. At this fearful sight, Mendaña ordered all the soldiers to be confessed, and to set the example he himself confessed to the Vicar in public.

Soon the ships neared an island south of the volcano. It was roughly rectangular, about twenty-five by fifteen miles. On all sides but the western, densely wooded volcanic slopes rose to a height of 1800 feet.

On September 7, fifty small canoes came out to the ships. The people in them were very black, not at all like the Polynesians of the Marquesas. They wore shocks of frizzy hair, which was often caked in lime and urine to dye it yellow or red. They were completely naked. All were tattooed with lines blacker than their skin; they had designs on their faces as well as their bodies. They wore many necklaces of very small beads of bone and fish teeth, and plates of mother-of-pearl hanging from various parts of their bodies. They carried bows and arrows, darts with three rows of barbs, and heavy wooden swords.

When the Governor saw their dark color he again jumped to the conclusion that at last he had reached the Solomons. But this forbidding and inhospitable group, which he named Santa Cruz, was still about 240 miles east of the southern Solomons. He tried to speak to the natives in the language he had learned nearly thirty years before, but they did not respond, and in fact Mendaña never did attain an understanding of these formidable savages.

The natives in the canoes would not come aboard the ship but, incited by a tall old man, fired off many arrows which whistled harmlessly through the sails and rigging. In return the soldiers discharged a volley from their arquebuses. Some of the black men were killed, many others were wounded, and all fled to shore in great terror, to hide among the trees. In the tradition of this fleet a new-found people had once more been greeted with a volley of bullets.

The three ships could not find a safe haven, and at night almost drove onto the rocks and coral heads that lined the shore. The soldiers got into a panic, but would not lend a hand in hauling up the anchors. Disdainfully the sailors shouted, "Let the brave Peruvians go below, and may those who do the work get the credit!" They managed to make sail and get the flagship into the open seas, where she heeled over and almost swamped with the waves coming aboard. The incident did little to abate the rivalry between soldiers and sailors.

For two days they floundered offshore, hoping to find a harbor, and at night heard from the shore the noise of music and dancing, the beating of drums and tambourines of hollow wood. Then they found a sheltered anchorage by a village in a bay on the north side of Santa Cruz, a bay which the Governor in gratitude christened Graciosa, the name which it still bears.

Another group of natives, wearing red flowers tucked in their hair and nostrils, came out to visit the ships, and some of them were persuaded to come aboard. Among them was a tawny-skinned, tall man of fine presence, with blue, yellow and red plumes on his head. He came forward and asked by signs who was the leader of the Spaniards.

Mendaña took the chief by the hand and told his name, whereupon the native replied that his was Malope and indicated that he would like to exchange names as a sign of friendship—an old Melanesian custom. Thereafter, when anyone called the chief Malope, he would say no, his name was Mendaña but the leader of the Christians was called Malope.

Mendaña dressed Malope in a linen shirt, and the soldiers gave the other natives some feathers, little bells, glass beads, bits of cotton and even playing cards, all of which they hung around their necks. They also showed the Melanesians some mirrors, and with razors shaved their heads and chins, and with scissors cut their toenails. The black men begged hard to be given these magic tools of metal, the razors and scissors.

Four days later the soldiers went ashore to visit Malope's village, where crowds of natives greeted them with joy. The soldiers were disappointed with these signs of peace, though; they felt they were growing rusty at their profession and informed their leaders that they wanted to make war instead. The day after this visit, a boat was sent to load water at a stream, and some concealed natives shouted and fired arrows, which wounded three Spaniards. At once Mendaña ordered the Campmaster to land with thirty men and do all the harm they could with fire and sword. The natives stood their ground until five of them were killed, then the rest fled. The Christians cut down some palm trees and burned some huts and canoes before they came back to the ships, bringing three pigs they had captured.

Early next morning the Campmaster returned with forty soldiers to punish the natives further for the attack. The party arrived secretly at the village, surrounded the huts, and set them on fire. Seven natives who were inside defended themselves bravely; six were killed and one, badly wounded, escaped by running.

That afternoon Malope came to the beach and cried out to the Governor, to complain that this punishment was a mistake. He made clear by signs that the houses and canoes that had been burned belonged to him, but that the natives responsible for the attack were bad men, his enemies from the other side of the bay. He went away sadly, but returned on another day and friendship was restored.

One day in a violent explosion the volcano pulverized its rocky top, so that even though the fleet was now ten leagues distant, explosions shook the vessels. Thereafter mighty thundering was heard for days, and dense smoke overarched the sky.

The ships found a better anchorage along the bay, but soon five hundred enemy natives came to the beach and hurled darts and stones at the sailors. They were chased back by a boatload of soldiers led by Doña Isabel's brother, Captain Lorenzo Barreto. The Captain, although he had no orders to land, followed the natives into the jungle.

The Campmaster, watching from the ship, shouted that the soldiers' lives should not be risked in this way, and that an officer who disobeyed orders ought to be punished. This remark touched Doña Isabel's family pride, and she exclaimed that, since Don Lorenzo was her brother, there was no limit to his powers on the military side. But the old Campmaster went ashore with thirty men, caught up with Don Lorenzo and told him he was not fit to be a captain. When Doña Isabel heard of the scolding, her remarks about the Campmaster added to the bad blood that was building on each side.

The Campmaster stayed on shore that night, and next day ordered the soldiers to clear a flat place near a large stream and build a settlement there. At this command most of the unmarried men began eagerly to chop down trees and bring palm branches to thatch the huts they were building.

But the married men felt that they would be happier if they moved the natives out of their houses in the village and took over these ready-made homes for themselves. They went to Mendaña and complained of the Campmaster's decision, and the Governor grew angry because he had chosen a different site for their town, on a bare point near the entrance to the bay; but the Campmaster insisted that his choice prevail.

Everybody bustled around setting up tents and huts in a spirit of optimism. But this feeling did not last long, because many of the settlers could not help thinking how this place suffered in comparison with the remembered delights and comforts of Lima; and thus, wrote Quirós, the devil began to spread discontent and dissension among the colonists.

It would have been better if the Governor had lived ashore to watch how things were going there; but no house had been built for him and his wife, so they kept their headquarters on the flagship. The Governor commanded that the natives be well treated and their houses and property respected. But many of the colonists said that they had already spent much money to get to this place, and they wanted to start collecting some profit from their venture. Thus Mendaña was daily pestered by complaints from all sides, and the discontent grew.

The colonists should have been happy on this island of Santa Cruz, for it provided the elements of a bountiful life for those who were willing to work in peace and harmony. The Melanesian inhabitants, after the initial battles, had become quite happy in their relations with the Spaniards. They laughed all day, brought presents to the Spaniards, tilled gardens and raised pigs and fowls, and caught many fish from their outrigger canoes, hollowed out of a single log. They also showed the colonists how to raise many kinds of bananas and other fruits, and how coconuts and sugar cane could be harvested. They ate breadfruit and a starchy root which they roasted and made into biscuits. They plaited bags and sails and mats from palm leaves, and wove a fabric to be used as cloaks. Compared to other Pacific natives, they were healthy and slept well at night, for no mosquitoes were observed on this island.

The Spaniards ashore got into the habit of demanding food from the natives, and soldiers would raid the villages and return with coconuts and bananas and as many pigs as they could round up. Chief Malope was very helpful and persuaded his natives to come and work at building houses for the Spaniards, so that their own would not be taken from them.

But in what could have been a successful colony, there was constant trouble. The Campmaster was in charge on shore, and he did nothing to put down the grumblings that continually arose, until a petition was circulated secretly by the soldiers, asking that Mendaña take them away and find a better place, or go to the Solomon Islands where the gold and pearls were waiting to be collected.

When Mendaña realized that a pitiful end was inevitable for a project that should have succeeded magnificently, the poor old man began to fail. His health was further damaged by the merciless feud between his wife and the Campmaster, and if a coup de grâce was needed, it was found in the endless bickering which his doddering personality had allowed to grow up in every quarter. However, when the petition was presented he tried to draw himself up in a last gesture of authority and announced that what they had done was nothing less than an act of mutiny. They were founding a city, he said, not trying to reach a spot where an idle man could pick up emeralds, diamonds and rubies from the ground. Great cities were not built in a day, he preached, for some sturdy pioneers always had to construct the foundations.

The soldiers responded to such sentiment most effectively. They simply grabbed an unoffending villager and stabbed him to death, hoping thereby to force the black men into a war that would cut off the food supply, so that the expedition would have to go somewhere else in search of provisions. They reasoned also that if the natives attacked, the Governor would have to send ashore the cannons for defense there, and these could then be turned against the ships.

Other malcontents proposed to make holes with augers in the ships' bottoms, so that nobody could go back to Peru and report their bad behavior. The soldiers were afraid that the sailors would put to sea and desert them, and to calm their fears the Governor had to take all the ships' sails and lock them up under guard, where in the excessive heat they began to rot.

The soldiers now forced others to sign their mutinous petition and to promise that, if things degenerated into an open conflict, they would use their guns on the side of the Campmaster and against Mendaña. One soldier boasted in public: "The Campmaster is my fighting cock; everyone is afraid of him. Let us take his side in this war." Another complained maliciously: "The clothing of Doña Isabel was made to be worn for two years. Must we stay all that time on this lost island? And I have no wife to take by the hand, as Don Alvaro has his wife."

Several times Mendaña rose from his sickbed and went on shore to demand that the Campmaster keep better control and put down this rising mutiny. But the fiery old Campmaster snorted that he was a gentleman and that if it had not been for him, all these rascals would long ago have deserted the Governor. The Campmaster also introduced his own complaint. Doña Isabel, he charged, was spreading evil rumors about him. Moreover, he protested that the Governor had not supplied enough axes and machetes for the building work, and that he had not been given clear orders about how the fort should be built and the town laid out.

Meanwhile, throughout the little settlement, the pioneers were bickering bitterly over which family should have the best allotment of land, and what their titles should be and how their estates would be entailed for their heirs. A month had not yet passed since their arrival, and already the colony was split into two factions—those who wanted to stay and those who were determined to escape from Santa Cruz even if it meant mutiny and open civil war.

At dawn one morning Doña Isabel's brother Diego hurried out from land in a small canoe bearing frightening news. He gasped that he had uncovered a plot whereby the men on shore were going to kill Mendaña and the entire Barreto family, as well as any who remained loyal to them. He said the plot arose from the determination of those ashore to abandon Santa Cruz and move on to the riches of the Solomons.

Hardly had this intelligence been digested when the Campmaster came out to the flagship to make fresh petty complaints about new injuries to his authority and his pride. Doña Isabel whispered sharply to her indecisive husband: "Kill the Campmaster or have him killed! What more do you want? He has fallen into your hands, and if you do not, I will kill him with this knife!" Driven by his wife, Mendaña was ready to strangle the old man and hang him from one of the masts, but the Campmaster suspected some plot and, moving his guards about him, cautiously withdrew to the shore.

The time was obviously at hand when the Barretos could no longer endure the existence of the cantankerous old Campmaster. Therefore it was determined in family conference that Captain Lorenzo Barreto and three faithful men would assassinate the old man. Mendaña agreed to go ashore and give the murder a semblance of legality by raising the royal flag and announcing that justice was about to be done.

But at dawn on Sunday, October 8, before the plan could be put into effect, a shout came from the shore to demand that a boat be sent to the beach. Doña Isabel jumped from her bed, shouting, "Alas! They have killed my brothers, and now they ask for a boat so they can come and kill us!" Those on the ship then saw a party of thirty soldiers emerge from the trees and wait.

Mendaña, wracked by disease and barely able to walk, arose from his sickbed and took a boat to the beach. There he asked the party of soldiers where they were going. The lieutenant in command said they were ordered by the Campmaster to go to Malope's village to seek food. Something in their manner made the Governor warn them not to hurt Malope or take any of his property, for the chief was the friend of the Spaniards. The soldiers ignored him with a harsh laugh, and marched off.

Then Mendaña forced himself up to the place where the fort was being built. The Campmaster, who was having his breakfast in his tent, came out unarmed and without his coat and hat. When he saw who was approaching, he became suspicious and shouted for a servant to bring him his dagger and sword. But it was too late. The Governor gave the signal for the attack in this way: he sighed, raised his eyes to heaven, put his hand on the hilt of his sword and cried, "Long live the king! Death to traitors!"

One of his men grabbed the old Campmaster by the collar and stabbed him twice, once in the mouth and once in the breast. Another gashed him in the side. The Campmaster gasped, "Oh, gentlemen!" and tried to get to his sword. Felipe Corzo, captain of the galiot, hacked at the old man with a huge machete and nearly cut off his right arm.

The Campmaster fell to the ground, pleading, "Leave me time to confess!"

"Well might you feel contrite!" said one of the killers.

The Campmaster lay writhing on the ground, crying, "Jesus María!" A woman settler came up and helped him to die in peace.

The body was left in the dust, with the white locks dabbled in blood. The Governor's drummer, desiring a new suit of clothes, stripped the body and left it naked. The Campmaster's epitaph may be found in the words of Pilot Quirós: "The Campmaster was very zealous, a hard worker and good soldier, and in all enterprises he was the first. . . . Though old, he was vigorous, but very impetuous. He knew how to think much, but he could not be silent, and I believe that for no other thing he was killed."

Mendaña, himself dying, proclaimed that the Campmaster's death was approved by him, and that all others would be pardoned in the name of the king. But this was little to the liking of Captain Lorenzo Barreto, who led his men in a search for other traitors, and one of the Campmaster's aides was struck down. Captain Corzo chopped off this man's head and also the Campmaster's head, and others of the party went around seeking enemies to kill, shouting, "Long live the king! Death to traitors!"

Many of the women came out from the camp, fearful for the lives of their husbands; some prayed, and others wrung their hands and lamented. The sergeant major came out of his tent, and in order to prove his loyalty by a valiant act, he gallantly slashed the Campmaster's little page boy on the head. Other innocents would have been killed except that the Chief Pilot, still trying to act as peacemaker, protected them from the fury of the gang.

Captain Corzo now took the two heads and stuck them up on poles at the guard's outpost. He then went out to the flagship and announced to Doña Isabel that he had given a good blow against the Campmaster and had cut off two heads. "It is terrible that for so long we endured presumptuous fools," he told her. "Now that the Campmaster is dead, there is nothing to keep you from becoming the wife of a marquis!"

The Vicar went ashore with the sailors to rally to the flag of the Governor. When he heard that the Campmaster was dead, the Vicar put down the lance in his hand and agreed to celebrate the mass. After he performed the service, he spoke to the people and told them not to be scandalized by the deaths, for the act was ordained. They should be quiet and obey the Governor, and all would be well.

When the loyal ones assembled at the outpost, the Governor ordered that the heads should be taken down from the poles and that everything should look as it was before the killing. He still had to placate the thirty men who had gone to Malope's village, and he did not want them to suspect anything.

One of the thirty soon returned and reported that they had gone to the house of Malope, who had regaled them with all the food he had. Malope was friendly and felt se-

cure, and was not aware of trouble until a Spaniard, with
no provocation whatever, raised his arquebus into the friendly chief's face, and fired.

As Malope lay on the ground, another soldier put him
out of his pain by cleaving his skull with a hatchet, saying,
"We have never done a better thing. Malope obviously intended to commit treason."

When the soldiers, unaware of the assassination of their
leader, returned with the good news that they had slain
Malope, Mendaña's men grabbed them and held them prisoners. The lieutenant in charge was put in irons. After being
allowed to confess to the Chaplain, he was beheaded and
his body covered with branches. Later it was thrown into
the sea, despite the weeping and pleading of his wife.

Then the Governor called before him the soldier who had
killed Malope. This man prayed for pardon, and swore that
he would serve the Governor well thereafter. The Chief Pilot
begged that the soldier's life be spared, but the Governor
asked, "How am I to pay for the death of my friend Malope
except with the death of this man?" The Pilot suggested a
stratagem: show the natives the heads of the two men who
had already been killed. Thus the gentle Quirós saved the
life of the murderer.

Now the Vicar asked that in charity the two heads be
buried, and Mendaña agreed. They were left exposed on the
beach, however, and next morning were found with all the
flesh and skin gone, for dogs had eaten them. The head of
the executed lieutenant still remained, though, and the Governor ordered a party to take it to Malope's village, where all
the natives were bewailing the death of their chief. The
Christians showed them the bloody head and with signs
tried to explain that vengeance had been exacted for the
murder. The natives left their mourning ceremonies and ran
into the woods. The head was left at the door of one of the
huts, and the party returned to the ship.

The murderer of Malope, imprisoned on board, began to
suffer from the pangs of conscience, because his friends
asked him, "Why did you kill that good native without cause?"
and others said that he should be drawn and quartered for
such an act. He turned his face to the wall, refused to eat
and drank large draughts of sea water. Within a few days
he was dead.

Now each day Mendaña, like his ill-fated colony, grew
worse. In order to revive him, his men took him to a house

ashore; but the new residence was dangerous, for many natives, enraged over the death of Malope, kept in hiding near the Spaniards and greeted any man who moved with arrows, which wounded many. But more deadly than the black men was the unprecedented disease which now began to fell one Spaniard after another.

The first of the party died on October 17. He was the hard-working Chaplain, and the Vicar, the only remaining priest, cried aloud because, if he too should have to die, he would have no one at hand to shrive him. That night there was a total eclipse of the moon, and the colonists could not help feeling that this was an ominous sign, for they were alone in a vast ocean many leagues from Peru, and their friends were beginning to die.

Mendaña was now so weak that he could scarcely sign his name to his will, which had been written out for him. In it he nominated his brother-in-law, Captain Lorenzo Barreto, to be captain general of the party. He named his wife, Doña Isabel, as his heiress, and in addition he made her Governess of the whole expedition, for he carried with him a special decree from the king granting him power to name as his successor any person he chose.

On October 18 the Governor was clearly dying. The Vicar brought a crucifix and before it the Governor seemed to bend his knees in spirit, since physically he could not move. While joining in saying the Miserere and the Credo, Governor Alvaro de Mendaña, who had discovered the Solomon Islands, the Marquesas and Santa Cruz, passed from a life devoted to the service of his God and his king. Doña Isabel and her relatives felt the loss keenly, as did most of the company; but some people secretly rejoiced, for now it might be possible to abandon the cursed settlement.

Mendaña's body was placed in a coffin covered with black cloth, and carried on the shoulders of eight men of the highest social rank. The soldiers stood with their arquebuses in reverse position, according to the usage customary at the funeral of a general. With muffled drums, the procession went to the church that was being built, and the Vicar performed the services. Then the people returned to console Doña Isabel on her widowhood.

Doña Isabel quickly assumed the title of Governess, in charge of the whole expedition. Never before had a woman been the head of a Spanish exploring enterprise, but unfortunately, as the Chief Pilot pointed out, this great responsibility did not change her character or bring her more wisdom.

Yet there was increased need for her to make wise decisions, for now the Santa Cruz disease struck down two or three people every day. The Vicar walked about the camp, crying out, "Is there anyone who wants to confess? There is a man who does not know whether he is a Moor or a Christian; others have committed sins so foul that I will not name them. We have among us sickness, war, famine, and discord, and we are far from any remedy. Confess yourselves, and with repentance appease the anger of God, Who has brought us this terrible chastisement!" Day after day he went about giving the sacrament to the sick and burying the dead.

Meanwhile, the fighting with natives went on. The soldiers who were not stricken with illness burned more villages, and finally captured some women and children and held them as hostages. But their menfolk came and asked that they be returned to them, and in order to avoid more trouble the Spaniards yielded the hostages.

Now a new petition was circulated, begging the Governess to leave the island of Santa Cruz. This time the Vicar himself wrote out the petition and announced that nobody would be killed for signing it.

The sick continued to die, stretched out in the clutches of the unknown disease and delirious with long fever, which did not kill suddenly but which ultimately struck most of the people on the shore. Those on the ships did not fall prey to this plague, which probably resulted from the changes which had been made in the lives of the colonists. They had exposed themselves to heat and cold, and eaten strange foods, and worked bareheaded in the sun in wet clothing and slept on the ground in the night mists. No doctor had accompanied the expedition, and death seemed inevitable.

Aboard the flagship, even the resolute Doña Isabel appeared lost in a fog of irresolution. She was unwilling to abandon the settlement that had once seemed so promising, yet the toll of death showed her how necessary some drastic action had become. She became aware of this when Chief Pilot Quirós rowed out from shore and asked that the Vicar join him at the settlement.

The Vicar answered, "I cannot go; can you not see that I am dying too? And I must die unshriven, for the good Chaplain has gone before me." But when it was explained that Doña Isabel's brother, Don Lorenzo, was dying, the fever-wracked Vicar agreed to go ashore. He was wrapped in a blanket and taken by canoe to the beach. Then he was carried to the bedside of the Captain General, and confessed him. That night Don Lorenzo was much worse, and at daybreak on November 2, 1595, he died. He was buried with the same military honors that had been given his brother-in-law, the Governor. Now it was obvious that Santa Cruz was doomed.

Perhaps not even the wisdom of Solomon could have solved the problems that had arisen on this unlucky island. Five days later, Doña Isabel decided to terminate the settlement, for the sickness was so bad that ten determined natives might have attacked the village and killed everyone ashore. The Governess ordered that all the sick people should be carried to the ships, along with the royal flag. Thus the promising colony of Santa Cruz was abandoned and, as Quirós wrote, left in the claws of the devil, who had held it previously for so long. Mendaña's men had been ashore only two short months since the fleet had first sighted the smoke of the volcano that brooded over these Melanesian islands, and now the enterprise was ending in total tragedy.

Before the three ships left, they stocked up with provisions. Thirty men went across the bay to the charming and fertile little island that the Spaniards had called The Garden. There they captured five native canoes loaded with biscuit made from a starchy root. They also killed many pigs, and collected coconuts and bananas. The soldiers abused the natives, who then dug pits in the earth and lined them with sharp stakes, on which one soldier hurt his foot.

On the flagship, it was now the Vicar's turn to die. He called for a crucifix and, with no one to shrive him, bravely commended his own soul to God. He was buried in the waters of the bay, so that the natives, now completely out of hand, could not dig up and insult his remains.

The Governess gave her decision to the Pilot. The ships would sail westward in search of the Solomon Islands, on the chance that the vanished consort ship might be found there. If it were not, then the remaining vessels should head for the city of Manila in the Philippines, where there was a Spanish colony. There Doña Isabel would recruit new priests and more settlers, and return to finish founding the town at Santa Cruz.

Pilot Quirós told her that since some of the sailors were coming down with sickness, and since the hulls and rigging of the ships were rotten, it would be sensible to abandon the galiot and the frigate, which were not decked over, and put their crews aboard the flagship. But Captain Corzo of the galiot objected, for he had secretly developed his own plan for getting his ship away from this doomed venture. The Governess, whose stinginess was now becoming a mania, fell in with Corzo's plan, for she did not want to lose the money value of the two smaller ships, which now belonged to her, and she insisted that they come along.

Some of those who were still healthy now came forth with a gruesome plan. Since they objected to having sick people on the flagship, they proposed to dump them all on the little frigate. But the humane Quirós remonstrated at this cruelty, and the sick ones were allowed to remain on the flagship. However, when some loyal men crept ashore at night and dug up the body of Mendaña to be taken to Manila, the healthy settlers insisted that it be put aboard the frigate. "With this," wrote Quirós, "ended the tragedy of the islands where Solomon was wanting."

The ships departed from Santa Cruz on November 18, 1595. Manila was nine hundred leagues away, but it was easier to reach there than to try to make the long northern circle back across the Pacific to Peru. The ropes of the vessel were so rotten that the falls carried away three times when the sailors tried to get the longboat on board the flagship.

But in spite of such an ominous beginning, the people aboard ship were overjoyed to see the last of hated Santa Cruz, where in one month forty-seven persons had died. According to Quirós, they turned their eyes to the abandoned huts of the settlement and cried, "Ah, there you remain, you corner of Hell, which has made us mourn for lost husbands, brothers, and friends!"

The voyage which began with these frustrated cheers was destined to become one of the strangest in Pacific history, for Doña Isabel quickly showed herself to be strong-willed, capable and utterly inhuman. The journey developed its true character when on the first day the skilled boatswain and four ordinary sailors fell ill with some new disease that completely incapacitated them and brought them to the point where death seemed imminent. The seamen who remained healthy warned Quirós that the three ships were unfit for service, they were filled with dying men, and the food and water were short.

Nevertheless, Quirós followed Doña Isabel's orders and searched westward for the Solomons, where wealth had to be waiting, but for once God was generous, and they missed the islands. Had they pushed a few leagues further west, they would have come upon the Solomons in a state so weak that they would probably have ended up in the ovens of cannibals. The Solomons, which had last been seen by Mendaña on August 17, 1568, were thus lost to the outside world until the English explorer Philip Carteret rediscovered them in 1767.

Near the unseen Solomons, Doña Isabel decided that, since no land was in sight and since the missing consort ship could not be found, her fleet should head for Manila, as planned. They sailed northwest to avoid the big island of New Guinea, which previous explorers had reported as the abode of "black people with frizzled hair, who are cannibals, and the devil walks with them."

North of New Guinea, great waves knocked the ships about. Then, three weeks after leaving Santa Cruz, they crossed the Equator. It was so cold at night that they had to use blankets, although in the daytime the sun beat unendurably on the planks of the deck.

The condition of the flagship was now so bad that the Governess feared it would fall apart, for the mainmast was sprung. She ordered Captain Corzo of the galiot to remain close by, to rescue the people in case the flagship foundered. But that night, in accordance with Corzo's plan, the galiot disappeared, and was not seen again during the voyage. Later, Quirós heard that Captain Corzo had sailed off and left them, and that he and his men had landed safely on the Philippine island of Mindanao.

Starvation and sickness hung over the two remaining ships day and night. The ration for each person was half a pound of flour, which was mixed with salt water and baked in the ashes of the galley fire. The water ration was one pint of fluid, which stank with the bodies of drowned cockroaches and was almost undrinkable. Even so, the people prayed pitifully for more water; some begged for a single drop, pointing with their fingers at their swollen tongues, looking like the pictures of Lazarus in the Bible. The worst aspect of the sickness was the open ulcers that covered the bodies of the stricken ones. The noise of mourning never stopped. Scarcely a day passed when one or two did not die in the mud and filth of the flagship's hold, and on some days three or four were thrown overboard. So few sound men were left that it was a problem to find enough of them to haul the bodies up from between decks.

Only a few of the sailors were healthy enough to work the flagship, and these were kept incessantly busy, splicing and sewing the decayed sails and rigging. One day the sprit-sail and all its gear fell into the sea, and could not be got back aboard. The topsails had to be taken down and used to mend the mainsails, which were the only ones that could be used. For one spell of three days one big sail was flapping about uselessly, because no hands were strong enough to try to hoist it with a rope that had already been spliced thirty-three times.

What was worse, the ship's hull gaped open and the waves ran in and out; the vessel floated only because her timbers were of an excellent South American wood which never seemed to rot. But still the Pilot drove his stricken ships onward through the uncharted seas of the middle Pacific.

The sailors, although they were given double rations because they had to man the pumps four times a day, suffered from exhaustion, and some of them hid themselves so that they would not have to attempt the impossible hour after hour. They cared little for their lives, it seemed; one of them told the Pilot that he could no longer endure always being tired, and that they might as well shut their eyes and let the ship go to the bottom. The Pilot told him that if he dared to jump overboard, the devil would get him, body and soul.

While the passengers and crew were enduring these torments, what was Doña Isabel doing? She occupied her dead husband's quarters, where she was attended by servants, but more important, she kept tight control over her private storeroom, which contained ample supplies of wine, oil, vinegar and flour. She also had a calf on board, and several small pigs. When starvation began to kill off the passengers, they naturally appealed to Doña Isabel for fragments of the stores she had stowed away for her own use, but she met each appeal with the reply that this food was hers.

When Quirós, in despair at seeing his sailors die at the pumps, received a cold rebuff from the Governess, he suggested that if she prized money so much, she might sell the food to the dying men, and he himself would give her re-

ceipts for any stores she issued and pay her when he got to
Manila. He warned the lady that if his men did not maintain their strength, the ship would perish and all would die,
and Doña Isabel would die too.

The Governess refused the offer. She said that the Pilot's
obligation to her, as the one who had raised funds for the
expedition and was in full command, was greater than his
obligation to these lowly sailors, and she suggested that if
he hanged a few of them to the yardarm, the rest would
learn to hold their tongues. But Quirós came back several
times and urged her so strongly that at last she issued
two jars of olive oil. That was soon used up, and the complaints against her continued.

The remaining soldiers were also despondent as they faced
the fact that many days must pass before they could reach
Manila. They swore that they would gladly exchange this
existence for a death sentence in a prison, where at least
they would be fed, or for a bench in a Turkish galley,
where they might at least hope for rescue or ransom.

The weather now grew so unbearable that many passengers died for lack of water, and strict inspection was maintained to insure that not a drop was wasted. Quirós himself
stood on guard to check each cupful as it was issued to the
dying. His rage was great, therefore, when he observed that
Doña Isabel was wasting large amounts in laundering her
dresses. Once when she sent her large jar back to be
filled again for washing clothes, Quirós cried that it did not
seem right for her to use so much water for such a useless
purpose when there was so grievous a shortage.

"Can I not do what I please with my own property?" she
demanded angrily.

"The water should be shared by all. You should cut down
your allowance," he pleaded, "so that the soldiers cannot
say that you wash your clothes with their life's blood."

The governess reacted by taking from him the keys to
the storeroom and giving them to one of her own servants,
so that she could continue to have all the water she wanted.
Many men on the ship muttered that the Pilot should not
allow himself to be ruled by a woman. If the matter were
to be put to a vote, they assured him, the crew would elect
the Pilot to lead them. But he answered, "Let her enjoy her
legal title for the brief time that remains."

Yet, fearing that the starving people might break open
the storeroom and loot the supplies, the Pilot returned once

more to argue with the lady. She answered: "Keep them away from me. They are always coming to me with complaints that I do not wish to hear."

For once the Pilot spoke out bitterly. "I know that it was you yourself and your brother that plotted to kill me at Santa Cruz, and you sharpened the knives. I'm not ashamed of my advice to you, and I excuse you for your lack of sense, for you are a woman." Then he added an observation which has ever since amused historians. "Very few women, I realize," he said, at his wits' end, "are as intelligent as Dido, Zenobia, and Semiramis."

In contrast to Doña Isabel's harsh behavior was that of an old man who had joined the enterprise somewhat by accident. Of him Quirós writes: "There had come on this expedition a venerable old man and good Christian, who in Lima had been a hermit and had served in the hospital of the natives. His name was Juan Leal [Loyal John], which he was through all events. This servant of God and worthy man, in poor health, for he was himself convalescent, devoted himself to the service of the sick with cheerful faith. He showed that his bowels were full of charity, for all that was done for the sick passed through his hands. He bled them, cupped them, made their beds, helped them to a good death, prepared and accompanied their bodies to burial, or got them out of danger; a man, in short, who did well in word and deed, though deeply feeling the numerous miserable sights he beheld. . . . But he died alone and forsaken, like the rest. He had gone about dressed in sackcloth next to his skin, and reaching half down his legs, with bare feet, and long hair and beard."

It was discovered that the little frigate was in even worse shape than the flagship, and was unable to maintain position, even though three men were sent aboard to help at the pumps. Several times the Pilot pleaded with the Governess to allow the people on the frigate to come aboard the flagship and let the leaky little vessel go adrift, but he could not get her to agree, for she remembered her investment in the doomed frigate and insisted that it complete the journey to Manila, where she could sell it.

She had her way, but the frigate did not quite reach Manila. One night, after Quirós had begged her in vain to pick up its crew, the little frigate with the body of Mendaña disappeared from sight and was not seen again. A long time later Quirós heard that the lost frigate had run aground in the Philippines with all sails set and the crew lying dead and stinking on the decks.

Next occurred one of the most incredible events of this expedition. Only one ship, the *San Jerónimo,* remained, and it almost wrecked itself on an immense, cruel reef which nearly took away the bottom. But early in 1596 Quirós made a landfall at Guam, whose natives rushed out in canoes bearing coconuts, rice, large fish and water. They offered to provide almost endless supplies to the starving men in exchange for old pieces of iron, which they needed badly for tools. But the trading ended abruptly when the Spaniards reverted to the custom of this voyage and wantonly shot two of the natives dead in an argument over an old iron hoop, whereupon the Guamanians sadly paddled away, taking with them the life-giving foods and the water that would have saved dozens of souls.

The sailors, seeing their salvation disappear, were mad to get ashore and obtain provisions for the last leg of the journey to Manila, but they were powerless, for they had no ropes by which to drop the longboat into the water, and Quirós refused to let them toss it overboard with no chance of recovering it, for it might turn out to be their only means of keeping afloat.

With a courage that few men could have commanded, Quirós resolutely set his face westward and ordered his starving, scurvy-ridden crew to drive the *San Jerónimo* on to Manila. In this way they left the island of Guam, whose food and water had been at their fingertips only to be lost through their brutal folly.

The deaths on this long haul through the central Pacific were lamentable, but Doña Isabel kept to her cabin with plenty of food and water and affected not to know of the misery. At last the Philippines hove in sight, but the crew was too exhausted to cheer. Most of the company were too weak even to be propped up to view the peak of the high mountain in sight; they were feeble skeletons who could only lie on the deck and whimper. They begged for a double ration of water to celebrate, but the Pilot told them this was not possible, for they must continue to ration the supply.

There were still many perils to be faced in threading the barrier of islands that dotted the route to Manila. If the ship foundered on one of the many reefs, anyone who might escape drowning would find ashore a horde of savages who would shoot him so full of arrows that he would look like St. Sebastian.

Doña Isabel in her private cabin now turned to piety, and with a book of devotions in her hand often raised her eyes to heaven and begged for divine mercy, but prudently she refused to issue any of her food. Nor did she, even now, ease up on discipline; and when, among the Philippine Islands, a married soldier sneaked ashore to get food for his starving wife, the Governess ordered him to be flogged as an example to the others, even though she knew that in his condition such a punishment meant death.

The boatswain interceded with the Pilot: "The Lady Governess, instead of ordering floggings, would do better by giving us food from the stores that she keeps for herself. All we have on this ship is flog here, hang there, plenty of orders, and no food!"

The Pilot went to Doña Isabel and pleaded that the guilty man had lost four children and all his possessions during the expedition, and that it would be unfair for him to be left without anything and to die without honor. She said that the man had disobeyed her orders and that he should suffer for it. But finally, due to the pleadings of Quirós, the prisoner was set free with a warning.

The ship was still twenty leagues from Manila when a boat was sent ashore to seek food. The natives fled, for they feared this to be an English ship, like that of Thomas Cavendish, who had frightened them in 1587 and had captured the Manila galleon. The men returned to the flagship without having found any food.

Acting as his own pilot in these dangerous, island-littered waters, Quirós threaded a channel only a stone's throw across. After this escape, he had to meet another crisis. The starving soldiers had assembled at the Governess' storeroom and were demanding their rations, or else, they threatened, they would break into the supplies locked inside.

Again the Pilot pleaded with the Governess to order that her food be served out to save the lives of the people. If she insisted upon money for it, he again offered personally to sign a promise to pay her for the food when they got to Manila. It was not just, he argued, that while there was still food on the ship the men should die for the lack of it.

"Sir captain," the lady answered coldly, "have you spent forty thousand pesos on this expedition, as I have? Or have these mutinous men agreed to underwrite all the costs? My poor husband has been badly repaid for all the expense he went to in making these discoveries!"

"My lady," said the Pilot, "I spent all my property, and each of these men has spent all he had to spend. Many have given up their lives, and spent all they had. That which belonged to my good friend the Governor, and which now belongs to your ladyship, must be used to bring us all to Manila."

Doña Isabel, hating the Pilot for his sentimental interventions, finally consented that her cherished calf might be slaughtered to feed the starving crew.

Then two boats full of natives from one of the Philippine Islands came along and offered food for barter. The Pilot exchanged two pairs of his shoes for two large baskets of rice, and shared this food among the people. The Governess had a chance to barter for two more baskets of rice, which would have saved many lives, but she thought that the bargain offered by the natives was too dear, and she let the canoes go back to shore.

When the *San Jerónimo* was almost in sight of Manila, the sailors finally demanded that the vessel be run up on the shore, as they were totally unable to work her further unless they had something to eat. All their food and water were gone, though the Governess still kept two sacks of flour and a little wine. Doña Isabel would not give in. She not only refused to distribute the food, stating that she was determined to sell it in Manila in order to buy masses for the soul of her dead husband, but she also commanded the sailors to keep the ship moving.

At this dreadful moment a boat came out from the shore, rowed by natives but containing four Spaniards of the colony, who seemed to the ship's people like four thousand angels. The Spaniards leaped aboard and saw the people lying sick, covered with revolting sores, barely hidden under rags and surrounded by misery. The visitors were so deeply moved by the horror of the ship that they could only exclaim, "Thanks be to God!"

One of the Spaniards descended to the sick bay and the women lying there screamed out to him, "Give us food! We are mad with hunger and thirst!" He came on deck again, and there in a pen he saw Doña Isabel's two pigs. He stared at them, then at the dying, and cried, "If you are starving why don't you kill those pigs?" He was told that the pigs belonged to the Governess. "What the devil!" he exclaimed. "Is this a time for courtesy about who owns the pigs?"

The Governess was thus shamed into ordering the pigs to be killed and eaten; but one starving soldier was heard to mutter, "Oh, the power of avarice, which will turn to stone even the heart of a gentle and pious woman, when the need is so clear and the remedy is so cheap!"

Then another boat, sent by the governor of the Philippines, arrived with fresh bread, wine and fruit, which was shared out and gobbled up immediately. The long night ended, and next day a barge arrived laden with fowls, calves, pigs, bread, wine and vegetables. On February 11, 1596, the ship anchored at the port of Manila. Pilot Quirós, with a sick crew on the verge of mutiny because of misery and starvation, had brought his sinking ship, with rotten spars and rigging, safely across more than four thousand miles of unknown ocean, from Santa Cruz to the capital of the Philippines.

Throngs of charitable Spaniards visited the ship, bringing food and other gifts. They had heard that this vessel had come from Peru to bring away the Queen of Sheba from the islands of Solomon. When they saw the great distress of the survivors and heard their story, they praised God that so many had been spared. On the journey from Santa Cruz fifty persons had died. "It is to be noted," concluded the Pilot philosophically, "that if the people who died had not died, those who survived would not have arrived with more than twenty jars of water and two sacks of flour left over."

Within a few days, ten more of the ship's company succumbed from the effects of their sufferings. But these deaths were forgotten in the many festivities that were held in Manila to celebrate the safe arrival of the Governess, who posed as the heroine of the expedition. She graced a procession of parties and gay ceremonies as guest of honor. She was comfortably lodged in the city, and when her year of widowhood had barely passed, she married again.

Her new husband was a young cavalier named Don Fernando de Castro, who was a cousin of the governor of Manila and a distant relative of Mendaña. The young man took possession of the goods and privileges of his wife, as was legally proper. In Manila the newlyweds raised money so that the *San Jerónimo* could be refitted and provisioned for the long voyage home to South America, since no other ship was available to take them back. Curiously, Pilot Quirós went home in the same vessel, but after what had happened on the fatal voyage to the South Pacific, it may be imagined that his relations with Doña Isabel were somewhat strained

It was clear that she and her new husband were determined to retain title to the islands discovered by Mendaña in the South Seas, and that they planned to return there and take up their kingdom. At first, Doña Isabel's petitions to His Majesty to be allowed to carry on the great work of Mendaña were received favorably, but gradually difficulties were interposed, and she never returned to seek the rich islands of King Solomon. What enraged Doña Isabel most was that at the same time the king rejected her plea, he decided to put the Solomon Islands expedition under the command of the skilled Portuguese pilot, Pedro Fernandez de Quirós. This peaceful, humane and zealous explorer, who dreamed of finding a great Southern Continent and becoming a second Columbus in the Pacific, was thus able to sail on the famous voyage of 1606, during which he discovered the Tuamotus and the New Hebrides, while his second in command, Luis Vaez de Torres, first sighted Torres Strait and came within thirty miles of the unsuspected continent of Australia.

Doña Isabel finally swallowed her disappointment and settled down in Peru as the wife of Fernando de Castro, by whom she had several children. Later she took her family back to her ancestral home in Galicia, where she supervised the setting up of an elaborate estate in the country. In the evening of her life we can hear her telling her offspring, "Had it not been for the greed and envy and meanness of a gang of low-born rascals, your mother would today be queen of the islands of King Solomon!"

7

Bully Hayes,
South Sea Buccaneer

An amazing American tore back and forth across the Pacific during the middle years of the last century, terrorizing nearly half a world and leaving in his wake a forecastle full of horrifying stories. He was charged with murder and piracy and bigamy and blackbirding, and the foul destruction of his entire family. His name was whispered at night on lonely atolls to frighten children. Native chiefs prayed to ancient gods that they might be spared visits from this terrible man. Police and warships of many nations tried to track him down, but he either eluded them or talked his way to freedom, and after thirty years of unparalleled depravity he died of natural causes—that is, he was murdered and thrown to the sharks by his cook, whom he had bullied once too often.

Today, looking soberly at the career of this unbelievable man, it is almost impossible to separate fact from legend, for there is no true account of his desperate adventures and upon a slim thread of proven incident has been hung all the romantic canvas of a great ocean. Nevertheless, an honest attempt should be made to isolate the true history before the sifting of legend becomes completely hopeless.

From the first day on which the present authors, in their separate ways, embarked upon the alluring Pacific, they have been haunted by stories of this sometimes diabolical, sometimes ridiculous man. From the wilds of New Zealand, where he roamed, to the loneliest islets of the farthest reef, where he marauded, they have heard improbable stories of his outrageous career. Never, so far as they can recall, have they ever heard a dull yarn, and they now welcome this opportunity to review the available sources. With the rollicking echo of the great ocean setting the rhythm for them, they herewith present all that is nowadays known about William Henry Hayes.

He was born in Cleveland, Ohio, in 1829, son of a grogshop keeper. As a boy he stole $4,000 from his father, it is said, and ran away to become a sailor on the Great Lakes. He married early. This woman, whose name we do not know, was his official wife, but when he became involved in a horse-stealing affair he left town hurriedly with a tarnished reputation and a strange lady he had picked up near his father's saloon. There is some evidence that he skipped out of New York as a passenger on the ship *Canton* on March 4, 1853, and here the confusion really begins.

For into the port of Singapore, the capital of rascaldom, the *Canton* moved smartly on July 11, 1853, under the command of twenty-four-year-old Captain Bully Hayes. How he had got control of the ship no one knows, and whether he was then the rightful owner is uncertain, but as we shall see, this matter of papers never bothered Hayes, and one week after arriving in Singapore, he sold the *Canton* at a good price.

He reappeared dramatically in Singapore on December 21, 1855, as master of the American bark *Otranto,* his papers apparently in order, and with a load of cargo he had picked up at Swatow. Disposing of the *Otranto,* on March 10, 1856, he mysteriously bought back the *Canton,* which gave him legal title to her, and promptly painted out her old letters and renamed her the *C. W. Bradley, Junior,* after the American consul at Singapore. This tribute to an American official is important, for all during his years of outrage in the Pacific, Hayes was able to hoodwink American officialdom, which at times seemed to be his best defender and often his only defense against long overdue justice. Bully loved consuls.

On April 1, a fit day for the deed, he mortgaged his new ship to the firm of Dare & Webster, chandlers, for $3000 and next day left for a profitable voyage to Shangai. It looked as if Singapore had acquired a competent and industrious new captain, so that on his return to that city in November, 1856, Hayes stayed two days in port and loaded the *C. W. Bradley, Junior,* with every conceivable cargo he could lay hands on, promising full payment next day. The otherwise canny British merchants of Singapore appeared willing to trust any ship sponsored by the American consul, and the cargo was a rich one. Before dawn on November 20 Hayes fled Singapore's island-studded harbor without clearing customs, without papers, without orders of any kind. He had discovered how easy it was to "pay your creditors with the foresheet." He was well on his way to becoming the Pacific's foremost absconder.

A few weeks later he turned up in the steaming tropical city of Batavia, in Java, where he sold his rich cargo and refilled the *C. W. Bradley, Junior,* with the choicest items from the warehouses of hardheaded Dutch merchants. Properly suspicious of Hayes, these shrewd men demanded payment before he returned to his ship. He willingly paid them in full, using forged drafts upon the Singapore chandlers, Dare & Webster.

Up to this time the arrival of Captain Hayes in any port had signaled the beginning of some clever and profitable fraud, but his next call showed another side of the dashing young American. He entered society. Not only was he a master thief of Singapore merchandise—he was an even greater thief of women's hearts.

Fremantle, at that time a little convict colony perched on the western coast of Australia, nestles on a hook of land where the life is hospitable and the climate delightful. Captain Hayes sold off his stolen Java goods in Fremantle and settled down to enjoy at leisure the gay life of the town. Trim-looking, impeccably dressed and always affable, he soon proved that his arrival at any party was the highlight of the evening. He sang extremely well and displayed a courteousness to women that was unusual in the Australia of that day. He was clearly the lion of Fremantle society and celebrated that fact by becoming formally and sentimentally engaged to the harbormaster's daughter.

Dashing young Captain Hayes took his ship on several passenger trips to Adelaide, and made out handsomely on the fares because overland travel between that city and Western Australia was impossible owing to the forbidding desert that interposed its thousand miles of desolation. But the profits that Hayes made on these trips were lost when the

sleuths employed by Dare & Webster of Singapore caught
up with him and forced him to sell the *Bradley* at auction.
The ship brought only enough to pay the mortgage of
£1250.

The people of Fremantle, far from being suspicious at this
turn of events, considered the sale merely a business re-
versal and invited Hayes to move his belongings ashore, where
he enjoyed such a hilarious time that he celebrated his warm
feelings toward Australia by jilting the harbormaster's
daughter and on August 25, 1857, marrying the liveliest and
prettiest widow in town, Mrs. Amelia Littleton.

The following year, supported by his new—and bigamous
—wife's high spirits, Hayes successfully fought off a horde of
creditors from three countries and finally escaped them by
submitting himself manfully to insolvency proceedings in
the Australian courts. On March 16, 1858, while still an un-
discharged bankrupt, Hayes pulled one of his neatest tricks
and escaped jurisdiction of the Western Australian courts.

Learning that the schooner *Waitemata* was weighing anchor
for Melbourne, Hayes primed a crony to launch the rumor
that he had got away that morning on a brig that had
sailed for Newcastle. The creditors hastily chartered a tug
and rushed vainly in pursuit, but while they were returning,
sad and seasick, they passed the *Waitemata* setting forth on
its way to Melbourne with Hayes aboard. His loyal wife
later joined him in that city.

There he persuaded Daniel A. Osborn, owner of the British
ship *Orestes,* to give him command. How Hayes, an American
with no certificate of maritime competency, managed to
clear customs on September 2, 1858, for Vancouver is a
mystery. After the ship had left port Osborn apparently reflected on his foolhardy choice of a captain and dispatched
warnings to various British consuls, but their intervention was
not required, because the *Orestes'* supercargo, Clements,
found the behavior of his captain so extraordinary that he
had the American thrown off his own ship in Honolulu, on
the charge that he had swindled several of his passengers on
the trip.

Honolulu, now a bustling port under the rule of King
Kamehameha IV, was almost too easy for Hayes. Within a
few weeks he had passed worthless drafts, borrowed from
prominent citizens and enlisted the money of business adventurers. With $2000 in cash, he and his wife left for San

Francisco in one of the bark *Adelaide*'s most expensive cabins.

Anyone familiar with Hayes could predict what story the San Francisco *Bulletin* would sooner or later carry. On August 31, 1859, the paper informed its readers: "The brig *Ellenita*, Captain Hayes, ran off on Sunday night without clearing papers, and leaving creditors to the amount of several thousand dollars in the lurch. The captain pretended that he was about to sail for Melbourne, and obtained credit for the repair of the vessel and large amounts of stores, besides the baggage of intending passengers, with all of which he put off on an unknown and unlawful voyage." Of course, he left many creditors, including M. S. Morrison, to whom he still owed $300 on the purchase price of the brig. Adding a new wrinkle, he also swindled Mr. Morrison out of some forty tons of beans. Bully left his wife Amelia behind, abandoning her to the mercies of the San Francisco water front.

Cruising the Pacific in his fine new ship, Captain Hayes found that he needed to replenish his water stores, and so put in at the Hawaiian island of Maui, where he not only acquired water but also a good deal of gold for goods he smuggled ashore at night. On September 18 he was arrested by Sheriff Peter Treadway of Lahaina, but Hayes talked fast and persuaded the burly sheriff to come aboard the ship and see for himself that there could not possibly be any contraband on the *Ellenita*. After the sheriff had been heavily plied with liquor in the cabin, Hayes weighed anchor and cleared the port. Then, wakening the pudgy sheriff, Hayes told him coldly, "Go back on shore without me or stay aboard and take a long trip to Tahiti." The sheriff studied for a moment, then climbed down into his boat and started rowing.

Actually, Sheriff Treadway made a wise choice, for a month after he went ashore with the hootings of Hayes's crew in his ears, the *Ellenita* foundered in heavy seas. The cargo of stolen beans shifted and plugged up the pumps. Hayes, with eleven others, navigated the lifeboat into Samoa in four stormy days. A makeshift raft carried the other sixteen crew members for twenty terrifying days through sharks and storms and blazing sun. The men survived only by eating raw shark's flesh, and finally made landfall on lonely Wallis Island with the loss of only one man.

By one of the strange coincidences that marked Hayes's life, the men from the boat and the survivors from the raft were reunited seventy-seven days later, when a British warship and an island trading brig sailed simultaneously into Sydney Harbor on New Year's Day. There was a drunken reunion, but Captain Hayes's celebration was quickly over, for Australia was at last catching up with her adopted son from Cleveland.

On January 6, the Sydney *Morning Herald* reprinted a scathing biography of Hayes from the Honolulu *Advertiser*. Next day the same paper reported that Hayes had been charged with assault on a fifteen-year-old girl named Cornelia Murray on board the *Ellenita* soon after leaving San Francisco. The case was dismissed, however, for lack of corroboration.

On the ninth, the Sydney *Empire* came out with an exposé under the heading: "The Career of a Remarkable Scoundrel." Hayes was therein described as "thirty-two years of age, six feet high, fifteen stone weight [210 pounds], and of rather plausible, bluff exterior, which with many, it would seem, has enabled him to pass off, until a settlement came, as a very honest jolly seaman, and he is a man who at times spends his money, or the money in his possession, very liberally. . . . The success of this enormous mercantile humbug (he having possessed himself probably to the amount of $20,000, or to the value thereof, if not twice as much, in the last eight years, without any equivalent but impudence and promises) is the more singular from the fact that he is a man of the most meager education, and possessing no particular qualities, except rare cunning, attended by an unlimited command of impudence, and a somewhat more than average degree of physical power."

In response, in the *Herald* for January 12 appeared a rambling letter signed by Hayes—but one which his illiterate hand was clearly incapable of framing—denying all charges except fooling Sheriff Treadway. In the same issue four other letters appeared in Hayes's defense. Subsequently it was found that all five had been written by a friend who had sailed with Hayes on the *Bradley*.

The fundamental character of Hayes was now becoming widely known throughout the Pacific. He was a cheap swindler, a bully, a minor confidence man, a thief, a ready bigamist, and about to prove himself a ravisher of young girls. The Sydney Police Court accordingly heard charges against Hayes in connection with a £53 fraud executed some time before in Samoa, but the case had to be dropped because of faulty jurisdiction. However, Australian creditors combined against him and he was popped into Darlinghurst Prison, from which he was duly released as an insolvent debtor.

At this point Hayes descended to the ridiculous and became a member of a blackface minstrel troupe; this style of entertainment had lately been introduced from America and had proved quite popular at back-country race meetings and stock shows.

At intermission time between the minstrel acts, Hayes spent his time in the barroom seeking out gullible investors, and soon uncovered a wealthy country gentleman who was willing to finance the purchase of the sturdy bark *Launceston* in April, 1861.

This ship left Newcastle with a cargo of coal intended for Bombay, but when Captain Hayes reached Surabaja, on the north Java coast, temptation proved too great and he sold the coal for his own pocket and took on a charter cargo of sugar and coffee. But at this moment an article in a Singapore newspaper arrived with details of the gruesome commercial history of the American captain, and the frightened merchants and underwriters of Hayes's cargo offered to pay him full freight to the next port if he would only give them back their goods. Bully agreed, but after they had relaxed their guard, he slipped out of port with a cargo worth fully $100,000 plus £500 he owed his agents.

He and the *Launceston* then vanished and the ship was next heard of when it returned to Java under different owners, who sold it for ready cash.

Hayes, who never explained how he had lost his ship, now turned up with a new trick, as reported by the Melbourne *Age* on September 9, 1862: "The notorious Captain Hayes, with the bark *Cincinnati,* visited Sydney, and after engaging passengers for Dunedin, New Zealand, and receiving their passage money, sailed away without a single passenger."

But Hayes was himself a passenger when, on September 13, the *Cincinnati,* under another captain, sailed from Newcastle, up the coast. Bully now began a phase of his career that combined high adventure, art and another fling at bigamy. Among his fellow passengers aboard a ship heading for New Zealand was a traveling company of vaudeville artists, including a Mr. and Mrs. Glogski, a handsome widow named Mrs. Roma Buckingham, her brother, her daughter and four talented sons called The Masters Buckingham. After a five-day passage, Hayes married Mrs. Buckingham and became the loving stepfather of her five children.

He became a member of the vaudeville troupe and seems to have enjoyed a splendid season in New Zealand, but the lure of the sea was too strong and in some unaccountable way he turned up several months later as master of the *Black Diamond*, out of Sydney. With his reputation broadcast throughout the Pacific, how he could find an Australian owner willing to entrust him with a costly ship baffles the imagination, but soon the *Black Diamond* was loaded with the seven-fold Hayes family and, appropriately, a cargo of coal which was to be delivered within a few days up the Australian coast.

This time an authentic cyclone tore away Bully's sails and put three feet of water in his hold. Running the crippled ship before the wind, Hayes fought out the storm for fourteen days and wound up clear across the Tasman Sea near Auckland, New Zealand. "An act of God," Hayes said and promptly sold the cargo, took on a new one, and early one blustery Monday morning when no one was looking slipped out of the harbor with all bills unpaid.

Tragedy struck on August 19 when the *Black Diamond* was hiding in Croisselles Bay, off New Zealand's South Island. The crew was busy loading firewood and calking leaky seams, so Bully borrowed a yacht and went for a sail with his latest wife, their thirteen-month-old baby girl, Roma's younger brother and a maidservant. Caught in a squall, the boat sank instantly, and Hayes saved his own life by swimming to shore. His family drowned; only the body of the baby reached land. Bully's enemies openly accused him of murdering his whole family, but no evidence could be established.

The New Zealand residents were sympathetic to the bereaved captain, but the mortgagor of the *Black Diamond* was demanding his money, and a whaleboat full of special constables sailed to Croisselles Bay and there boarded and seized the vessel. Bully, taken unawares, could do little more than turn the air blue with inquiries concerning the reason for this early-morning call. The *Black Diamond* was sailed to the nearby port of Nelson and was lost to him, but on October 2 he sneaked out of town on the *Phoebe*, despite a writ against him from a laborer to whom he owed money for chopping firewood.

Where did he hide? Probably only Bully Hayes would have adopted the scheme, for he rejoined the Glogskis and toured with their show, The Buckingham Family, which must have aroused guilty feelings in Roma's widower, if anything could.

But Hayes did not stick with the troupe for long. He had often boasted in bars that one of his strongest points was his ability to pick up a ship when he needed one, and a beautiful young stewardess to keep him company. In the little coastal town of Akaroa he stole the tiny cutter *Wave* and lured on board a sixteen-year-old Irish orphan named Helen Murray, his come-on being that she would accompany him to the port of Lyttelton to join some other girls whom he was taking on an important theatrical tour of China.

But little Helen Murray was more than a match for Bully. A storm overtook the cutter as it headed up the coast, and for several days the girl fought off Hayes's courtship, screaming to be put ashore. She would not go below with him and remained on deck even when gales blew, clinging to the mast during one bad spell when waves washed the deck.

Hayes resorted to violent language, threatening that she must go below with him or he would throw her off the ship. When she persisted in defying him, testified one disgusted witness to his brutality, "he dragged her most violently, tore off her clothes, and eventually lifted her into a boat to take her ashore. The night was wet and cold, and with a view to compel her to go on board again on his own terms he represented her to the pilot as a character that no respectable man would admit to his house."

Another boatload of constables caught up with Hayes in January, 1865, but he talked his way clear of charges that he had abducted Helen Murray and had stolen the *Wave*. However, his reputation suffered a damaging blow when one of the constables noted that the buccaneer carried in his cabin a pair of curling irons that presumably were in constant use to curl the long locks that covered his ears.

On February 1, 1865, as the Civil War was drawing to a close in America, Hayes walked into the ship registry office in Wellington, the capital of New Zealand, and claimed sole ownership of the schooner *Shamrock*. This so astonished the officials that they started inquiries to find out how this amazing man had acquired a new ship. It was discovered that Bully had been paying wild court to a New Zealand lovely who had put up the needed £500. She was widely known to the saloon trade, a contemporary newspaper confided, as "The Bull Pup."

Hayes and his new ship disappeared for a few months, then returned with a cargo of oranges, lemons, pigs and hand-carved curios. On his next appearance he offered the people of Lyttelton more oranges and lemons, some coconuts, grown hogs, rich shells, imitation canoes, colorful hunks of coral, long-tipped spears, war clubs and well-woven house mats. And thus it was discovered that Bully Hayes had finally worked the region where his fame would never die. He had been to the South Sea Islands.

Apparently he traded well, for he now imitated his earlier rich experience in Fremantle, Australia. He moved ashore at the port of Lyttelton as a respected sea captain, tasted the joys of a refined society and married his fourth wife, Emily Mary Butler, by whom he quickly had twin daughters. The babies were named Laurina Helen Jessie and Leonora Harriett Mary and were reared in Apia, the sweet, somnolent capital of British Samoa. Both girls later married. Undoubtedly Bully Hayes has grandchildren living in the Pacific region today. A son, Fred, later born to the couple, was to try to carry on his father's trading business in the South Seas.

To celebrate the birth of his twins on May 2, 1866, Hayes sold the *Shamrock* and bought the sturdy brig *Rona*, which he mortgaged for £970—a sum which, of course, he never paid. He made a quick trip to Fiji and another to Rarotonga, but as he was unloading this cargo the mortgagors of his ship caught up with him. It was the last day of 1866, and the port officials decided to allow him to celebrate New Year's Day a free man, which he did by auctioning off his entire cargo for cash, unloading it at night and slipping out of the harbor while those ashore were engaged in year-end festivities.

At this time the Maori War, which ravaged New Zealand for years, flared up, and Hayes made a tidy sum by smuggling powder and lead to the natives at hidden coastal anchorages. To mislead searchers, he stowed the powder under the ship's cabin and littered the floor with straw. A single dropped spark would have blown the *Rona* to bits, so no one ever thought of looking there for live powder. After a particularly successful blockade-running cruise, Hayes pocketed his profits and left New Zealand for good. It is said that the entire shipping industry sighed with relief.

He soon appeared at Savage Island, south of Samoa, where

the missionary ship *John Williams* had been wrecked on January 8, 1867. Hayes bought the wreck for $500 gained in running guns, but was unable to get the ship afloat. The salvaged cargo, however, made the buccaneer a good profit. He then agreed, for a price, to carry the surviving missionaries to their island posts. On the voyage Bully ordered his mate to go aloft, and when that seaman began swearing audibly, Hayes bellowed: "Come down, you rat! Don't you know you are on board a missionary ship? If there's any swearing to be done here, I'll do it all!"

The Reverend James Chalmers wrote later in his autobiography that on this trip Bully was "a perfect host and a thorough gentleman." But he reported that several times the skipper lost his temper and did highly unusual things, "acting under the influence of passion more like a madman than a sane man." Chalmers then related how Bully nearly killed his supercargo during a quarrel by battering him about the head with a bag containing several hundred silver dollars, final payment of the missionaries' fares. Hayes then pitched the money disgustedly into the sea, shouting that it was not fit for a decent man to keep since it had touched such a skunk as his supercargo!

Bully Hayes was now thirty-eight years old, an intrepid sea captain and a confirmed confidence man. He probably could have continued for years, stealing ships and mulcting chandlers, but he was about to launch upon a new kind of adventure that would account for his principal fame throughout the Pacific. All that had transpired up to now, lurid though it was, served merely as preliminary to the main action of his life, and as he stands poised at his personal crossroads, let us try to reconstruct the man as his contemporaries saw him.

The only picture of Hayes that may be authentic is a color sketch made in 1912 by the famed Australian artist and novelist Norman Lindsay, which Louis Becke, the Australian writer who lived on Hayes's ship for months, agreed was a faithful likeness. It shows a muscular, bull-necked man with dark hair, mustache and beard, and the face of a determined pugilist. We are not even sure of the exact color of the hair. Becke said it was black; but others say it was brown, and one book consistently calls him a "blond giant." However, most of the accounts by those who knew Bully personally do agree on other main features.

Becke recalled that at his first meeting with Hayes he saw

"a tremendously powerful man, with a heavy and carefully trimmed beard. . . . I noticed that he had wonderfully bright blue eyes that seemed full of fun and laughter."

Wrote Edward Reeves in 1898: "I remember Hayes in New Zealand in the sixties. . . . He enjoyed stealing a few pounds as much as seizing a merchant ship and making crew and passengers walk the plank. . . . He was a stout, bald, pleasant-looking man of good manners, chivalrous, with a certain, or rather uncertain, code of honor of his own—loyal to anyone who did him a good turn; gentle to animals, fond of all kinds of pets, especially of birds." But George Britt, who once arrested Hayes, remarked: "He was a bad-looking man—a fine, well built man, but there was something bad about his eyes. You could not move without their following your slightest motion."

Other descriptions, from people who did not know him at first hand, include a passage from Frederick J. Moss: " 'Hayes was a great, big-bearded, bald-headed man,' said one of my Ponape informants, 'weighing 236 pounds, with a soft voice and persuading ways.' He was an American, and must have been of what Americans call the magnetic type. 'Mad as a hatter at times,' said one of the men who sailed with him."

Stonehewer Cooper wrote: "Captain Hayes was a handsome man of above the middle height, with a long brown beard always in perfect order. He had a charming manner, dressed always in the perfection of taste, and could cut a confiding friend's throat or scuttle his ship with a grace which, at any rate in the Pacific, was unequalled."

Miss Carolyn Gordon-Cumming, an English lady who was visiting in Apia, Samoa, at the time of Bully's death, saw in the French convent there the twin daughters of "the notorious Bully Hayes, of whose piratical exploits I have heard many a highly seasoned yarn from the older residents of Fiji, where he occasionally appeared, as he did in all the other groups, as a very erratic comet, coming, and especially vanishing, when least expected, each time in a different ship, of which by some means he had contrived to get possession; always engaged in successful trade with stolen goods; ever bland and winning in manner, dressed like a gentleman, decidedly handsome, with long silky brown beard; with a temper rarely ruffled, but with an iron will, for a more thoroughgoing scoundrel never sailed the seas."

W. B. Churchward, consul at Samoa in 1881-85, remarked: "My informants told me that although more brutal than any beast when enraged, this pirate could, when he liked, assume a courteous behavior and address positively fascinating, and calculated to deceive even the greatest skeptic. Although self-educated, he could converse fluently and cleverly on all ordinary topics and if he were judged by his handsome and gentlemanly personal appearance, the lie direct would be given to the multitudinous reports of his lawless career. To see in 1876 an elderly, well-dressed man in missionary black frock coat and tall hat with a flowing gray beard sweeping his expansive chest, above which smiled a handsome and benevolent countenance fit for a bishop, and be told that the entire person was that of an undoubted pirate who was far from being free of having committed murder, would astonish any man in his sober senses. Yet such was Bully Hayes in his best rig on shore in the colonies. In spite of his many ruffianisms, some of which were of so gross a nature as to preclude mention, Hayes had many friends, even among those whom he had swindled, at all events in Samoa. Hayes was commonly believed to have indulged somewhat in murder. . . . Yet I never heard in any conversation a positive statement of his having done so."

Perhaps the best conclusion comes from Charles Elson, who was mate aboard the little ship *Lotus* when Bully met his death: "Despite his evil life Hayes carried something big in his soul. Nature used the extremes of emotion when she molded him. To the student of human nature Bully Hayes is a pathetic figure. Only fifty years of age when slain, he might have attained an honorable career had he but learned self-discipline early in life. He was indeed a strange mixture of a man."

It was in 1867 that Bully delivered the missionaries to their appropriate islands, and thereafter for some months the outer world had no news of the buccaneer, who seemed to have disappeared. It was rumored that he had run a valuable cargo to Hawaii, but Honolulu had heard nothing of him, and was glad. Others claimed that he was back in China, but those ports did not see him, and no one in Swatow regretted his absence. There were other rumors, and then the ugly news broke.

In December, 1868, Hayes's ship *Rona* arrived at Papeete, the languid capital city of Tahiti, where Bully announced in a loud voice that below decks he had 150 prime natives for sale as contract laborers. With this he kicked open the hatches, and in the hold the planters of Tahiti saw the first

cramped, sick and struggling mass of virtual slaves that
Hayes would steal in the remaining years of his life. He had
gone into the blackbird business, recruiting South Sea natives to serve as plantation hands.

He summoned the whimpering Savage Islanders on deck
and they filed forth, blinking in the sun, their long black
hair straggling to their brown shoulders, with despair mark-
ing their normally happy faces. It was as if they had been
grabbed from the Stone Age and hauled unwillingly into
the dollar economy of the present. They had no idea where
they were, nor for what reasons, nor for how long. All these
Polynesian men and women knew was that for every one
who lived to reach this strange, soft port, another had died,
either from white men's diseases or from the fiery sticks
that shot death or from beatings or from lack of food on
the long voyage eastward from their island.

They were among the first blackbirds stolen from Savage
Island and their captor, Bully Hayes, was about to become
the greatest of the blackbirders.

Slavery reached the Pacific just as it was about to die out
in the United States, for it was our Civil War that disrupted
the world cotton trade and made cotton growing in northern
Australia enormously profitable. Therefore in the 1860's
Australia suddenly required many hands to work the cotton
fields. When the cotton boom was over, many more blackbirds were needed for the Queensland sugar plantations. Toward 1870 the demand for Kanakas became very great, from
Hawaii to Queensland, from Tahiti to Fiji, and at one time
there were more than fifty vessels in the trade of blackbirding. The abuses became so horrifying that the British
government put five small gunboats on patrol to overhaul
ships that might have unwilling slaves aboard. When this
failed, the Queensland government ordered that every labor
ship have an official aboard to see that the law was observed; but at least one member of the blackbird trade
stated that many government observers were drunk nine
days out of ten and did as much recruiting as anybody,
collecting good bonuses from labor-hungry plantation owners.

The laborers were recruited—for a pretense of legality
was scrupulously maintained—by adventurous sea captains
who were supposed to roam the islands inviting strong young
men to work on a distant plantation. No force was to be
used, the incoming islander was called a contract laborer,

and when his term was over he was supposed to be sent back home to the island of his origin.

The classic example of how these ground rules were observed came in 1871 when a respectable and even pious Melbourne doctor, James Patrick Murray, chartered the brig *Carl* in order to go among the South Sea Islands recruiting help for the plantations of Fiji.

The doctor was one of the first to use the trick of having his men reverse their collars, carry black books under their arms and go ashore disguised as missionaries. When the congregation was assembled to hear the word of God, the good doctor flashed his guns, drove the islanders into his boats and bolted them under his ship's hatches.

When this device no longer worked, he had his crew lash stout ropes to cannon butts, anchors and other heavy objects. Then, by displaying trade goods, he lured dozens of native canoes to the side of his ship, whereupon his sailors dropped the anchors and cannons plumb through the canoes, destroying them. The ropes were belayed, however, so that the iron weights could be retrieved and dropped next time.

Meanwhile, boat crews sped among the capsized natives and dragged them in as prime bodies for the canefields. If a man was clearly wounded from the falling iron, so that he would be of little use as a field hand, he was allowed to drown, or was even struck over the head with an oar so that he might not swim back to shore.

With his hold full of Solomon Island natives—there was barely room for each man to lie down—Dr. Murray sailed off toward Fiji to market them. But on the hot, rolling passage to the southeast, the men below decks became frightened and started to cry out. Moreover, they were starving, for the customary ration was one old coconut every other day for each two men. Their complaining voices were annoying to the crew, and the natives also banged on the locked hatches with bunk poles.

One morning a tough crew member casually asked Dr. Murray: "What would people say to my killing twelve niggers before breakfast?"

"My word!" the doctor laughed. "That's the way to pop them off."

The crew took revolvers and shot the natives in the dark hold. Whenever a black head could be spotted, a bullet was sent through it.

"Shoot them! Shoot them!" the pleased doctor encouraged his men. "Shoot every one of them!"

Whenever a noise came from the hold, another fusillade was launched, but by this time such panic reigned below decks that the doctor felt he ought to teach the black men a permanent lesson. Accordingly he grabbed an auger and bored holes through the bulkheads of the fore cabin, whence he and his crew used revolvers to fire right into the heart of the mob, picking off any natives who looked as if they might cause trouble. It is recorded that during the massacre the doctor encouraged his fellow hunters by lustily chanting "Marching Through Georgia."

When the morning's shoot was ended, the doctor ordered breakfast, and when the meal was served, offered prayers, as was his custom.

After the food had been removed, a ladder was lowered into the hold and those natives still alive were allowed to crawl on deck, where Dr. Murray had them lined up for medical inspection. Coldly he went down the line and studied the wounds.

"This man is worth saving," he said. "This man is not."

When the natives were divided into two groups, Dr. Murray said in a clear voice, pointing to the maimed who would probably not bring a good price at the slave marts, "Throw them over."

The first to be thrown to the sharks, which trailed all ships in these warm waters, was a young boy who happened to have six fingers and six toes, which signified to the natives that their gods had marked the boy as their particular ward. When he was lifted to the rail the natives raised such a lament that the men holding the sacred child paused, but Dr. Murray stepped forward and struck the boy in the face, whereupon he toppled backward into the dark waves.

The spell broken, the other wounded men were pitched overboard, where their trails of telltale blood soon attracted the sharks.

Then the hold itself was entered and the dead bodies were hauled on deck and slid into the deep. In all, about sixty men were slaughtered that morning, at least sixteen by the doctor's own admission having been thrown to the sharks while still alive.

Although the tale of horror aboard the *Carl* became well known, Dr. Murray was never brought to trial, for he was allowed by a shocking miscarriage of justice to turn Queen's evidence, but his testimony against his crew members was so pusillanimous that they too escaped the justice they merited. It was left to Dr. Murray's father to pronounce sentence on his son. In a letter to a Sydney newspaper he said: "As regards Dr. Murray, the celebrated *Carl* man-catching approver whom I have for years cut off as a disgrace to creed, country, and family—your condemnation of that cruel, unhappy being I fully endorse and add, although opposed to capital punishment on principle, that if any of the *Carl* crew murderers ever ascend the gibbet for the seventy kidnaped and cruelly slaughtered poor Polynesians, Dr. Murray should be the first, as head."

Dr. Murray's grisly performance was merely the worst example of blackbirding. A catalogue of horrors could be compiled depicting the way in which sea captains of all nations plundered human lives in the Pacific in the forty years following 1863. To Australia alone 1500 natives were taken annually during that time.

Any native paddling his canoe in the South Seas could become a target for the blackbirders. Swift boat crews were trained to dart into a mass of canoes, cut out three or four with the ablest-looking young men, smash the canoes, haul the struggling swimmers into their boats and pitch them below decks.

It was especially profitable to kidnap whole congregations where missionaries had taught natives the blessings of Christianity, and the reason we know so much about the depredations of the blackbirders is that their operations were mostly directed against natives who had already been converted, because the docility taught by the missionaries made them more tractable in the fields. Only the repeated protests of dedicated missionaries finally mobilized public opinion against the blackbirders.

By far the cruelest device used by the blackbirders was that of subduing a hostile island by tossing ashore two or three natives infected with measles. Within a week this horrible disease, absolutely fatal to these people, would sweep an entire island. Men and women, quaking with fever, would dig pits in the sand and allow the cold sea water to cool their burning bodies, whereupon they would contract pneumonia and die. One of the authors of this book lived for several years on Melanesian islands where blackbirders had ravaged the populations, and he saw many flowering, lovely valleys in which a thousand people had once lived, but where six now huddled by the shore in desolation.

It would be too mournful to narrate the individual stories of islands whose entire male populations were carted off to slavery. Manihiki, Penrhyn, Fakaofo—the roll call is one of senseless horror, because when the total depopulation of an island was ordered, it was inevitably found that the slavers had acquired many captives they could not use, and these had to be tossed overboard.

But one expedition is remembered with particular remorse, for it exterminated an entire culture and left standing in the Pacific a haunting memory of the white man's extreme cruelty in this area. This depredation was performed by the worst of all the blackbirders, those from Peru, whose completely vicious behavior was challenged only by depraved captains from Chile.

Just as the American Civil War initiated slavery in the western Pacific, so the discovery of the properties of fertilizer encouraged the slave trade in the eastern half of the ocean, for entrepreneurs in Peru and Chile found that the guano deposits on rainless, rocky islands off their coasts provided the world's best and most concentrated source of cheap fertilizer. All they needed was labor to dig the solidified bird droppings.

Harder work has probably never existed in the world, and travelers reported that the rocky shores at the foot of the guano cliffs were customarily strewn with the bones of Indians and Pacific islanders who preferred to leap to certain death than to work another day under the lashes of the Peruvian overseers. It was to these guano pits that the natives of Easter Island were taken in 1862.

Of a known population of three thousand, about one third were carried off, including all able-bodied men, all priests, all male members of the royal line and all who could read the symbols of the unique and once powerful Easter Island culture. Of these thousand men, nine hundred perished quickly, coughing out their lungs in the guano pits. European governments forced the return of the remaining hundred, but measles broke out aboard ship, and only fifteen got back to Easter Island, where their latent measles erupted in a terrible plague that killed half the remaining population.

Thus in a brief space the Peruvian slavers had destroyed two out of every three people on Easter Island, and it is one of the great tragedies of the Pacific that among those dead were all the learned men. No one was left who could decipher the history of Easter Island. No one knew how to carve the gaunt stone statues that symbolize this ancient culture. An entire people had been paralyzed psychologically and has never recovered.

It was this filthy business that Bully Hayes now entered, and it seems from sketchy evidence that on August 29, 1871, Hayes was involved in one of the most hideous aspects of the entire trade. On that day a black slave ship, supposed to be Bully's, hove to off Florida Island, facing Guadalcanal in the Solomons. When five natives from Florida paddled out to inspect the ship, swift boats were dropped into the sea and were rowed quickly toward the Florida canoe. While the missionary Charles Hyde Brook stood on the shore, hiding his face in horror, the Florida men were beheaded, their bodies tossed into the sea and their heads collected in a heap to be taken back to the black ship.

The facts of the affair cannot be denied. Their meaning is obscure. It seems likely that the two boats dropped from Bully's ship contained one or two white men each—members of Bully's crew—and several head-hunting warriors from some tribe to the north of Florida. Certainly Bully's men were not chopping off heads, for there was no market for such items. But equally certainly, he had brought savages from one island to another and had not only permitted but had made possible a head-hunting raid. According to the records, this was often done by blackbirders in order to curry favor with chiefs, so they could get a hold full of natives for sale elsewhere.

Whether or not it was Hayes's ship that the Reverend Mr. Brook watched that day cannot now be decided. An investigation conducted by Lord Belmore in Sydney led him to conclude that it probably was, and he so reported to London on November 23, 1871. At any rate, Bully Hayes was now up to his neck in blackbirding, and for the rest of his life this was to be his main occupation. He seems to have made a good deal of money at his calling.

At the beginning of his career as blackbirder an ominous coincidence of such improbability occurred that certain religious people throughout the Pacific held that it could only be interpreted as God's divine intervention. Hayes had made so much money blackbirding that shortly he had two ships in the trade, the brig *Rona* and the brigantine *Samoa*. On

March 22, 1869, his two ships left the same port in the Society Islands—one headed north for California to pick up trading materials with which to lure natives aboard, and the other for blackbirding operations among the Samoan Islands to the west. Hayes was not destined to reach California, for the *Rona* sank at sea, and after two agonizing weeks of drifting, Hayes and his crew sighted an island which they correctly took to be Manihiki Atoll.

It was a minute speck in the vast Pacific, so small that it contained altogether only about a thousand acres, none of it much above sea level. It was nevertheless with some relief that Hayes led his starving men ashore, where to their astonishment they were hailed by loud cries from a band of shipwrecked sailors, who rushed down the blazing coral sands to meet them.

On the beach there was a moment of utter disbelief as the two groups of men halted and stared at each other. Then one of the sailors already on Manihiki cried, "My God! It's Bully Hayes!"

The greetings grew solemn, for one of the Manihiki sailors pointed grimly to the other side of the lagoon, where a ship lay piled on the reef, a total loss. It was Captain Hayes's second blackbirder, the *Samoa*.

Thus both of Bully's ships, one headed east, the other northwest, and departing at the same time from the same place, were lost and the castaway crews marooned together on one of the tiniest islands in the entire Pacific. A coincidence like this would have reformed most men, but Hayes supervised the building of a makeshift longboat out of salvaged timbers, and after a perilous voyage with little food and less water, his two crews made Samoa, without the loss of a man.

As soon as he got ashore Hayes started to look for a new ship. "There's money in blackbirding," he insisted and soon stepped aboard a dirty old schooner, the *Atlantic*, which he drove full speed back to Manihiki, where he kidnaped most of the islanders and brought them to Samoa as slaves. But at Pago Pago, in what was later to become American Samoa, a brave native chief, Maunga, strode out into the breaking surf and single-handedly upset Hayes's landing boats, whereupon the Manihiki blackbirds escaped.

Hayes was brought to judgment at Apia, where, in February, 1870, Consul Williams found him clearly guilty of stealing men and women and remanded him to Sydney for sentencing and jail. It seemed that Hayes's career as a black-birder was over.

But before Bully could be shipped to an Australian prison, another notorious American, probably even more cruel than Hayes, brought his ship into Apia and hell broke loose. Captain Ben Pease had met Bully Hayes, according to one account, when the two adventurers were commanding gunboats in the Imperial Chinese Navy. "The two became friends," wrote Louis Becke, "and in conjunction with some mandarins of high rank levied a system of blackmail upon the Chinese coasting junks that brought them—not the junks—in money very rapidly, and Hayes's daring attack on and capture of a nest of other and real pirates procured for him a good standing with the Chinese authorities. Pease soon got into trouble, however, and when a number of merchants who had been despoiled succeeded in proving that his gunboat was a worse terror to them than the pirates whom he worried, he disappeared for a time."

Pease's ship, a 250-ton brig specially built for the opium trade, was called the *Water Lily*, of Aberdeen, when Pease sailed her into Manila in 1868 in a damaged condition. The firm of Glover, Dow & Company bought her in Manila, renamed her the *Pioneer* and retained her captain. Pease proceeded to become famous as the first man to bring blackbird labor into the Fiji Islands.

Hayes broke his parole and bolted from jailless Apia on his pal's ship, which sailed on April 1, 1870. Pease—a Satanic-looking rascal with a black spade beard—was a more openly piratical operator than Hayes. His ship was heavily armed with cannons and breechloading rifles, and was manned by a large crew. The bulkhead to the big fore-hold was loopholed so that if the Kanaka recruits that often inhabited it caused any commotion, they could easily be shot down by rifles. Pease was accustomed to land a big armed party on a new island and take off any coconut oil he could find there. After rescuing Hayes from the law in Apia, Captain Ben steered for Savage Island, where by means of forged orders he and Bully obtained £300 worth of produce owned by J. and T. Skinner of Sydney.

Then, cruising the Bonin Islands, the pair fell out—over a woman, of course. Pease had bought a very beautiful girl from one of the chiefs for $250, which he told Hayes he did not intend to pay. Bully, with rare propriety, insisted that his partner either pay the sum or else give back the girl. He rescued her at pistol point and started to take her back ashore, but decided to ask the girl if she were afraid of Pease. When she said "no," Bully told her to follow his brother captain; but thereafter the two distrusted each other.

For some months, Hayes and Pease cruised the Western Carolines, mysteriously filling the brig with coconut oil and hawk-bill-turtle shell that brought $6 a pound. Then brazenly they sailed their ship right back to Apia, where Bully was still under arrest, and sold the cargo at a fat profit.

How was Hayes able to get away with this? It was said that he had bought off Consul Williams, with whom he now became chummy, and the charge was dropped. In fact, Williams, unworthy descendant of the angelic John Williams, foremost missionary of these regions, probably helped Hayes get his next job, a commission from the world-famous German firm of Godeffroy & Son, out of Hamburg, who dispatched Pease and Hayes to the Line Islands for more blackbirds, offering $100 a head for all the laborers landed in Samoa.

No one has solved the mystery of this savage trip, but when the brig *Pioneer* returned to Samoa, Captain Pease could not be seen and Bully Hayes was in sole charge. Pease, he explained, had tired of blackbirding, had sold his ship and had retired to China. People speculated, but the new captain's big right arm prevented suspicions from becoming charges. It was rumored that Pease had been caught by an American warship and taken to the United States as a pirate. Others claimed he had been killed in the Bonins. Many people believe that he was captured not by an American warship but by a Spanish one, from which he either jumped or was thrown while wearing full leg irons, which dragged him to his death. All we know for certain is that a monster vanished, and another turned up in possession of his ship.

Hayes now painted the ship a gleaming white, possibly to discourage identification of her as the *Water Lily,* which had been described as a black ship during the head-hunting episode. He hoisted over her the American flag, to which he was not entitled, and in a burst of fatherly affection rechristened her the *Leonora,* after his favorite daughter. Along with Cook's *Endeavour* and Bligh's *Bounty,* the *Leonora* was to rank among the most famous ships in Pacific history.

Bully now entered the serious business of hauling semi-yearly cargoes of coconut oil, copra and blackbirds—all obtained by fraud—into Samoa, but this grew tedious to a man of Hayes's temperament, and we find him in the legend-laden Tuamotu islands east and south of Tahiti. There he persuaded a dozen soft-eyed *vahines* to take a free pleasure cruise with him to Tahiti, where he was certain their charms would be more appreciated than at home. But when they were afloat, Hayes changed his mind and decided to skip Tahiti.

"We don't want to trouble the French authorities with extra work," he explained, and headed for the Marquesas, where he sold off four or five of the willing ladies to local lovers, either white or native. Hayes always threw a marriage party, with plenty of gin, as part of the bargain.

Any girls left over after such a cruise, and Hayes made many, would be dumped ashore somewhere with one of Hayes's famed testimonials. For many years after Bully's death, when a ship arrived in the Carolines or the Palaus, ladies would troop out to the dock to make the sailors welcome, each bearing tied to her pretty forehead with ribbons such interesting recommendations to the seafarers as this one, which has been preserved:

To All Whom It May Concern:
   I, William H. Hayes, hereby certify that the bearer of this, Marutahina of Vahitahi, was with me for four or five months, and I can confidently say that I can recommend her to any one in need of an active young wife, general help, or to do chores. She is a very good girl, and the sole support of her mother—an old thief with a tattooed back who lives on Reka Reka.

Hayes was reported in the Gilbert group in the fall of 1870, but nothing definite was heard of him until March 29, 1871, when the *Leonora*, bound for Hong Kong, put into the unlikely port of Bangkok in distress. After repairing leaks at the cost of most of her cargo, she cleared on April 26.

Back at his Samoan headquarters, Hayes was surprised on February 19, 1872, when two boat's crews from the U. S. S. *Narragansett* boarded the *Leonora*, took possession of her, and escorted her master to the warship to answer charges of oppression of the Caroline Islanders and of carrying too large a crew and armament for a peaceful merchant craft.

But after examining Hayes's crew and papers for three days, Captain Richard Meade could not find sufficient evidence to warrant shipping Bully to San Francisco for trial. No arms were found, and the crew was actually under complement. Bully's threats and fear of his heavy fist had probably intimidated most of the witnesses. Consul Williams also hampered the investigation at every turn in order to protect his crony, and Captain Meade's report implied that Williams had deliberately held back the required proof. After his acquittal, Bully rushed back to the *Leonora* and dressed her out with flags to celebrate his exoneration. He then gave the crew liberty, and they painted the town, seeking from pub to pub any witnesses against their captain. When they found one, they beat him up to teach him respect for the law. And legends continued to spread in the South Seas concerning the cunning of Bully Hayes.

Hayes himself contributed to the legend that had grown up around his name and kept it alive with barroom tales that displayed both his boastfulness and his capacity for invention. One of the most commonly heard is that he contracted in Hong Kong to take a load of Chinese immigrants to Australia, where a head tax of $50 had to be paid on each. He received the money in China, and then devised a means whereby he would not have to pay it out. Inside Sydney Harbor, at Watson's Bay, Bully choked both his pumps, started his fresh-water tanks, and set his colors at half mast, union down, to show his sore distress. When a tug came to his assistance and offered him a tow, his humanity overcame his selfishness, and he shouted: "Just take off and save these poor souls first, and I reckon we can beach the ship before you come back!" The tug, scenting rich salvage, took the Chinese into port and her captain paid the tax. Of course, when he returned, Hayes's ship was nowhere to be found. The story sounds rather like a barroom dream, for it seems especially incredible that a tug captain, even if he had the money, would pay out a heavy head tax on immigrants rescued by him.

This Chinese story, like many others, was probably circulated by Bully himself to show his smartness. One of his most goggle-eyed listeners was W. Akerstein, who led the party that took the *Black Diamond* from Hayes in 1864. Bully hinted to Akerstein then that Hayes was not his real name

that he made a voyage to Sydney in the *Sir Charles Napier*
in 1842 and that he served a prison term from 1843 to
1848 in Van Diemen's Land for forgery. He said that once
he was in a boat with £500,000 worth of gold and no food,
as a survivor of the famed *Madagascar*, a ship which cleared
Melbourne for London on August 12, 1853, with ninety passengers and a cargo that included 64,660 ounces of gold,
and was never heard of again.

Another frequently heard legend—which Bully certainly
would not have helped to circulate—is the yarn of the barber of Arrowtown. This New Zealand gold diggings provided
little in the way of entertainment, and bets were rife concerning the question of whether Hayes, then running the
United States Hotel, had one ear or two—one had presumably been cut off in his early years by a loser in a poker
game who accused Bully of cheating. A half-starved little
cockney was set up in business on Main Street behind a
striped pole, and one day word spread around that Bully
was in the chair.

After a bit of chatter, during which Hayes expressed a
strong preference for long locks over the sides of the head,
the barber daringly snipped off the hair that concealed the
stump of Bully's left ear. All the bloods of the town had
been listening in with delight, and rescued the terrified barber from instant pulverization, while Bully went wild and
wrecked the shop.

A few days later, the variety company of the Bucking-
hams, angry because Bully had married their leading lady,
put on an act called "The Barbarous Barber," in which Bully's
humiliation was parodied and vaudevillized into a comedy
classic; during the show, the audience chanted in unison
what were supposed to be Bully's words: "A little off the
top—you can leave the sides as they are!" One modern Hayes
expert comments on this episode: "Probably the only correct
statement in the foregoing is that Hayes had only one ear,
but he may have been born minus that organ."

But we must get back to the facts. And 1874 is a good
year to pick up the story, for it not only represented the
height of Bully's prosperity, but it was also the year when
he signed aboard an Australian lad of eighteen who would
later become the foremost chronicler of the South Sea trader
and Bully's personal Boswell. It is from the accounts of this
gifted youth, Louis Becke, that we know how Bully lived
at the peak of his power.

Hayes had made a few changes on his ship since the days when Captain Ben Pease stalked the quarter-deck of the brig. Topside the *Leonora* was flush-decked, with sleek, yachtlike lines. All ropes, all gear were meticulously ordered, while below the trade room, to which Hayes invited island chiefs when mulcting them of their coconuts and turtle shell, was kept like an ultra-neat country store. The hold, of course, was a horrible place where the blackbirds were stowed, and many Caroline and Solomon and Line Island natives died there on the long voyages and were pitched feet first into the consoling Pacific.

A feature of the *Leonora* was the main cabin, luxuriously fitted out with a fine collection of ancient and modern arms, the former for ornament, the latter for instant use. From his youth Hayes had been fond of old weapons and now he was rich enough to indulge his fancy, his artistic eye enabling him to display them effectively. And to liven the ship, Hayes usually carried with him one or two French poodles, which he spoiled outrageously.

The ship was kept spotlessly white by a polyglot crew of thirty, an unusually large number, since spare hands were required to kidnap natives, cut out canoes or storm island beaches in search of copra to be highjacked. The men were allowed two privileges that were rare at sea: they could buy as much gin, beer and rum as they could drink; and each man could have one native woman along, except the Chinese carpenter—he had two.

At sea the heavy hand of Hayes kept order and by means of the severest punishment prevented insubordination, but as soon as the anchor was down he allowed utter riot to take over the ship, and it always did. The clamor of yells, oaths and blows rose from the gambling circles in the forecastle, while women's wild screams sounded throughout the ship.

In these days Captain Hayes always had one or two young native girls with him, changing them from island to island. He was a rugged man and his fine figure relieved the monotony of atoll life, so that he never had trouble convincing island belles to cruise with him for a month or so; but since he rarely put back in to the same island before tiring of the girls he had picked up, his castoffs dotted the Pacific. But as in the Marquesas, he always endeavored to hook up any dismissed island beauty with some onshore lover who would at least give her a place to sleep.

In the notorious *Leonora*, heavy with arms, trading goods

and women, Bully was aimlessly prowling the South Pacific toward the end of 1873, and at the beginning of the new year crossed the Equator and put into Mili Atoll, one-time refuge of the *Globe* mutineers. It was here that he signed on Louis Becke.

In the southern Gilbert Islands, where Bully hoped to steal coconuts, he found the natives gripped in a famine. So he gave them food, and the first five who came aboard ate so furiously that they died. Then Bully, rationing his gifts, took more than one hundred starving men aboard his ship and transported them, at their request, to work on the German plantations at Ponape, where there was food. Before departing the starvation islands, however, he gave the remaining people nearly a ton of rice and many casks of biscuits, saying beatifically, "You can pay me when the sky of brass has broken, the rain falls, and the land is fertile once more."

One morning in March, Bully's men sighted the high and verdant hills of Kusaie rising from the sea miles in the distance and their spirits lifted, for this was one of the loveliest islands in the Pacific. Set apart from other groups, nobler by far than the atolls, this considerable island contained pleasant valleys as well as excellent harbors, which were favorite stopping places for the whale ships of the world. Sailors loved Kusaie, and Bully's men were no exceptions.

But when the *Leonora* put into the spacious harbor of Lele, the crew found the island in an uproar. Five white men, accompanied by a gang of savage natives from ill-named Pleasant Island to the south, had backed the wrong side in an uprising on Pleasant and had been banished in whaleboats. Ultimately they had reached Kusaie, whose natives were famed for their gentleness, and had reduced the island to a shambles.

The Pleasant invaders were savage fighters, each clothed only in a thin girdle of leaves and armed with a Snider carbine and a short stabbing knife. Their women, who had shared banishment in the whaleboats, were tall, handsome and even more deadly in brawls than the men. With nothing better to do, these dreadful savages, led by their five white companions, were systematically killing off the Kusaie men, raping their women and taking over their plantations.

This was the kind of situation Bully Hayes loved. After consulting with wizened old King Togusa ashore, Hayes wrapped himself in pugnacious dignity and, facing the five

ruffians, delivered his ultimatum. Either they would stop this
disgraceful behavior and release every Kusaie woman, un-
harmed, or the *Leonora*'s heavy guns would blow the marauders to bits. When the gangsters capitulated, Bully charged
the king a hefty fee, payable in coconut oil, for his services.
Then, in an aside to one of the traders, speaking in Spanish,
Bully explained that he was not going to betray his fellow
merchants, but they ought to cut out the rioting—and as
for his fee, he might as well earn the king's oil as let the
missionaries have it. Then, in a further gesture of comrade-
ship, he agreed to haul the whole troop of invaders to
Eniwetok, where they could collect coconut oil for him.

Thus at one swoop Bully rescued an island, got a free
cargo of oil and enlisted a group of traders to work for
him on Eniwetok.

But two nights later, as the overloaded *Leonora* sought
temporary shelter in another bay before her departure for
Eniwetok, a monstrous hurricane overwhelmed the harbor,
and Bully, with his ship hemmed inshore by two Yankee
whalers, could not maneuver her into the gale. Unable to
run out to sea, the proud and lovely *Leonora*, one of the
finest brigs that ever sailed the Pacific, was dismasted and
shattered on the jaws of the reef, and then pounded her
heart out and sank in fourteen fathoms of stormy sea.

Thanks to Bully's excellent seamanship and personal bravery, most of the passengers and crew escaped, including
Louis Becke, who helped get ashore a considerable amount
of stores, especially liquor, arms and ammunition.

At first Bully was all business. He smothered his grief over
the loss of the *Leonora* by building a big house that would
serve as a combined trading station and harem. Then he
presented the king of Kusaie with a formal bill for 48,000
coconuts in compensation for damages he had suffered
when the natives stole goods drifting ashore from the wreck.

On sunny days Bully would stand at the door of his
spacious dwelling and command his subjects like an emperor. His salvaged boats scurried along the shore to collect the tribute of nuts, which were unloaded at the stone
wharf he had built. In the middle of a tree-lined plaza,
also constructed by Bully, the women from Pleasant Island
would husk the nuts, split them open and pulp the kernel.
The pulp was then put in troughs and allowed to rot, while
the oil percolated into casks set below.

But a few weeks of this placid operation bored Bully,

and in his tedium he indulged in violent brawls with the five white traders he had earlier subdued. Then, in irritation at his enforced stay on Kusaie, he began to plunder the island as it had never been plundered before. He ordered young girls abducted and hauled into his harem. He stole everything of value he could find. He swore and raged and indulged in the most violent behavior.

Then he began to suspect treachery—for indeed it was strange that he was not assassinated—and in fits of extreme rage had some of his crew flogged until their backs were raw meat. One day he started out alone and declared war, unarmed, upon an entire village, driving the natives before him like sheep, felling with one great blow of his fist any man that tried to resist him. Then he personally captured half a dozen young girls and herded them along the beach to the quarters of his men, advising them to keep the girls until their families ransomed them.

Spurred by such behavior on the part of their leader, the lives of the *Leonora*'s men degenerated into a seven-month orgy of pandemonium, mutiny, violence and the most horrible oppression of the gentle brown-skinned natives. Hayes and his men outdid anything that even New England whalers had accomplished on this languorous island.

Those were the days when an American missionary, like some prophet of Israel, lamented: "Murdered men's bodies were picked up on the beach every morning . . . and the poor natives of Lele fled in terror of their lives."

The debacle at Kusaie ended dramatically when the British steam corvette H. M. S. *Rosario* put smartly into the harbor. Captain Hayes dressed in his best, combed his long side locks and went aboard to pay his respects to Captain A. E. Dupuis. "Good morning, gentlemen," he said expansively. "I am Captain Hayes of the brig *Leonora,* cast away on this island."

Captain Dupuis coldly studied the American and said stiffly: "Indeed! Then you are the very man I am looking for. Consider yourself my prisoner."

Becke later reported: "Bully was arrested on ninety-seven charges—every count, I believe, except leprosy."

Hearings were held before Captain Dupuis. Mr. B. G. Snow, representative of the American Board of Commissioners for Foreign Missions, advised the captain that "the course you contemplate in taking him to Sydney and delivering him up to the American authorities there will not only be approved, but applauded. It will certainly relieve our Micronesian seas of one of the greatest sources of annoyance we have had during the twenty and more years I have been a resident missionary on these islands."

Aside from that of annoying Mr. Snow, few charges could be supported against the redoubtable Bully. The disgruntled Danish ex-mate of the *Leonora,* N. Nahnsen, who had been dumped ashore at Kusaie by Hayes, deposed that at Pingelap in March, 1872, Bully had held a chief as a hostage for the delivery of two girls and 7000 coconuts, but had magnanimously settled for one girl and 5000 coconuts. An American, Henry Gardiner, and the *Leonora*'s halfcaste Fijian second mate, Bill Hicks, swore that, at Providence Island in July, 1872, Hayes had taken a ten-year-old Pingelap girl ashore and had violated her with brutality. But the charges were not proved.

When Hayes was no longer around, King Togusa of Kusaie supported the prosecution with the following letter:

> Strong's Island, Sept. 30, 1874
>
> To Capt. A. E. Dupuis, Kaptin Inglish Man of Wa *Rosario*: My Kind Friend,—I am glad to see your ship to my island at this time. I think because you come Kaptin Hayes he go. I am very glad for this. What for he fraid mon o wa? Spose he good man he no fraid. We think Kaptin Hayes one bad man. Spose he no run away, I like very much you take him on board your ship and carry him off. . . .
>
> Togusa (X his mark),
> King of Strong's Island

But Dupuis found that Hayes was so greatly feared by white and brown people alike that none would accuse him of criminal acts, and Dupuis would have exceeded his instructions by taking off an American on such charges as cruelty to native girls, who in those days had no rights whatever. It was doubly dangerous for a British warship to arrest a Yankee in 1875, when England had recently paid compensation of £300,000 to America for a breach of international law in the *Alabama* case. Hence Dupuis was remarkably careless in guarding Bully Hayes, and was not at all sorry to hear that Bully had escaped from Kusaie on the night of September 27, heading for Pingelap with another American, Harry Mulholland, in a fourteen-foot oak-built boat, one of those saved from the wreck of the *Leonora.*

Before departing Kusaie, Hayes wrote letters to various of his traders to tell them about his situation. The following of September 26 to Marshall, his agent on one of the Ellice group, is a sample of the unedited Hayes prose:

Friend Marshall,—I have lost my vessel on this last March, and I have never seen a sail since tel now. I am sezed heer by a ship of war; am goion to Sydney. But they cannot do anything with me I am sure. If not, I will be with you soon again. I have given to Mr. Beck, late clerk at Mrs. Macfarlan's stor, my power of attorney to settle with you. . . .

So Bully Hayes fled from Kusaie a free man, in an open boat with scant water and barely enough food to keep him going to the next islands. He was drifting north of Kusaie when he was spotted by an American whale ship, the *Arctic*, headed for the Spanish island of Guam.

Bully, strolling the rutted streets of this foreign colony, was now about forty-five years old, weighing well over two hundred despite his privations on the sea, sunburned, and graced by the long curls which hung about his ears. He would have to start his fortunes from scratch, for he lacked almost everything he needed. But he felt sure that this sleepy island would be a fertile new field for his business methods.

He was wrong. What happened next is the only incident in Hayes's long career of which he appeared to be intensely ashamed. Twice in one day he was outsmarted, and instead of stealing a ship, he had one stolen from him. And all because of sentiment.

Drawing on credit, Bully purchased the fifty-ton schooner *Arabia*, which cleared Guam on April 8, 1875, on a trading mission to the south. The goods to be traded, it turned out, were escaped convicts who had paid Bully $24 a head in advance. Normally Hayes would have accepted the money and fled, but since these passengers were convicts, Bully felt a spiritual obligation to them and actually loitered off the island until they could reach his ship. A few could not make it that first night, so Hayes unwisely drifted offshore during the dark hours, intending to pick up the other convicts at dawn.

But someone had alerted the Spanish military, and twenty guards had remained hidden through the night, waiting for Hayes. When he rowed ashore for the last convicts, the soldiers jumped him. Blandly he explained that he always came ashore at dawn to take a bath in the surf, and he might have got away with this unlikely story, but the convicts aboard the *Arabia*, uncontrolled in his absence, disclosed themselves and Hayes was plunked in jail, incommunicado.

The offshore convicts, seeing their captain taken and the soldiers about to send a boat out to recapture them, sensibly turned pirates. Cutting the cable and hoisting sail in a trice, they outdistanced the soldiers and struck for the high seas. Bully gazed his last on his new ship as it disappeared in the distance in the hands of the pirates. Later he heard that they had abandoned his schooner in the Palau group and made their way by other craft to Sydney, from which safe vantage they could revile the Spaniards freely.

Hayes was not so lucky. He was taken in chains to Manila, where a Spanish judge handed down a nine-month sentence for aiding escaped convicts, and it was while Bully was in the calaboose in that city that we have our most famous description of the buccaneer, and also the most uncharacteristic.

Captain Joshua Slocum passed through Manila on his solitary way around the world in the little yacht *Spray;* and as a courtesy to the doughty sailor the Spaniards showed him their prize prisoner, Hayes, the American pirate.

"Hayes," reported Slocum, "became a chum of the governor of the prison, and also struck up a warm friendship with the priest, who baptized him in the Roman Catholic faith while he was locked up. Now that he was converted to the true faith, Hayes found an all-powerful friend in the Bishop of Manila. The buccaneer was a penitent, and he made a most impressive and moving figure. Fever had twisted and shrunken him until I recognized him only by his long beard and his unusual height and breadth. The light, free spring of his gait was gone, and he was a picture of the shuffling monk. To behold the old freebooter, penniless, reduced by sickness, tall, gaunt, with a flowing white beard half a fathom long, marching barefooted, at the head of a religious procession, and carrying the tallest candle of them all, softened the hearts of his enemies, if he had any in Manila. His accusers retracted their charges, and were covered with confusion. After his release Hayes obtained passage home from Manila on the ship *Whittier*, bound for San Francisco. The U. S. consul vouched for him as a destitute American seaman."

The only bright spot in the Manila incident is the fact that even under those conditions Bully was able to convince American consuls that his heart was pure. As if in payment for our officials' sublime faith in Hayes, he now turned his attention to American shipping, and what he accomplished there is well documented.

Penniless, he landed in San Francisco in the spring of 1876 and immediately became fascinated by the water front. Striking up an acquaintance with a married couple named Moody, he proposed a partnership which would purchase the thirteen-ton schooner *Lotus* and make a triple fortune in the South Seas. He painted a vivid picture of himself as captain, the Moodys as passengers, and a fine Scandinavian cook to dish up the victuals. The gullible pair envisioned enjoyment and riches, tropical isles, and practically endless wealth now being held by stupid native chiefs who just loved to be defrauded.

On the midnight of October 7, when the tiny vessel was ready to sail, Hayes remembered that the *Lotus'* chronometer was still ashore, being repaired at the watchmaker's. Moody was sent ashore to pick it up, and when he returned to report that somebody from the ship had collected the chronometer that very afternoon, he saw that the *Lotus* was gone, and his wife, Jenny Ford Moody, as well.

On the run south, Hayes did not get along well with the man who had signed on as cook. He was a young Scandinavian named Peter Radeck, known along the water front as Dutch Pete. Hayes kept the cook standing sea watch as well as running the galley, and often beat him.

Arriving in golden Apia, his best-loved port in the Pacific, Hayes was welcomed like a king, and with some reluctance he left Samoa on January 2, 1877, headed for Kusaie, to pick up the coconuts he had accumulated there. Louis Becke claims that he was also going to dig up a sum of money that he had buried on Kusaie after the wreck.

The best account of what happened on this voyage was given by the mate of the *Lotus*, Charles Elson of Honolulu, who aside from Dutch Pete and Jenny Moody was the only other person aboard. The cook was still being tyrannized by the captain, and had been flogged for trying to desert at Jaluit.

The *Lotus* left that island on March 31, 1877, and encountered a bad storm. Elson, wearied by his trick at the wheel in the little cockpit astern, was sleeping below. He was wakened by the sound of revolver shots. He rushed up, and in the dark made out the figures of Hayes and Dutch Pete fighting on deck above the cockpit. The cook held an object shaped like a cross—either an iron tiller or a wooden boom crutch—and swung it full on the captain's skull.

Bully's clenched hands dropped to his sides, his head fell on his breast, his knees sagged, and as the *Lotus* swept into a trough of the sea, his massive body lurched backward into the ocean. He may still have been alive, but nobody turned the ship around to go and look. Appropriately, Bully Hayes had found an unmarked grave among the sharks of the Pacific. The keels of his stolen ships would cross those waves no more.

With Bully Hayes definitely gone, Dutch Pete collapsed in terror, then tried to tell Mate Elson what had happened. The final version was not clear, but it seemed that Hayes felt that his cook had not obeyed an order smartly enough and had cried, "I'll kill you and throw you overboard!"

The burly captain leaped forward to carry out his threat, but Dutch Pete slipped out a revolver and fired several rapid shots. Some must have hit Hayes, or Pete would never have had time to snatch up the heavy cross and crush the buccaneer's skull. It is only fair to state, however, that Louis Becke always contended that "the woman and the mate deliberately planned his murder. . . . Hayes tumbled back into the cabin, then, still breathing, he was dragged up on deck and dropped overboard."

Mate Elson took the *Lotus* back to Jaluit, where it slowly rotted on the reef. Instead of being charged with murder, Dutch Pete was hailed as a public hero. In fact, the authorities made no inquiry into Hayes's death, so content was everyone with his passing. Dutch Pete drifted off with the flotsam of the South Seas, but Mrs. Moody made her way to Honolulu, where she died in poverty and blindness.

Often throughout the Pacific, Bully Hayes, in order to forestall pursuit or arrest, had announced his own death. Now, when he was really dead, it was years before old hands in the islands would believe it. Confidently they expected the fiery fraud to turn up on their shores seeking coconuts or pretty girls, and as they waited, they began to embroider the legend of Bully Hayes. It is now possible to winnow out most of the substantial facts, but quite impossible to kill the legend.

Two almost opposing views of William Henry Hayes can

be found. Louis Becke, who knew Hayes better than any other writer, summarized his character as "an extraordinary combination of bravery, vice, kindheartedness, and savagery." Elsewhere he said: "I have spoken of Hayes as I found him—a big, brave man; passionate and moody at times, but more often merry and talkative (he was an excellent raconteur); goodhearted and generous in one hour, hard and grasping in the next. He was as suave, as courteous and as clever as the trained diplomatist when occasion demanded the arts of civilization. He would 'haze' a malingerer unmercifully; but he never omitted a nod of approval or a word of praise to the sailor who did his work well. With women his manner was captivating; and no one entered more heartily into a romp with little native children, whom he allowed to do anything they liked with him. . . . Nine tenths of the tales that have been told of and written about him are purely fictitious. He has been held up to the public as a bloodthirsty pirate of the worst type and accused of crimes he never dreamt of. . . . He was a much maligned man, and scores of writers who never saw him in their lives have made a good deal of money by their monstrous tales of his alleged murders, abductions, poisonings, and piracies."

An opposing view was registered some years later by A. T. Saunders, an Australian journalist who studied all the facts he could find and concluded: "That Hayes was a cowardly 'bully' I am satisfied. He was ignominiously captured by a Samoan chieftain in 1869, was arrested, and the *Black Diamond* taken from him, by Akerstein at New Zealand in 1864, and in 1865 Britt and others took the cutter *Wave* from him, also in New Zealand. . . . Hayes was a sneak-thief when he could not cajole or bully. I know of no instance when he did not deceive and rob those who trusted him. He bolted from Adelaide in 1858, Frisco in 1859, from Auckland in 1864, Hokitika in 1867, and Samoa in 1870, having deluded and defrauded people who had trusted him." It has even been whispered to Bully's discredit that he never was much of a hand for guzzling liquor, and that he preferred to leave such befuddlement to his chosen victims.

At any rate, these are our conclusions: There is no evidence that Bully Hayes ever murdered any white person, "except," as one apologist argued, "his wife Roma, and that ought not to count against him." The likelihood that he caused her death by drowning is remote. It has never been proved that he killed personally any of the blackbirds that he captured in the South Seas, but it is likely that he did. Certainly, many must have died on his slave ships.

There is no evidence that Hayes ever captured a ship on the high seas in an authentic act of piracy, and when one considers how easily he came by ships through guile, one concludes that he would have been crazy to take one by force. Still, the disappearance of Ben Pease, and Bully's grin of satisfaction when he turned up in command of that cruel man's ship, tempts the mind. But we know nothing specific.

Bully was frequently charged with having made victims walk the plank in the style of eighteenth-century pirates. He never did. He may have told young girls whom he kidnaped from remote islands that they had to sleep below with him or he would send them to the plank, but hundreds of sea captains of the time seemed to have followed that practice and, so far as we know, none of the girls drowned.

All other charges, as Louis Becke might have said, were proved "except leprosy." The number of ships he stole cannot be accurately computed. The slaves he impressed must have run into the thousands. The money he got by fraud probably totaled well over a million dollars, all of which he wasted. That he invaded peaceful ports and stole all the coconuts he could find, we know for sure. That he subdued and debauched whole islands we find reported by trustworthy witnesses. That he kidnaped and raped children is on record. He was a known bigamist three times over, and if one counted his island marriages, he was probably guilty one hundred times more.

But the fact that will probably live longest about the buccaneering Cleveland citizen was this—he had one ear and kept the stump of the other covered by long curls, which he tended with a lady's curling iron.

8

Louis Becke, Adventurer
and Writer

There are several ways to test a stranger's contention that he knows the Pacific, but there is only one sure way.

You might ask him to identify the four famous ships of this ocean—(*Vittoria, Endeavour, Bounty, Leonora*)—but some people don't like ships and pay small attention to them.

Or you might require the variant names of certain well-known islands—Penrhyn (Tongareva), Easter (Rapa Nui), the Marianas (Ladrones), Pleasant (Nauru), Stewart (Sikaiana)—but many travelers do not easily associate names in this way.

One of the best tests of Pacific knowledge is to ask which groups contain the following famous individual islands. Where was Robert Louis Stevenson's Abemama? (Gilberts.) Where is Rapa Iti, the island which is rumored to have ten lovely girls for every eligible male? (Australs.) To which group does Bikini belong? (Marshalls.) Where lies the forbidding cannibal island of Malekula? (New Hebrides.) The weakness of this test is that men who navigate vessels will always be able to answer better than others, who may in different respects be better informed.

The best quiz for starting an argument is to ask which islands are associated with certain outstanding missionaries who made history in the Pacific. Where did the saintly John

Williams meet his death? (Erromanga of the Martyrs.) What group did the extraordinarily able Shirley Baker dominate for a generation? (Tonga.) Where did the fiery priest Father Laval rule for thirty-seven years? (Mangareva.) Where did sagacious Hiram Bingham operate? (Hawaii.) But, of course, this test fails completely when the traveler growls, "I never discuss missionaries."

There is only one test that never fails. Simply ask the stranger, "Who do you think is the best writer about the Pacific?" From his answer you can tell every time if he knows what he's talking about.

If he says, "James Norman Hall," you know he loves the high romance of the ocean, but you cannot be sure he knows the ocean itself.

If he replies, "Robert Louis Stevenson," you probably have hold of a man who has read nothing since childhood, but who loved what he read then. Many travelers tour the Pacific spurred mainly by such youthful reading, but they rarely see much and their knowledge remains partial.

If your traveler replies, "Herman Melville," you are in trouble, for while Melville is unquestionably the greatest writer to have dealt with the Pacific, it is shocking how many people discuss *Moby Dick* and *Typee* and *Omoo* without ever having read them. In the Pacific you quickly find that you can't trust people who claim Melville as their favorite author. Their answer, as police sometimes report of witnesses, is too good.

Nor should the answer, "Robert Dean Frisbie," be accepted. There is a growing cult, in which one of the authors confesses membership, which holds that Frisbie was the most graceful, poetic and sensitive writer ever to have reported on the islands, but other critics hold that his charm was too tenuous. Certainly his later books deteriorated pathetically.

There is only one correct answer. Almost without fail, people who know the Pacific will choose as their favorite author Louis Becke. And equally without fail, those who do not know the great ocean will not have heard of Becke.

The present authors state without equivocation that if one wants an honest, evocative, unpretentious and at times fearfully moving account of the Pacific in its heyday, he must read Louis Becke. They do not claim that Becke was a great writer, for he was markedly limited in both scope and skill. They do not claim that he ever wrote one completely satisfying book, for all his works are chaotic. Nor do they even claim that he could invent colorful characters, for his are monotonous. But they do insist that in some strange way this unlettered Australian absorbed the essence of an ocean and preserved it in his books. Around the world, men who have wandered the Pacific go back again and again to the works of Louis Becke, and as they leaf through the graceless stories of this awkward man, suddenly they are gripped in a veritable typhoon of nostalgia.

For Becke could describe the grubby foreshore of an atoll, or the waters rushing into a lagoon through a break in the reef, or a trader's lonely shack, in such salt-stained and wind-ripped words as to make anyone who knows these things cry out in almost anguished recollection of his youth, "Ah, that's the way it was!" Louis Becke is the laureate of the prosaic, the curator of things as they actually were.

Consider the typical Becke yarn, "A Basket of Breadfruit." It takes fewer than two thousand words to tell and has neither a beginning nor an end, but it immediately drags the reader into island life and for the moment he is a South Sea trader, hurrying his small schooner inside the perilous reef.

It happened in Samoa, at the time when Malietoa was trying to gain control. The trader had taken his vessel into Apia and was about to return to his post on another island when he idly stopped to watch a group of native girls chewing kava root and spitting the narcotic juice into the bowl from which toasts would later be drunk.

When he was teased about not having a wife he said that he was ready to take one if a girl could be found who was untouched by scandal; whereupon an old woman presented her beautiful granddaughter. The crowd agreed that she was a girl above reproach, but the maiden was so humiliated by the laughter that she fled, followed by her grandmother.

Some hours later, as he was about to sail off, he was met on the beach by the old woman and the girl, who was solemnly offered to him as a wife, either to marry or to take Samoan style. All the old woman wanted was passage in the boat for herself and her basket of two large, ripe breadfruit.

The trader thought, "This is well for me, for if I get the girl away thus quietly from all her relations I will save much in marriage presents," but during the dark trip he found that he would have escaped giving presents anyway. All the

girl's relatives, except her grandmother, had been killed in
recent fighting. A day and a half ago her one brother and
a cousin were killed, and their heads had been shown at
Matautu. Since then she had grieved and wept and eaten
nothing.

This news touched the trader and he produced a tin of
sardines for a midnight snack, but he could find no biscuit,
so instead of ransacking the stores below deck, he decided
to cut open one of the old woman's breadfruit. But when
he slipped his hand into the basket, under the wrappings his
fingers touched a human eye.

Striking a match hurriedly, he peered into the basket and
found not breadfruit, but two heads with closed eyes, and
white teeth showing through lips blue with death. The old
woman had begged the heads from the enemy and was taking them back through the lines for ceremonial burial in
their ancient village.

The trader was angry at this deception, but the girl explained that Malietoa's troops would shoot them if they tried
to run the blockade. So some trick was necessary. That
was all. Then the girl ate the sardines and, leaning her
head against the trader's bosom, fell asleep.

The incident probably happened, and Becke narrated it
with precision, for to anyone who knows Samoa there is
an inescapable ring of truth about the setting, the style of
expression and the mood. But if Becke had a passion for reporting island life honestly, that passion diminished markedly
when he wrote about himself, for practically every statement he offers as autobiography has to be questioned. He
cites four different birth dates, according to the age he
wanted to be when retelling a particularly good yarn.

The prosaic records of the Registrar-General of New
South Wales prove that he was born on June 18, 1855, and
that his name was properly George Lewis Becke. His parents were named Frederick and Caroline Matilda Becke. His
father was clerk of petty sessions in the old town of Port
Macquarie, about two hundred miles north of Sydney. Louis,
as he preferred to spell his name, was the youngest of six
children. He was disposed to go off and camp in the bush,
or watch his aboriginal black friends spear five-foot fish in
the coastal lagoons. Before he was ten he had twice run
away from home and had to be brought back by the mounted
police. Fear of brutal teachers in school and Sunday school

left him with a stammer that he was never able to overcome.

His father, black-bearded and stern, believed that the boys of the family should master the practical arts of boat and camp, although the kindly mother and sisters spoiled them in between times. The family was none too prosperous, and life in provincial Port Macquarie was boring. "I have often thought," Louis wrote later, "that that town only wanted a small cathedral to make it, *facile princeps*, the dullest and most God-forsaken hole on the whole Australian continent. It was built by convict hands in the days of the cruel System, and nothing but an earthquake or a big fire will ever improve it."

The family moved to Sydney about 1865 and got a house in Hunter's Hill on a point jutting into the Parramatta River directly opposite Cockatoo Island, then a prison. Ten-year-old Louis often gazed across at the gloomy buildings perched high on the treeless island, guarded by pacing red-coated sentries. The sound of the prison bell was in his ears, and he not only watched the long lines of wretched men marching to and from their toil in the dry dock or among the sandstone quarries, but twice was taken with his brothers to visit the men inhabiting the cells hewn from solid rock.

On foggy nights, when the guard boats rowed around the island to prevent escapes by water, the children would go down to the rocks to listen. Once, on a winter dawn, Louis heard a shot from a sentry's rifle, followed by the clamor of the escape bell and the gasps of a fleeing creature, exhausted by his swim through the icy water, clinging with bleeding hands to the slimy shore, too weak to drag himself further. Becke's disdain for authority in later years might perhaps be traced to his early sympathy with victims of the convict system.

The boy attended the Fort Street School on Observatory Hill in Sydney, and there obtained the brief but sound education that was to last him for the rest of his life and to get him clerical posts on many a South Sea schooner. Years later, when critics charged him with ungrammatical writing, the successful author replied: " 'I never was taught no grammar.' . . . And had I let this lack of knowledge worry me I would never have earned a stiver at literary work."

When dealing with Becke's life after the age of twelve, his autobiography absolutely falls apart, for if one lists the adventures he claimed for himself one soon discovers that there could not have been enough years in Becke's teens to accommodate all that his imagination invented.

Here are some of the things he claimed, in various interviews or reminiscences, as his adventures before the age of nineteen. When he was only twelve he and his brother Vernon embarked on the great Pacific to seek their fortunes. They left Newcastle, N. S. W., on the bark *Lizzie and Rosa,* commanded by a little red-headed Irishman, a savage bully who boasted of being a Fenian and who was hated by the thirty passengers. From the day they sailed, the crew had to man the pumps, but the captain refused to turn back. The leaky old ship met such a series of adverse gales that it was forty-one days before they sighted the island of Rurutu in the Tubuai group, where young Becke got his first glimpse of a South Sea island.

Here the ship's company, in a starving condition, demanded that the captain supply them with some of the fresh provisions offered by the natives, but the captain was so stingy he would purchase only one small pig, and that for his table alone. The crew, weary of decayed pork and weevily biscuit, came aft and requested better food. When the fiery little captain refused, the mate, a hot-tempered Yorkshireman, exploded and knocked him down.

The monkeylike captain rushed below and reappeared with a brace of old-fashioned Colt revolvers, one of which he pointed at the mate. Calling upon him to surrender and be put in irons, he fired toward the mate's head. The bullet missed. The crew rushed the skipper, seized him, and held him under the force pump until he was nearly drowned. Only their respect for the captain's wife, a lovable woman who was sharing the trip, kept the crew from killing the man.

Louis and Vernon had been eager spectators of the mutiny, but thereafter became so bored that they decided to desert the ship, and had to be locked in their cabins in the port. With the captain confined in a stateroom, the crew worked the ship to Honolulu in twenty days, under the guidance of the mate from Yorkshire. There the mate and all the crew stood trial for mutiny, but were acquitted by the court, mainly through the testimony of the passengers.

Finally the old crate reached California, after a passage of 140 days. Here in San Francisco, in a Front Street saloon, the great adventure of Becke's life began, for he met the famous buccaneer, Bully Hayes. It was an exciting moment, but Hayes did not hire the boy at that meeting, and they were to part for a few years, until a much wilder adventure occurred in the far Pacific.

Adrift in San Francisco, Vernon Becke found a job on a sheep ranch and Louis became captain's clerk on a steamer running to Lower California. Using his savings to buy a share in a trading ship, he then cruised the Marshall Islands for several years. "My partner was a grand old seaman," he said later, "but no navigator, and I was only a youngster and no navigator. It was not long before the skipper burst out drinking, and went mad from delirium tremens. Although I was but a lad, the native crew (three Hawaiians and one Manihiki sailor) begged me to take charge and tie up the old man, who had jumped overboard three times. We made a strait-jacket and put him in it; and a day later sighted an uninhabited atoll." After treatment ashore, the captain kept sober, cutting down his ration to only half a bottle of gin a day.

On the way to the Palau Islands they rescued a canoe load of Marshallese who had been blown hundreds of miles off their course. Of seventy who had set out, only forty remained alive. Becke provisioned them so that they could sail homeward, and exchanged names with their chief, as a gesture of friendship. Many years later, when Becke was about to die on the island of Majuro, he was nursed back to health by this same chief.

At the end of his first trading cruise, Becke returned to Australia and joined the Charters Towers gold rush in northern Queensland. For two years he drifted about, learning, among other things, locomotive driving, amalgamating metals and practical blacksmithing. But he felt the lure of the sea and returned to Sydney, where he bought a trading cutter and, making his base at Samoa, operated as a smuggler of arms and ammunition during the Samoan civil war. It was here that he re-established acquaintance with Bully Hayes, who was then in the blackbirding trade in the brig *Leonora*.

Unfortunately, most of this lurid autobiography is impure invention. Young Becke could not have done all these things before he was nineteen, for it would have taken him at least seven years to accomplish so much. Dates and ship registries prove that only four years and five months elapsed between the time he left home on the *Lizzie and Rosa* and his departure from Samoa to join Bully Hayes on an atoll in the Marshalls.

The *Lizzie and Rosa* left Newcastle on July 23, 1869, when Louis was actually fourteen. Again, a careful search of the Archives of Hawaii and newspapers of the period give no evidence that his ship put into Honolulu in the summer of 1869 or that a trial of the entire crew for mutiny was held. It seems unlikely that so stirring an event would have passed unnoted.

However, the San Francisco *Bulletin* for October 20, 1869, does record the arrival of the *Lizzie and Rosa* from New South Wales. But she arrived via Tahiti and required only eighty-four days for the uneventful trip. Only six names are recorded on the passenger list, and "Becke" is not among them; however, since he traveled by steerage, it is possible that only first-class passengers were named. He certainly reached San Francisco, for the 1871 street directory lists "George Becke, messenger." And he soon returned to his home, for records in Sydney show that "G. L. Becke, clerk, of San Francisco," arrived as a second-class passenger on the *City of Melbourne* on July 24, 1871, from San Francisco via Fiji. He thus reached home at the age of sixteen.

It is probably true, as Becke said later, that he had got acquainted with a Rarotongan native who was an A.B. on the bark *Rotumah* and who on March 21, 1872, helped him stow away on that ship, bound for Samoa. There he worked for about two years as a clerk in the store of Macfarland and Williams, and perhaps did some smuggling on the side. At Apia he met Hayes, but we shall postpone briefly our account of Becke's adventures in company with the notorious buccaneer.

Rivaling his experiences with Hayes was a sojourn in 1880 on Nanumanga in the Ellice group, where he worked as trader for the Liverpool firm of John S. De Wolf and Co. The chief of that island had ruled that only one white man could live there among the two hundred natives, and Becke was the man. But after a year, because of a quarrel, he closed his store, dismissed all his workers, and lived alone except for a little native girl, Pautoe, whom he had adopted and who kept house for him. In a letter of July 8, 1880, he wrote to his mother: "I rise every day at 4 A.M. and bathe and then Pautoe gets my breakfast—generally flying fish or lobsters—and fills my pipe (I smoke a pipe now) and cleans the house while I smoke and instruct her how to use a broom and wash plates, etc., without breaking more than two at one wash-up."

In another letter he described the beachcombing type of trader: "I forgot to say that I had a visitor here in the *Vaitupulemele,* a trader from an adjacent island, Niutao— George Winchcombe. Four years on Niutao and cannot yet talk the language; in fact, I had to interpret for him. Such a man to talk, my ears are tingling now. I don't know how much more I would have suffered if it had not been for a case of gin I produced and by liquoring him up freely I got a little respite. He is a fair sample of too many island traders, fond of liquor and never happy without some grievance to relate against the natives. These are the men that give the missionaries such a pull over *all* traders."

At the end of his year on Nanumanga, the trading station was destroyed in a hurricane, so Becke moved to neighboring Nukufetau and set up a store there on his own account. Leaving there in August, 1881, he was shipwrecked on Beru Island in the Gilberts and lost most of his possessions, including a cherished box he had made from pieces of the wreck of Hayes's *Leonora.*

Returning from Beru on the *George Noble* with a poisoned foot whose pain the ship's doctor could not alleviate, Becke met, during a stop at the island of Abemama, the famous King Tembinok, whom Robert Louis Stevenson was to describe in a notable essay.

After a brief stay in Sydney, Becke was induced to try his luck in the cannibal isles of New Britain. He arrived there in time to witness the collapse of the last expedition sent to that place by the notorious Marquis de Rays. Becke's account of the death of Captain Gustave Rabardy differs from the usually accepted version. He states that Rabardy, game to the last, died of fever in the stifling cabin of his ship, the *Génil;* "his dying words to the writer of this sketch, as he grasped his hand for the last time, were, 'I have tried—and failed. I had not one competent officer with me to help me to maintain my authority or shoot some of the ruffians who have ruined the expedition.'" No other source supports Becke's contention that he was present at Rabardy's death, but the young man was an unknown at the time, and his appearance might have gone unremarked.

Becke was assigned the most distant trading station at New Britain, and during his stay some horrible massacres were perpetrated by the cannibal natives. He also suffered sickness, for he wrote his mother in November, 1882, from Majuro in the Marshalls, that he was nearly clear of the malarial fever he had picked up in New Britain.

Now began the years of vacillation. He would sicken of island life with its cannibals and malaria and would wander disconsolately back to Australia for some ill-paid land job. Once he tried to raise chickens on a snake-infested tract. Once he decided to be a bank teller in North Queensland, but of this attempt the manager reported to headquarters that Becke was frequently absent from his cage and fought with the accountant; that he showed utter lack of business capacity and a distinct disinclination for work; that he once left £900 in the hands of a barkeeper so that he could go off and watch a fight; and finally, that he dressed unconventionally and kept kangaroo dogs on the bank premises. The young man cheerfully admitted each count of the indictment and begged to resign so that he could return to his beloved islands.

The decade beginning in 1882 saw him wandering among the "Gilbert and Sullivan Islands," as they have been malappropriately called. He met a diversity of creatures, both white and brown, and was a fellow to romantic rascals and ruffians like Paunchy Bill, Joachim Ganga, Paddy Coney and Joe Bird. He also knew Cappy O'Keefe, who had carved out a little kingdom for himself in the Carolines and who was finally to disappear in his tiny schooner *Santa Cruz*.

Becke never lost his boyish urge for action and craving for new scenes; his curiosity never flagged. Furthermore, he was honestly fond of the brown men and women of the islands and had a happy knack of getting into their confidence. Thus he acquired his deep knowledge of their languages, customs and beliefs.

The reason why such men as he could not return permanently to civilization is perhaps explained by a passage in a novel he later wrote about Bully Hayes: "Return? not they! Why should they go back? Here they had all things which are wont to satisfy man here below. A paradise of Eden-like beauty, amid which they wandered day by day all unheeding of the morrow; food, houses, honors, wives, friends, kinsfolk, all provided for them in unstinted abundance, and certain continuity, by the guileless denizens of these fairy isles amid this charmed main. Why—why, indeed, should they leave the land of magical delights for the cold climate and still more glacial moral atmosphere of their native land, miscalled home?"

Nevertheless, Becke remained torn between civilized Australia and the primitive tropics, and in the final outcome the former won, for on February 10, 1886, at the age of thirty, he sedately married Bessie Mary, daughter of Colonel Maunsell of Port Macquarie, the town he hated. Becke promptly took his wife to the islands, but like most white women, she suffered a decline there, and by 1892 the couple were back in Sydney. Louis, himself stricken by recurrences of fever, was unable to get a job, except the painful, ill-paid work of grubbing out stumps.

Quickly his ambivalence drove him the other way and he was contemplating a return to the trader's life, even if it killed him; so on October 1, 1892, he wrote to a firm at Efate in the New Hebrides asking for a station, stating that "I am thirty-five years of age [he was thirty-seven], am married (with two children), am well up in all branches of the island trade, a good rough carpenter and used to sail small craft, but cannot navigate." Had the answer been favorable, Becke and his family would have returned to one of the most lethal groups of islands, "the white man's grave," and he would probably never have written a line of the rambling volumes that are treasured today.

Disconsolate and without a job, he met one morning an Australian explorer and author, Ernest Favenc, famed for his daring expedition in 1878 into the center of that continent, between Blackall and Darwin. Favenc had set out with two other white men and a black aborigine and had explored north as far as Creswell Creek, only ninety miles from the telegraph line. But the weather was unbearably hot and his three horses perished from lack of water. When the men's rations ran out, they lived for weeks on wild ducks, blue bush and pigweed, until thunderstorms brought relief and they won through to the coast at Darwin.

Favenc, writer of novels, short stories and history books like *The Explorers of Australia*, listened to Becke's yarns and said, "You ought to be a writer." He took Becke down to the offices of the Sydney *Bulletin* and introduced him to the celebrated editor, J. F. Archibald.

Born in Australia, John Feltham Archibald was the son of an Irish sergeant of police, but feeling imbued with the Gallic spirit he changed his first names to Jules François, and

as such combined with his friend John Hayes in publishing
a new magazine, the *Bulletin,* which is still an influential
weekly in Australia. The two were constantly in trouble and
once were in jail together, unable to meet the costs of a
libel action. But they were popular figures and were released when their fines were paid by public subscription.
Archibald, a man of medium height, frail, mercurial, bearded,
sardonic in expression, was a brilliant journalist with a wicked
gift of satire and a forbidding manner, but his innate personal charm and loyalty drew many talented associates to him.
Later, Becke always paid high tribute to his first editor,
who, he said, "taught me the secrets of condensation and
simplicity of language."

This famous editor, after listening to Becke relate a few
experiences, asked him to write something for the columns
of the *Bulletin.* But Becke had never written a story. "How
does a bloke go about it?" he asked.

"Write just as you are telling me now; they will make
dashed good yarns!" advised Archibald. Taking him at his
word, Becke went to his scantily furnished room on William
Street and, on a table made of gin cases, scrawled out half
a dozen stories.

They were accepted by the *Bulletin,* and Becke wrote half
a dozen more. These tales, under the title *By Reef and Palm,*
were published in London in 1894, the year of Stevenson's
death.

For the London appearance of his book, Becke felt that
he required some celebrated writer to prepare an introduction. He wrote therefore to the Earl of Pembroke, who had
sailed through the South Seas in 1870 in his yacht, *Al-
batross,* and had ended up wrecked on one of the islands.
The earl and his friend Dr. G. H. Kingsley had published
a volume about their cruise called *South Sea Bubbles,* which
was widely read and still, twenty years later, was remembered, particularly because it had given some offense to
the missionaries and their supporters. When Pembroke
agreed, Becke sent him some highly colored and imaginative
autobiographical material, which Pembroke inserted bodily
in the introduction, thus misleading most later seekers after
the facts of Becke's career.

By Reef and Palm, which the author sold outright for
£65, went through many editions and is still being reprinted.
It was the first of some thirty volumes written by Becke,

who in addition turned out six historical novels in collaboration with a Sydney journalist, Walter J. Jeffery.

Although he was destined to be a wanderer all his days, Becke's path now lay in more civilized lands as he pursued his career of writer; but for his material he generally depended upon his recollections of years of Pacific roving. In 1896 he borrowed £200 from Archibald and lit out for London, where he was something of a sensation.

British interviewers of the "Rudyard Kipling of the Pacific," as Becke was called, found him a man of the world with few frills and a graceful habit of "shouting" for drinks all round. He was pictured as slight and sinewy, about five feet nine inches tall. He lived surrounded by blue clouds from the plug tobacco in his pipe, and told his yarns with an expressive drawl and the remains of his boyish stammer: "I knew a m-m-missionary once . . ." He struck a person as somber and melancholy, and looked as if, when roused, he could well take care of himself. "His face is tanned a dark brown by years of brazen suns" ran one interview; "he has a restless, roving eye; his hair is black streaked with gray; his mustache is heavy; his nose has just an aquiline curve to it; his neck is bit deep with fiery wrinkles; his hands—ah! his hands are enormous for such a slim-built fellow. They look strong enough to crush a coconut, or a skull."

Becke's career as a free-lance writer was well paid, although he sold his books outright rather than on a royalty basis. He dashed off his volumes and articles, including book reviews and "London Notes," in the extemporizing, yarn-spinning style he had taught himself. During most of the last twenty years of his life he turned out at least one book annually, and contributed to many newspapers and magazines in England and Australia, sometimes using the pseudonyms "Ula Tula," "Te Matau," "Papalagi" and "A South Sea Trader." Like most writers on the South Pacific, he received many hundreds of letters from male readers asking how to get to the Pacific islands, the cost of living there and so on. "But," he adds, "they invariably wound up by some very pointed questions concerning the ways of the Brown Woman. . . ."

Notable, a generation before the revival of critical interest in Herman Melville, was Becke's lifelong advocacy of the whaleman of the *Acushnet*, "the one man who knew his subject and knew how to write about it." In his introduction to a 1901 edition of *Moby Dick,* which he thought one of the best sea books ever written, Becke said: "His writings possess that power and fascination that no other seawriter, excepting Marryat, can exercise. He was of the sea; he loved it. Its hardships, its miseries, its starvation, its brutalities, and the grossness and wickedness that everywhere surrounded him in his wanderings through the two Pacifics, held but little place in the mind of a man who, ragged and unkempt as was too often his condition, had a soul as deep and wide and pure as the ocean itself."

Becke's generous treatment of other writers was in marked contrast to the disgraceful plagiarism he himself suffered. Unknown and penniless, several years before his first book was to come out, Louis was staying in the home of Thomas Alexander Browne, who under the pseudonym of "Rolf Boldrewood" had won deserved popularity with such books as *Robbery Under Arms* and *The Miner's Right.* Browne was working on a novel about the islands, and for a cash payment of £12 10 s. and a gentlemen's agreement to pay more upon publication, Becke supplied Browne with a manuscript he had written about his exciting life with Bully Hayes. This was to be used as raw background material for a Boldrewood novel. But Becke wrote so well that Browne adopted his material, virtually unchanged, as the main body of his novel, *A Modern Buccaneer,* which appeared in 1894 without a word of acknowledgment to Becke. The best part of the novel, in Becke's straightforward style, deals with the adventures of a supercargo serving under "William Henry Hayston"—a pseudonym for Bully Hayes—and his experiences among Pacific isles, including the wrecking of the brig *Leonora* at Kusaie.

On August 6, 1894, Becke complained to Browne: "You bought the manuscript for the purpose of weaving the incidents in my narrative into a romance of your own. . . . I certainly did not imagine that the manuscript would go, without alteration, into your book as your work. It was a shock to find that instead of my material being used as a framework for *A Modern Buccaneer,* to be clothed in your picturesque language, it was used *verb et lit* and actually constitutes the book itself. *I* thought that under your skillful hands the story would be so changed and improved as to render *my* work entirely unrecognizable."

Becke then consulted his solicitor, "Banjo" Paterson, who

as Australia's greatest balladist supplied the words of its unacknowledged national anthem, "Waltzing Matilda." Paterson advised Browne to admit publicly Becke's contribution, which was done in an advertisement in the Sydney *Daily Telegraph* of November 3, 1894, as well as in the one-volume edition of the novel that appeared in 1895. But Louis never got any of the promised money from the sale of the book. In Browne he had met a "modern buccaneer" worse than Bully Hayes!

Through the years, Becke changed his residence from London to Ireland to France, and traveled in Jamaica, the eastern United States, and Canada. But he missed the islands. They haunted him and lured him back to their sun-swept coral beaches. So in 1908, at the age of fifty-three, he and his entire family turned up in Wellington, N.Z., full of plans to carry out a twenty-month scientific expedition through the Pacific islands. Louis was now a member of the Royal Geographical Society and an earnest researcher. The expedition actually sailed, and by December had reached Fiji, armed with phonograph recording devices for taking down the native songs and stories of Melanesia. But for some unknown reason, the big adventure collapsed, and Louis Becke went disconsolately back to New Zealand.

The family returned to Sydney in 1911. Becke's health had been deteriorating for some years, although there survives a large newspaper advertisement in which his portrait is accompanied by a testimonial praising Jones' Australian Oil as a sovereign remedy for his muscular rheumatism, as well as for occasional bruises and sprains. He does not look well in the photograph, although his eyes are as luminous as ever. About this time Norman Lindsay described Louis as a "thin, hawk-faced, emaciated man with a ragged, drooping mustache, muffled up in an ulster and speaking in a husky voice that had lost all resonance." Actually, Becke was suffering from cancer of the throat.

For a time he was in a private hospital, but he recovered enough to take up residence at the Hotel York—indistinguishable from dozens of other Sydney licensed premises. On the morning of February 18, 1913, a chambermaid found Louis Becke dead in his chair, with the manuscript of an unfinished short story scattered on a table in front of him.

Once, when recalling his halcyon days in the islands, Becke may have had a premonition of the manner of his death, for he wrote: "Denison [Becke's fictional *alter ego*] often wishes he could live those seven months in Leassé over again, and let this, his latter-day respectability, go hang; because to men like him, respectability means tradesmen's bills, and a deranged liver, and a feeling that he will die on a bed with his boots off, and be pawed about by shabby ghouls smelling of gin." Louis Becke should have died at sea or on one of the golden atolls he had served as a solitary trader. There he could have been appropriately buried. Instead, he was interred with a Church of England service in a smug Sydney suburb, attended by his widow, a nephew and three elder brothers. The grave, in the highest part of the Waverley Cemetery, is still remembered and tended by those who love Australian literature. There is one redeeming feature: the spot overlooks the swells of the sparkling Tasman Sea.

As a boy growing up in Sydney, Louis Becke had dreamed of becoming a pirate; and before he was twenty, he was charged with piracy. Unquestionably the climax of Becke's life came when he was eighteen and served under Bully Hayes, but the facts of his association with that wild buccaneer are difficult to pin down. In three different works Becke speaks of specific meetings with Hayes, and by combining them we can construct a rough timetable. In "Bully Hayes, Buccaneer," published the year before Becke died, he reports having met Hayes in a San Francisco saloon and says that "five years later" he became Bully's supercargo. In "Skippers I Have Sailed With" he says, "During the two years I was with Bully Hayes we visited many hundreds of islands." In September, 1914, the magazine *Adventure* posthumously published a Becke letter about Bully: "I knew him when I was quite a boy, and sailed with him as supercargo and labor-recruiter for over four years."

Thus we find that Becke knew Hayes in many different places, sailed with him for over four years, and visited with him many hundreds of islands. Unfortunately, each of these statements is false. Here are the facts.

It is doubtful that Becke could have seen Hayes in San Francisco, since there appears to have been no date when the two seamen were in that city at the same time. Becke probably did see Hayes once or twice while the young Australian was working as a clerk in Mrs. Macfarland's store in Apia, Samoa. On December 3, 1873, Becke was sent by this same Mrs. Macfarland to deliver a worm-eaten ketch, the

E. A. Williams, to Captain Hayes, who was waiting in the Marshalls, where he had cooked up a shady deal to hoodwink an unsuspecting native chief by palming off the worthless ketch for good money.

Becke sailed to Mili Atoll and delivered the ship to Hayes on January 17, 1874, on which date his service in the *Leonora* began. He could not have sailed on the ship for more than fifty-seven days, for on March 15 the vessel was totally destroyed in a hurricane, after which Hayes and Becke were ashore together as castaways until the warship *Rosario* arrived at Kusaie and the two were separated forever. But even during these six months ashore, Becke saw little of Bully, for as we shall learn shortly, Becke soon deserted his wild captain and went to live by himself at Leassé on the other side of the island. Of this time Becke wrote: "And the memories of the seven happy months he spent there remain with him still, though he has grown grizzled and respectable and goes trading no more."

So Becke was not with Hayes for four years; he was on the roster of the *Leonora* for fifty-seven days, and most of them were spent ashore at one or another island. He did not touch "many hundreds of islands," though; possibly they put in to three after leaving Mili. And he did not associate with Hayes for "over four years"; he knew him for eight months, by far the larger number of which were passed as a fugitive from the wrath of that unpredictable buccaneer.

But Louis Becke was not a liar; he was a writer. And Bully Hayes was the hero of his red-letter days. From here on, in retelling the adventures of that youthful time, we shall not again question in niggardly manner what happened on the memorable cruise of the *Leonora*, for what Becke wrote in his various accounts of it was mostly true, and all who love the Pacific quickly fall within the spell of that robust episode. This is what should have happened to an eighteen-year-old lad as he set forth from Samoa to deliver a rickety sixty-ton ketch to the greatest buccaneer of his day, who was waiting for him far across the expanses of the Pacific.

The trip to the northwest was a miserable affair. After forty-two days of rolling through Pacific swells under the command of a gin-sodden Dutch captain, the *Williams* staggered into Mili Atoll, where the *Globe* mutineers had landed exactly half a century before. There, on the shore where

Sam Comstock had planned a cathedral, waited bearded Bully Hayes, cursing at the long delay in his plans. "We'll sail that ketch to Arno in the morning," he fumed.

But as soon as Hayes piloted the leaking ketch into the anchorage, Becke packed his gear and informed Bully that he refused to sail another day in the *Williams,* unless she traveled on the deck of another vessel. Bully poked his thumb through her hull, consulted Ah So, his Chinese carpenter, and decided to beach the *Williams* and abandon her.

"We can keep her from sinking that way," he announced, "and maybe come back later and sell her. But I can't wait around for the chance. Now, young Becke, you have no way to get back to Samoa. Why not sign aboard as my supercargo?"

In this way Louis Becke joined up with Bully Hayes, who was later to be his most memorable literary creation. One incident of the saga occurred a few minutes after Becke first boarded the *Leonora.* Three men, hard cases put ashore by the captain of a New Bedford whaler, came out and asked Bully to ship them. He refused in such unnecessary language that the leader of the gang offered to put a head on him. Hayes at once had the deck cleared and, taking the men in turn, knocked out each of them in one round. He then gave them a glass of grog apiece, and sent them ashore with a bottle of arnica to rub on their bruises.

It was in the *Leonora* that Becke voyaged to Kusaie, that soaring, lovely island where he was to spend the happiest months of his life. Until his death, his mind constantly returned to Kusaie and the delectable days he spent there among the friendly brown people.

His introduction to Kusaie was dramatic. As late as 1825 the island had contained about eleven thousand handsome, virile and warlike natives. Then European diseases, particularly measles, ravaged the inhabitants, followed by American missionaries who introduced clothes, which in turn brought pulmonary diseases. When Becke landed there, only four hundred people survived. The frightened, worn-out men confided that in the old days they had been afraid of nobody, but since so many strange things had happened to the island, they had become bewildered and all the fight had gone out of them. Now they were being persecuted and killed off by a gang of invaders from Pleasant Island.

King Togusa, a wizened old man of about sixty, crippled by rheumatism, received Hayes and Becke in his thatched

palace beside the cosy harbor of Lele. He was dressed in a
black frock coat, white duck trousers and patent-leather
shoes. While Louis chatted with the handsome and flirta-
tious Queen Sa, the king drank Bully's brandy and explained
how the invaders held Kusaie in a grip of terror.

Hayes, as we have shown in the preceding chapter, quickly gained control of the situation and agreed to take the
invading Pleasant Islanders, and the white traders who led
them, to settle on one of Bully's favorite islands. Just before
the *Leonora* got under way in the harbor, the old king and
his young queen came aboard to make some purchases in
Louis Becke's trade room. After buying about $200 worth of
printed cloth and cutlery, the king retired to drink brandy
in Bully's comfortable cabin, while Louis, as he said later,
"had the distinguished honor of fitting on and selling Queen
Sa a yellow silk blouse and two pairs of patent-leather
shoes."

The overcrowded brig then departed for Port Lottin, a
few miles to the south, to take on final provisions before
leaving Kusaie. At 7:00 A.M. they dropped anchor in fourteen fathoms abreast of the inner reef of that port, with
two New Bedford whalers, *St. George* and *Europa,* between
them and the deep but narrow passage out to the open sea.

By dusk young Louis, who had been weighing and paying
for the pigs and yams being loaded, began to think of the
dinner to which he had been invited on one of the whalers.
Just then, the trade wind that had been blowing all day
suddenly lulled—a dangerous sign at that time of year. The
barometer began to fall rapidly.

Hayes, weather-wise, sent over a boat to warn the whalers
and advise them to head out to sea, but they decided not to
risk towing through the jaws of the reef, since they were
at good moorings. That meant the *Leonora* could not escape;
and she was left in a bad spot, close to shore, with almost
no room to swing. The rising swell prevented them from
shortening her cable, for it would soon have parted.

Bully ordered the royal and topgallant yards sent down,
decks cleared of lumber, boats slung inboard by the davits
and native passengers sent below, out of the way. Although
not a breath of wind was stirring, the mountainous swell
threw the brig almost on her beam ends. The air was so close
and oppressive that the Pleasant Island natives could be kept
below only by threats that the first one to come on deck
would be shot. When some of them begged to be allowed

to swim ashore and spend the night, Hayes let them go. At once ten men and six women sprang overboard into the shark-infested waters and swam toward the village of Utwe, invisible now in jet darkness.

Then, as if belched from a cannon, a hot gust hit from the south, rising to hurricane force. The sea was tremendous. Louis Becke had never heard anything like the thunder of the surf on the reef, now only a couple of cables' lengths from the brig. The sound of the huge seas as they tumbled upon the hollow crust of coral made his hair stand up like wires. A strange humming undertone terrified the fierce Pleasant Islanders, and the rest of them begged Hayes to let them come on deck, because "the belly of the world was about to burst." Bully consented, and in a few minutes the natives, after stowing their Snider carbines in Becke's trade room to protect them from the salt water, thronged the heaving deck.

The trade room had become a mess because of the rolling, and the floor was a jumble of broken cases of liquor, gunpowder, concertinas and women's fancy hats. Beckoning a couple of native sailors to help him, Louis was just going to clean it up when Bully Hayes called sharply to his officers to stand by.

From the northwest came a droning roar, and in half a minute the *Leonora* heeled in the fury of the first gust of wind, rain, spume and palm leaves. She brought up on her anchors with a jerk. Blown sheets of water lashed her bows and waist.

Bully Hayes stood in the stern, sounding the depths, as calm as if he had been trout fishing. "Don't bother about the trade room!" he told Louis quietly. "Get all the arms and ammunition you can ready to put in the boats. I can't give her more than another ten fathoms of cable—there are a lot of coral mushrooms right aft, and the first one we touch will knock a hole in our hull. We'll get smothered in the seas in another ten minutes—if the cables don't part before then!"

During a strange lull, in which the glass fell steadily, Becke began loading heavy trade chests with chronometers, sextants, charts, the ship's books, some silver plate and about six thousand silver dollars. He also stowed in some Winchester rifles and cartridges. He was helped by a young Easter Island half-caste girl named Lalia. The other natives were terrified, but Lalia took a cutlass from the rack and, cursing freely in French, English, Spanish and whalemanese, threatened to murder every one of them if they did not hurry.

Louis got the first box sent up the companion and into one of the whaleboats just when a sea crashed over the waist and all the women but Lalia bolted. Sea after sea tumbled in over the bulwarks with crashing clamor, carrying away the forward deckhouse and sweeping it overboard, killing four men in the main rigging, and flooding the cabin.

The ship rolled, and two starboard guns broke away and rammed to port, carrying away the two guns on that side. The same sea knocked the longboat overboard, but half a dozen Rotuma sailors leaped over and, using canoe paddles, saved her from the crunching coral. Becke was ordered to take charge of her, but before he could do so, a second comber fairly buried the ship. Becke and the Chinese carpenter, Ah So, saved themselves only by tangling in the falls of one of the quarter-boats.

The dismal drone of the gale rose again. Louis heard Hayes shout to the carpenter to stand by and cut away the masts, for the seas were now sweeping the deck like a torrent. Soon the *Leonora* gave such a terrible roll to port that it seemed the end had come. Six big water tanks amidships had gone adrift. But the big masts were hacked off and sent plunging overside, and the brig stood up again.

Meanwhile, from the shore an old sailor, a castaway from some long-departed man-of-war, had brought out his longboat, manned by half a dozen of his half-caste sons, to try to rescue a number of the women and children. The rescuers could be seen only by the glare of the foam-whipped sea. Then suddenly the longboat and all its hands vanished in the dark, and during a five-minute lull, Hayes urged the remaining women to jump over and make for the shore, as the brig's deck was now awash.

While Louis stood by, one powerfully built mother from Ocean Island, whose baby had been lashed to her back with bands of sennit, rushed up to Hayes, shouting, "Captain, if I die, I die!," rubbed noses with him and leaped over the stern into the surf. She was found next morning on the beach, dead of cruel coral gashes, but beside her was the baby, alive and sleeping soundly, for with her dying energy she had sheltered it under a bower of grass and leaves.

The end was near. The brig had been moored with her head toward shore. Now the stern hawsers parted one af-

ter another. The *Leonora* spun like a top, and headed into
the wind on her short cable, with the breakers on the reef
less than fifty yards astern. The big coral heads which had
been safely distant now showed like huge fangs in a sneer-
ing mouth as the ring of broken water rose and fell right
under the vessel's counter.

The native girl Lalia was almost exhausted, but she had
refused to jump into the ship's lifeboat, saying she would
stay with Louis and help pack the remaining valuables. She
ran below, and in a few minutes reappeared with a powerful Pleasant Island native named Karta, carrying the Chinese
cook, Ah Ho, who was paralyzed with fear and drink. In
fury, Hayes tossed the cook overside, but he landed near a
boat whose crew amazingly picked him up.

Becke went below once more with Lalia to haul up another of the boxes, and aided by Karta had got it halfway
up the companion ladder when the last cable parted. The
brig reared her stern high in the mountainous sea and came
down with a terrific smash on a coral boulder. The rudder
was ripped from the stern post and sent clean through the
deck.

Lalia fell backwards into the cabin and the heavy chest
slipped down on top of her, crushing her left foot cruelly
and jamming her slender body underneath. Karta and Becke
tried vainly to release the tortured girl until, hearing their
cries, some Rotuma sailors ran down and got her clear. She
had fainted, and was put on the steward's bunk.

As this final chest of treasure was tossed into a boat, the
brig came down again on the coral head with an impact
that smashed a big hole in her timbers under the starboard
counter. She began to fill.

"It's all up with her, boys!" roared Bully stoically. "Jump
for the boats—but wait for a rising sea, or you'll get smashed
on the coral." Most of the natives preferred swimming in the
seething water to taking a chance in one of the darting
boats. More than a few were drowned—despite the fact that
it is pretty hard to drown a Micronesian—or else were
banged against the razor-sharp reef until they bled to death.

Louis Becke suddenly remembered that Lalia was still
below, and with Karta and a Manila man went to rescue
her. She was sitting up in Ah Ho's bunk in the dimly lit
cabin, her hair unloosed, her eyes shining with terror. The
cabin had three feet of water sloshing about.

Becke lifted her out. She tore off her dress, stripped to

the waist, and hand in hand with him succeeded in gaining the companionway just as a cascade came down and put out the lamps. The same wave brought in the body of a little native boy who, crouching on the stair, had been crushed to death by the wheel falling on him when the rudder carried away.

Half drowned, Becke struggled to the deck, with Karta carrying the girl in his arms. The *Leonora* was now broadside to the reef and well under water forward; the after part was hung up on the coral mushroom, wounded by every wave. Bully Hayes snatched the girl from Karta's arms just as the ship lobbed over on her bilge and a thumping swell swept the mass of them over the stern. As the backwash lurched seaward again it rolled the brig off the reef, to sink under the jagged ledge in fourteen fathoms, with only the stump of her foretopmast sticking above the swells.

Nothing of the brave Manila man was ever seen again—except his right arm and shoulder, all that the sharks of South Harbor had left of him. Hayes reached shore in the longboat, which was swept over the inner reef by a giant roller, and at once began to direct the work of salvaging the goods from the sunken brig.

The girl, Lalia, Becke and Karta clung to the fragments of a boat and drifted into a mangrove swamp a mile down the shore. They were badly knocked about. Louis was so generally bruised and skinned by coral that he would never have reached shore had he not been buoyed up by Karta and the courageous Lalia, who clung to him when he wanted to let go and drown quietly.

At dawn, the castaways saw, as they gazed seaward, that the two whale ships which had ridden out the hurricane in safety were scuttling through the narrow passage and out to sea. Their captains wisely feared that, since Bully Hayes had lost his own ship, he would not be too particular about taking another near to hand. And they were right; Hayes and the other hard-boiled survivors would have been happy to seize one of the ships of the blubber hunters. But the Yankee skippers, knowing Bully's evil reputation, outwitted him and left him and his crew marooned on Kusaie.

Ashore, a reign of terror began, and the Pleasant Islanders continued their persecution of the gentle Kusaieans. "One night, therefore," Becke later told a newspaperman, "our other South Sea islanders attacked these Pleasant Islanders with rifles, knives, stones, and bludgeons, and I went out under the idea that I could put a stop to the fray. They were all fighting like madmen, and I was promptly knocked down and a knife stuck in my head. It went right through the bone."

We have seen in the chapter on Hayes how he ran wild on Kusaie, indulging in behavior that bespoke a madman. Becke observed this insanity with growing alarm, and then one day realized that there was no hope. Bully had found that one of his trade ledgers was missing. Jumping from his seat in rage, he roared that he had not lost it himself. He strode into his bedroom, driving the women out with savage oaths, and next moment reappeared with his arms full of chronometers. Standing in the doorway he tore the costly instruments from their cases and dashed them to pieces on the coral flagstones at his feet. Then, vowing that he would set a torch to the trading station he had built and roast everyone in it, with his hands beating the air and his face grimacing with passion, he staggered like a drunken man to the beach and sat alone on a boulder.

This was enough for nineteen-year-old Louis Becke. He boldly informed Hayes that he was going to leave him.

"Where will you live?" Hayes growled.

"Across the island, away from here," Becke replied.

"You're a damned young fool to take things so hotly," Hayes grumbled, but when he saw that his young aide was determined, he put his big arm around Louis and handed him a quart of gin. With this fatherly gift, he bade Becke the best of luck.

For the remainder of his months on Kusaie, while the rest of the island reeked of mutiny and drunken violence, Louis Becke spent an idyllic existence as the guest of the dying tribes who lived near Coquille Harbor at the poetic village of Leassé.

Here he dwelt in a small grass-thatched hut and led a somnolent existence that would haunt him for the rest of his days with a memory of peace. He wrote of it: "At daybreak he would awaken, and, lying on his bed of mats upon the cane-work floor, listen to the song of the surf on the barrier reef a mile away. If it sounded quick and clear it meant no fishing in the blue water beyond, for the surf would be heavy and the current strong; if it but gently murmured, he and Kusis and a dozen other brown-skinned men . . . would eat a hurried meal of fish and baked taro, and then carry their red-painted canoes down to the water, and, paddling out through the passage in the reef, fish for bonito with thick rods of *pua* wood and baitless hooks of iridescent shell.

"Then, as the sun came out hot and strong and the trade wind flecked the ocean swell with white, they would head back for shining Leassé beach, on which the women and girls awaited their return, some with baskets in their hands to carry home the fish, and some with gourds of water which, as the fishermen bent their bodies low, they poured upon them to wash away the stains of salty spray."

And then, as if the gods of the Pacific were determined to include everything possible in Louis Becke's great adventure, it ended in the most dramatic way possible. A British warship, the *Rosario,* put into Kusaie determined to bring Bully Hayes to justice. The captain, with a full complement of marines, formally arrested Louis Becke on a charge of piracy. In Samoa the storekeeper, Mrs. Macfarland, had accused him of stealing the worm-eaten old ketch *E. A. Williams,* which he and Hayes had abandoned on the reef at Mili, and he was put in confinement and hauled off to Australia to stand trial as a proper pirate. But fortunately he had kept a copy of the power-of-attorney given him by Mrs. Macfarland, and this proved that he had been within his rights in disposing of the ship according to his best judgment. At the ripe age of nineteen he thus cleared his name of piracy, and was free to move on to other Pacific adventures.

It was from such experiences that Louis Becke wrote. His protagonists are usually white men caught up in tropic life. They are traders, sailors, drunken captains, beachcombers. They customarily have native wives, though few of the stories deal with romantic love affairs. The native wife is accepted as a matter of course and rarely is there much moralizing about the problem. Marriage in the Western sense is not usually indulged in, but liaisons often last through twenty or thirty years.

The traditional Becke hero has sometimes had to flee a more stable society because of murder or theft or drunkenness; more often he is merely a drifter. In the islands he faces new problems of violence, and it is a rare story that does not include some extraordinary outburst of passion, which is reported in matter-of-fact phrases. A murder is rarely built up into fictitious levels of interest; a beachcomber murders someone and that is that.

There is no standard Becke villain. One time it will be a native who has gone mad and murdered nearly twenty helpless victims. Another time it will be a surly white man, or an evil supercargo, or a revengeful mate. A surprising number of Becke's stories end in sudden and even gruesome death but without the effect of horror or even regret. That was the way men died in the late-nineteenth-century Pacific and the author is merely relating a normal experience.

All critics of Becke's work have mentioned the monotony of his plots, and this stems from the fact that he used the same kind of protagonist repeatedly. This Becke island man is not a philosopher, not a poet, nor a heroic figure, nor a deviser nor an empire builder. He is simply an average man caught up in the average situations of a wild and violent ocean. Part of Becke's charm is that one can start almost any story and be instantly in the middle of it, because the chief character, whatever his name, is the same familiar hero one has met endlessly before.

Becke's women are even more standardized. The white women—and far more of these appear in his stories than the reader at first realizes—often exhibit courage, but they are a dreary group, wasting their lives away on remote islands. The native women are surprisingly undifferentiated. They wander in and out of stories, support their men in crisis, bear children and say little. Often they are not even named. Rarely does one catch a glimpse of why a white man marries a brown woman other than for convenience, and after reading a batch of Becke yarns, one concludes properly that it was nothing but convenience that motivated most of these matches.

Becke was a very poor novelist and it requires a patient reader to plough through to the end of one of his more lengthy tales. The characterizations are not skilled, the incidents are apt to be repetitious, and the interlocking of major and minor plots is completely unsophisticated. If the author had written novels only, he would now enjoy no reputation whatever.

But as a short story writer—if that designation be elastically defined—Becke had real power. It is deceptive. The newcomer to Becke, trained in the great Russian, French or American masterpieces in this form, will surely be thrown off balance by Becke's casual opening paragraphs: "I stayed once at Rotoava—in the Low Archipelago, Eastern Polynesia —while suffering from injuries received in a boating acci-

dent one wild night. . . ." But with surprising speed Becke
lures his reader into a real situation. With apparent deficiency of art he states bluntly the apex of his story, then
adds some irrelevant ending, and the yarn is done. But
when the reader thinks back upon his reading experience, he
acknowledges that in some strange way Becke has conveyed
a sense of the island setting, a feeling for the dreadful
averageness of the characters involved, and a lasting appreciation of the varied life of the Pacific.

It is probably unfair to call these artless tales short
stories—they are more properly sketches; but some impart
a surging power. Sharks devour a group of wanderers; a
drunken sailor rows off into the night with his enemy's child,
a lover who has been badly wronged tips his hat to the woman who did the wrong; a murdering deserter commits suicide rather than face recapture. These incidents remain viv-
idly in the mind.

Technically, Becke was adroit in setting the stage for his
yarns. He roams the entire Pacific, refers to the most memorable islands, the staunchest ships, the worst buccaneers. With
admirable spareness he indicates exactly where each action
takes place: "One night, as the bark was slipping quietly
through the water, and the misty mountain heights of Bougainville Island showed ghostly gray under myriad stars,
Rothesay came on deck an hour or two before dawn."
Through such indications of setting, Becke takes his reader
endlessly back and forth across the Pacific as no other writer
can.

He was not good at sustaining dialogue, but often his awkward and stilted reports of what men said invoke a feeling of
the period, and if they lack dramatic tension, they send forward the mood and the sense of time. It is difficult to find
any Becke dialogue referring to values; it is the talk of men
who face perils or who have such mundane problems as murder and piracy to attend to.

It should therefore be obvious that Louis Becke does not
warrant comparison with gifted writers like Melville and
Stevenson; nor with polished storytellers like James Norman
Hall and the colorful John Russell. He lacks the poetry of
Robert Dean Frisbie and the rare artistic integrity of his New
Zealand successor, Katherine Mansfield. Nor does he have
the social conscience of his Australian contemporary Henry
Lawson.

But what other author born and brought up in the Pacific

region in the nineteenth century is better than Becke? He merits a secure place in the literary history of the Pacific, primarily because his very lack of polish reflects the rude and lawless period in which he lived. (To most old Pacific hands it is positively impossible to get a single breath of ocean air from Stevenson, for example.) And in his ability to end a story with some apparently irrelevant afterthought, which somehow sums up the entire yarn, and the age, and the ocean, too, Becke is without compare. Once he told a very rambling tale about a garrulous old man who had sailed with Will Mariner to Tonga. The story is utterly tedious, but at the finish Becke throws in an unanticipated paragraph which reflects his art. He has the old man write a farewell note to Becke and the visiting ship captain: "And now, Mr. Denison and Captain Packenham, as I think we shall never meet again, I want you to be good to my [sons] Tom and Sam, and warn them both against the drink. It is kind, generous gentlemen like you who, meaning no harm, send so many half-caste lads to hell."

Nobody but Louis Becke could have written such a paragraph.

9

Will Mariner,
the Boy Chief of Tonga

When one reviews the tragedy and defeat that attended most attempts to find in the Pacific the earthly paradise that Europeans and Americans sought, it is refreshing to come upon the story of a young English boy to whom, in the years 1806 to 1810, the dream was given in richest fulfillment. Not only was he able to go to sea at the age of thirteen as a full-fledged privateersman marauding in the New World, but he experienced one of the strangest adventures in the Pacific, rising to the rank of an authentic boy chieftain and military counselor to the ruler of one of the most interesting groups of islands. His story has always fascinated the Pacific wanderer, for this youth proved that it could be done. A boy could survive the massacre of a ship's crew and in a few months become lord of all he surveyed.

His story became known in 1811, when a successful London doctor named John Martin happened to overhear some exciting news. Dr. Martin, inspired by reading about the voyages of Cook and others in the Pacific, had become a sort of amateur ethnologist, and had just learned that a young fellow had sailed into the Thames after four years of living on the remote Tonga Islands.

Dr. Martin immediately took steps to meet this lad, who was now barely twenty-one years old. His name was Will

Mariner. He was tall, fair-haired and bronzed by his years in the tropics. His manner was rather taciturn, but after several attempts Martin, who was not much older than he, got him to talk. Young Will had an amazing memory, and under the doctor's questioning revealed a familiarity with the Tongan language and customs greater than anything hitherto known in Europe.

Unfortunately, Will could not relate much then, for he was scheduled to leave on a voyage to the West Indies; but Dr. Martin got him to promise that, while away on the trip, he would note down everything he could recall about his life in Tonga. When he returned to London, the doctor worked with him day after day, writing a book that would reveal the boy's astounding story. Will was not inclined to embroider his tale, for to him the events seemed neither odd nor romantic. "Having been thrown upon those islands at an early age," wrote Dr. Martin, "his young and flexible mind had so accorded itself with the habits and circumstances of the natives that he evinced no disposition to overrate or embellish what to him was neither strange nor new."

From his shipboard notes and through frequent cross-questionings, Will Mariner reconstructed his adventure for Martin, who offered it to the public in a lengthy work. This book, *An Account of the Natives of the Tonga Islands, in the South Pacific Ocean,* first appeared in 1816 in two volumes. It was so much in demand that a second edition was published the next year, and a third came out in 1827. Today it is treasured as a work of first importance in Pacific ethnology, as well as a stirring narrative of wild adventure.

Will was the second child of Captain Magnus Mariner, who had served on the British side in the American Revolution as owner and master of a privateering ship under the orders of Sir William Cornwallis. Afterward, the privateer business became unprofitable, and the captain settled in London and married. His son Will was born at Highbury Place, Islington, on September 10, 1791. He got a better education than most lads of his position, for he spent five or six years at Mr. Mitchel's Academy at Ware in Hertfordshire. When Mitchel died, the boy returned home well grounded not only in the three R's but also in history, geography and French.

Will had always shown a fondness for an active life and a thirst for information about the world. His sports were usually those of a daring sort. He read many books of travel, and often used to say that he would like to live among savages and meet with strange adventures. But he was not in the mood then to go to sea, and according to the custom of the time, in 1804, when only thirteen, he accepted a post in an attorney's office.

About six weeks later, Captain Isaac Duck came to dinner and changed Will's mind. Duck, now about forty, had come to bid farewell to Magnus Mariner, under whom he had served his apprenticeship. He was about to sail as master of the *Port-au-Prince*, private ship of war. His orders were to cruise for prizes in the Atlantic. If not successful, he was to double Cape Horn and harry enemy shipping in the Pacific, meanwhile filling in the time chasing whales.

Captain Duck's enthusiasm aroused Will's desire to go on this voyage. On the spot a position was devised for him, that of captain's clerk; so that when the *Port-au-Prince* sailed from Gravesend on Tuesday, February 12, 1805, Will Mariner was aboard.

The privateer *Port-au-Prince* was a three-masted square-rigger of nearly five hundred tons. She mounted twenty-four long nine-pounders and twelve-pounders, besides eight twelve-pound carronades on the quarter-deck. She was a formidable vessel. The large complement of ninety-six men allowed for the chance that prize crews might have to be released to man captured vessels.

No enemy ships were encountered in the stormy Atlantic, however, and Captain Duck, who was sick part of the time, navigated the *Port-au-Prince* around Cape Horn and up the west coast of South America. Here some Spanish brigs fell easy prey. The undefended Spanish colonies were likewise ready victims of the loot-hungry crew of the privateer.

For example, one day the privateersmen came upon the Spanish town of Ilo, at the southern extremity of Peru. Ilo was a tiny port at the mouth of a stream which emptied there the sand which it had picked up on its wanderings through the mountains and deserts that separate Lake Titicaca from the sea.

The men of the *Port-au-Prince* stormed ashore, captured the port and completely sacked Ilo, burning the little city to the ground. The church was plundered and yielded forth a rich booty of silver candlesticks, chalices, incense pans and crucifixes. From Ilo the *Port-au-Prince* moved northward to the Galapagos Islands, where whales were sought in vain, and thence back to the little town of Tola, at the mouth of the Rio Santiago in modern Ecuador near the Colombian border. The governor of Tola was a man of the world who knew how to put his enemies at their ease, the principal weapon in his artillery being an uncommonly pretty daughter of sixteen, Margarita, who had just completed her education in a nunnery. She spoke fairly good English, and she and Will were able to chat together. He was more than a year younger, but toughened by the life of a privateer. When Margarita heard of the sack of the church at Ilo, her eyes widened with horror. She told Will that, after such sacrilege, his ship would never reach England again.

Unfrightened by a prediction which turned out to be true, Will tried to pass it all off as a joke. When she asked if he had taken part, he said that he had only knocked down as many silver images as he could conveniently reach. When she scolded him, he warned her that in England she would be punished as a witch. For this she boxed his ears.

Later he brought Margarita a fine cheese—a delicacy in that place. In return she gave him some gold buckles for his shoes, but reminded him that according to her prophecy he would not live to wear them very long.

Heading north of the Equator, the *Port-au-Prince* alternated piracy with whale hunting. Lack of luck caused them to switch to the slaughter of sea elephants at Cedros Island off Lower California. During this massacre, Captain Isaac Duck's growing illness became acute. He died on Monday, August 11, and two days later was buried ashore on Cedros.

The command now fell upon Mr. James Brown, the whaling master and one of the stupidest men ever to try to take a ship across the Pacific. There is no record of this pathetic man's age, appearance or previous service, but his performance with *Port-au-Prince* has made him notorious in maritime annals. On the first afternoon of his command he demonstrated the monumental incompetence that was to mark his career, for less than an hour after his men had buried their beloved captain, he ordered them to the messiest job aboard a whaler: the nauseating work at the try-pots of rendering out oil from sea-elephant carcasses.

At sea the crew found that their ship had sprung a leak in her side, and it was decided that they should head for the Hawaiian Islands and make repairs on her there. At Honolulu the reigning monarch, Kamehameha the Great, who had won fame by uniting all the islands under his vigorous rule, visited the ship. He took a liking to young Will Mariner and asked him to remain there as his secretary.

This was a marvelous offer for a fifteen-year-old lad, but he turned it down. His sense of duty as captain's clerk made him remain aboard to keep safe the records that would allot the proper share of prize money to each of the crew, including the dead captain's heirs.

The *Port-au-Prince* sailed south from Honolulu on October 26, but the leak still persisted. The crew, supplemented by eight Hawaiians, had to man the pumps much of the time. Captain Brown, no navigator, was heading for Sydney, the nearest big port, but in this emergency sought to put in at Tahiti. Because of an adverse current he missed the Society group and had to make for an alternative target, the Friendly Islands. The leak had now increased to a rate of eighteen inches of water every hour, and the pumping required to keep afloat was punishing.

The Friendly Islands that Captain Brown sought are strung out for a distance of about a hundred and eighty miles north and south, with the 20° S. parallel of latitude running through their center. Known today as Tonga, the islands for the most part are flat coral reefs, lifted by volcanic action in ancient times, and surrounded by beautiful fringing reefs. Several of the islands are volcanic cones rising from the centers of lovely atolls. There are three main groups: Vava'u, with one high island, to the north; Tongatapu, with the most substantial island, to the south; and Ha'apai, with no major island but with a multitude of glorious islets, in the middle. Captain Cook had been well received among the low-lying islands of Ha'apai, and Captain Brown steered for the passage there. Toward the end of November, 1806, a month out from Honolulu, the *Port-au-Prince* dropped anchor off the northern end of Ha'apai's central island, Lifuka, the very spot where Cook had stopped in the *Endeavour* thirty years before and had been greeted by these Polynesian people.

The Friendly Islanders lived up to their name. Sending presents in advance, the head chief, Finau, came out in a large canoe and paid a formal call on the captain. His interpreter was a Hawaiian named Kuikui, who had voyaged to Manila in an American whale ship and thence to Tonga. Kuikui, who was to play an infamous role in what was about to transpire, assured Brown repeatedly that the people of Lifuka were all good folk, and that the captain need not worry if many of the islanders came out to visit the ship, because they had seldom seen such an important vessel there. While High Chief Finau was politely sipping brandy in the captain's cabin, Kuikui sought out the eight Hawaiians in the forecastle, and privately slipped them the word that they would be safer if they went ashore for the next few days. The Hawaiians had been well treated aboard the *Port-au-Prince* and immediately suspected that Kuikui was warning them of an attack. They went at once to Captain Brown on the quarter-deck, advised him to be on his guard, and said that it would be wise not to let too many Tongans on board at any time.

Captain Brown had been charmed by the soft-spoken chiefs, and his dull and stubborn mind simply could not comprehend the possible dangers. He rebuffed the Hawaiians and said that these Tongans were clearly not treacherous, and that their name proved they had always been friendly to white men. He even threatened the Hawaiian spokesman with a flogging. Their advice thus rejected, the Hawaiians went ashore and thereafter pestered Brown no more.

That night all the Tongans left the ship, but the crew had little rest, for the vessel was kept afloat only by pumping continuously. Next morning was Sunday, and Brown's anxiety was so great that he ordered all the heavy guns to be moved aft, so that the carpenters could get at the bad spots.

The men, tired out and yearning for the delights of the shore now in view, and encouraged by the "pernicious invitations" of the natives, complained bitterly. They marched aft in a mutinous manner, argued that they had always been allowed to go on liberty in port on Sundays, and asked leave to land at once.

Captain Brown came out on the quarter-deck and told them they might all go to hell if they pleased, but not before they had carried out his orders to careen the ship. Then James Kelly rushed to the gangway over the ship's side waving a dagger looted in South America. "By God, I'll run through the guts of the first bastard that tries to stop me from leaving this ship!" he shouted. He and three other men jumped into a passing canoe, taking their clothes with them, as if they intended not to return. Soon they were followed by fifteen more mutineers—for that is what they had now become.

The remaining men got to work moving the guns aft, and with the leaking holes in the bow at last exposed, the water stopped pouring in and the labor of pumping was somewhat reduced.

During the day, as the men worked, they noted that more and more natives were boarding the ship, armed with clubs and spears. By afternoon the decks were thronged with Tongans, who acted so threateningly that the crew came aft to report that they suspected an immediate attempt to capture the ship. This was, in fact, true, as was afterward discovered. For the moment, however, the plot was frustrated, unwittingly, by Will Mariner.

He and Captain Brown and Mr. Dixon, the mate, were in the cabin entertaining two young chiefs. Will, bored with trying to talk to natives who did not know English or French, strolled out into the steerage. There he met the sailors coming to warn the captain. He was impressed with their story, and he went back and urged their case so strongly that even Brown's sluggish mind was aroused to the possibility of an attack. The captain agreed at least to walk out of the cabin and look over the situation. He walked arm in arm with one chief, while Dixon strolled next to the other native. Thus the party marched out on deck.

Accidentally, Will had broken up Chief Finau's plot, for it was Finau who had sent his two young henchmen to the captain's cabin. A canoe had been ordered to stop beneath the porthole, and the natives on deck were to go to that side of the ship and shout at those below. The captain and any other white men in the cabin would surely go to look at what was going on. While their backs were turned, the two young chiefs would draw short clubs from beneath their garments and brain the officers. This would be the signal for the natives forward to attack the crew and massacre every white man aboard.

When Will got up and went out of the cabin, the chiefs feared that the plot had been discovered. When they were led out on deck, the natives were even more sure that the tables had been turned and that they faced instant death. Their faces went as pale as their brown skins would allow. Brown asked them to order the crowd of Tongans off the ship. The chiefs did so instantly, and even threw overboard the clubs they had concealed. Obediently all the natives jumped into their canoes and headed for shore.

Brown, with ill-timed delicacy of feeling, realized that the two chiefs, now disarmed, were looking with fear at a rack of boarding pikes, tomahawks and muskets on the quarterdeck. With incredible stupidity, Brown ordered that these weapons be sent below, as a gesture of friendliness.

At dusk Brown committed an even greater act of folly, for he refused the request of the crew spokesmen to post armed sentries and prevent the natives from swarming aboard and interfering with the repair work. Brown, bewitched by words, had it in his stolid head that the Friendly Islanders were truly friendly, and refused to permit even normal precautions.

At dawn on Monday, December 1, 1806, hordes of natives began to come off to the *Port-au-Prince*. By eight o'clock no less than three hundred men armed with clubs and spears swarmed over the ship. A little later Kuikui, the interpreter, came aboard and invited Captain Brown to pay a visit ashore and enjoy the entertainment which had been arranged by the chiefs there. Brown accepted heartily, stepped into a canoe, and was last seen walking up a path into the fringe of coconut palms.

Now there was to be no more delay. All that remained was for the Tongans to slaughter the crew, and the *Port-au-Prince* would be theirs, along with her guns and gunpowder, iron and brass metal—untold wealth for a Polynesian tribe.

First to fall was the mate, Dixon. Prudently, he was ordering several canoe loads of natives not to come aboard, as there were too many on the ship already. A club bashed in his skull. There was a wild yell of *"Maté! Maté!"* and the massacre began. Owing to Captain Brown's orders, not a single crew member was armed, and not one of those on deck survived the sudden attack.

Young Will Mariner was below, about to begin writing up the daily log from his rough pencil notes. He went to the hatchway to mend his quill in the daylight, and heard the cry of "Kill! Kill!" Looking up, he saw Dixon fall in his blood.

Will dashed for the gun room close by, where he could lock himself in and get a musket from the chest there. Evading a Tongan who clutched at him as he went by, the boy shook clear and dived down the narrow scuttle to the deck below.

Here he found Robert Brown, the ship's cooper, paralyzed with fear. Will pulled him along to the hatch of the powder magazine, and they jumped down and shut the hatch over them. When the shrieks and groans of the clubbed victims were followed by a deathly silence, Will had time to think.

Since they faced certain death anyway, the boy bravely decided that they should blow up the ship and destroy it, along with the murderous natives. To do this, he had to get to the gun room, where he might find a flintlock musket to fire into a barrel of powder to explode the magazine. Will peeped out, saw the coast was clear, and rushed to the gun room. There, to his dismay, he saw that the boarding pikes brought down the evening before had been carelessly heaped on the musket chest, and that removing them would make so much noise that he would betray himself.

There was nothing to do but to go back to the magazine and think out some other plan. The cooper was in such a state that he was of no help. Will decided that sooner or later they would be discovered. Better to go out boldly and face fate like a man, he reasoned. It would be easier to get the killing over quickly, while the enemy was still hot with slaughter, rather than to risk later torture.

The cooper agreed, if Will would lead the way. The boy threw open the hatch again, stepped aft to the gun room, and opened the hatch into the captain's cabin immediately above.

Peering through, he saw the backs of Kuikui and a young chief, who were bending over the captain's bunk to examine the sword and pistol fastened on the bulkhead. Will jumped into the cabin. When they turned at the sound, he held out his hands to show he was unarmed, and uttered the Hawaiian greeting he had learned—*"Aloha!"*

Will then asked Kuikui, in mixed Hawaiian and English, if he would be killed. If so, he was ready to die. Kuikui answered that he would not be hurt, and asked how many more white men lurked below. Will said there was only one, and called up the cooper. The two captives were then led by Kuikui to the upper deck, where Will saw for the first time the results of the massacre.

Seated on the companion hatch was a middle-aged Tongan warrior, naked to the waist. One side of his hideous face was twitching with a convulsive tic, and his eyelids blinked over his bloodshot eyes. Both he and his big ironwood club were spattered with human blood and brains, and over one shoulder was slung a blood-soaked seaman's jacket. Beyond him were laid out in a neat row on deck the naked bodies of twenty-two of Mariner's late shipmates. Only two of the battered faces were recognizable.

When the number was reported to the chief in charge, he ordered that the bodies be thrown overboard to the waiting sharks. The only two white men left alive on the *Port-au-Prince* were the cooper Robert Brown and Will Mariner. The chief looked over the survivors, ordered that Brown should be left alive on board, and gestured Will to a waiting canoe. On the way to the beach, Will's guard stripped him of his shirt, leaving most of his body bare to the blistering heat of the tropical sun.

The canoe landed and the boy was led along a path to the village of Koulo. By the path lay the naked, clubbed body of foolish Captain Brown. One of the natives asked by signs if they had done right to kill the captain. When Will could not answer, one of the Tongans lifted a club as if to lay the boy dead on the grass too. But his captor hurried him along and took him aboard a large sailing canoe.

While waiting there, Will saw a small boy wade out to the canoe and point to a fire burning a short distance away under the palms, uttering the word *"Maté!"* Will, remembering Captain Cook's stories, feared—mistakenly, as it turned out—that these people were cannibals, and that he had been saved on the ship only to be cooked and eaten on shore.

Half an hour of waiting went by, and then he was led up to that fire. There on the ground lay three more bodies—those of the first men to mutiny and go ashore without leave. Will was now more certain than ever that he was to serve as the main course of a cannibal feast. He was so dazed that his relief was not great even when he saw some dead hogs hauled up to the fire and put into the underground oven, their bodies filled with hot stones.

Will was then stripped of his trousers and taken to the north point of Lifuka Island. Then he was compelled to wade over a quarter of a mile of dead coral and sand to the adjoining island of Foa. Since his boots had also been taken from him, the knife-edged coral cut his bare feet cruelly. Soon the natives came out of the villages the party passed through, to jeer at the white lad's blistering nakedness, to push him about and spit at him, and to throw sticks and pieces of sharp coconut shell at his body, which soon streamed with blood. This went on until a kindly woman gave him an apron of large ti leaves to wrap around his waist.

At the large village of Lotofoa, his captors stood around drinking kava, but none was offered to exhausted, thirsty Will. A man arrived in haste to lead the boy to High Chief Finau, ruler of Ha'apai, who would decide Will Mariner's fate.

Will was taken to Finau's house. It was long, with rounded

ends, having walls of woven bamboo grass. The high-pitched roof was thatched with palm leaves and rested on many rafters supported by heavy posts, and the whole was tied together with sennit fiber. Will and his guides entered in the middle of the long side, and at once the party sat on the palm-leaf mattings covering the ground, as a sign of respect for the great chief.

Poor Will was garbed only in green leaves, his white skin burned scarlet, his fair hair unkempt, his face grimed with the dust of the powder magazine and the filth thrown at him by the villagers. As he hobbled into the house, a group of women at the chief's left set up a cry of pity.

Finau, an imposing figure, sat on a fine mat. He beckoned the boy to him in a kindly way, and put his nose against Will's forehead, a Tongan salutation between equals. Then he told one of the women to take the boy outside to wash himself in a pond of clear water. After he had a good bath, Will's smarting wounds were soothed by a rubdown of sandalwood oil. The woman then clothed him in a large square of soft *ngatu,* or beaten-bark cloth, spread out a mat for him in a house, and fanned off the mosquitoes as Will, exhausted beyond endurance, fell asleep.

The change in Will's treatment derived from a fact unknown to him. When Finau first came aboard the *Port-au-Prince* he had taken a sudden liking to the yellow-haired boy, who, he thought, was the captain's son. He admired the air of courage in the lad, tall and strongly built for his age, and had given orders that during the taking of the ship, Will Mariner's life was to be spared.

Will was awakened in the middle of the night by the woman, who realized that he had been given nothing to eat all day and offered him a supper of coconut juice, a cooked yam and a slice of pork just out of the dirt oven. Will ate the yam greedily, but feared to touch the pork, thinking in the dark that it might be human flesh. When he awoke from his second slumber at dawn, his scratches were beginning to heal and he could face the new life that had come to him on the island.

Finau sent to ask Will to accompany him aboard the *Port-au-Prince.* There Will was delighted to find about a dozen of her old crew, who had survived because they had been in villages ashore at the time of the massacre. Twenty-six of the crew, in all, had been saved in this providential way. Later, Finau had spared them in order to have someone to work the guns of the captured ship, since none of the Tongans could do so.

Finau's plan was to beach the vessel and strip her of all fittings. The distance from deep water into an opening in the reef opposite the nearest village was only a mile and a half, but the passage was jagged with coral patches. Four hundred natives were swarming over the ship, but they could not sail her to shore. Faced by a seemingly insurmountable problem, High Chief Finau consulted young Will, who ordered the mob to sit down and keep quiet, while the white men worked the sails and steered the *Port-au-Prince* shoreward through the maze of the reef, until she grounded a few yards from the village.

During the next few days the ship was dismantled. Two of the carronades were brought ashore, along with eight barrels of gunpowder and all the remaining cannon balls. Every scrap of metal was hacked away and saved; even the hoops were knocked off the barrels of whale and sea-elephant oil in the hold, so that the precious oil floated on the water to a depth of several feet.

On December 9, spring tides enabled the natives to warp the doomed *Port-au-Prince* close to the shore to her last resting place. She was then set on fire, so that the woodwork would burn away and reveal the iron and copper bolts with which her timbers were fastened. She burned for hours.

Unknown to the Tongans, all the guns were still loaded. In the middle of the night they became heated enough to discharge themselves. The natives arose in alarm as the ninepounders and twelve-pounders exploded, believing that the whole island of Lifuka would be sunk beneath the ocean. With the aid of his Hawaiian interpreter, Will reassured them that all would be well. From this day on he was constantly consulted as an authority on white-man matters.

After calming the natives, Will strolled down in the moonlight to see the last of his ship. She had now burned to the water line, and as he watched, a sizzling heap of metal sank under the waves. Mingled therein was a mass of fused silver, where coins and church plate had been stowed in the strong box. In melancholy Will recalled Margarita's prophecy at Tola, that the ship and all her crew would be destroyed for the sacrilege in robbing the church at Ilo. Now it was certain that his floating home, the *Port-au-Prince*, would never reach England again. All the crew's gains, in oil wrenched from two years of whaling, with the destruction of hundreds of sea creatures, had vanished in smoke. The privateersmen who had destroyed other ships had now lost their own.

While Will had been helping to dismantle the ship, he had taken the opportunity of bringing ashore in his sea chest, hidden in his own belongings, a number of books and papers—including the precious log of the *Port-au-Prince*. After the ship was burned, Will stayed in Finau's house, where the chief often found him reading or writing down his experiences. One day Finau asked Will to hand over all his printed matter. The boy did so, but took the precaution of hiding the log book under his sleeping mat. It was well that he did, for he soon found that all his other books and papers had been burned. An escaped convict from Botany Bay, named Morgan, had blamed the nine missionaries stationed on Tongatapu to the south for causing a pestilence by means of the witchcraft of white-man's books; and through the promptings of Kuikui, Finau had ordered the destruction of all the records of the English sailors.

With the burning of the ship began Will Mariner's four years' residence on a South Pacific island. But he was not to remain very long in the role of a common captive. At the behest of High Chief Finau he stayed indoors for about a week, until the highly inflamed emotions of the common people of the place had a chance to subside; for Finau had startling plans for the lad's future.

Will got his first premonition of this on December 16 when he was invited to go shooting rats on a nearby island. This was a noble recreation which utilized the bow and arrow—weapons that had not been generally used in war until the Tongans had recently learned from the Fijians how to make large war bows to slay an enemy. During the hunt, Finau revealed his soaring ambitions to the white boy. Now that he possessed guns and white men to fire them, he was going to campaign in the European manner in a concerted attempt to bring all the Tongan islands under his sway.

When Captain Cook arrived in the Friendly group, he had found that they indulged little in warfare, but during the interim since his visit, the placid islanders had learned several bad habits from their fierce black neighbors of Fiji to the west, where the Tongans had sailed to obtain sandalwood for oil. In Fiji they not only were taught the use of the bow, but also improved their throwing of the spear and imitated the Fijians in painting their faces and dressing in a way to inspire terror among their foes. The Tongans also picked up the loathsome idea that to eat one's enemy was a manly and satisfying practice.

For years the men of Ha'apai had engaged in a ritualized annual attack on the major southern island of Tongatapu. Customarily such excursions involved little fighting and less death, but this year the warriors of Ha'apai had a major surprise in store for their cousins in Tongatapu. Ambitious Finau ordered Mariner and three other survivors to get four of the twelve-pound carronades ready for action. The Englishmen set to work and mounted the heavy guns on new carriages with high wheels made by native carpenters. The chief was fearful that the usual mode of Tongan fighting, consisting of sudden rushes and frequent retreats, would not fit in with his new type of warfare. Mariner and his comrades promised that they would remain with their guns in the forefront of the battle if the Tongan fighters would promise to stand firmly with them and not run away.

One day, while Mariner and the other Englishmen were collecting the shot salvaged from the burned ship and cutting sheet lead for other ammunition, Chief Finau asked Will if he had a mother living. When the boy said he had, the chief appeared grieved that he should be separated from a mother's care, and forthwith appointed one of his wives to be Will's adopted mother. This woman, the same one who had bathed his wounds the first day, took great joy in looking after him and furnishing him with food and other necessities, and soon gave him as much parental affection as if he had been her own son.

Kuikui, the villainous Hawaiian, was still agitating to have the survivors of the ship killed, including Will, on the plea that if an English warship should arrive and hear of the massacre, a terrible revenge would be taken on the Tongans. But Finau felt that the foreigners would be too forgiving in nature to hold such grudges. Besides, in his grandiose plans he had reserved an important role for the white men.

But although the survivors were not murdered, they lived miserably. Wherever they went they were subjected to insults. Their lack of food was most pressing, and they did not know how to supply it honestly in this strange land. Thus they were starving in the midst of luxurious gardens full of vegetables, of banana and breadfruit and coconut trees in profusion, of pigs and fowls running underfoot everywhere.

The white men thought that to take any of these would be stealing—a crime which in England was still punishable by death. Pressed by hunger, they raided at night, but finding that Will was in favor with the chief, they got him to implore Finau to arrange for them to get meals regularly. They would work for them if required.

When Will told Finau of this, the Tongan was dumbfounded by the request and inquired how people got food at home in England. Will replied that every man earned food for himself and his family by his own labors. What happened in the case of strangers without homes and gardens? Will said that although a man might occasionally invite his personal friends to take a meal with him, no one would ask complete strangers—people wandering about on the roads—in to eat. Finau roared against the ill nature and selfishness of such foreigners. He told Will the Tongan custom was much better. Here anybody, friend or stranger, who felt hungry would merely go to a house where the people were eating and drinking, sit down without any invitation, and eat his fill.

At once the starving sailors took advantage of this genial custom. But as word of their plea to Finau spread, it became a standing joke, and when a native dropped in to a village hut, the host would say: "No, we shall treat you after the manner of the white men. Go home and eat what *you* have, and we shall eat what *we* have!"

At this time Finau II, as he was known throughout Tonga, controlled the middle and northern groups of islands, but, as he had confided to Mariner, his heart was set upon taking over the greatest group, Tongatapu and its outlying dependencies. Preparations for war were accordingly hurried along. Spears, clubs and slings were collected, and all the great canoes—some of them holding as many as a hundred men—were overhauled and made ready for the seventy-mile voyage.

Finau II, now about fifty-five, was a giant of a man, six feet two inches tall and muscular in proportion. His skin was a warm olive brown; his hair was straight and glossy, falling back from his very high forehead. His penetrating eyes could be gentle, but when they flashed fire, his subjects did well to beware. His nose was large and aquiline, and except for his skin color and prominent jaw, he might have passed for a handsome European.

He was a man of high mental powers and was intensely

interested in new ideas. His chief trait was a ruthless desire for supreme command. To gain his ends he could be treacherous—for example, some years before he had helped his half-brother, Tubou-niua, to assassinate the rightful hereditary ruler of Tongatapu, a cruel tyrant, and to murder by night every man, woman and child in that chief's house. Finau was cursed by a rage so fierce that he had given orders to his courtiers to hold him down when these fits struck him, so that he would not commit some act that he would later bitterly regret. Yet he could still be sympathetic with suffering, and kind to such a captive lad as Will Mariner. His passionate attachment to his own children was later to be the cause of his downfall. He seldom smiled, but his laughter, when it came, was so loud and deep that it was renowned through the islands under his sway.

Finau II now directed that Will should appear in Tongan dress with a chief's *vala*, or skirt, of fine patterned bark cloth, falling from waist to calf, with a wide, twisted girdle. His naked chest was as brown as that of any Tongan, and his bare feet had hardened since his first painful walk ashore. He was quick at languages, and the liquid Tongan words rippled off his tongue.

Finau's admiration for the lad, still not yet sixteen, was so great that he now bestowed upon him the name of a beloved son who had died at about Will's age. Thenceforth the name of Will Mariner was no longer pronounced in the islands. He was known to all the people as Toki Ukamea, the Iron Ax. Since his adopted mother was the daughter of a chief, Toki also took status as one of the *eiki* of Ha'apai, and he was able to bathe on the lovely leeward beaches reserved for those of high rank.

It was as Chief Toki, therefore, that Will embarked on his first military campaign. Finau's half-brother, Tubou-niua, came down from Vava'u with thirty canoes of warriors to join the fleet of fourteen large double canoes of Ha'apai and many small ones. The four mounted carronades were loaded aboard the four largest double canoes. Most of the warriors had adopted the terrifying Fijian custom of covering their bodies with horrid designs to scare their foes. Since all Tongan men were tattooed in a close black pattern from the line of the navel to the knees, they looked as if they were wearing black short pants.

On the way south the fleet stopped at the islands of Uiha and Nomuka, and Finau II reviewed his troops ashore.

He made a heartening speech to his men in his famous voice, which could be heard for a very long distance, and told them that the new style of fighting required them to stand their ground and defend the cannons, which could not be quickly moved. This the warriors promised to do, and the fleet of 170 canoes set forth upon the last stretch of sixty miles of open sea.

Late one evening the fleet reached a small island which stands on the reef fronting the north side of Tongatapu, about a mile from the shore. Across from this insignificant island was a sanctuary in which some of the highest chiefs were buried, including the great Finau I, father of the present leader. All the chiefs of the fleet and their attendants, including Will Mariner, dressed in mourning and accompanied their leader to the grave of his father, where the proper ceremony was held and the priests explained to the spirit of the former ruler the purpose of the present war party.

When they returned to the camp on the islet, they saw the enemy forces across the channel on Tongatapu, brandishing their clubs and yelling ceremonial threats, as in former years.

Tongatapu considered itself unassailable because of the great fortress which had been built on top of the hill at Nuku'alofa, and Finau realized that if he sought a real victory, he must destroy this strong place. It was circular and surrounded by deep ditches that shielded a central citadel which was protected by platforms latticed with woven bamboo. Under ordinary conditions of Tongan warfare such a stronghold could withstand a long siege.

Finau and his fleet arrived opposite the fort, where a large party lined up on the beach to oppose the landing of the Ha'apai army, now wading across the reef to shore. Fifteen survivors of the *Port-au-Prince*, armed with muskets, covered the operation. Their first salvo killed three defenders and wounded several more. The second salvo caused most of the Tongatapu warriors to bolt in terror back to the fort, and those few brave ones who stood firm were driven back by Finau's warriors as they splashed to the beach.

The carronades, slung on poles, were then landed and quickly remounted on their wheels. Other natives brought the powder and cannon balls ashore, while the white gunners followed with flint and steel and slow match. Finau took up the position of general in command, sitting on a chair (looted from the *Port-au-Prince*) on the reef in a foot of water, and directed the proceedings. He had been asked by his chiefs not to expose himself, as he usually did, fighting in the van.

Firing commenced on the wickerwork stockades of the fort, but owing to the yielding nature of the bamboo lattices, the cannon balls went through them, leaving few marks. Finau had never seen a bombardment before, and had expected that the whole fort would be pulverized. He sent for Mariner and demanded to know why this had not happened. Will explained that even though there was little damage visible outside, when Finau got inside he would see that things were much different, for it was known that the fort was packed full of warriors and their families, who must be suffering from the cannon balls.

Finau therefore commanded an attack to be made on the outer defenses, while two strong parties were sent to stand by the two landward entrances to the fort, to deal with anyone trying to escape. The frontal attackers set the fences on fire and the flame spread furiously. Finau's men penetrated the defenses, and the carronades fired blank charges so as to scare the enemy without hurting the attackers. When those inside the fort tried to flee, many were killed by ambushes at the rear exits. Soon the frontal party got to the innermost stockade, and there they clubbed down men, women and children with equal ruthlessness, according to the methods recently learned in Fiji. In less than an hour this famous fort, strongest in all Tonga, had been completely destroyed, and its garrison lay groaning and dying amid the whoops of the victorious men of Finau II.

This chief now climbed the hill to observe the smoking ruins, and was amazed at the havoc wrought by the gunfire. Several large canoes had been shattered, while 350 corpses lay around, many of them dismembered by cannon balls. A few of the enemy who had been taken alive said that the balls, not content with destroying the inner houses, had glanced off the house posts and went rushing around seeking someone to kill. Thus fell the fortress which had withstood all attacks for more than eleven years.

The white cannoneers, headed by Mariner, now urged Finau to follow up his victory—to pursue his retreating foes, destroy every fort in the country, and wipe out all enemies so that he would be proclaimed *hau,* or military leader, of all Tonga. Such European tactics, however, would have been contrary to all Tongan teaching. First the army would have to get the priests to consult the gods of Tonga as to the next move.

After full ceremony, the chief priest went into a convulsion and then spoke the message of the gods. Finau, before he could do anything else, must first restore and rebuild the fort of Nuku'alofa which he had that morning destroyed! Appeal from such a judgment was unthinkable.

The process of gathering the required material would have taken many days had it not been for the use of steel axes stolen from the *Port-au-Prince*. Then Finau summoned all his army to start the rebuilding. Without bothering to haul away the hundreds of decaying bodies that littered the site, the army amid the stench began erecting the new fort, which was defended on each side by one of the carronades that had done such good service.

The wars in Tongatapu had destroyed all the crops, and Finau sent his canoes back to Ha'apai to obtain provisions. Meanwhile he put out foraging parties, and when his men were harried by a party of the defenders of the land, Finau ordered two hundred of his best warriors to destroy them. In the fight that followed, many of Finau's warriors were decoyed into an ambush, and the rest ran for their lives. Among these was Will, who had the bad luck to tumble into a hidden pit six feet deep. Fortunately it was not lined with rows of sharpened bamboo spikes, as was the usual practice. With the enemy on their heels, four of his comrades stopped and hauled him out of the pit, and one of them was killed on the spot by an arrow. Will and the remaining three resolved to sell their lives dearly, but luckily some of the other men of the war party appeared and routed the attackers. When the band at last reached the safety of the fort, they were exhausted and hungry beyond belief.

They had brought back fifteen prisoners, and since the canoes had not yet returned, some of the Ha'apai chiefs who had lately been in Fiji proposed that they appease their hunger by killing and roasting some of their captives. Despite objections from most of the army, this was done, and cannibalism was introduced into Tonga. Will was not yet enough of a savage to partake of such a dish, however, and starved for several more days until the canoes, loaded with provisions, but delayed by storms, at last arrived.

It was now nearing the end of July, 1807, and Finau II was called back to Ha'apai to take part in the lifting of the tabu which had been in force for eight months after the death of the Tui Tonga, supreme hereditary ruler of all the island group. Finau decided to leave the fort of Tongatapu under the command of a local chief who had surrendered and had tendered his allegiance to Finau. But no sooner had the forces of Finau headed north than flames from the hill showed that the faithless chief had burned down the fort to show his hatred of the invaders from Ha'apai.

The anger of Finau was partly diverted when Will Mariner showed him some white man's magic. Will had left a written message with a chief at the fort, to be given to the captain of the next ship that might stop at that island. The letter warned all ships not to trust the Tongans and told of the dire fate of the *Port-au-Prince*. It also proposed that the visiting captain seize some chiefs as hostages until Mariner and his friends were given up to them.

The vengeful Hawaiian, Kuikui, had gotten hold of the message and now told Finau what his favorite, young Toki, had done. Finau handled the paper wonderingly, for he had never heard of writing; then he gave it to a white lad named Higgins and asked him what it meant. Young Higgins, who like the others could now speak Tongan fairly well, with quick wit pretended to translate it and said that it merely asked any English captain who might visit the islands to request that Finau allow all the castaways to go back in his ship, saying that they had been kindly treated by the chief, but that, after all, they would like to go back to their own land.

Finau agreed that this was a natural sentiment. He remained interested, however, in the mystery of how black marks on a paper could reveal secret thoughts, and calling Mariner to him, asked for demonstrations. When the foreign lads revealed that they could communicate to each other ideas about things which they had never even seen, the chief's bafflement knew no bounds, and he decided that this whiteman witchcraft was a dangerous thing and that he would never permit it in Tonga, or the islands would soon be filled with conspiracies and scandals.

The lifting of the tabu was accomplished successfully and Finau then turned his attention once more to winning the title of *hau* of Tonga. Craftily he sought to clear his way by assassination, the main means of political change in Tonga. He had recently become suspicious of his half-brother Tubou-niua, who had been his instrument in the killing of the reigning Tui Tonga in 1797. Tubou-niua, who had done the deed to bring liberty for his country, was in many ways a noble and honorable man, and as governor of the northern islands of Vava'u had contributed his troops to Finau's assault on Tongatapu. But Finau could not tolerate any rival, not even his brother. Yet he refrained from personally killing Tubou-niua, for fear that murdering such a popular man might cause his own downfall.

Again he found an instrument—this time a low-born son of the Tui who had been killed by Tubou-niua. This young man was known to be seeking vengeance, and when the returning armies were in Lifuka, Will Mariner, who was a good friend of Tubou-niua, begged that noble chief to go armed and watch out for knavery. But Tubou-nuia disdained any act that might seem to show that he distrusted his brother. "It is better to die than to live innocent and yet be thought capable of treachery!" he responded proudly.

One night Will Mariner was returning with Finau, in company with the unsuspecting Tubou-niua, from a trip to a nearby village. As the party, walking in single file in the moonlight, stepped beyond the village fence, five men leaped forth with uplifted clubs and fell upon the unarmed Tubou-niua. The first blow missed his head and struck his shoulder. He shouted: "Oh, Finau, am I to be killed?"

Finau, several yards ahead, turned and ran back with feigned efforts to defend his brother; but as part of the plan, several of the attackers seized Finau and pinned him against the fence. It had all been carefully plotted; the leader of the assassins was found to be the low-born son of the former Tui. The doomed Tubou-niua used only his bare hands and arms to protect himself from the blows of the clubs that fell upon him until both arms were broken. Then the leader of the thugs felled the chief to the ground and clubbed him until long after his life had departed from his body.

Will Mariner, last in the line, thought at first that Finau was being murdered, and although unarmed, rushed ahead to help his friend. Had he succeeded in reaching the scene of the murder, he would have been killed also, but fortunately for him, he was grabbed by one of the attackers, a big savage who held the boy's arms at his sides until the gruesome business was over.

The guilty Finau then addressed his forces with the high power of oratory for which he was famous. Unctuously, he pretended to give a straightforward explanation of the whole bloody business. He admitted that he knew that the avenger had plotted to kill Tubou-niua and that he, Finau, had even pretended to assist him, in order to satisfy the man for a time, hoping thus to prevent the murder. Unfortunately, the crime had been committed too quickly for him to prevent it.

After he finished there was silence for half an hour in the council, but no one dared to object for fear that he also would lose his life. Will Mariner, as a foreigner who would escape the dire tabu of handling a dead body, sorrowfully prepared the corpse of Tubou-niua for burial, a ceremony attended by more than sixty canoe loads of mourners.

Finau then declared that the slain man's place as governor of Vava'u would be taken by Finau's aunt, Toe-umu. But when the men of Vava'u returned home with the tale of the murder, this loyal woman was horrified, and demanded that Vava'u at once declare war upon her perfidious nephew. Thus Finau's hopes of becoming *hau* of all Tonga were again thwarted, and he lost not only Tongatapu but Vava'u as well.

Preparations for war were interrupted by the arrival of Finau's eldest son and heir, Moenga, who as part of his education as a young chief had been sojourning for five years in Samoa. Moenga, who was to become Will Mariner's closest friend, was at this time about twenty-two years old. He was tall and athletic, with an open countenance and a cheery sense of humor. He was the finest flower of Tongan nobility, and was intelligent as well. The prince was curious to learn all the lore of the *papalangi*, or strangers, and Mariner was strongly attracted to him from the start.

Having awaited his son's return for several years, Finau had set aside two charming ladies, daughters of chiefs, to be his wives; and it was decided that Moenga should marry both of them as soon as possible. Moenga had already brought back two wives from Samoa, but for a young prince of his position a couple more could easily be justified.

The wedding preparations—and the feasting and dancing after the ceremony—delayed the civil war for several weeks. Then Finau assembled an army of six thousand men, their bodies and faces painted with horrifying designs after the Fijian fashion. Again the high chief roared his instructions, and emphasized that the *papalangi* method of fighting with the aid of big cannons would be followed. When his peace overtures failed, Finau's fleet finally landed at Vava'u, along with the four famous carronades and eight white gunners, all under the command of Will Mariner.

But in this campaign the two sides were more evenly matched than at Tongatapu, and during the months of ceremonial warfare that followed, the fighting settled down to a tiresome siege marked by desultory skirmishes for possession of one yam patch or another. In one of these raids Will was wounded in the foot by an arrow. At last Finau resorted to involved diplomacy by which the fighting was ended and he, acknowledged by the people of Vava'u as their *hau,* was able to withdraw to Ha'apai without loss of face.

During this expedition Will Mariner and the young prince Moenga had become fast friends, and together advanced their education in gentlemanly accomplishments, which included not only the use of club and spear, but also boxing, wrestling, swimming, diving under water for long periods, handling a canoe, casting a fishing net in the shallows and the graces of Tongan singing and dancing. Young Chief Toki, as the white lad was now always called, had justified Finau's interest in him, and had become in all respects a polished courtier of the Tongan court.

At this time a chief turned over to Finau his estates on the island of Vava'u. Will, weary of being a landless hanger-on in the high chief's household, asked Finau to give him the lease of these northern lands, as well as twenty-one workers, over whom he would have the powers of life and death. Finau agreed, and thus the boy who had been a lawyer's apprentice became a landholding chieftain on a South Sea island.

His plantation was half a mile wide and ran inland for about a mile and a half. The region was one of the loveliest in the lovely isle of Vava'u. Toki's domain included gardens of yams, taro and sugar cane, and was shaded with shapely coconut palms, green breadfruit trees, gray casuarinas and spreading banyans. It ended at a towering cliff overlooking a sparkling bay, the view from which was the subject of many a romantic Tongan song.

His idyllic existence as a landed proprietor was interrupted by the news that a whale had gone ashore on a reef near Vava'u. Now the tooth of a sperm whale was considered to be a treasure of untold value among the natives of the South Pacific, and at once Finau, accompanied by Will and others, headed for the reef to cut out the teeth from the lower jaw of the dead whale and share them like fabled jewels.

It was now almost three years since the burning of the *Port-au-Prince*, and for the first time a foreign ship was reported in these waters. Will went to Finau and told him that he was called on a quest even more important than the winning of a whale's tooth. Could he depart for his homeland on this ship? He was loath to leave his great friends of Tonga and his foster mother; but he yearned to see again his own father and mother, and the *papalangi* people among whom he rightfully belonged.

Will Mariner's heart beat wildly as Finau gave the necessary permission, and ordered three fishermen to take Toki in a good canoe and put him on board the ship, which lay ten miles out to sea.

After four hours of hard paddling, Will's canoe came alongside the ship, which turned out to be the *Hope*, of New York. On the deck waving at him were three of his former shipmates, who had been taken on board at an earlier stop up the coast and had warned Captain Chase about the massacre of the *Port-au-Prince*—that was the reason the cautious shipmaster was out at such a distance from the land of the dangerous Tongans.

From his small canoe Will hailed the ship and asked to be taken aboard. Captain Chase gazed sullenly down at him. "We can't take you, young man," he growled. "We have more hands aboard than we know what to do with."

Will couldn't believe his ears. "Not take me? I am the only white man left here," he pleaded, ignoring other survivors on other islands. "If you have three of my mates there on deck, why not take me?"

"It's no use saying any more. We can't take you, and that's that." The captain turned his back and walked away.

In a frenzy, Will offered to bring out any provisions that the captain might need; but the master of the *Hope* was not listening.

Plunged into despair, Will was now in great danger. If it became known ashore that the captain had refused him the passage, all Will's hard-earned prestige would fall to the ground, and he would be returned to the status of a low peasant. Fortunately, the three fishermen had been so busy staring at the rigging of the *papalangi* vessel that they had missed the drift of the short conversation. Will put on a cheerful face and told them that the ship was bound for a country far from his own, and that he had determined to stay in Tonga after all, until some other ship came out that was bound for his homeland of Bolotané.*

Shouting to his three shipmates to send messages to his parents in London that he was still alive, Will, sick at heart, ordered the fishermen to begin the long pull back to the islands, as the *Hope* filled her sails and steered away to the westward without the sad castaway.

Finau and his chiefs marveled at the lad's return, but swallowed his excuses. The main surprise was that he had brought them no presents from the ship. For some days afterward he was the butt of many a joke. "What a lot of steel axes he has brought back for us!" they would remark. "And beads and mirrors will become all too common among the girls of Vava'u, now that Toki has returned with such a load of gifts!" Poor Will lamely explained that he had been so upset at finding that the ship was not going to Bolotané that he had forgotten to ask for presents. But Finau consoled him, and promised that he should surely depart on the next ship bound for home.

Early in 1810 the surprising news came that the governor of Tongatapu, weary of strife, was offering to acknowledge Finau as the military ruler of all the Friendly Islands, and this governor came to Ha'apai and in a great ceremony submitted himself to Finau's overlordship. Thus, without further war, Finau realized his high ambition of becoming *hau* of all Tonga.

But within a few weeks his joy was spoiled. One of his daughters, a little girl of six to whom he was wildly devoted, fell ill. In despair, the high chief supplicated all the various old gods of Tonga, and dragged the ailing child from one shrine to another. Day after day the child drew closer to death. The oracles of the priests finally uttered the grim word that Finau must be punished for his notorious disdain of the ancient religion, and that either his beloved daughter must die or he, Finau, must die in her place.

Frantic with despair, the chief had the girl hauled to still other god-houses, but while he was taking her in a canoe to another island, the little girl died.

In his angry grief, Finau decided to show his resentment

*All the South Sea natives had trouble with the word Britain. In Honolulu, for example, one of the main thoroughfares is Beretania Street.

by offering openly to the gods the most violent insults that
he could invent. Disdaining the usual funeral, he wrapped
the body of the girl in muslin looted from the *Port-au-
Prince* and put it in a cedarwood chest belonging to the
dead Captain Brown. This casket was carried with the chief
for days, wherever he went. Then Finau sent four of his
trusted warriors, who like him were skeptical about the old
religion, and ordered them to seize and bind the high priest
and then to kill him in any manner they pleased.

But before the high priest could be executed, the gods of
Tonga exacted a fearful revenge. Finau's final outrage was
too sacrilegious to be endured, and as he lay down to rest,
tired by the long festival of defiance—celebrated as if the
girl's death were an occasion for rejoicing—he was seized
with a sudden fit of choking. His jaws shook, he groaned
in great agony, his lips became purple with pain. The gods,
it was clear, had taken him by the throat.

His son Moenga, in a desperate effort to ward off the
threat to his father's life, hurriedly chose one of the lesser
babies of Finau and strangled it in a pious manner. But
this atonement came too late. Will Mariner, at the dying
man's bedside, placed his hand on the chief's heart. There
was one more convulsion, and then Finau II lay empty of
life, a victim of the vengeance of the outraged gods of
Tonga.

The *hau* of Tonga was buried, along with his beloved
daughter in her little cedarwood casket, in a vault near Will's
estates in Vava'u. Mariner could not help revealing a genuine
grief at the loss of this violent man, who with all his bar-
baric faults had been a good friend to the *papalangi* lad
he had saved from death on the ship and had raised to a
high place in the island world. But Moenga told Will that
it was unfitting to a warrior to show womanly tears, and
there were more manly ways of mourning. He pointed to
warriors who ran about knocking themselves over the head
with clubs, and gashing themselves with sharp shells until
the blood ran. Then every mourner went home, shaved his
head and burned a two-inch patch on each cheek; he
rubbed in the juice of a certain berry to make the wound
bleed, and thus the sore was kept open for twenty days
thereafter.

In an impressive ceremony of kava drinking, Moenga was
invested with the kingly title of Finau III, and took his
place at the head of the chiefs. Here was a ruler of a com-

pletely different sort from his violent and treacherous politician of a father. The young man was devoted to the peace and happiness of all his subjects, and advocated a return to the cultivation of the fruits of the soil and the simple arts of woodworking, weaving, and dance and song. Yet he was not unaware that some of the chief's were envious; and, watchful for revolution, he kept his closest friend, Will Mariner, at his side at all times with pistols primed and ready to defend the young king.

The proper number of months of mourning passed, and now the time came for Finau III to perform the ritual of "breaking his head" in front of the tomb of his father. While the party of chiefs were dressing for the ceremony and laying out the weapons with which they were expected to wound themselves, Will Mariner entered the house and thoughtlessly indulged in a loud sneeze.

This omen was so frightful that instantly the warriors realized that they would be affronting the gods and invoking disaster if they went any further in the ritual. Finau III was gripped by one of those storms of rage that he had inherited from his violent father, and roared at his best friend the most frightful Tongan oath he could think of.

Will, realizing what he had done, firmly answered: "Your father would not have believed in such nonsense, and I am surprised that you do." Finau grabbed a club and would have killed Will in an instant, but his chiefs held him down and others hauled Mariner out of the house to safety.

The warriors hastened to assure Finau that the sneeze was, after all, merely a *papalangi* sneeze and should not be allowed to affect their Tongan religious duties. They went forth and began wounding themselves on the head in a violent fashion. Finau, now somewhat reassured, outdid them all. He took a sharp saw, salvaged from the *Port-au-Prince,* and gashed his head frightfully until blood poured forth in streams.

Will withdrew to his estate and, advised by his foster mother, who felt keenly that he should maintain his dignity, resolved not to be the first to make advances of peace toward the young king. Thus he refused to accept any messages to return to the court, and at the end of ten days, Finau himself walked into Will's house, greeted him warmly with a Tongan nose rubbing and begged his pardon for his outburst of anger. The two great friends were reconciled.

Thereafter the young men were inseparable. But although Will Mariner was now the comrade of a king, and a wealthy landholder in an island paradise, he was not happy; for he yearned to see once more the thronging streets of London. His disappointment that Captain Chase had refused to rescue him was still sharp.

Thus his heart leaped up one evening in November, 1810, when, returning home in his canoe, he caught sight of the sails of a European ship against the sunset. At once he ordered his three men to paddle him to the strange vessel, promising that they would be made rich for life by the gifts they would receive.

The head canoe man, Teu, replied that they had seen the ship before but had not told him, because it was well known that the chiefs of Tonga would kill anybody who helped their beloved Toki to leave their land. Again Will ordered the men to paddle him to the ship, but they began whispering together, and then Teu swore that, although they held their master in high respect, they could not disobey their tribal rulers. Teu picked up his paddle and began pulling for the shore.

This was too much for Will to bear. He had been given the power of life and death over these men. It was also well known that, although Teu was a reliable boatman, he had killed two of his children because they were unwanted, and had also, during a time of famine, killed and eaten his own wife. In rage Mariner grabbed up his musket and lunged out with it at the disobedient serf. The barrel was old and worn around the muzzle, and the weapon stabbed into Teu's belly as he knelt at his paddle. With barely a groan, he fell senseless in the bottom of the canoe.

The two others, frightened by Toki's threat that he would shoot them, and unaware that if he fired at either he could not quickly reload, fearfully began paddling toward the distant ship, just barely visible in the dusk. The journey was long and anxious. Guarding himself from the dying Teu and watchful to see that the other men did not jump overboard and abandon him, Will Mariner urged on the exhausted paddlers through the long night.

At dawn the canoe came alongside the ship, and Will leaped into the main chains. He was almost knocked overboard by the sentry placed there. The man naturally supposed that natives were attacking the ship, for here confronting him was a brown-skinned man with long hair knotted inside a turban of bark cloth, wearing only a short skirt of ti leaves.

"I'm an Englishman, a survivor of the *Port-au-Prince!*" Will shouted. An officer standing by came up.

"I am Captain Fisk, of the New South Wales brig *Favorite*," he announced. "I heard in Sydney about the massacre. I'll take you to China, if you are willing to work your passage."

Will agreed at once, and was given a pair of pants and a shirt, so that he could dress like a white man for the first time in four years. But when he washed the shirt, which was filthy, and hung it to dry in the rigging, it was stolen from him, and for the remainder of the voyage to Macao he was to go about naked to the waist.

Will asked the captain to give food and presents to his men in the canoe, who then began the long paddle home with the dead body of the unruly Teu. They took also a steel ax as a present for Finau. Captain Fisk was impressed by Will's story that he was a friend of the ruler of these islands, and anchored the *Favorite* off Vava'u, where a crowd of Will's native friends came out to visit this marvelous ship.

Among the visitors was Finau III, who brought five hogs and forty giant yams as provisions for his comrade and Will's shipmates on the voyage toward home. The Tongan chief was so impressed by the luxury of the ship that he spent a night aboard, and two days later, when the *Favorite* was weighing anchor, he asked Captain Fisk if he might go with Will to Bolotané and learn the sciences that had made the English people so great.

Quite reasonably, the captain refused, pointing out that here Finau was a king, but in England he would, because of his skin color, be put in a lower class and would be given none of the respect that he had taken as his right from the time of his birth.

Finau's beautiful sister came sightseeing on board ship and her lively remarks, translated by Will, greatly amused the crew. She pretended that she would go to Bolotané and asked if she could wear her usual dress there—a skirt of bark cloth and nothing above it. "But perhaps it would be too cold for that, anyway!" she prattled. "I might have to spend all my time in one of those hot-houses that Toki tells me they use to raise plants in from warm climates. And my brown skin would keep me from getting a *papalangi* husband. It would be a great pity to leave so many handsome chiefs in Vava'u and then go to live a single life in England!"

Mariner performed two important tasks before his departure from Tonga forever. The first of these was to persuade Captain Fisk to ship any of the other survivors of the massacre who wished to leave the islands. All those who desired to go were summoned and taken aboard the *Favorite* as members of the crew. Several, however, chose to remain in Tonga, saying that they preferred to live in this tropical, hospitable land rather than to go back and starve in cold, unfriendly England. Among these was one of whom Mariner reported: "Thomas Waters was not disposed, however, to return to England. He was an old man and he reflected that it would be a difficult matter for him to get his bread at home, and as he enjoyed at Vava'u every convenience that he could desire, he chose to end his days there."

The second duty was to recover the log book of the ill-fated *Port-au-Prince*. This record was the only evidence in existence of the claims for prize money from the capture of enemy ships during the cruise, and without it there would be no chance to obtain the shares that represented the whole wages of the survivors for the past four years. Will sent ashore two trusted natives who brought back the famous log book to him. He had hidden it in a barrel of gunpowder—the only place where a curious Tongan might not search for concealed documents.

Almost four years after Will Mariner had first sighted the Friendly Islands, he bade farewell to these fatal shores with a joy tinged heavily with regret. He was leaving behind a private estate, a royal comrade and a host of brown friends whose lives had been mingled with his own. But now Toki wanted to go back to the land of the *papalangi*.

Did he leave behind a sweetheart? In his book Mariner discoursed learnedly on the marriage customs of the Tongans; but nowhere among its thousand pages is there a hint that he loved a Tongan girl.

More than half a year later, voyaging by way of Macao and the Cape of Good Hope, Will Mariner landed at Gravesend—the same port from which, a boy of thirteen, he had sailed with high hopes some six and a half years earlier. He took the ferry to the London side of the river, and sought out his home. But he received a brutal welcome. He was grabbed by a roving press gang who were collecting likely lads to serve forcibly in His Majesty's navy. A prisoner, he was rowed out to a hulk in the river, and more than a week passed before his father, Captain Magnus Mariner, was able to pull strings and get his long-lost son released.

Thus, in a Thames hulk, ended the great adventure of Will Mariner. His mother had died not long before, still believing that her son was a captive on a far Pacific isle; but his father greeted Will joyously. He had said farewell to a little boy; and here was returned to him a man, full grown and bearing the marks of danger and deep experience.

After Will's return to England, his former schoolfellows were hardly able to recognize him. His love of adventure seemed to have been so sated by his savage existence that, as a result of hardships and perils suffered too early in life, he yearned only for rest and quiet. During the five years between his return and the publication of the famous book, usually called *Mariner's Tonga Islands*, he embraced the quietest shore life he could find, as an accountant in a merchant's office.

In May, 1818, he married Margaret Roberts, daughter of a Welsh banker. He then became a stockbroker, going daily to his office in Hercules Chambers at the Stock Exchange. Eventually he retired from business and went to live at Gravesend, in view of the spot from which the *Port-au-Prince* had sailed in his boyhood on the famous voyage.

The Mariners had six daughters and five or six sons. Tradition has it that all the men were drowned at sea, leaving no children. Thus no direct male descendants now live to carry on that fitting and melodious surname of Mariner, so suitable for a family destined to follow the sailor's craft.

Will's wife lived until 1871, after a widowhood of eighteen years. Will, after his hairbreadth escapes and perils on the oceans of the world, had died ironically. He was drowned when a little skiff overturned on the river Thames.

10

Leeteg,
the Legend

Shortly after the end of World War II an airplane pilot
flying low off the coast of Japan saw an impressive sight. A
volcano arose from the surface of the sea, writhed and
twisted in the sunlight, spewed smoke and rock, then in
great convulsions of incredible force lifted an island from
the bowels of the earth and into brute being.

When the pilot returned to base he was badly shaken, for
he had seen what no one had previously witnessed. He had
seen the earth being born, and the sight was unnerving.

The present authors feel much the same way about the
subject now to be treated. They observed the birth of a new
legend that will echo throughout the Pacific for years, and
in retrospect the whole affair is amazing, for this man
boldly set out to clothe himself in fable. "I have boozed
more," he boasted, "fought more, laid more girls, and thrown
more wild parties than anyone else on the island, but it's
all good publicity and gets me talked about plenty, and that's
what sells pictures."

The legend begins on any Tuesday in Tahiti. The little
inter-island boat *Mitiaro* has set out from the neighboring
island of Mooréa around eight in the morning, and for
nearly four hours it has been ploughing through some of the
most glorious waters in the world. Behind lie the noble peaks

of Mooréa, those unexcelled volcanic minarets whose green points dance in the tropic sunlight. Ahead lie the lower and softer hills of Tahiti, whose valleys slip quietly down to the sea, forming black beaches of stark and sweeping charm. No boat in the world plies a more legend-strewn path.

And none is more uncomfortable. There are no seats this morning, for they are jammed by crates of chickens, while overhead, threatening the frail canopy, half a dozen pigs have been lashed together and are squealing their way to market. Forward a group of girls in blue and green *pareus* tucked tightly about their breasts sing old songs as a weary man, propped up against a sack of fruit, strums a guitar and beats time with his foot. He is too perpetually drunk to create a legend, but behind him, leaning against the rail, stands a man of quite a different sort.

He is short, with unusually abbreviated legs and small feet. He stands not more than five feet three and wears a woven Manihiki hat whose flopping brim keeps the sun and spray from his round face and prevents one from seeing his sparse black hair that is just beginning to gray. It is a kindly face that peers out from beneath the island hat. The mouth is ample, the lower jaw juts forward slightly; the chin is fleshy, the nose large. The eyes are a steely blue, and although the man laughs from time to time, for he enjoys all that goes on around him, it is not a naturally mirthful laugh but one that is slightly nervous, as if the owner were a compulsive drunk who had not yet had his morning bottle.

Actually, for five days each week the traveler is abstemious, but on Tuesday mornings, as the *Mitiaro* approaches the dock in Papeete harbor, he senses the approach of good whisky and begins to fidget. For this is his habitual day to tear old Papeete apart, to chase half-naked girls down the street, to punch policemen, to knock Chinese down and to curse at sailors. Gentle, tolerant Tahiti has known some epic brawlers in its day, but none to surpass the strange man who waits impatiently to begin the assault.

It would be difficult for a stranger to identify this short-legged man. He looks like a planter from southern France, but he speaks almost no French. Others will say, in later years, that in appearance he is a twin brother of America's Senator McCarthy, but he boasts not a drop of Irish blood. He is a German, of American birth, and when he calls out to a friend on the *Mitiaro* he uses the nasal twang of Arkansas.

"Behave yourself today," the friend warns him.

"I will," the roly-poly man calls back in his high, flat voice, and everyone within earshot laughs, for it is a certainty that by midnight he will be lying somewhere in a gutter or in jail, his shirt torn off, his eye aflame from some stray fist and his friends gone. It is going to be one hell of a day, this Tuesday in Tahiti; and now, as the rickety *Mitiaro* approaches the pleasure capital of the South Pacific, the chunky little man grimaces in delightful anticipation of the forthcoming brawl.

By noon the dock at Papeete is crammed with islanders who have wandered down to see the boat land. Brown girls and yellow men, and white women with parasols to fight off the midday sun, and traders and bums wait for the gangplank to be lowered; and in the interval two island girls who have been dismally seasick on the bouncing boat jump over the railing of the launch and onto the dock. Unsteadily they run away from the sickening memory of their voyage and disappear in the crowd.

Then, as the gangplank hits the dock, a horde of passengers descend with chickens and bananas and laughter and kisses. There is shouting and much weeping and men making appointments with pretty girls, and finally there is this rather plump forty-nine-year-old American in a Hawaiian shirt and shorts, with a funny hat pulled down about his eyes and a bundle of black velvets under his arm. As he lands in Papeete all the habitual drunks shout greetings, but the more sedate shopkeepers ignore him, for it is apparent that as soon as he gets his velvets safely out of the way, he will start to debauch the town.

Ignoring those who have turned away, he walks slowly through the crowd, limping a little, for he is just recovering from a bout of elephantiasis and one leg is a little swollen. In the old days, this leg would have continued growing until it was thicker than a tree, but now the drug Heterasan controls the disease so that it is no longer disfiguring.

The American walks slowly to the post office, where he mails a huge batch of letters and his lengths of black velvet, on which have been painted in glowing colors a series of handsome Polynesian heads. He is careful of the velvets, for although they used to be worth about $4 each, they have recently skyrocketed to around $5,000 each, and he is becoming rich. He then goes to the Banque d'Indochine, where like a sober businessman he cashes the cabled drafts that have reached him that week from many parts of the world, and drawing a few thousand francs, he stuffs them in his pocket. The rest he deposits to his growing account and signs his name to the receipt in careful blue letters: Edgar William Leeteg.

Then he walks happily through the midday sun of Papeete to a small house where two handsome children eagerly await his weekly visit. As soon as they see him they start to shout, "Papa! Papa!" and then drag into the flowering yard a beautiful woman with long black hair at whose home Leeteg boards his children. She bows to him and he greets her warmly.

Leeteg draws the children around him and listens to their stories of the week's triumphs. "I had a pretty good week, too," he says, throwing a fistful of francs on the table.

"That's too much, Edgar," the lovely woman says.

"Children always need money," he laughs. "Anyway, you know me, I'll booze it away tonight."

Everyone laughs at this and the daughter, a beautiful thing about to burst into womanhood, says, "You were very bad in Papeete last week, Father. You almost wrecked the party at James Norman Hall's."

"This week no booze," her father promises. He then kisses his children, says good-by to the beautiful woman who takes care of them, and steps forth into the golden tropical sunlight. "You kids listen to her," he admonishes. "She knows what's best for you."

From the garden the children wave good-by to the chunky American with the little feet as he walks, with increasingly quick steps, toward the water-front bars.

Leeteg has performed his business and family duties for the day. He has mailed his paintings, dispatched his two dozen letters, evened things out at the bank and seen his Tahiti family. He is ready for some fun, and as he turns a corner onto the main street of Papeete—that wild, poetic street that faces the quay and resembles no other in the world, for yachts tie up stern to, right in the middle of town—he sees that a new white craft has docked and now rests with its after parts jutting into the street not far from the Chinese store where he buys his canned goods. On its stern appears, in fine lettering, *Philante*.

"Yeeeeiiii!" he explodes in a shattering cry of sheer joy. *"Philante,* watch out!"

With dancing little steps, for his short legs will permit

no other, he dashes across the street, over the grass and up the gangplank, allowing his momentum to carry him onto the deck, where he grabs a marlinspike and begins hammering on everything he can reach. "Get up, you goddam sonsabitches," he screams. "Get up! Get me a girl!"

From the interior of the yacht a young American sailor appears and the painter leaps at him like a bear and carries him to the deck. "Case!" he bellows. "Where's a girl?"

Spectators have now gathered along the shore and are watching the brawl. The two Americans tumble noisily about the yacht and the artist keeps shouting for girls. Finally, from the crowd on shore a native girl from the island of Raïatéa identifies the troublemaker and shouts, "Leeteg! Leeteg!"

The brawling painter stops, looks down into the crowd and spots the girl, a playmate of former riots. Quickly he runs down the gangplank, grabs her by the hand and hauls her onto the deck. Other members of the crew, awakened from their midday naps, appear and a soft-spoken Englishman pleads, "Edgar! Not again this week!"

"I'm not gonna drink a drop!" he promises.

"Seriously, we have a meeting here this afternoon. Don't tear the ship apart again today."

There is a moment of hesitation and then the girl jerks Leeteg's hand. "Come along," she whispers. "We go Quinn's."

"Hey, that's a good idea! We'll all go Quinn's."

He leads a motley gang toward Tahiti's famous bar, and hangers-on, who have been dozing in the sun, suddenly become alert when word goes round that Leeteg has some money. The party now has about a dozen able members and soon bangs its way into Quinn's Tahitian Hut, where Leeteg commandeers three split-bamboo alcoves and starts setting up drinks for the house. He pours his down in huge gulps and by late afternoon is almost blind drunk.

In a stupor he rolls from Quinn's to Col Bleu and then by taxi out to Les Tropiques for dinner, after which he hires two cabs and takes the entire gang out to the Lido, east of town. Everywhere he buys liquor for the crowd, not one of whom he can recognize by now, but toward midnight he steers himself uncertainly back to the *Philante*, dragging three island girls along with him. Trying to find the gangplank, he falls into Papeete Bay, from which the *Philante* crew drag him shivering and apparently dead.

But for Leeteg the night is just beginning. Stripping off

all but his underpants, he runs through the streets yelling
for girls, and finally one of his old mistresses, fatter and
with fewer teeth, catches him and hauls him into a dingy
hotel, where she hides him before the police can arrest him.
Another long-time girl friend has meanwhile assembled his
wet clothes at the quay and now takes them to the hotel,
where the first native woman interprets this as trespass on her
man of the night. Accordingly she belts the newcomer over
the head with a shoe.

A majestic brawl ensues in which the two water-front
girls try to gouge out each other's eyes, whereupon Leeteg,
though in a stupor that prevents him from ever understanding who the two girls are, tries to make love to each. Suddenly they turn on him and scream in French, "We'll kick
his balls off!"

Their rage now has a common target and they begin to
assault him. With bottles, shoe heels and a little knife they
try to smash him and carve him up, outraged by their memories of old offenses against their love and their youthful
dignity.

"We're going to kill him!" they scream.

The landlady hears the crashing of the furniture and
forces her way into the room. She finds the American
sprawled on the floor, bleeding heavily from several wounds.
At first she thinks him dead and adds her screams to the
night; but the corpse rises, looks at himself shakily in a dirty
mirror, and starts to rub the blood away from his face.
He smears it further. Then, pushing aside the three shouting women, he lurches naked into the darkened street.

A big policeman, speaking a patient patois of French,
Tahitian and English, ambles slowly over, puts a fat, protecting arm around the chubby artist, and says, "Another
big night, eh, Edgar?"

He leads the American to another hotel and asks the
landlady there to put him to bed. She has performed this
deed of charity often before, but tonight she shies away
from the bloody face and refuses.

"Please," the policeman says in French. "The night is
over. Put him to bed."

"Throw him in there," she growls.

There is a commotion, of course, before the painter can
be got into the bed, so that in a room down the hall a
woman who once lived with Leeteg hears that he is back
in town. Quietly she slips away from her man of the evening,

scurries along the hall, and darts into Edgar's room. Her man misses her and begins to bellow, "Teuru, come back here!"

When there is no reply he suspects that she has gone to Leeteg, so he roars down the passageway and begins to bang on the artist's door. "Goddam you, Teuru! Come out here."

There is a soft giggle inside and he becomes infuriated. "I'll kill you! I'll kill you!"

He does not specify whom he is going to murder but after a while the patient policeman appears and tells him to go back to bed. "My girl's in there!" the outraged man reports.

The policeman studies the man, studies the door. "You better go back to sleep," he advises.

When all is quiet, Leeteg's door opens. He appears wrapped in a woman's *pareu,* and after him tiptoes the water-front girl he knew years ago. They slip along the darkened hallway and out into the fragrant tropical night. A breeze has set in from Mooréa, and the palms along the shore are bending against the moon. Silently the accidental lovers steal out of the hotel and across the main street, and make a dash for the *Philante.* This time Leeteg is in much too bad shape to negotiate the gangplank, and again he pitches into the bay.

"He's drowning!" the girl screams in French.

The policeman walks unhurriedly up, looks over the situation and calls, *"Philante!* You got a boat hook?"

A tiny light appears aboard, followed by Case, the American sailor, who fishes the drowning artist from the bay. Unsteadily, Leeteg climbs aboard, refreshed by the cold water. "You got any girls here?" he mumbles.

"Christ, what hit your face? Looks like a shoe heel."

"You got any girls?"

The owner of the yacht appears in shorts. "Oh, dammit, Edgar. Not all night again, please."

"You got any girls?" Leeteg asks huskily.

"Shall I take him to jail?" the policeman asks.

"No, we'll bunk him down somewhere."

"Where are the girls?" Leeteg demands in a roar.

Up the gangplank hurries the dark-skinned girl who rescued him from the hotel. "Hello, Teuru," the *Philante* men say.

"We sleep him here," she says solicitously.

But at that moment Leeteg collapses on the deck and it

takes two sailors and the girl to drag his leaden body into the saloon, where he promptly and happily begins to snore. The girl covers him with a blanket and lies beside him. Then she too falls asleep. A bright rosy glow begins to rise on the peaks of Mooréa and a fishing boat puts into the magic harbor with its night's catch, while a church bell rings across the town.

Tuesday is over in Tahiti.

This account does not exaggerate Edgar Leeteg's regular Tuesday performances during the middle years of this century. He rioted, dissipated his energies, destroyed his health, fornicated with anyone he could find, often wound up in jail or hospital, and awoke on Wednesday with a clear head. That he survived even a year of such abuse is a miracle. That he died in the middle of such a night was appropriate.

The immediate impulse that launched such astonishing performances is found in his report to a friend: "I've rolled up enough fool adventures here to perpetuate my memory for years to come." No one can read Leeteg's painstaking accounts of his binges without realizing that the artist planned them, carried them out and wrote about them with one purpose in mind. He wanted to be talked about and remembered as a wild character. He wanted to become a legend.

What were the details of the legend he worked so hard to create?

His grandfather Lütig (Lutteg, Leeteg) had been a graveyard sculptor in Germany, his great-grandfather an architect. Leeteg was born in East St. Louis, Illinois, on April 13, 1904, the son of a butcher who worked across the river in St. Louis, but Leeteg once claimed that his first breath was a whiff of the Chicago stockyards, a city which he later admitted he had never seen and didn't want to see. At sixteen he went to work for an uncle in Little Rock, Arkansas, after which he shifted to many jobs: cotton picking in Louisiana, foundry work in Illinois, herding cows in Texas, odd jobs in Alaska.

At twenty-two he landed a good position with Foster & Kleiser, a large outdoor advertising concern in Sacramento, California, where he mastered the art of working from a small photograph or drawing which was to be expanded until it filled a billboard. He was especially skilled in making the required enlargements with his unaided eye and at depicting, even on billboards of mammoth size, human figures that created the illusion of roundness. He favored bright colors and prided himself on producing a billboard whose parts were in harmony. After he became a successful artist he was often accused of being nothing but a hack letterer; actually, he was not much good at lettering and could not have made a living that way, but he was already highly skilled at copying photographs of the human figure.

Toward the end of his life, a Boston publisher asked him to write his autobiography, and the world lost a lusty volume when he completed only a few pages and quit the effort. His words do explain, however, how he stumbled upon Tahiti.

"My first trip to Tahiti was a vacation of six weeks in 1930. I chose Tahiti from a bunch of travel folders because the $134 round-trip fare by the Union Steamship Co. fitted into my year's savings for a vacation. Even at that my vacation was almost cut short upon arrival because the Tahiti government demanded $20 of the $54 I had in my pocket as a landing tax for a sojourn of over three days.

"I could have returned by the northbound steamer within three days, but I tightened my belt, sold my boots and camera, subsisted on a bowl of soup and bread bought for two francs nightly at a Chinese restaurant, and borrowed $8 from another American, C. C. Campbell, who operated a combination curio shop, rooming house, and real estate office in Papeete. I faced foodless days when a policeman caught me riding one of Campbell's bicycles one evening at dusk and hauled me into court for riding without a light. The court summons set a date which would be later than my departure date. Campbell advised me to request the court to set the date forward rather than for me to sneak away like a cur avoiding punishment. So I asked for a trial date that would be prior to my departure. It was granted by a surprised official. At the trial my English testimony in a French court got me short shrift and a fine of five francs, which was not exorbitant to my lean purse until I discovered upon paying my fine that it meant sixty francs including costs. As an explanation the official told me that ink and paper for entering the court proceedings cost money.

"Certainly the tropical splendor of Tahiti exceeded the glowing words of the travel folders. I hiked into jungle-choked Fautaua Valley and got lost looking for the waterfall. I rode the hundred-odd miles around Tahiti and to Tautira, the most beautiful native village. At a hotel near there

I contracted ptomaine poisoning from a free breakfast given by a somewhat surly proprietor. At the time I thought his generosity strange; afterward I reasoned differently when I fell from the bicycle and lay beside the road doubled in abdominal pains until the retching came. The proprietor had evidently learned where his favorite maid had slept the previous night. Few people passed where I lay moaning on that country road, but of the few who did, none stopped to ask the trouble or offer aid. Tahiti seems to have a dearth of Good Samaritans. What charity is dispensed in Tahiti today is principally given by the American residents. The last night of my Tahiti vacation was in the company of another American and two island belles at the old Tiare Hotel, now dismantled but in those days the bright spot of the island.

"Campbell trusted me with some souvenirs but the real Tahitian souvenir was given me by the little gal of the night before. I became increasingly aware of her souvenir as the boat steamed ten days back to San Francisco. No, I can't say that my first acquaintance with Tahiti made me vow to return some day. Adding up and balancing the pleasure and the pain, I did not then care if I ever saw the place again.

"When I returned from my Tahiti vacation I became aware of the effects of the 1929 depression upon my job with Foster & Kleiser Co. Some of my fellow workers and union brothers voiced regret that I came back to share the meager amount of work available. Another young man who had been taking over my work as pattern-maker was bitter that I was taking my job back. He complained that he was married and I was not, therefore he needed the work more than I did. As a more efficient and willing worker than some around me I now came in for more criticism for not slowing down. I was on trial at my labor union for working a few minutes overtime to complete a job in the country which otherwise would have necessitated another long trip the following morning. Fidelity to my work earned me the promotion to foreman of the hand-painted poster department. I could fire the men who worked under me. When they shirked and slowed down production I did fire some. Jobs became bones that the so-called brothers fought over. Work was spread out thinly a few days a week to keep all the men on the payroll. Still, jobs were bones that brothers fought over. One morning when I came to my work on a poster, the head designer, and my best friend, was working on it. 'My kids have to eat!' he shouted at me to hide his embarrassment.

"All this was building up a bitterness in me. Letters were coming to me from Campbell saying there was opportunity awaiting me in Tahiti. A company was forming to build a theater in Papeete and he had wangled me the job of doing the decorating and subsequently the lobby advertising. They had great plans. With the passing years I learned that people of Papeete always have great plans, none of which materialize; the pleasure they derive is from the dreaming, the profit from those they can convince of their dreams. The little lady who bequeathed me the souvenir mailed me a can of guava jelly and an offer to share her plantation with her. Neither was good. The jelly was spoiled by the customs poking an enquiring knife point into the can.

"At this critical time I received a small inheritance due my deceased father, all that was left of his father's estate in Germany. I had been trying to establish my claim to it for fourteen years. Finally a plea to Hitler himself freed the money. No, I didn't sell our America nor myself to soften the dictator's heart; it was probably just a brotherly tie between one housepainter and another that appealed to him. The lawyer went with us to his bank to cash the draft and took his half at the cashier's window. The remaining half called for a decision as to how best to spend it. Mom and I talked it over again and again. Shall we use it to eke out a thin and thinning weekly pay check? Or shall we cut loose from the struggle and find a new hunting ground? Where to go? The depression was everywhere. As secretary to my union I received scores of printed requests such as 'No work in Chicago,' 'Union clearance cards will not be received by local such-and-such.' But there lay the last letter from Campbell offering opportunity in the Garden of Eden. The decision was not so hard after all. We packed our few belongings, bought new clothes. I stole several brushes from the plant where I was in charge of supplies. I washed out a dozen mayonnaise jars and filled them with paint from the stockroom. Then with a trusting gray-haired mother, a portable phonograph, and a dozen jars of assorted paints, I tossed my job to my hungry friends and set sail for Tahiti . . . where the happy failures go. And for me as well as the other odd hundred Americans in Tahiti, life began for us from the moment we waved at the sea of happy faces that meet every ship coming to Papeete."

There the autobiography ends and the legend begins. For in Tahiti he found an atmosphere so congenial and a police force so tolerant that he finally decided to take out French citizenship. "In America I would be in jail all the time," he reasoned. "Here I am accepted for what I am." He also loved the island for its crazy pattern of life. "Never bet on anything in Tahiti," he wrote, "excepting that the sun sets in the west."

During his first years in Tahiti he lived not on Mooréa but in Papeete, where his mother tried running a restaurant, but went broke. He spent his free time with a crowd of hard-drinking, wild-loving, hell-raising friends. He worked primarily as a sign painter but accepted any jobs that were offered, and lived miserably without one spare franc. When actual poverty was at hand, Mrs. Leeteg returned to the United States, but her son stayed on. He had not yet begun to paint on velvet.

The legend says, "One day, perhaps just after the daily rains had chased their hundred rainbows off to Bora Bora, Leeteg entered a store and, if he behaved in character, went at least so far as to chuck the salesgirl's chin.

" 'Give me some monk's cloth,' he said. 'I need it to paint on.'

" 'We're all out of monk's cloth,' replied the girl, sure at first she had lost a sale.

"Then she remembered the commodity that was overly bountiful on her shelves and that the proprietor had told her to push.

" 'How about some velveteen?' she said. 'Could you paint on that?'

"Could he? . . . In time Leeteg was to stumble upon the technique that made his paintings live with the glow of human flesh.

" 'Stumble upon' is not the precise term for what happened unless used in the sense that is applied to the manner in which a chemist discovers a new 'wonder drug' after countless hours of compounding chemicals, for Leeteg worked hard at perfecting his technique.

"One Frenchman in Tahiti, seeing some of Leeteg's paintings placed on his terrace to dry, settled for a romantic answer to the question, 'What is the secret to the method with which Leeteg mixed his paint?'

" 'I know what it is!' the Frenchman exclaimed. 'It is mixed with God's own sun.' "

That's how the legend says he got started.

Armed with a technique well suited to Polynesian subjects, Leeteg now faced the difficult job of creating a market for his work. In bars the velvets were popular and occasionally a drunk sailor would buy one for $4. Today those early Leetegs sell for $2,000, and it is fascinating to imagine the shock some sailor's wife in Baltimore is going to get some day when she opens that trunk in the attic.

On a trip to the United States to bring back his mother, who would live the rest of his life with him in Tahiti, Leeteg paid his passage by working as a sign painter in Honolulu, where he also peddled his velvets, which no one seemed to want. His price was now $20 and he specialized in nudes, but he was not entirely committed to velvet, for when he won first prize at the Hawaiian Orchid Fanciers' Show, it was for an oil painting of orchids done on canvas.

By 1938, on a later visit to Hawaii, he was an established velvet artist, but again he had to take a sign-painting job in order to live. During the Christmas rush of 1939, Leeteg's boss called on him for a large Santa Claus.

"What's Santa Claus look like?" the chunky artist asked.

"You know—Santa Claus."

"Show me what he looks like and I'll paint him," Leeteg insisted, and so someone dug out a Santa Claus painted by the dean of illustrators of the time, J. C. Leyendecker. Leeteg grabbed the small picture and within a few hours produced a blow-up that was startling. An admiring fellow worker recalls, "It was better than Leyendecker himself had done. It looked as if Santa were going to speak. We put it in the lobby of the Waikiki Theater and kids thought it really was Santa."

A man took Leeteg aside and said, "If you can paint like that, why do you paint signs?"

"I paint what I can make a living on," Leeteg replied.

"But your velvets? Don't they sell?"

"When velvets sell, I'll paint velvets."

Almost by accident, Leeteg picked up a devoted pair of patrons for this style of work. Mr. Wayne Decker, a happy, extroverted jeweler from Salt Lake City, was eleven generations descended from John Alden and Priscilla Mullens and an elder in the Mormon Church. His business having prospered wildly, he had formed the unlikely habit of carting his entire family—wife, three sons, two daughters—on junkets around the world, and on one memorable starlit evening he was dining with his entourage in the Royal Hawaiian Hotel on the sands at Waikiki. He had just danced with Clara Inter, the performer famed under the name of "Hilo Hattie," and was strolling down a corridor of shops. Under a spotlight in one of them was a painting on black velvet of the girl with whom he had just danced. She was in her garish costume as "the cockeyed mayor of Kaunakakai," and her eyes seemed to be snapping and her lips laughing aloud.

Decker had to leave for Australia early next morning, but when he returned to Honolulu some months later, he eagerly sought out the shop, intending to purchase the painting. The shopkeeper only dimly remembered the piece. He did not know where it had gone, or even who had painted it.

Nearly a year later, Mr. and Mrs. Decker strolled ashore at Papeete. To their delight, the tourists found, hanging on the wall of a souvenir store, no less than fourteen paintings on black velvet, obviously by the artist who had rendered "Hilo Hattie." Both were delighted, and especially admired a portrait of "Hina Rapa" in her big yellow hat.

The Deckers decided overnight that they must have this one to hang over their library desk back home in Salt Lake. They rushed ashore to make the great purchase. And when they entered the store, they saw that every one of the fourteen paintings was gone! Later they discovered that the proprietor of the Seven Seas night club on Hollywood Boulevard in Los Angeles had made a special trip to Papeete to obtain these works as decorations for his club.

But Leeteg was asked to get in touch with the Deckers, and he did so. The first meeting of patron and artist was recounted by Mr. Decker himself. "A short, stocky chap in a wide straw hat disengaged himself from a group of people, and with a smile as wide as the hat he greeted me. 'You must be Mr. Decker. Crawford told me when I found the loudest Hawaiian shirt I'd ever seen, it'd be you.' I admitted the identity and invited him aboard.

"We visited for a couple of hours. He left the ship with five of my loudest shirts and all the loose money we had in the crowd. I don't remember how much it might have been. The tears were running down his face. He said I was the first man who had really trusted him since he had been in Tahiti.

He assured me I wouldn't be sorry, that he'd outdo himself in doing another 'Hina Rapa' for us. He would send it to me when he was satisfied it was his very best."

Eventually, the new painting arrived in Salt Lake City, along with five other fine examples of Leeteg's portraiture on velvet. The Deckers were more enthusiastic than ever, and immediately sent a check with an order for at least ten paintings a year, at any price within reason. This arrangement lasted till Leeteg's death, and the Deckers built up a collection of more than two hundred velvets, three fourths of which now are on show in their Salt Lake City home.

Leeteg survived as an artist through the encouragement and financial support of this couple from Utah, whom he had seen only briefly. It was the Deckers who provided the money with which Leeteg built his Mooréa home. They sent funds when Edgar's mother had to go to Hawaii to recuperate from a near-fatal illness. It was the Deckers who commissioned the artist's work through the lean years, and left a standing order: "Send us one of everything you paint."

Although Decker reprimanded Leeteg whenever the quality of his work slipped or colors faded in transit, the Salt Lake City jeweler never wavered in his belief that he had discovered an artistic genius. He wrote shortly before Leeteg's death: "Edgar, please know that to me you are the greatest living artist in the world. I want everyone to see you as great as I do. I am very proud of your work and love nothing more than showing it to my friends. To me it is out of this world and I find my friends are equally impressed."

The chance meeting with Decker assured Leeteg's survival, but it was an accidental meeting with a much different kind of man that assured his fame. In the early 1930's, while working as a sign painter in Honolulu, Leeteg met a tall, gangling, happy-go-lucky, tattooed submarine sailor named Barney Davis, who on shore leave played the accordion at the Princess Theater, where Leeteg's company had quarters. The two were natural companions, for both liked bootleg beer, funny stories, women and music. Davis could simultaneously play *Sobre las Olas* on his accordion, accompany himself with one hand on a pipe organ, eat a ham sandwich, and drink a glass of foaming beer. This Leeteg considered just about tops in human accomplishment.

At this time Davis was unaware that Leeteg painted anything but signs, and for about fifteen years lost sight of the

Tahiti artist; but when Davis opened a Honolulu art shop in 1947, he was pestered by sailors who wanted "one of those velvets like they have in the bar." Davis went down into the rugged section of the city to inspect the velvets, which had already begun to cause a commotion in Hawaii. Once they had been traded to the barkeeper for drinks and sandwiches, and they still made a handsome display above the mirror. The artist? No one knew where he lived.

Then a Mormon missionary returning from Tahiti—where that church has always been strong—wandered into the art shop and unrolled two fine velvets, better than anything Davis had seen so far. The missionary knew Leeteg and that afternoon Davis rushed off an air-mail letter containing $500 with instructions for Leeteg to send regular shipments of his work.

The business relationship that resulted was notable for two reasons. Davis sold velvets like mad and paid Leeteg large sums of money, and Leeteg in return sent Davis long letters in which the most intimate aspects of life were discussed. That we know so much about this inflammable artist is due to his outpourings to Barney Davis.

His first letter set the style for all that followed: "Maybe I'd better give you the straight about the Leeteg rumors in Hawaii, although the publicity I get from the adverse rumors seems to help rather than hinder the sale of velvets.

"As long as I'm rutting and drinking I'm not dead, so that rumor is easy to kill.

"I've never been in Chicago and was never a bum or a beachcomber. But let it go at that. I don't mind being a bum and/or a beachcomber if it increases my sales.

"I'm not a dopehead either though I've visited dens with tourists on slumming parties. However, all good artists from Tahiti are supposed to be inspired by drugs.

"I don't use spray gun, or projectors, or stencils or any mechanical means in producing my velvets and this dastardly lie you should correct with your clients.

"I worked as pattern maker, designer, and pictorial painter for Foster & Kleiser Outdoor Advertising Co., but did no lettering then. Was not good enough at it. But did all Tahiti's signs and decorating until five years ago when I quit to devote all time to velvets. I also did posters for Waikiki Theater and helped decorate the Toyo Theater. Ordinary artist's oil paints are used on velvets and applied with ordinary artist's brushes.

"The truest or nearest to the truth of all the rumors you listed is that the models are my wives. Technically I'm not married to any of 'em but I do lay a goodly number. . . . Am really married—much to my regret—but am separated from her now.

"Tell me all this—I like it. Lot of the more malicious lies originate with a guy . . . who once lived here and is trying to imitate my velvets in Hawaii now with zero success."

The last phase of Leeteg's life was now beginning. He painted velvets as rapidly as his energies permitted and airmailed them to Davis, who sold them at increasingly high prices. More important, so far as the Leeteg legend is concerned, Davis launched a publicity campaign that will probably never subside in the Pacific.

He made many smart moves. First he suggested that Leeteg sign all pictures "Leeteg, Tahiti," and from then on in both advertising and conversation Davis referred to his artist in that manner, or more simply as The Master. He also invented the tradition, afterward adopted by many purchasers, of invariably writing BLACK VELVET in capital letters. He bombarded Honolulu papers with stories about Leeteg, printed handsome brochures in which the paper looked and felt like velvet, reproduced the more popular Leeteg subjects in superb photographs that sold in large batches at $15 each, and started referring offhand to Rembrandt, Goya, Rubens and Hals when seeking some basis of comparison for The Master's work. And that Leeteg was the inheritor of Gauguin's mantle he took for granted and got the public to do the same. It was Davis who coined the phrase, "The American Gauguin."

It was a good, clean relationship, one that made Leeteg rich in both money and accolade. There were bickerings about price—Leeteg wanted a bigger cut of the profits—but they always subsided and Davis acquired more than two hundred velvets. Early in the life of the arrangement Davis turned all bookkeeping over to an accountant, who saw to it that Leeteg got paid regularly. Since the artist had been careless and unbusinesslike in his previous sales, handing his work over to any tourist who said, "I'll sell these for you," and since he had lost thousands of dollars on people whom he never heard from again, he appreciated Davis' honesty. "You and God are all the allies I need," he wrote, and his appreciation for what the Honolulu dealer accomplished was expressed almost weekly, and in moving words.

He also relied on Davis for artistic guidance, and although Davis spoke like the immortal dealer—"Send me what will sell"—he also warned whenever quality slumped; and Leeteg acknowledged this: "Apology for feeling miffed at your letter saying the seven velvets which finally arrived were below my standard. Thanks for standing up and telling me something that is for my own good. I really thought those seven were above par and they looked fine when I sent them—that's why I could not savvy your dissatisfaction with them—until I found out what was wrong—*the colors sank into the velvet dye.* . . . You are right as rain about the necessity of my concentrating on the luminous qualities in my velvet. With my head full of art ideas I was getting sidetracked from the one feature that puts velvet in a class by itself—their *luminosity.* I promise to stay on the *right* track hereafter."

One of the greatest pleasures enjoyed by Leeteg in this relationship was Davis' glowing faith that Leeteg was the greatest painter of contemporary times. At no time did Davis waver in this opinion, and one of the authors of this book can testify to the fire with which Davis, then unknown to him, telephoned in 1950, shouting, "Christ, you've got to come down here right away! I've uncovered an artist who's as good as Rembrandt." Occupied with other things, the writer did not obey the summons, which was repeated in 1951: "Look, goddamit, this man Leeteg is more exciting than Gauguin. He's a new Rubens, believe me." By 1952 Davis was impatient and growled, "Look, you sonofabitch, these velvets are only a block from where you're sitting. Come over and see the new Goya." Again it proved impossible and in 1953 Davis reported simply, "He's dead. You waited too long and now he's with the immortals."

In 1954 Davis launched a writing campaign that finally lured the writer into his handsome gallery, which had been converted into a shrine for Edgar Leeteg. There were velvets, for $5,000, Leeteg letters, a handsome photograph in color of the Leeteg outhouse, color snapshots of the artist raising hell with one of his models and fine reproductions of Leeteg originals.

Some of this overpowering belief rubbed off on Leeteg, and while there is excellent written evidence that he positively refused ever to think of himself in terms of Rembrandt or Rubens, he did start speaking of himself as the American Gauguin. In 1952 Davis visited Tahiti and one resident reported: "It was like a cyclone. He played his accordion. Any number anybody requested, he played *Sobre las Olas*. But what set Tahiti agog was his opinion of Leeteg. We'd never thought much of him down here but Davis announced flatly that he was as good as Rembrandt and the hottest selling artist of modern times. Tahiti is still gasping. As somebody said the other night, 'My God! Suppose Davis is right! Suppose Leeteg really is good!'"

There were, of course, adverse aspects of the relationship. At one time Leeteg wrote: "Will do several for you of 127 . . . and then discontinue this number as my photo is faded with age and every time I strain my eyes on such a one—or one too small a copy as 108—I have a little less eyesight, so better take my word for it when I say I can't do a certain number, although I'll take a chance on eyestrain for just a couple more. The more I abuse my eyes the sooner I'll be blind. Take your choice. I don't give a damn."

But shortly before his death Leeteg summarized his business experience with Davis: "Am fixed fine financially now. Limit the January remittance to three hundred maximum and lay the rest in your safe for me." The fact is that Leeteg was barely scraping by on Wayne Decker's subsidy when he established relations with Davis. He wrote that in 1946 his velvets were selling for $25. When he died, some were bringing over $7,000. For this transformation Barney Davis was largely responsible, and it was free use of the names of Rembrandt, Hals, Gauguin, and Rubens that fortified his customers in accepting the high prices he named. After all, if a millionaire who knows nothing about art is contemplating an outlay of thousands for something he could have bought for fifty dollars a few years back, a word like Rembrandt is most reassuring.

The Leeteg legend had other facets that insure its survival. His most famous model also happened to be the girl he loved throughout his life. She was a lively, adorable island child whose winsome little face has become fairly well known in many parts of the world. Her arrival in the Leeteg household was the best thing that ever happened to the artist emotionally; her forced departure became a deep, inconsolable tragedy. When she had gone a friend reported, "Long ago Leeteg confided to me that he recognized as the most tragic circumstance of his life his failure to find the right woman. . . . Isn't it indeed tragic to think that while, perhaps, there exists for most of us a true mate, yet such are the mischances of life that in the majority of cases we are destined to miss each other like 'ships that pass in the night.'" She had been the girl for Leeteg, but he had allowed her to be driven from his home, and for the rest of his life he paid a heavy penalty.

After her departure he married—he had had two previous wives in the United States—and picked up dozens of others Tahiti style, but he found no lasting gratification. His later riotous behavior merely demonstrated the emptiness he suffered.

His epic fights with his neighbors, Tahitian and European alike, added to the legend, for they protested against his fantastic building program, his boisterous parties, his drunken Tuesdays and almost his very existence as an alien in the colony. He, in reply, scorned them, calumniated them, ground their noses in the dirt when he had a chance. He had to suffer lawsuits, threats, ostracism, but he always bounced back with some new outrage to command attention. And he loved every minute of the fighting. "To hell with their petty jealousies," he wrote to Davis. "If I busied myself with such pettiness I would not get any farther than they do. I'm intending to *go places* and I can't stop to kick at the curs snapping at my heels." He used the vilest language to describe his enemies and gloated indecently when he triumphed over them: "The *Philante* is giving us some good publicity here making these green-eyed #$%&%#$& groan when they brag about your gallery and how Leeteg rates in Hawaii."

His running fight with academic artists degenerated into abiding bitterness. It had started in Honolulu when Academy of Arts judges turned down some of his velvets as not being art but more like leather tooling or embroidery. He stormed the exhibition, cursed his rivals, accused the judges of assigning themselves all the prize money, and issued a statement which forever precluded acceptance of his velvets by Honolulu artists: "The tourists who gape at the current exhibition are probably of the opinion that they have seen better similar art on the end of a stableboy's shovel."

Later he stated his views even more forcefully: "Please don't bother submitting any of my work to art societies or museums as I hold them long-haired bastards in contempt since I know a lot about how and why they operate. Leave them to plug for their own darling daubers. We don't need them and they are just cheap fourflushers in frock coats. To hell with them even when they come to you. Tell them

Leeteg is very particular about hanging his paintings in a museum in the same room with some of the stuff that is now classed as art. If this modern crap is art, I prefer not to have my stuff labeled as art, but just call them beautiful but not art, or beauty because it is not art. Fight back at these snobs. I do and I've went a long way without their help. It's really a drawback to tie up with them. We are selling our pictures and they cannot sell their works so they put them in museums so people will have to look at it when they come to see the real art of the old masters there. But Rembrandt and Rubens would get the brushoff if they approached the art guys with their works today. I could tell a lot about these #$%&$&#%@ in pince-nez, but I just boil when I talk about them S.O.B.'s."

A most regrettable by-product of this hatred for academic artists was his lifelong bitterness toward two inoffensive Honolulu artists, Ben Norris and Madge Tennent, to whom he turned again and again through the years with savage diatribes. They had won prizes the year his velvets had been disqualified. The intemperate language he used prohibits quotation.

So the legend grew, pretty much as Leeteg had originally intended. Often he wearied of his role and would write that his exhibitionism was wearing him down, but of course it kept people talking about him, which, he said, was the important thing. One of the authors met Leeteg once when he was in such a mood. The interview started in typical Leeteg fashion, with the artist announcing in Quinn's Tahitian Hut, "I suppose you're one of those #$&$%@#@ who's gonna write a book about Tahiti and tell a lot of #%&#&$% lies and spoil it for honest @#%&$@% like me!" Then he got offensive and claimed that nobody could understand the South Pacific, not even Leeteg, who had laid more native girls than the writer could count. Finally he subsided and in a gentle mood of reflection said it was a tough life, a very tough life. He said he got very tired at times and he guessed that the writer had already discovered there were never enough hours in the day to complete the work one intended. But the conversation in Quinn's ended when he spied a sailor who had offended him. "Hey, you contemptible #@%&$@#," he bellowed, and late that night he was dragged into the writer's hotel, a bloody mess.

In many ways he was a very gentle human being and

spent his money lavishly to help others. Whenever he received a sizable check from Honolulu he would spend a share of it buying the paintings of Tahiti artists whose work was not selling. Then, on the *Mitiaro* heading back to Mooréa, he would stand at the gunwales and toss the canvases into the wind like playing cards. He kept urging Davis to sign on younger artists, but he hated bitterly anyone who presumed to copy his work on velvet: "I think that when all the velvets arrive you will have enough for a real exhibit, and maybe follow this by an announcement of $50 prize (deduct from my account) for the best velvet painted by a Hawaii artist. Exhibit them along with one or two of *my best* and let the public make comparisons, *but after the exhibit is over tell the winner his stuff is not good enough for your gallery*. This will end most of my up-and-coming competition. Also have all the entries in your hands two weeks *before* the exhibit, which is enough time for their colors to dry thoroughly and fade if they are going to fade and crack. Savvy?"

The Leeteg legend reached its climax in February, 1953. The yacht *Philante* had returned and was again stern to at the quay, and Leeteg had a series of monstrous nights with two members of the crew, Reggie Chambers and Herb Case. Once when the latter was cruising in Mooréa waters, Leeteg spotted him, hauled him off the boat, and made him stay at Villa Velour for three days. Case says, "We had a party every night till two, but at six Edgar was at his easel."

When Case left, Leeteg promised, "I'll see you in Papeete this week-end!"

"You mean you're coming over on the Saturday *Mitiaro?*" Case asked.

"Sure! Gotta give you boys a party before you sail."

When Case reported this, Chambers and the captain said, "Jesus, we've got to keep Leeteg out of here Saturday. You know how he can bust up a party, and we've got to entertain the government officials."

"We just won't tell him about the party," Chambers suggested.

"He can smell a party at ten miles," Case warned.

And sure enough, the *Mitiaro* had docked only ten minutes that Saturday, February 1, 1953, when squat, roly-poly, short-legged Edgar Leeteg trotted briskly up the gangplank, roaring, "Hear there's a brawl organizing!"

Chambers recalls that he and the captain took Leeteg aside and put it to him straight. "This is a formal affair, Edgar, and you're not welcome."

"I ain't gonna drink."

Everyone laughed at this and Leeteg raised his hand solemnly. "I'll sit here and act like a gentleman."

"Like you did at James Norman Hall's?" somebody asked.

"I was drunk that day. Today, nothing."

So the *Philante* let him stay and Chambers says, "He was the perfect guest. He bowed to all the officials and didn't curse the ladies."

At dusk, when the formal guests had departed, the *Philante* crowd decided to go west of Papeete for a farewell dinner at Les Tropiques. Lew Hirshon, leader of the American community, and his beautiful Tahitian wife were driving their cars and invited Leeteg to join them, but Leeteg preferred to climb on the back of a blue Harley-Davidson motorcycle owned by Herb Case, and together the two friends roared through the tropical night. Leeteg shouted, "First time I've ever been on one of these things sober!"

At Les Tropiques the party separated into two rooms. Hirshon acted as host in one, Leeteg in the other. He gathered about him a gang of barflies and native girls and began to raise hell. "I promised to stay sober until the guests left, but now we'll have some white wine." He started to guzzle from the bottle, then primly put it down. "Tonight I'll stay sober, in honor of the *Philante*." He tried to get some dancing started, prancing about the native girls in tiny steps, but there was no music and the project faded. When the bill came, he characteristically wanted to pay it all.

The two parties broke up simultaneously and it was agreed that everyone would roister out to the Lido, where some of Tahiti's wildest brawls occur. Again Hirshon offered to drive Leeteg, since it was obvious that Herb Case wanted to carry his *vahine* on the back of his motorbike, but Leeteg liked the feel of wind on his face and shouted, "I'll ride here, on the back seat." Accordingly he shoved Case's girl into one of the cars and climbed aboard the motorcycle.

It was not a back seat he had; the motorcycle was an oversize single-seat job on which a passenger, usually a girl, perched while she wrapped her arms about the driver's body for protection. This Edgar did, but at the start the wheels spun in the Tropique gravel, and he almost fell off.

Therefore he grabbed Case more tightly, and in this way they roared onto the highway.

They had gone only a few hundred yards when Leeteg cried, "We'll turn off and see Ten Francs!" referring to a retired admiral whose name—du Saint Front—when pronounced rapidly sounded like Two Five Francs. He was Leeteg's only firm friend in the French colony, and on most visits to Papeete, Edgar sought him out for counsel.

What happened next is unknown. Some claim that Leeteg, dead drunk, started throwing his hefty body around. Others say he grabbed Case so tightly the motorcycle veered. Case says he thinks Edgar grabbed at the handle-bar grip to turn up toward Admiral du Saint Front's, accidentally turning the throttle. No one knows.

We do know that the motorcycle, partly out of control, went into an S-curve leading to a bridge by the school, that it struck a concrete abutment, and that Leeteg was thrown head-first into a low cement wall. The back of his head was split open, and he was instantly killed. At the hospital the attendants, when they saw him bloody and still, said, "He's been on another drunk," but when they saw the back of his head completely smashed in, they laid him out in a big zinc tray and covered him with a sheet.

The automobiles had carried the rest of the party on to the Lido, and there the news was sent that Leeteg was dead. The *Philante* crowd hurried back to the morgue and saw the stiffening little body. Then the party broke up to look after two dissimilar jobs. Lew Hirshon, who had never approved of Edgar Leeteg, said he would take care of the funeral and offered his family crypt for the burial.

While Lew Hirshon attended to the funeral, the *Philante* crew hurried to the yacht, got up a full head of steam, and sped across the bay to inform Edgar's mother, on Mooréa, of what had happened. But when the yacht tied up at Villa Velour, the crew discovered that Edgar's elderly mother was too ill to make the rough journey to Papeete. "When we suggested that she return to Papeete with us," Reggie Chambers reports, "she said weakly, 'I can't leave Mooréa!' So we held the funeral without her."

The services took place in a church, where the pastor delivered such·a lukewarm eulogy that Hirshon, always impetuous, swore during most of the service and was heard muttering, "This is a hell of a way to bury a man." At the end of the prayer he said in a loud, sharp voice, "What a hell of a way to dismiss an old friend!"

The procession was led by a black hearse with cut-glass windows, drawn by black-draped horses. Out toward Les Tropiques the cortege went, and up the hill to the cemetery to where a pergola formed a dismal arch, under which the lead horse balked so that it had to be led by hand. Hirshon growled, "By God, everything's going wrong at this funeral." But the worst was now at hand.

At Hirshon's vault a perfunctory prayer was mumbled and the casket was slipped off the hearse and into the crypt. It had gone only six inches when it jammed. Extra hands were called for and it was started again. Once more it jammed and Hirshon cried, "For God's sake, can't you see it's too wide?"

It was, and a hurried consultation took place, after which a messenger ran down the hill to borrow a chisel. While flies droned in the tropic heat, the mourners fidgeted and tried to find shade under coconut palms. In a few minutes the runner, sweating furiously, produced a hammer and chisel, and for the next interval the cemetery echoed with the dull hacking sound of the workmen chipping away all the plaster-of-Paris decorations on the right side of the casket.

The workers were not skilled and Hirshon groaned, "I wish they would hit that chisel squarely just once." Then the job was done and with a strong shove Edgar Leeteg was laid to rest, at which Hirshon mumbled prayerfully, "Thank God! I hope when they bury me they do a better job."

Within a year he had his wish and now lies sleeping in the crypt beside a man he had never especially liked. There they are, two fiery Americans, each of whom had come to Tahiti in the 1930's and each of whom had stayed for the remainder of his life.

No epitaph was placed over Leeteg's grave, but he had given himself one in his letters to Barney Davis: "That fornicating, gin-soaked dopehead, The Moron of Mooréa."

We have not yet mentioned the major controversy that raged over Leeteg, for it was a technical problem and deserves to be discussed at length. Critics, and French and American government officials, claimed that Leeteg's velvets were not art, contending that he painted them by means of projecting photographs onto the velvet and filling in the backgrounds with an airbrush, leaving a few highlights to be added by hand. In defense of his right to enter his work into the United States duty free as fine art, instead of under heavy charges as mass-produced artisan's work, Leeteg finally enlisted the help of a museum official, whose report became the justification of Leeteg's plea to customs officers that his work was art.

Willis Shook, of the Art Institute of Pittsburgh, reported to the government: "I sat beside him and watched him begin, develop, and complete several paintings. I am quite willing to state under oath that he draws the figures from life, freehand, paints them in exactly as does any artist producing work that is called 'fine art.' He uses no mechanical aids whatever in the production of his paintings, neither airbrush, stencil, reflector, projector, nor any other means other than his eye and hand. I have seen no such magnificent effect in any other artist's work."

The story that he stumbled upon the medium through the help of a Chinese salesgirl who substituted black velvet for monk's cloth is also incorrect. In conversations with Bill Erwin, the Honolulu artist, he repeatedly stated, "When I was still living in St. Louis I went to a museum and saw some very old velvets. Italian maybe? The artist had used heavy paint on thick velour. It had caked, of course, and up close the pictures looked like hell. But from a distance everything fell into place and the contrast between the places where the paint was thin and the caked areas gave a wonderful feel of life. Right there I had the idea that you could get even better effects if you didn't pile the paint on all at once but applied it in very thin layers. I experimented with this and found that it worked O.K."

In one letter Leeteg stated that he had started painting velvets in 1933, but in another he said 1935. We know, however, that by the earlier year he had already sold a few paintings in this medium.

It is not difficult to paint on velvet, for thousands of Victorian young ladies used to decorate lush purple and blue chunks of the stuff for chair backs. Flowers and deer on crags silhouetted against a dark sky were popular. And as Leeteg had already discovered, Renaissance artists often dabbled in the art.

What is difficult is to paint well on this fabric, and the reason most serious artists abandon the effort is twofold. First, paint cakes so that the liveliness of the cloth is killed by globs of oil which harden and thus imprison the individual threads of the piling. This means that velvet is a self-defeating medium; its living quality and its ability to reflect light from many different angles are destroyed by pigments. Second, the black dye used in making velvet is so harsh that it materially modifies the chemistry of other pigments. Bright red becomes a dull rust, clean blue a dark and muddy purple, and white a dirty gray. Even when the dye chemical does not organically affect the paint, its power is so great that in order to mask it, one must use so much pigment that it cakes. It is understandable why artists prefer canvas, which instead of fighting oil and pigment seems to augment them.

What are the compensating virtues of velvet? First, shadows do not have to be painted; they merely have to be left in the design, whereupon the black dye of the velvet shows through. Since ordinary media require the artist to paint both the highlights and the shadows, velvet cuts the work in half. Second, if each strand of the pile can be kept free and not caked to its neighbor, the result is a painting which seems to have an added dimension. Any shift of light, any breath of wind gives the work a vitality that a flat piece of canvas cannot attain. And finally, black velvet gives the effect of lushness and opulence. The authors do not know why this is so; possibly it stems from our Renaissance culture, when nobles were accustomed to dress in velvet; possibly it is a carryover from the Victorian era, when people who lived in big houses used velour for their draperies. Regardless of the reason, many people consider velvet paintings ideal for a night club, where a sense of opulence is required.

Leeteg solved the technical problems of painting on velvet—actually, he used velveteen most of the time, originally from France, later from New York—and ultimately turned out paintings that were technically flawless. Each strand of pile stood free with its own specks of color. The dye of the velvet had been neutralized so that it no longer chemically affected the pigments. And the entire painting was kept in balance. Many artists contend that anyone who wanted to could have mastered the problem of oil paints on velvet if he had applied himself. Leeteg did it.

Usually he worked from a photograph, drawing upon his experience as a sign painter, which provided the basic techniques that carried him through life. He did not use living models directly for several good reasons. They were expensive and, as we shall see, he would have required one during at least six different stages of each painting. In Tahiti no girl would commit herself to six days of work in advance, anyway. In fact, Leeteg would have been lucky if he could have talked the girl into coming back once. Nor were Tahitian girls apt to remain in a steady attitude. It was difficult even for photographers to catch them in repose. And finally, the problem of lighting, which is all-important in velvet work, would be impossibly difficult with a lively, capricious model. Even for his portraits of distinguished local citizens or rich travelers, he invariably used a photograph.

At the beginning of his career several witnesses saw him using the sign painter's helper, a pounce pattern, for transferring the main outlines of a photograph to velvet. A pounce pattern is a thin sheet of paper on which the design is punched with little holes and which is then powdered with talcum. When laid over a velvet and tapped briskly, it produces an outline in powder from which the artist can work. For some reason, in the art world a man who uses a pounce pattern is looked down on as lacking in the basic skills of his trade, and Leeteg apparently shared this feeling, for in later life he sketched freehand in chalk, and the results were better.

His palette was described by one friend as "the brightest I have ever seen" but it contained only white and seven colors, which he used directly from the tubes without any kind of mixing.

There is argument as to whether Leeteg used an additive or a dryer. He told Erwin that he did not and in a well-known letter he denied using any. After his death a group of enterprising gentlemen wished to forge Leetegs, since they were bringing around $3,000. The artist they employed could draw like Leeteg; he understood Leeteg's palette and on canvas could produce a fine Leeteg. But he was unable to master the velvet until a traveler who had known Leeteg in Mooréa suggested that the forger buy from France a secret preparation which he said accounted for Leeteg's success with this medium. Accordingly, the cabal purchased quite a few bottles of Stoffine Wood, and when this was mixed with Leeteg's palette, painting on velvet became relatively simple. Copies made with Stoffine Wood are now being widely distributed.

Leeteg sketched his pictures with extremely light brush strokes. Deftly he brushed a pure, basic color onto the velvet so that each pile caught its share. If he made errors, he could at this stage correct them with a solvent while the paint was still wet. But when the sketch was done, no further corrections were possible, and from then on he had to work with a sure hand. He could not thereafter indulge in the gesture which is so popular in movies about artists. He could not stand back and study his work, then slop a rag in turpentine and rub out the offending areas. If areas offended, he could either throw the velvet away or else adjust his entire concept and build a new picture around what he had. For that reason he became highly skilled in applying paint exactly where he wanted it.

After the sketch was done, the velvet was allowed to dry in the sun for several days. Since the entire painting process took at least two weeks, it is obvious that Leeteg, in order to fill the demand, would have to keep as many as half a dozen velvets in process at one time, and it was not unusual for passengers on the *Mitiaro* to see that many drying in the Mooréa sun as they passed Villa Velour.

When the sketch was dry, the next layer of paint was applied; and of this procedure, whereby as many as eight successive layers might be thinly applied, Leeteg wrote, "The purpose of my method of painting velvet in successive stages using black material is to mix my colors on the velvet, not on the palette. . . . It is really an offshoot of Impressionism somewhat on the manner of Childe Hassam." It was also the style adopted by such diverse geniuses as Tintoretto and Cézanne, both of whom Leeteg liked. In fact, his knowledge of classical art was extensive, and through notebooks which he compiled he studied Matisse, Renoir, Picasso, and others.

After each subsequent application of thin paint, the velvet was allowed to dry thoroughly, and for this purpose only sunlight would do. Therefore he rarely worked indoors, but usually on the concrete veranda of his home.

He was often charged with having set up an assembly line whereby he did half a dozen copies of the same subject at the same time, but there is no record of this, for he approached every painting as a new adventure, and when he had done a particularly fine copy of a subject he would announce that fact gladly in his letters: "Finished 'Hina Rapa' today. A real super-duper." Any version that turned out especially well was tagged a super-duper, and he realized that upon these his reputation would rest.

A minor controversy always raged in art circles concerning the technical facts about Leeteg's work, but a greater one centered on his habit of duplicating the same painting over and over again. Of his most popular subjects he did upwards of twenty-four copies each. Of "Hina Rapa," the boisterous portrait of a bare-breasted hoyden in a big yellow hat, he told Erwin, "I've done her twenty-seven times and I'm sick of her."* It is therefore rather difficult to define what an original Leeteg is, because later versions of a subject were often better than the first.

Leeteg never concerned himself with this problem. He said, "I'm here to paint what the public wants." Barney Davis established a numbering system in which all subjects were listed, and if the public wanted six more copies of Number 118—"Hina Rapa"—they were ordered by cable and in due time provided. He would also alter a basic design to please a special customer, so that when Mary Morton, a Honolulu friend from the old days, wanted a copy of popular Number 115, she specified that she wanted the girl to look as if she were about to cry. Leeteg added tears and produced one of his very finest velvets. On another occasion a gentleman wanted a "Hina Rapa" for his den but insisted that the girl appear with an oversize bosom, for the delectation of his guests. Leeteg charged extra for this version of 118 and always referred to it as his "Girl with the Four Gallon Tits."

Many critics feel that Leeteg's willingness to paint whatever was required disbars him from serious consideration as an artist. The present authors are quite willing to discuss the possibility of Leeteg's being thrown out of the fellowship, but not on that score. After all, Hiroshige did dozens of versions of a single subject in his wood blocks. Veronese was told what colors and what subjects must appear in his massive religious paintings. Since we live far removed from the time when the great Renaissance artists lived, we forget that they were ordered to provide Crucifixions in which Jesus was clearly bleeding, Virgin Marys where the breast did not show, and donors' portraits which were to look ten years younger. And as Admiral du Saint Front pointed out, "Admittedly, Cézanne painted two dozen canvases or more of the Montagne Sainte Victoire." Throughout the history of art, some artists have had a fiery integrity which permitted

---

*Al Ezell, Leeteg's original Hawaii agent, thinks Leeteg may have done "about a hundred copies of Hina." He owns one of the finest, as well as many other super-dupers.

them to do only what they felt inspired to do. Others, including Van Dyck, Rubens and Rembrandt, often painted what they were told to paint. And equal merit has always rested in both schools. One cannot imagine Albert Ryder painting anything to order. One can imagine Rubens doing so, for some of his orders have been saved. Therefore one can question Leeteg's judgment in modifying his subjects to suit his customers, but one cannot for this reason disbar him from the rank of artist.

He might, however, be disbarred for a more substantial failing. Let us consider eight of his finest subjects; we find that every one was copied from other men's work.

Of his two greatest popular successes he wrote: "The photos of 'Hina Rapa' [Number 118] and the 'Old Chief' [Number 112] were taken some nineteen years ago. Both subjects are now dead. 'Hina Rapa' photo I bought from Bowers originally who ran a photo finishing shop and probably snitched it from some brought in for processing by a French naval officer. Anyway, Bowers is dead, too. So far as I know this photo has never been published excepting in our ads. The 'Old Chief' was photo'd by Simpson who is alive and in Papeete. I'll get the rest of the dope from him when I again see him in town and relay it to you. To the best of my knowledge, neither has been copyrighted anywhere."

With his next three big successes he ran into trouble. They were lifted bodily from a book by William S. Stone, a neighbor of his, called *Tahiti Landfall*, published in New York in 1946. This book was illustrated with photographs taken by a Tahiti photographer, Igor Allan. The photographs were hailed by many critics as being the best to come out of Polynesia for many years and three in particular were praised: a portrait of a native adzeman, a picture of a frenzied drummer boy, and a shot of a girl drinking from a coconut. The composition and lighting were superb and shortly they appeared for sale as Leeteg velvets: "Native Adze Man" (Number 136), "Drummer Boy" (Number 137), "Coco Drinker" (Number 127). Allan was astounded and when he could obtain no satisfaction from the artist was goaded by several Tahiti residents, who were tired of Leeteg's antics, into sending a bitter letter to the Honolulu *Star-Bulletin*, in which he charged Leeteg with plagiarism and added:

"I have received an illustrated clipping from your paper

dated November 4, 1950, headed 'Edgar Leeteg of Tahiti Is Hailed as Worthy Successor to Gauguin.'. . .

"Much has been written about Leeteg by a group of individuals who are interested in collecting commissions from the sale of his velvets. I, personally, know Leeteg well, for he has approached me continuously to take photographs for him. . . .

"The accurate fact is that Leeteg took a course on how to paint signs and was employed as a sign painter. Essentially, his work has remained sign painting to the present day."

Leeteg's reply in its original version was unprintable and attacked Allan savagely for having raised the question of plagiarism. It was always Leeteg's contention, acquired from the opinion of a lawyer, that if an artist changed even one item of a photograph, he was free to use it at will, without payment, for then no copyright existed, but that when the work was done, he, the artist, was free to copyright the painting. He felt that photographers who wanted payment for subjects which were later used to earn him up to $10,000 were chiselers and blackmailers.

His published reply to Allan read in part:

"In fairness to hundreds of Honolulans who hang my velvet paintings in their homes, kindly print this reply to the attack made upon these velvets by Russian-born Igor Allan and printed (Why?) in your letter column of March 13.

"While it is true that the painting reproduced for the late Col. L. G. Blackman's article of November 3 was 'copied' from one of the splendid photographs of Allan's appearing in *Tahiti Landfall,* the balance of his assertions are false. . . .

"Copying from a photograph requires more skill than working from a model because the painter must recognize and corrrect distortions and poor values as well as add coloring and detail from his knowledge and imagination.

"When this is done properly, the painting is not a copied photograph but a work of art embodying the artistic skill, perception, and feeling of the painter."

Later he circulated private blasts at Allan which show a blasphemous man willing to stoop to any level to destroy a rival.

Leeteg's "Beach Boy" (Number 156) was an instantaneous and riotous success, for it showed a happy kid in a coconut hat. Copies were ordered in batches and people in Honolulu photographed the velvet to send snapshots of it to their friends. Unfortunately some of these negatives were sent to a Honolulu photographer to develop, and in this way short, quick little K. K. Tagawa first discovered that one of his prize shots was being sold as a velvet. He had taken the picture one day on the beach at Maui and had known, even before he developed the negative, that he had captured a prize-winner. Consequently, he paid the boy a model's fee and found that his judgment was right. His print won first prize in Australia, other prizes elsewhere, and many mentions. It appeared on page 97 of *Paradise of the Pacific's* 1950 holiday issue, and on page 249 of the 1952 edition of *Photography Annual.*

From one of these sources Leeteg had copied the print without asking permission, without giving credit, without offering any fee and without acknowledgment of any kind. When Tagawa protested, Leeteg exploded: "As for my friend Mr. K. T. Kagawa [*sic*], to hell with him and his precious photo as it certainly is not worth $100 (the price of my cheapest velvet) for me to paint just two velvets from it. However, I usually pay photographers here about $1.50— 100 francs—for the use of their pictures for each velvet painted. At this rate I owe Kagawa $3 and debit it to my account. Offer him $3 as full payment for using his photo twice. Tell him I will not use his photo any more. If he wants to sell the reproduction-on-velvet rights to his net-thrower photo to send me a small contact print of it (I can only work from enlargement because of failing eyesight) and if it is usable for my work I'll buy an enlargement from him at my usual rates. But I won't be shook down for a free velvet by anyone—not even a governor."

Later Leeteg's agent offered compensation to Tagawa—whose name Leeteg always misspelled—but Tagawa did not accept it. Today, looking back on the incident, the photographer says, "I understand fully that in law I cannot complain if an artist copies my photograph in oils, but my photographs have caught the spirit of the islands so well that many artists want to copy them and all except Leeteg had the decency to make some kind of deal with me first. I always tried to be cooperative and almost invariably gave permission. For example, when Bill Erwin, whom I didn't even know, wanted to use my photos as a basis for his velvets he came to me directly and offered a deal. He was willing to pay money but I suggested that he paint a portrait of my mother, which he did. I think it's worth about $200."

Tagawa feels sure that Leeteg pinched "Beach Boy" from *Paradise of the Pacific* because in that same issue was a handsome photograph by another Honolulu photographer, Herbert Bauer. It showed a Hawaiian cowboy, an elderly man with handsome face, peering into the sun. Around his neck he wore a kerchief and it was this that attracted Bauer's father when the latter saw a Leeteg velvet, "Hawaiian Cowboy" (Number 117), in the window of Hawaiian Things, a curio store, sometime later. He called his son about the plagiarism and young Bauer recalls, "I stopped in to see Leeteg's agent, who was very excited about a new batch of velvets he had just received from Tahiti. He was saying that this man Leeteg was the American Gaugin and gave me a powerful sales talk, but I reached into the velvets and said, 'You can't call a man a real artist who steals his ideas from another man's photos.' Later we reached a settlement and I got $15 for my photo. The only thing I'm ashamed of now about this whole deal is that I took the money. I should have said that Leeteg needed it more than I did if he was too careless even to ask for permission to use my work." Bauer also points out that other artists have used his photos as the basis for their work, but that they usually ask his permission and pay him for the privilege.

Leeteg's most famous single subject, his portrait of Christ (Number 154), was a different story. From Hawaii a friend sent Leeteg's children a plaque to remind them to pray before bed, and on this plaque was a miniature head of Christ taken from the phenomenally popular series of religious paintings done in this century by the living American artist Warner Sallman. It was about the size of a postage stamp. Later, when a Mormon missionary visited Leeteg and asked if he had any religious subjects, Leeteg offered to reproduce Sallman's head on velvet. The result was a sublime representation of Jesus in a style which preserved the sickly sweet quality of Sallman while infusing it with an honest strength.

From the moment this velvet was completed all who saw it recognized it as a gem of popular religious art, and four more times Leeteg copied from the minute original. The five copies—Davis says there are only four—are not identical, and each has its peculiar quality. For a popular vision of how people like to think Jesus looked, there could be no finer interpretation than Leeteg's, and in artistic competence it goes far beyond Warner Sallman's original. Unfortunate-

ly, this time he had copied a work that was itself copyrighted, and he found that if he persisted in doing so he
was going to get in trouble. So his greatest velvet, which
he could have reproduced endlessly and at substantial profit, was proscribed, and in a letter to his agent he acknowledges this: "Just completed the 'Beach Boy' and you won't
have any trouble unloading this one. Will start a second
one soon. Hope it will be as good. Also have a Sallman
Christ head started—without background. Don't invite trouble by displaying it in your window. Actually I always feel
like a thief when I copy another man's painting and do it
only from hunger."

We are not here concerned with the ethics of Leeteg's
behavior. The facts are available for anyone's conclusions.
Nor are we involved in the question of using photographs as
a basis for art. Utrillo did so with superb results and so
did Leeteg. But we are concerned over the fact that Leeteg's
finest work was usually copied from other men on whom he
relied for precisely those details of light and shade and
composition and design which have traditionally been held
to be an artist's main accomplishments. It would seem that
Leeteg was markedly deficient in his capacity to conceive a
subject, to organize it and to see it through to the finished
painting. "Beach Boy" is a delightful velvet primarily because K. K. Tagawa posed the child properly and caught his
abandoned joy in a splendid design. The reason Leeteg's
"Adzeman" is truly dignified and grand is that Igor Allan
posed him so as to bring out these qualities, and one feels
quite certain that Leeteg himself would have been unable
to conceive the universal style of his portrait of Christ had
not Sallman first done his sentimental version. A deficiency
of such magnitude is serious when one wants to advance
the claims of an artist, and it is this deficiency which prevents Leeteg from occupying the place that his adherents
want to give him.

We are still faced, however, with the tantalizing question:
Was Leeteg a great artist or was he a hack journeyman?
His velvets lack completely the plastic sense and the control
of both planes and surfaces that marked the work of men
like Rembrandt and Velasquez, and those who would find
such virtues in Leeteg's work cannot know the canvases of
the masters. In technique it does compare favorably with
the lesser work of French portraitists of the eighteenth century but is immeasurably far behind their British contem-

poraries like Hogarth, Reynolds and Gainsborough. There is, though, a curious similarity in both style and concept to the portraits of Raeburn, and had Leeteg lived in that age, he might possibly have painted as Raeburn did.

How does he compare with Gauguin, with whom he is so often linked? The similarity lies mostly in the dissolute lives the two men led and in their love for the Tahitian people. Gauguin used a strong, brilliant palette; Leeteg's, when the velvet had subdued it, was almost somber and some of his finest paintings seem monochromatic. Gauguin was a master of landscape; Leeteg stuck mostly to big heads, and when he did try landscape it was apt to be formless and lacking in design. Gauguin rebuilt all he saw and remodeled it into his vision of life; Leeteg simply made his vision prettier than the original and displayed none of the great disruptive force which abounds in original artists like Gauguin. The Frenchman was not a great designer, but he was a forceful one; whereas Leeteg relied mainly on others. Finally, Gauguin was consumed by a personal fire that burned over onto his canvases; Leeteg also had this fire but it never touched his velvet.

On the other hand, Leeteg surpassed Gauguin in his ability to place a head within a rectangle; he did this as ably as any artist who ever lived, and in this capacity alone he reminds one of Holbein. It is a curious fact that his ability to bring his well-placed head slowly out of a shadowy background recalls Rembrandt's favorite treatment, though there any analogy ends, for Leeteg's execution reminds one neither of Holbein nor of Rembrandt. Only his power to evoke the mood of Polynesia recalls Gauguin, for travelers who love the islands do attest to his skill in luring them subtly back into the shadows of remembered lagoons.

It is totally unwarranted to call Leeteg the new Gauguin, if competence in painting is the justification for the comparison. And to compare him with Hals, Rembrandt, Rubens or Goya is to abandon objective standards completely. He frequently announced that his idols were Rolfe Armstrong and Norman Rockwell, and like them he aspired to be a fine pictorialist: "Decker wrote me today saying he was not satisfied with my last seven velvets because they were too dark, so burning the midnight oil studying up on what is art was a mistake too. However, all painters usually make the mistake of getting *too* arty and the successful ones are those smart enough to see their mistake and return to what is popular. Norman Rockwell is one such. In future I will do bright ones like those which made my work popular; but even brighter since I found a new color that gives light."

Anyone who studies Leeteg soon learns to expect the unforeseen; nevertheless, at one point the authors of this account felt that they had pretty well plumbed the farthest reaches of his art. Then they happened to visit Wayne Decker's palatial home in Salt Lake, where, in the handsomely fitted-out basement they were shown nearly two hundred Leeteg velvets. All the standard subjects were exhibited, often in a super-duper quality, but as the rich procession came to an end the friend who had seen Leeteg only for a few minutes one hot day in Tahiti said, "Have you ever seen his masterpieces?" And he brought forth half a dozen superbly detailed portraits of Navaho Indians.

The impact was stunning and we were left bewildered by this contradiction: how did Leeteg, in the South Pacific, create as his finest velvets these portraits of remote Indians? Then Decker explained, "Edgar was always spiritually hungry for America, and begged me to send him reading material. I sent him *Time* and *Newsweek* and *U.S. News* and he devoured them."

"But how does that explain the Indians?" we asked.

"Well, once when I was filling up a bundle I had some empty space and chucked in a copy of *Arizona Highways*."

From the color photographs in this chance-sent magazine, Leeteg had copied his masterworks. As he told all of his customers, "Tell me what you like and send me a photograph and I'll do it."

From such honest statements, and from his worst work, one is tempted to dismiss Leeteg merely as a calendar artist, and many have done so. The present authors believe that he is better than that and expect his velvets to attain a position somewhat like the art of Albert Bierstadt and Frederick Remington—works of authentic Americana. But we believe Leeteg will be remembered chiefly because he lived such an extraordinary life. We must now consider some of the more startling aspects of that life.

Edgar Leeteg never outgrew his mother, and the tragic sense of loneliness and emptiness that haunted him after the age of forty came from a belated realization that he had clung to her able apron strings too long and that this had vitiated his life and estranged him from all other women.

Bertha Leeteg, a tall, handsome woman, was twenty-eight

when her only son was born, and from that moment her entire life centered in his. Her fear of his becoming entangled with girls probably helped the confusion that led to the disasters of his first two marriages, for no matter what girl Edgar brought home—wife or mistress—he finally got rid of her because the girl could not fit into his mother's plans. Late in his life, after numerous debacles, he sent a friend the following amazing analysis of the kind of wife he wanted: "Mom is ailing with flu and I want to make her last years comfortable by getting a mate she approves of and who will be kind and helpful to her."

At about the same time he wrote to Decker in Salt Lake City, "Sometimes I feel like taking back my estranged wife as she writes that she lost her teaching job because she staid home to nurse our sick baby. She is a very good mother. But I recognize that NO woman could get along with Mama long. . . . I get discouraged myself at times and say that the 4th commandment is the hardest to keep."

Mother Leeteg encountered her most difficult antagonist in a lovely model who came to Moeréa from one of the other islands, and who was by universal agreement the woman the artist should have married. But in the end Mrs. Leeteg forced her away and finally Leeteg retreated to that dismal and unsatisfying procession of broken-down models, wharf girls and chance pickups that characterized his later life.

But all observers agree that Leeteg's obsessive love for his tall mother, who stood above him both physically and emotionally, was the most touching aspect of his life. She controlled him, but his affection for her grew constantly. His main concern was to protect her from the unpleasantness of life, and few mothers have ever been treated with the constant and uncomplaining devotion that he lavished on his. "Am just up from the sickbed, heart and kidney trouble. Yesterday I began to put my affairs in order as best I could, just in case. . . . And in event the gossips are proved correct in their saying that Leeteg is dead, I want you to see that what money remains due to my estate is partly sent to Mom directly by certified check in *her* name, Mrs. Bertha Leeteg, and later I'll work out some way to see that my youngest son gets his share in monthly remittances."

As the years passed and his mother's health declined, Leeteg used to cut short even his drunken Tuesdays so that he might hurry home and comfort her.

This strange dependence possibly also accounted for his

building mania. He was aware that some inner compulsion drove him to erect homes, in which he never kept a wife, for he writes: "I may as well confess. . . . I'm off on another building spree, making a ritzy circular beer-drinking lounge and studio over my fish pond. Goddam. Barney, this building bug has got me, I just can't stop."

Many men experience this uncontrollable urge to build a house in which a family can find shelter from the pressures of the world and at the same time leave a mark to prove that the family once existed. But Leeteg's mania showed weird overtones: every house he built was a doll house. Here was a little house for himself; there a little one for his mother; this one a doll house for the wife that never materialized. All visitors to Villa Velour commented on the doll houses, painted in soft pastel colors, and many neighbors protested that with them—they almost formed a village of their own—Leeteg was ruining a fine bay. Action was started against him, but he brazened it out.

Then there was the matter of the outhouse. He vowed that he would build the most expensive, luxurious, and altogether resplendent privy in the Southern Hemisphere, and not since the days of the late Roman emperors has anyone enjoyed such a toilet. It was built like a low Polynesian temple, with thick masonry walls and massive buttresses. An enormous grille of metal was set into one side, across which swam twenty-six metal fish painted in seven different colors. The interior was imported Italian marble with a seating arrangement that would have satisfied Caligula. It was festooned with flowers and scented by the latest devices from Paris. From its commodious seats one could gaze on Paopao Bay and the softly swaying coconut palms. There were also books and magazines and fretwork to please the mind, and the edifice was painted in such subtle colors that once seen it could not ever be forgotten. The corrugated roof was painted a tile red, and was held up by a beige wall, which rested on a salmon pink base riding on a turquoise blue footing. And up the middle of the grille, holding the entire design together, rose a magnificent metal coral bush through which the dazzling fish intertwined. Bigger than an ordinary house, capacious enough to serve a platoon of men, it was Leeteg's noblest architectural creation and stands today to confound his enemies. They tried to prevent its building and claimed that it showed the crazy American had really gone mad, but Leeteg countered that a man ought to enjoy the kind of privy that suited his personality, and he won.

There is one other clue to Leeteg's character. He yearned to be held in line by outside pressures. He was happiest when his mother ordered him about, or when he could dedicate his energies to helping a friend who was in trouble.

When continued sales removed his financial worries, and when public acclaim assured him that he was an artistic success, he relaxed and immediately began to have those strong premonitions of death which fill his later letters. He also foresaw the Korean War and began to hoard huge stores of goods against the Third World War, which he anticipated momentarily. Then he was overcome with ennui and cried, "Barney, don't send any more money until you hear from me, I have all I need for a while, besides the goddamed stuff only breeds trouble for me. Wish I were a hobo again; they're a bunch of happy bastards; I no longer am."

His fear of disaster began to contaminate even his painting, and then something very good happened. Barney Davis, in building a new gallery for displaying Leeteg velvets, ran into debt and needed help. Suddenly Leeteg became his old energetic self and plunged avidly into his work, for now there was a reason: someone outside himself needed help. "Please, Barney," he wrote, "get your $20,000 paid off quickly as you can. That's what I'm working for now—to make it possible for you to get out of hock."

He needed restraint and obligation and when he faced none he sought it by sharing the hardships of others. He watched over his mother, loved his children, aided several former mistresses, and lent money to anyone who needed a franc. He was one of the most unselfish men Tahiti had ever seen, and Admiral du Saint Front summarized his character perfectly when he offered this eulogy: "To me Leeteg will always be the family man, the unselfish one."

It seems likely that Leeteg is destined to go down in South Seas history as the man who, in the midst of twentieth-century storms, found paradise. It would therefore be both appropriate and instructive to inquire into the definition of paradise and then to see in what degree Leeteg's experience matched this definition.

Summarizing the many legends of this great ocean, the authors conclude that when a man from a more mechanical society flees to the South Pacific he hopes to find these things:

a land where tensions are relaxed; a more rustic society uncomplicated by modern gadgetry; certainly a less expensive way of living; a quiet retreat where he can escape social pressures; an island home of exquisite beauty; and, whether we like to admit this in public or not, a greater sexual freedom than is customary in Western society.

As to the relaxation of tension, it is doubtful that Edgar Leeteg could ever have found, either in heaven or in hell, release from the tensions under which he lived, for these conflicts were his nature, and he jealously carried them with him wherever he went. True, he did avoid the exaggerated economic tensions of the American depression, and this was a prime motive in his move to Tahiti, but release from spiritual tensions he never found. He desperately yearned for a wife and home, but these eluded him. Nor did he ever discover any sensible basis for his relationship with his mother, and on this score his journey to Tahiti was disastrous, for island life drove him closer to his mother yet at the same time kept her more at variance with the world he had to live in. The mother-son-sweetheart tension at Villa Velour was always acute; it flamed into open spiritual warfare only when Edgar tried to bring some girl into the household, as either his wife or his mistress. Then the permanent hell that enveloped the place was visible to all, but it was no less a hell when it was hidden. Finally, the essential tension which Leeteg had built up between himself and society was also aggravated in Tahiti, not dispelled. He constantly warred with his neighbors, his friends, his women, his business associates, his rival painters and himself: "I will sink my teeth into any other artist as I love a feud . . . that's what gets a guy to the top, by besting his rivals who are trying to get to the top the same way." Since life in Tahiti was more communal than in the anonymity of San Francisco, the bitterness of Leeteg's reactions to his society was immediately known to the whole community and was reciprocated by many who would normally not have been involved. The South Pacific has wonderful therapeutic value, but it has never cured a soul which insisted upon reinfecting itself each day.

In some respects Leeteg did find the rustic life that modern men dream of with nostalgia. His determination to remain on primitive Mooréa when life would have been simpler in gay Papeete is proof that he cherished the less complicated life of the smaller island. Yet one is amazed in reading his letters to find that Leeteg spent much of his time worrying about exactly the same problems he would have worried about in St. Louis. Lawyers are charging him too much for his divorce. He has got to find a house that has electricity. Hadn't he better recover his children and move to some new location where the schools are better? With ease one can extract from any dozen Leeteg letters a composite that would sound almost as if it had been written by a young married woman in suburban America. The following household lament contains only Leeteg sentences:

"I busted my store teeth on a piece of French bread so must stay to home until Laverne takes the damned things over to a dentist and gets them soldered. Dentists already hiked prices. In wartime it is hard to get plates here. Mom asks if you can get her a pair of nurse's shoes size 5, low heels. I want a Maytag washer the worst way and wish I could get hold of a good Zenith radio. . . . The lumber I got is sap wood so poor I'll have to get plywood sheathing for the ceiling and walls to cover the cracks and uneven thicknesses of the boards. Otherwise the house is great, but the Chinese gal who sewed the drapes botched them so I'll have to get new; another $30 down the drain. . . . I will be glad to get the pinking shears. . . . I was worrying what to do about Laverne when she gets a little older. She is exceptional in school and should have her chance in life which cannot be gotten here. . . . Would appreciate your sending me two rubber hoses with spray nozzles attached which can be screwed on ½" faucet for bathroom use. My two beds and stove arrived and cost me just under $700. Too much. So no more ordering big stuff from America."

Life in Tahiti was rather more expensive than it would have been in St. Louis. Leeteg spent enormous sums on postage, air freight, customs and cables. Since he imported much of what he used, he never saved on the cheap local items. For example, since Tahiti is a French colony, wine was cheap, but he drank whisky, which was very costly. It is true that he paid little for the laborers who built his fantastic creations, but he had to employ many men to get the job done, so that the ultimate cost was high. And of course his building materials were almost prohibitive. Villa Velour, which would probably have cost less than $9,000 in America, cost about $14,000 in Mooréa. And as for the so-called bounty of paradise—free coconuts and breadfruit, fish crowding the lagoon—it never materialized. Most Westerners can eat very little coconut, for the milk gives them diarrhea, and few strangers like breadfruit. Besides, most trees are owned by someone who sells the fruit at a stiff price. There were fish in the lagoon, but Leeteg rarely caught any because his mother could not abide the smell. Two other things were free —lovely flowers and mangoes—and here Leeteg could have saved money, but he never acquired a taste for the fruit which some travelers hold to be the best in the world. The sad fact is that Leeteg ate almost exclusively out of tin cans. He had substantial tinned meats from Australia, tinned soups from France, tinned vegetables and fruits from America. Few housewives in St. Louis eat as much tinned food as Leeteg did in the wilds of Mooréa. Few have so deadly a diet. One reason was that he did not like native foods. More important, his mother preferred the ease of cooking out of a can. Since he had to buy his tins at great expense from Chinese merchants in Papeete, he spent more money for food in his lush and abundant tropical paradise than he would have spent in any standard American small town.

He also worked harder. He probably enjoyed his work more, but he had to spend longer hours than he would have been allowed to spend had he remained a good member of the sign painters' union in California. There he would not have been permitted to work six days a week, eight to ten hours each day. People who did not personally know Leeteg forget that he worked like a slave. All visitors to his home agree on this. Frequently he would rise at two or four in the morning to handle his extraordinary volume of mail, for he dedicated all good daylight hours to painting. Even on his weekly forays into Papeete he spent about half of each day taking care of his business: mailing parcels, cashing checks, cabling his agents and taking care of his children's education. From December 12, 1949, to his death 1154 days later, Leeteg painted 294 velvets, or about one every four days. Since it took him up to three weeks to finish each painting, he obviously carried a good many velvets forward at one time. Once he complained to Davis, "You tell me to go easy on the bottle and get down to work. Are you beginning to believe that stuff about me being an alkie? Which I appear to be for the benefit of the tourists. What the tourists don't see is me hard at it before my easel six days a week every week including Sundays."

For the greater part of his Tahiti experience, this unusual dedication to work earned Leeteg a very meager living. Much of the time he existed close to poverty and it was only in his later years that he lived well. Far from being a loafer's paradise, the South Pacific for Leeteg was a sentence to the hardest kind of work—and one in which the rewards were slow and the demands constant. When he did finally earn a decent return, he sensed that his capacity for sustained work was diminishing. Some of his saddest letters are those in which he reports his extreme tiredness accompanied by his premonitions of death or failing eyesight. "You misunderstood my letter about waiting for my dough," he writes. "I know you never made me wait. What I meant was that although I *should* not be made to wait *I would be willing to* rather than have you borrow on your insurance. Of course I gotta have enough to keep going here, too, but I don't want you to go into debt and then go bankrupt. Pay off those loans and stay solvent. After this month I will let some money stand with you each month. You may use this money without interest until I need it. I'll stick with you, too. But, Barney, don't try to expand your gallery now as I don't know how long I can keep up this pace without turning out sloppy stuff. I'm badly in need of a rest. You order six more 'Beachboys'—that's great business, but I make every one a super-duper."

Leeteg would have had a much easier life in California and would probably have earned more money and been able to spend it more profitably on the material things he craved. He found much happiness in Mooréa and subject matter ideally suited to his brush, but he certainly never found release from work or responsibility. Toward the end of his life he wrote, "If I was to leave here I would not be allowed to take over a hundred dollars out though my property holdings are worth around ten thousand not to mention my bank account and other assets. So this paradise is a sort of prison too, especially as Uncle Sam would not accept my kids."

So far as finding a retreat where he could work undisturbed is concerned, Leeteg's life in Tahiti falls into two segments. For many years he lived almost in isolation and nearly went crazy from the lack of friendship. His wife and his mistresses left him partly because Mooréa was so far from Papeete, and many residents of that city recall the days when any stranger would be invited or even dragged over to Leeteg's place for a visit that might extend to two weeks. In those days the *Mitiaro* hauled an amazing procession of freeloaders, drunks, wastrels, sex maniacs, and good storytellers to Edgar's hut, where they camped endlessly and drank his booze. And whenever he got a few francs ahead, he would hurry to Papeete so that he could escape the terrible boredom of his retreat. In later years, of course, this loneliness ended and he was deluged by visitors, but then they became such a nuisance that he had difficulty finding time to work. "Have been having my old trouble again," he protests, "visitors *every* goddam day. Sometimes twice a day with the result that I only started five velvets in October. Even getting mean don't help. Only thing to do is leave Mooréa and build so small a house in Papeete that there will be no room for overnight guests and also no reason for them to stay all night as there are hotels in town. One Australian brought his Tahitian bride here for three days and she pissed right on the floor—too lazy to go outside. I had to have a maid to scrub the whole house after he left. It's a hell of a life being host in Mooréa to the kind of people one meets here."

In fact, in order to hide his papers and velvets from his unwanted guests, he redesigned his house in order to build several hidden closets. But this gave him only partial relief, for now cruise directors started advertising in their brochures: "In glamorous Mooréa three days will be set aside for a romantic visit to the workshop of Edgar Leeteg, a real South Seas artist." And when these uninvited tourists did arrive, he had to house them, feed them, do their laundry, provide drinks and interrupt his work. But even so, he was never able to be firm, and tour directors could play upon his vanity and he would permit "just one more visit."

His hospitality was so abused, however, that finally he sent off to the Honolulu papers a cry of despair: "With the advent of air travel and the packaged tour, our hospitality has grown into a terrifying monster which is destroying us. . . . I don't want to be your sightseeing guide. My home was not built to be a museum with a free bar. . . . I'm tired, and you unreasonable uninvited tourists have made me so!"

Yet even after having published this letter, he continued to stop strangers in Papeete and invite them to Mooréa. Mom would grumble, native girls would amble by to see if a party was in progress, booze would vanish, and when the stranger left, Leeteg would have to work overtime to compensate for lost hours of sunlight.

Most white men in the South Pacific follow this cycle: retreat, call in the drunks, go crazy with the noise, retreat again, call in the drunks again. Leeteg was no exception, but finally the expense became so great that he cried, "Am sure of one thing. Will build my next hut on a hillside and won't even own a pair of shoes more than I can take care of easily. Am gonna get the few comforts and gadgets I want and call it a day. The house will be very simple and not too big." But two days before he died he was planning an addition to the doll's village he already had. He never broke the cycle.

In one respect Leeteg's flight to the South Pacific was outstandingly successful. The bay on which he settled is majestic. Its rugged shoreline bespeaks some ancient volcano whose sides have collapsed through centuries of marine erosion, leaving a body of cerulean water surrounded by a wonderfully broken shoreline. The mountains at the head of the bay look as if they had been stolen from a child's fairy tale, so grand and grotesque are they. And around both the bay and the foot of the mountain a natural vegetation of extraordinary luxuriance grows. The combination is at the same time so judicious and yet so opulent that many men would surrender the remainder of their humdrum lives to have known such beauty even once. There is no lovelier spot in the South Pacific than Edgar Leeteg's peninsula. Regardless of the vantage point from which it is viewed, his location for his home is a masterpiece, and in the debate that will continue as to whether or not he was a true artist, one of the most telling arguments will be that out of all the available land in the South Pacific, he chose the most magnificent.

There were drawbacks. In walking at night one constantly stepped on land crabs that exploded with a squishy noise. Storms sometimes lashed at the moorings of the doll houses, and mildew was a tyrant. Weeks might go by when fogs hung low upon the bay and the sun was never seen, and it is doubtful if any location should be considered satisfactory that could be reached only on the dismal *Mitiaro*. But even when mildew commandeered the place, the peninsula was glorious, and we can say without qualification that in Mooréa Edgar Leeteg did find a passionate, tempestuous, luxuriant beauty that most of us never know even remotely and few intimately. As he once said, "A man spends a good deal of his life sitting on the can, and at Villa Leeteg even the outhouse is beautiful."

It would be incorrect to think of Leeteg as one acquaintance described him: "That great, free, liberal soul who sought release from the confinements of life in the soaring freedom of the Pacific." Actually, he was a reactionary, and in his letters often referred to Roosevelt as the destroyer of America and of Truman as "that S.O.B. in the White House." His contempt for nonwhite, non-German people was notorious and his letters repeatedly speak of "niggers, chinks, them jap s.o.b's, them dirty jew-boys, kikes and dagoes." Most curious, he was never able to accept wholeheartedly the mores of Tahiti and often spoke as if he were a New England moralist: "Papeete receives 17 U.S. army men from a nearby base each weekend. Fine, clean boys. The wife of our consul, who is a refined and social lady, tried to arrange picnics and sightseeing trips for them but the chippies meet the boys at the wharf and thereafter they can be seen hanging out of a hotel window with a beer glass in one hand and a whore in the other—this continues until the furlough expires and that's all these boys get out of their lucky opportunity to see these lovely islands."

Nevertheless, Leeteg did find in Tahiti that sexual freedom which seems to form such a large component in the average man's dream of an earthy paradise. His testimony is unequivocal: "I lay most of my models." Lest this be interpreted as an unsupported boast he says in another letter, "Getting some choice stuff lately and missing more than I can use. Missed one lovely by being drunk and just wandering away from her. Can you imagine that? Why, it's enough to make me quit drinking." We have many intimate accounts of how he operated, one of the tenderest being: "Last Saturday and Sunday I was on an excursion to Little Tahiti, the wild, only partially explored part of the figure-eight shape of Tahiti. I doubt if more than a score of Americans ever saw this wild jumble of jungle-clad peaks with its dark rivers disappearing into narrow valleys and waterfalls leaping from the cliffs straight into the sea. There are no roads, only a footpath. I counted seven houses. Will send you a few snaps later. Boy, what a spot to play Robinson Crusoe. I took a honey along and we slept under the ironwood trees on a little island. How easily we whites slip into primitive native ways."

His typical experience was far less poetic: A couple of friends from Papeete were "my guests for ten days, at the same time as Doc Bridgman, who is a wonderful chap from New Zealand; then to make a full house I took in a strange gal who landed here from Paris looking for

Leeteg. She stayed four days. Doc bet me a gold cup that I would not get into her pants . . . so when you come again next year you can drink your champagne out of a golden goblet."

In these years he was willing to accept almost anything that came his way: "I've already got a swell l'il sixteen-year-old native gal lined up for some nudes. That's why I'm sick. I kept her all night to study her charms and strained myself. . . . Guess I gotta realize I'm getting old."

One of the most extraordinary aspects of Leeteg's sex life was his habit of reporting on the bedroom qualifications of his playmates, as judged by his own standards. One who knows the Pacific well is sometimes embarrassed on meeting an attractive young lady to remember Leeteg's evaluation of her: "Last week I dated a young thing that I had my tongue hanging out for for several years and when I got her in my bed she was the worst lay I had; was so disappointed I nearly decided to give up rutting and cut it off."

It would be sanctimonious to ask, "But did a grown man really enjoy this monotonous procession of island girls?" Leeteg says he did. He also admits that his private life was a shambles. He fought with his wives, lost his mistresses, suffered under his mother's domination, and in his later years rarely spent even one entire night with one girl. A sort of coconut Casanova, he was reduced to bouncing back and forth among the professional wharf rats who have always populated Papeete harbor. He lived in sad chaos and in one brief period seriously contemplated the following alternatives: he would re-establish his marriage with his third wife; he would have nothing more to do with her and would institute court action against her; he would woo his model again; he would marry a fine girl from New York; he would take over the mistress of a visiting yachtsman when the yacht sailed; he would bring to Mooréa a beauty he had stumbled upon during a Tuesday drunk; he would have nothing whatever to do with girls. Any one of these alternatives would have made sense. But he acted upon them all, at the same time.

Admiral du Saint Front, reviewing those difficult years, introduces a new and rather somber note: "Polynesian life is not quite, perhaps, what most people imagine: he could have found any amount of *vahines* to keep house for him, with all it entails, but not to have a discreet affair. He knew very little French, and practically no Tahitian, which did not make things easier. But above all there was 'Mom,' the children, and his unsuccessful previous attempts at a normal life. In this land of plenty, where he had no doubt, at one time, grazed at will, he could only get a few hurried and unsatisfactory mouthfuls."

Yet one is perplexed by this statement, for usually any man in Tahiti can find all the girls he wants. Indeed, that is probably why Leeteg lived there so long. His peculiar relationship with his mother necessitated a society in which casual girls were available, since permanent arrangements would inevitably be destroyed. Why, in the 1950's, should he suddenly have experienced difficulty in finding girls?

The authors were going to leave this tantalizing question unanswered, until they met by accident a Frenchwoman who had long lived in Punaavia. "Leeteg!" she cried. "How interesting that you are writing on Leeteg! He was a man of immortal misery, and I hope you can tell of the sadness in this man. In the end, you know, he was an outcast. Nobody would invite him to a decent home—except one very fine French admiral who could tolerate his ways. His language had become foul, his drunkenness complete. I used to see him on the street those drunken Tuesdays. His eyes were vacant and filled with lonely terror. Then I understood. A very good friend of Leeteg's"—and here she named one of the painter's most trusted companions—"came out to Punaavia and told us, 'You had better tell the young girls of Punaavia to stay away from Leeteg. You had better see to it that he has nothing to do with any girls who work in your home.'

" 'Why?' I asked stupidly.

" 'He has a terrible sickness,' this friend explained. 'He has the sickness which girls should stay away from.'

" 'Don't the new drugs cure that?' I asked.

" 'Not any more. He has worked his way through them all,' the friend explained. 'Penicillin, streptomycin, the sulfas . . .'

" 'What will happen to him?' I asked, for girls were his bread and water.

" 'It's all right,' the friend said. 'Within a year he will be dead.' "

This friend had visited all the villages advising young girls to stay away from Leeteg. He reached Punaavia with his message on the day before Edgar Leeteg climbed aboard the back seat of a motorcycle.

Selected Bibliography

Special thanks are due for bibliographic help from the University of Hawaii Library, Honolulu (Dr. Carl Stroven, Librarian, and Miss Janet E. Bell, in charge of the Hawaiian and Pacific Collection); from the Mitchell Library, Sydney, Australia (Miss Phyllis Mander Jones, Librarian); and from the Library of Congress, Washington, D. C. (Col. Willard Webb, Director of the Stack Division).

CHAPTER 1

LAY, WILLIAM, and HUSSEY, CYRUS. *A Narrative of the Mutiny on Board the Ship "Globe" of Nantucket, in the Pacific Ocean, January, 1824* . . . New London, Conn., 1828.

MORISON, SAMUEL E. Historical Notes on Gilbert and Marshall Islands. *American Neptune*, vol. 4, 1944, pp. 87-118.

PAULDING, Lieut. HIRAM. *Journal of a Cruise of the United States Schooner "Dolphin."* . . . *in Pursuit of the Mutineers of the Whale Ship "Globe."* New York, 1831.

STACKPOLE, EDOUARD. *The Sea-Hunters.* Philadelphia, 1953.

WHIPPLE, A. B. C. *Yankee Whalers in the South Seas.* New York, 1954.

CHAPTER 2

BECKE, LOUIS. The South Sea Bubble of Charles du Breil, in *Rídan the Devil.* London, 1899.

DUPERREY, LOUIS ISADOR. *Voyage autour du Monde* . . . Paris, 1825-30.

GROOTE, P. DE. *Nouvelle-France, Colonie Libre.* Paris, 1880.

Last Link with De Rays Horror. *Pacific Islands Monthly*, vol. 26, 1956, p. 127.

LESSON, RENÉ PRIMEVÈRE. *Voyage autour du Monde . . . sur la Corvette "Coquille,"* 2 vols. Paris, 1838-39.

LUCAS-DUBRETON, JEAN. *L'Eden du Pacifique.* Paris, 1929.

Marquis de Rays Link Broken. *Pacific Islands Monthly,* vol. 26, 1956, p. 159.

NIAU, JOSEPHINE H. *Phantom Paradise,* Sydney, 1936.

ROMILLY, HUGH H. *The Western Pacific and New Guinea.* London, 1886.

TUDOR, JUDY. The Marquis Provided the Millstone. *Pacific Islands Monthly,* vol. 19, 1949, p. 43.

CHAPTER 3

BLAIR, EMMA H. and ROBERTSON, J. A. *The Philippine Islands, 1493-1898,* vols. 12, 29, 36. Cleveland, Ohio, 1906.

BOXER, C. R. The Rise and Fall of Nicholas Iquan. *T'ien Hsia Monthly,* vol. 11, 1941, pp. 401-439.

CAMPBELL, WILLIAM. *Formosa Under the Dutch.* London, 1903.

DAVIDSON, JAMES WHEELER. *The Island of Formosa.* Yokohama, 1903.

DÍAZ, CASIMIRO. *Conquistas de Las Islas Filipinas.* Valladolid, 1890.

FERRANDO, FR. JUAN. *Historia de los Padres Domínicos en las Islas Filipinas,* vol. 3. Madrid, 1871.

HUMMEL, ARTHUR W. (ed.). *Eminent Chinese of the Ch'ing Period (1644-1912).* Washington, 1933-44.

KEENE, DONALD. *The Battles of Coxinga: Chikamatsu's Puppet Play.* London, 1951.

MONTERO Y VIDAL, JOSÉ. *Historia General de Filipinas.* Madrid, 1887.

PONSONBY FANE, R. A. B. Koxinga: Chronicles of the Tei Family. Transactions and Proceedings of the Japan Society of London, vol. 34, 1937, pp. 65-132.

REID, R. W. E. Piracy in the China Seas. Unpublished M.A. Thesis, No. 170, University of Hawaii. Honolulu, 1938.

SAN AUGUSTÍN, GASPAR DE. *Conquistas de Las Filipinas.* Madrid, 1698.

WYCHERLEY, GEORGE. *Buccaneers of the Pacific.* Indianapolis, 1928.

ZAIDE, GREGORIO F. *Philippine Political and Cutural History,* vol. 1. Manila, 1949.

CHAPTER 4

ANDRADE, ERNEST, JR. The Hawaiian Revolution of 1887. Unpublished M.A. Thesis, No. 317, University of Hawaii. Honolulu, 1954.

DAY, A. GROVE. *Hawaii and Its People*. Boston and New York, 1955.

FARENHOLT, A. The Hawaiian Navy and an International Incident. U. S. Naval Institute *Proceedings*, vol. 66, 1940, pp. 517-519.

GIBSON, W. M. *The Prison at Weltevreden*. New York, 1855.

HAWTHORNE, NATHANIEL. *Our Old Home*, vol. 1. Boston, 1863.

HORN, JASON. Primacy of the Pacific Under the Hawaiian Kingdom. Unpublished M. A. Thesis, No. 250, University of Hawaii. Honolulu, 1951.

House of Representatives Documents, No. 307, 34th Congress, 1st Session, 1856 (on claim of Gibson against the Dutch government).

The Shepherd Saint of Lanai. Pamphlet, Honolulu, 1882.

SOUSA, ESTHER L. Walter Murray Gibson's Rise to Power in Hawaii. Unpublished M.A. Thesis, No. 195, University of Hawaii. Honolulu, 1942.

STEVENSON, R. L. *A Footnote to History*. London, 1892.

CHAPTER 5

DAY, A. GROVE. *Hawaii and Its People*, Boston and New York, 1955.

EVATT, HERBERT V. *Rum Rebellion*. Sydney, 1938.

MACKANESS, GEORGE. *The Life of Vice-Admiral William Bligh, R.N., F.R.S.* Revised edition, Sydney, 1951.

CHAPTER 6

AMHERST, WILLIAM (ed.). *The Discovery of the Solomon Islands by Alvaro Mendaña de Neira in 1568.* Hakluyt Society, London, 1901.

MARKHAM, Sir CLEMENTS (ed.). *The Voyages of Pedro Fernandes de Quirós*. Hakluyt Society, London, 1904.

ZARAGOZA, JUSTO (ed.). *Historia del Descubrimiento de las Regiones Austriales Hecho por el General Pedro Fernández de Quirós*, 3 vols. Madrid, 1876-82.

CHAPTER 7

BECKE, LOUIS. The following works by Becke deal with Hayes in personal reminiscence or as a character in fiction: *The Adventures of Louis Blake*, London, 1909; Bully Hayes, *Adventure* magazine, New York, September, 1914; Bully Hayes the Pirate, *Bulletin*, Sydney, February 4, 1893; Concerning Bully Hayes, in *Bully Hayes, Buccaneer*, Sydney,

1913; The Real Bully Hayes, *Lone Hand*, Sydney, March, 1912; Some Skippers With Whom I Have Sailed, in *'Neath Austral Skies*, London, 1909; *The Strange Adventures of James Shervinton*, London, 1902; and The Wreck of the "Leonora"; A Memory of Bully Hayes, in *Ridan the Devil*, London, 1899.

"BOLDREWOOD, ROLF." [T. A. BROWNE]. *A Modern Buccaneer*. London, 1894. Based on a manuscript by Louis Becke.

CHALMERS, REV. JAMES. *Autobiography and Letters* (ed. Richard Lovett). Oxford, 1902.

CHURCHWARD, WILLIAM B. *My Consulate in Samoa*. London, 1887.

COOPER, H. STONEHEWER. *Islands of the Pacific*. London, 1888.

DUNBABIN, THOMAS J. *Slavers of the South Seas*. Sydney, 1935.

GORDON-CUMMING, CONSTANCE F. *A Lady's Cruise in a French Man-of-War*. London, 1882.

LUBBOCK, BASIL. *Bully Hayes*. Boston, 1931. A fictionized account.

MOSS, FREDERICK J. *Through Atolls and Islands in the Great South Sea*. London, 1889.

REEVES, EDWARD. *Brown Men and Women; or The South Sea Islands in 1895 and 1896*. London, 1898.

ROMILLY, HUGH H. *The Western Pacific and New Guinea*. London, 1886.

SAUNDERS, A. T. *Bully Hayes: Barrator, Bigamist, Buccaneer, Blackbirder, and Pirate*. Perth, Western Australia, 1932. Pamphlet.

SAUNDERS, A. T. *Bully Hayes, Louis Becke, and the Earl of Pembroke*. Adelaide, South Australia, 1914. Pamphlet.

STONE, WALTER W. Becke's Letter to Boldrewood. *Biblionews*, Sydney, March, 1952.

See also bibliography of Chapter 8 on Louis Becke.

CHAPTER 8

BECKE, LOUIS. The following works are of particular interest (all dates are of first London editions): *Adventures of a Supercargo*, 1906; *Adventures of Louis Blake*, 1909; *By Reef and Palm*, 1894; *By Rock and Pool*, 1901; *Call of the South*, 1908; *Ebbing of the Tide*, 1896; *The Jalasco Brig*, 1902; *Notes from My South Sea Log*, 1905; *Pacific Tales*, 1897; *Ridan the Devil*, 1899; *Rodman the Boatsteerer*, 1898; *Settlers of Karossa Creek*, 1900; *Under Tropic Skies*, 1904; and *York the Adventurer*, 1901.

DERRICOURT, WILLIAM. *Old Convict Days*. London, 1899. Foreword by Louis Becke.

FITZGERALD, J. D. *Studies in Australian Crime*, first series. Sydney, 1924, p. 115.

INGRAM, MARGARET ANNE. Louis Becke, a Study. Unpublished
 M.A. Thesis, No. 159, University of Hawaii. Honolulu, 1937.

MELVILLE, HERMAN. *Moby Dick*. London, 1901. Foreword by
 Louis Becke.

MILLER, E. MORRIS. *Australian Literature*, 2 vols. Sydney, 1940.

A New Australian Writer, Mr. Louis Becke. *Review of Reviews*,
 Australian edition, March, 1895, pp. 283-287.

PRIDAY, LEW. Trader Becke of the South Seas. *Bulletin*, Sydney,
 June 15, 1955, p. 25.

RODERICK, COLIN. *Introduction to Australian Fiction*. Sydney, 1951.

See also bibliography of Chapter 7 on Bully Hayes.

CHAPTER 9

Dictionary of National Biography. Articles on "Will Mariner" and
 "John Martin."

MARTIN, JOHN, M.D. *An Account of the Natives of the Tonga
 Islands, in the South Pacific Ocean . . . compiled and arranged from the extensive communications of Mr. William
 Mariner, several years resident in those islands*. London, first
 ed., 1816; third ed., 1827.

SOMERVILLE, Vice-Admiral B. T. *Will Mariner*. Boston, 1937.

CHAPTER 10

Correspondence of Edgar Leeteg with Bernard (Barney) Davis,
 Bill Erwin, and Mary Morton of Honolulu, Al (Papio)
 Ezell of Lihue, Kauai, and Wayne Decker of Salt Lake City.

RAMSAY, JOHN. Leeteg in Hawaii. *Hawaiian Life*, Honolulu, Feb.
 6, 1954.

SAINT FRONT, Admiral DURAND DU. Leeteg of Tahiti. *Hawaiian
 Life*, Honolulu, Feb. 13 and 20, 1954.

Index